Critical Essays on
Henry Adams

Critical Essays on
Henry Adams

Earl N. Harbert

G. K. Hall & Co. • Boston, Massachusetts

J Copyright © 1981 by Earl N. Harbert

Library of Congress Cataloging in Publication Data

Critical essays on Henry Adams.

   (Critical essays on American literature)
   Bibliography: p.
   Includes index.
   Contents: Democracy, an American novel / Mary A.
(Mrs. Humphry) Ward—The expense of greatness, three
emphases on Henry Adams / R. P. Blackmur—Henry Adams /
Henry Steele Commager—[etc.]
   1. Adams, Henry, 1838-1918—Criticism and interpre-
tation—Addresses, essays, lectures. I. Harbert, Earl
N., 1934-   . II. Series
PS1004.A4Z63   818′.409   81-2699
ISBN 0-8161-8280-9   AACR2

This publication is printed on permanent/durable acid-free paper.
MANUFACTURED IN THE UNITED STATES OF AMERICA

CRITICAL ESSAYS ON AMERICAN LITERATURE

This series seeks to collect the most important reprinted criticism on writers and topics in American literature along with, in various volumes, original essays, interviews, bibliographies, letters, manuscript sections, and other materials brought to public attention for the first time. Earl Harbert's volume is the first collection of criticism ever published on Henry Adams. As such its emphasis is on assembling the best existing scholarship on this writer as represented by the articles by Ernest Samuels, Mellicent Bell, J. C. Levenson, R. P. Blackmur, and Henry Steele Commager, among others. In addition, Professor Harbert includes a fine original essay by Margaret J. Brown on Henry Adams in Asia. We are confident that this collection will make a permanent and significant contribution to American literary study.

JAMES NAGEL, GENERAL EDITOR

Northeastern University

CONTENTS

Charles Vandersee, "Henry Adams, December 1885"   1
Introduction   3
Bibliographical Note   15
Reviews and Essays
    Mary A. (Mrs. Humphry) Ward,
    "Democracy: An American Novel"   19
    R. P. Blackmur, "The Expense of Greatness:
    Three Emphases on Henry Adams"   36
    Henry Steele Commager, "Henry Adams"   50
    Gene H. Koretz, "Augustine's *Confessions* and
    The Education of Henry Adams"   63
    Ernest Samuels, ["Introduction" to *Democracy and
    Esther: Two Novels by Henry Adams*]   76
    Ernest Samuels, "Henry Adams: 1838–1918"   84
    Millicent Bell, "Adams' *Esther*: The Morality of Taste"   104
    Charles R. Anderson, "Henry Adams, 1838–1918"   115
    Howard M. Munford, "Henry Adams: The Limitations
    of Science"   140
    J. C. Levenson, "Henry Adams and the Art of Politics"   150
    J. C. Levenson, "Henry Adams"   157
    Charles Vandersee, "The Hamlet in Henry Adams"   187
    George Monteiro, "The Education of Ernest Hemingway"   211
    Earl N. Harbert, "*The Education of Henry Adams*: The
    Confessional Mode as Heuristic Experiment"   220
    Earl N. Harbert, "Henry Adams's *Education* and
    Autobiographical Tradition"   236
    Margaret J. Brown, "Henry Adams: His Passage to Asia"   243
Index   259

Henry Adams,
December 1885

Charles Vandersee

An interesting error in a novel
nostalgic over the period
when everything in America went wrong
has Henry Adams on the lecture platform
in Washington, where he lived.
Although a prominent historian,
Henry Adams never lectured.
Or, he always lectured,
but never publicly.
Except once, in Boston,
on "Primitive Rights of Women,"
in December, 1876.

Probably the institution of marriage,
he said, had its origin in love
of property.
Both men and women were united in this:
whatever they loved best,
they wished to possess.
In Egypt,
in the most ancient inscriptions,
the love between husband and wife
is sometimes expressed
in delicate and touching language.

Three days short of nine years later,
Henry Adams died,
but then
led a dreary posthumous existence
for some thirty years more.
Such at least was the language he used
to hint at his feelings
when pressed to talk.

As he never stood up to lecture,
he never went to church,
so on that Sunday in Washington
he merely took his usual walk,

leaving his wife alone in her room
developing pictures, an amateur at work
in photography, the newest of the arts.
He came home
and found her on the floor dead,
having used the chemicals on herself.

The *Njalsaga*, he had said in his lecture,
like the poems of Homer,
turns on the character of a woman.
When he wrote the long story of his own life,
that same fulcrum he put to use,
with the most delicate of languages
("the wisest of men" had taught him),

          silence.

In "Henry Adams, December 1885," Charles Vandersee takes off from Gore Vidal's novel *Washington, D.C.* (V, i). Associate editor of the letters of Henry Adams, now in preparation at the University of Virginia, Professor Vandersee has also published poems in *The American Poetry Review, Sewanee Review, boundary 2,* and other magazines.

INTRODUCTION

This is the first collection of essays by various hands on the life and writings of Henry Brooks Adams (1838–1918). As a fourth-generation son in America's most famous political dynasty, Henry lived and died as a personage rather than a person, and his complex appreciation of this special position colored many of his judgments and actions throughout the years of his adulthood. How, after all, could Adams escape a heritage that included two Presidents and a Minister to England who served during the difficult period of the American Civil War? Of course he could not and he did not, although as the foremost figure in his own generation, Henry made a name for himself in literature rather than politics, as an observer rather than an actor in the history of his time.

The record that he left behind at his death in 1918 was a literary record—a modest yet impressive set of titles that have extended Adams's dialogue with the world into our own time. These writings of Henry Adams, in short, and not the details of his parentage or the actions of his life, have kept his name alive in the twentieth century. Biographers, historians, playwrights, poets, novelists, and literary critics, most of all, have found in these writings a richness of influence and example that invites exploration and understanding. Some of the most notable attempts to explain the achievement of Henry Adams have been included in this volume. Yet this, like any collection of commentary on so versatile a figure, must be regarded as a gathering of suggestions for possible approaches to more complete appreciation, and not as a definitive statement of method. Just as the best of Henry Adams's work in every genre managed to capture something of the elusiveness and privacy of his own personality, so the one common theme of the essays collected here is the unwritten message of all the authors to their readers: please turn again to the writings of Henry Adams and see for yourself just how much he has to offer us.

The literary reputation of Henry Adams is largely posthumous. As a whole, it represents a commentary on letters, essays, books (and a few poems) that he was not generally known to have written at the time of his death; especially on that classic of American autobiography, *The Education of Henry Adams*, which had not yet reached the general public when its author died in 1918. Only by putting out of mind his two novels, *Democracy* and *Esther*, his finely crafted personal letters, as well as the *Education* (and some lesser writings) can we understand Henry Adams's career and reputation in his own day. As a student of psychology and power, Adams was always concerned about his personal "image," and he did admit to playing a public role as a gentleman-historian and a self-

3

confessed "stable companion to statesmen," who somehow found time to set down on paper a nine-volume *History of the United States During the Administrations of Thomas Jefferson and James Madison*, biographies of Albert Gallatin and John Randolph, and that unique masterpiece of sentimental non-fiction, *Mont-Saint-Michel and Chartres*. Of course, Adams wrote other things as well, but these titles represented the chief pillars on which his reputation rested during his lifetime, when his authorship of the very popular novel *Democracy* remained an unconfirmed rumor and before the *Education* was known to a large audience. Critical reviews of the *Education* began to appear in print in 1918. Earlier, a private edition of this book, first printed in 1907, had been circulated in fewer than 100 copies among Adams's closest friends, many of whom responded in letters and notes sent directly to the author.[1] But before 1918, there was no significant public discussion of the book that has since come to be regarded as Henry Adams's masterpiece. In fact, because of the writer's cultivated pose of reticence during the years from 1892 until his death, the impact of his book as it was finally published in 1918 seemed all the greater. This poignant truth was noted by Henry Osborne Taylor, himself one of Adams's students at Harvard, who had first received a privately printed copy of the *Education* ten years before he was moved to call attention to public neglect of Adams's writings.

In the *Atlantic Monthly* for October 1918, Taylor summed up the moral of Henry Adams's life and the story of the *Education*:

> Perhaps no other American has left such a mass of clever writing, evolved through a life of thoughtful research and curious reflection, and died so unrecognized by the public, educated or otherwise. . . .
>
> Is it because the serious study of American history—other than local—has so few votaries that such a work as Henry Adams's nine-volume *History of the United States*, 1807 [*sic*]–1817, with its ancillary lives of *Albert Gallatin*, and *John Randolph*, and publication of *Documents*, should have drawn so little attention to the writer?[2]

Taylor went on to praise the autobiographical testament of his old teacher, "There is little more perfect in American literature than the opening chapter of the *Education*," and to argue for the overall coherence and historical relevance of its "latter part."[3]

In a concluding paragraph Adams's former student approached objective critical judgment, as he divided responsibility for the public's failure to acclaim this "New England Montaigne" between the nation and the man. Henry Adams had "avoided recognition willfully, not merely from the thoughtless, but from the sincerely thoughtful; and purposely he carried obliteration to a grave which has no stone to mark his name. None the less, the lack for recognition of Henry Adams throws a faint sidelight on the culture of his country."[4]

As a long-time friend, Taylor touched lightly and diplomatically on what he knew to be Adams's hypersensitivity to all public commentary and criticism—of his personal behavior as much as of his writing. This sensitivity often led him to avoid all forms of public recognition and to cultivate instead a reputation for reticence. In part, the explanation for this reticence may be found in the tragic suicide of his wife, Marian "Clover" Hooper Adams, in 1885, and in the intellectual, emotional, and biographical problem of living in the shadows of two Presidents, as a fourth-generation member of America's most prominent political family.[5] But another part of the explanation may be found in the pervasive force of Henry Adams's inherent skepticism, especially skepticism concerning his personal commitment to literature. In one of many of the delicately balanced polarities that describe the equilibrium of his intellectual life, Adams matched the strength of the ingrained family habit of writing against deeply rooted doubts about the value of what he was accomplishing. Without ever giving up the practice of writing, Adams managed again and again to turn away from all serious criticism of his work and to run before every gathering storm.

Henry understood this fact about himself; he warned his older brother Charles, who showed a different disposition, in a letter of 1869: "You like the strife of the world. I detest and despise it."[6] If he did not quite "despise" critical controversy, Henry Adams nevertheless sought to avoid such "strife" throughout his career as a writer. His cultivated pose of indifference sometimes seemed to belie all ambition for popular success. But beneath the surface reticence there were other, more complicated human feelings, such as the tacit yearning for approval and acceptance that emerges in *The Education of Henry Adams*.

The first important critical test of Henry Adams, author, was provided by the London press in 1862, when the *Times* and *Examiner* took turns ridiculing the 23-year-old son of the Minister to the Court of St. James. Henry had been exposed as the author of "A Visit to Manchester—Extracts from a Private Diary," which appeared along with an identification of the writer—despite explicit instruction from Adams—in the Boston *Daily Courier* for December 16, 1861. Writing as a critic of manners, Henry praised the polite society of Manchester at the expense of London, and the London press took its revenge by exacting in the end a heavy psychic toll from the sensitive young man, whose "Private Diary" had suddenly become all too public. In brief, Henry Adams felt himself humiliated by his first encounter with his critics.[7] As he confessed shortly afterward, when he began to contemplate a new and less controversial literary form, the historical essay, "I was roasted with pepper and salt by the English press. . . . [Now] my pen is forced to keep away from political matters, unless I want to bring the English press down on my head again."[8] Despite his wit, it is clear that Adams did not care to face the wrath of critics if he could avoid a confrontation. Yet, even in the process of being "roasted," he could not bring himself to relinquish the practice of writing for publication. Henry was, after all, an Adams and a grandson and great-grandson of writers as much as Presidents. For an Adams, the habit of placing words on paper provided nothing less than a fundamental method of ordering personal thought and experience, of making some pattern out of life.

But equally, Henry Adams's initial trial by his critics had its lasting effect; for him, "the impulse to withdraw from controversy . . . became a fixed habit."[9] As a writer, he went on to make himself the unacknowledged author of two novels, *Democracy* and *Esther*, as well as a careful historian who insisted on "trying out" his three most important non-fictional works, *History of the Administrations of Jefferson and Madison, Mont-Saint-Michel and Chartres*, and *The Education of Henry Adams*, in exclusive private printings designed to be "corrected" before the books were offered for general publication. Something of the aristocrat's disdain for popular success undoubtedly played a part in Adams's unusual career as an author; yet far more important was the effect of the "Manchester" incident in shaping his determination to play the literary game with special care—to remain after 1862 as noncontroversial a writer as he could. His careful revision of essays and books; his checking and rechecking of historical and scientific ideas and materials before and after he used them in his writings; and, perhaps most of all, his exaggerated claims for the objective and experimental techniques with which he professed to have replaced dogmatic finality in his writings—these important characteristics of his work document the permanence of his defensive response to critics in London and elsewhere. For, even while he preferred to remain out of sight and out of "strife," Adams could not keep himself from listening to what others were saying about him.

With these general observations in mind, we are prepared to review opinions of Adams's work that had appeared by the time of his death in March, 1918, just before the *Education* became a public statement. Leaving behind the English reception of "A Visit to Manchester" in 1862, we must look ahead to 1879, when the next significant commentary appeared. From 1870 until 1877, Adams had served Harvard College as a teacher of history, a position he left when he began research for *The Life of Albert Gallatin*, published in 1879.[10] This biography, Henry's first extensive historical effort, evoked an anonymous two-part review in the *Nation* for August 21 and 28, 1879, which introduced Henry Adams to the larger world as a subject for serious criticism.[11] The anonymous reviewer proved an unkind audience. He found *Gallatin* to be too specialized for the general reader, loaded with dull material, and enlivened only where the author broke away from reprinting papers and letters to speak in an interpretive voice of his own. When Henry Adams had finished reading these two issues of the *Nation*, he must have realized that his first book had failed to blend narration and documentation into a unified work. What Henry may not have learned, however, was that the reviewer for the *Nation* was his older brother, Charles Francis Adams, Jr., who did not let the younger man forget that family standards were very high and could not be satisfied with inferior literature: "This volume falls little short of being an outrage both on Albert Gallatin and on everyone who wishes to know anything about him."[12] The immediate effect on Henry must have been strong. But here, it is the longer-term influence of the review that interests us, for in every faulty particular specified by his brotherly critic—use of quotations, unity of tone, interpretation of documents, felicity of style—Henry's later work showed definite improvement.

His next published biography, *John Randolph* (1882), met with a more encouraging critical reception, as befitted a better and more interesting book. Yet enthusiasm was limited, and, while the response must have encouraged the serious historical interests of an author still in his early forties, it did not add up to popular acclaim for Henry Adams nor to unmixed approval among historians. An anonymous reviewer for the *New York Semi-Weekly Tribune* set the pattern for most critics, at least for those who did not interpret the book as simply another chapter in the Adams family crusade against the South and Southerners. The *Tribune* critic noted that while *John Randolph* displayed a "provokingly superior" authorial tone, it nonetheless remained a "lively and interesting volume" throughout.[13] Here was evidence that Adams had advanced his biographical art beyond the crudities of *Gallatin* as he sharpened his literary skills in preparation for the *History*.

Meanwhile, the real star among the galaxy of Henry Adams's writings in the 1880s and the most important of his books before the *History* was *Democracy: An American Novel*, published anonymously in 1880.[14] Building on the satirical techniques used in *John Randolph*, Adams now tried his hand at fiction, writing as a novelist of manners and mores. The chief targets of his satire were the politics and politicians of post-Civil War Washington, and these subjects proved immensely popular with the reading public. For the first time as an author, Henry Adams knew the feeling of popular success, even though he still refused to admit to authorship. Overall, the critical record of *Democracy* must have been reassuring; American and British reviewers gave the novel generous praise.

Today, it is difficult to summarize all that they wrote and even more difficult to decide just how their opinions might have affected Henry Adams. He certainly must have relished their compliments to his wit and cleverness, and glowed with their praise of his literary skills. His first attempt at the novel was compared to the mature work of Henry James and Anthony Trollope by one reviewer, and judged to be "distinguished by an ease and smartness in which English fiction is apt to be especially deficient" by another.[15] On the other hand, Adams must have been discomforted, at least momentarily, by the shrewd guess of Mary A. [Mrs. Humphry] Ward, reviewer for the English *Fortnightly Review*, who suggested "Mr. Henry Brooks Adams" as the probable author of *Democracy*. Her attribution, she claimed, was based on a comparison of the novel with "Civil Service Reform," an essay that Adams had signed and published in 1869.[16] Another comparative critic found that the anonymous novel *The Bread-Winners* (1883), a book Adams knew to have been written by his friend John Hay, offered greater intellectual and literary depth than did *Democracy*.[17] Here, the way was opened for Hay's good natured kidding at Adams's expense, but in other places the critical judgments of the reviewers touched on more serious matters. A largely unfavorable review of *Democracy*, published anonymously in the *Nation* in 1880 and since attributed to William Carey Brownell, focused on the familiar problem of artistic unity. Brownell's criticism was similar to the charges raised against *Gallatin*, and it foreshadowed a major theme in the most important discussions of the *Education* to be written in the next 50 years. Of *Democracy*, Brownell wrote, the "cardinal defect" is that "the love story and the political satire are not better blended."[18] Blending, of course, represented only one possible method for achieving artistic unity, but even while he was enjoying his first popular success as a writer, Adams must have realized that his shrewd critic had pointed to the single most significant failing in his vision and in his art: the resistance of experience to unifying explanation.

Whatever reception Adams might have anticipated when he published a second and last novel, *Esther: A Novel* (1884), this time under the pseudonym Frances Snow Compton (used perhaps to forestall guesses about authorship by Mary A. Ward and others), he was surely disappointed.[19] Neither the sales figures nor the critical reviews could have been comforting. Even though *Esther* appeared before reviewers had finished praising *Democracy*, the later novel made almost no impression on the literary community. The religious dilemma of its heroine simply did not rival the political satire of *Democracy* in popular interest, and in many ways it was an inferior book. Its chief weaknesses—pasteboard characters, preachy dialogue, stale religious philosophy, the contrived and inconclusive ending—must have been obvious to anyone who took the trouble to read it. In fact, only the attractive figure of the titular heroine, the Esther that Adams had inherited from Hawthorne and made his own by adding a highly personalized fictional representation of his wife, Marian, has managed to redeem the novel from obscurity.[20] One contemporary critic spoke with the voice of the general public when he found *Esther* above all "wanting in human interest."[21]

Eventually, his authorial disappointment with the reception of the book and his personal grief over Marian's death were combined in Henry

Adams's final pronouncement concerning the last novel he was ever to write: "I care more for one chapter, or any dozen pages of *Esther* than for the whole history [*sic*] . . . ; so much more, indeed, that I would not let anyone read the story for fear the reader should profane it. . . . "[22] In this retrospective defense of the failed novel, on grounds of personal reticence, we can sample Adams's philosophy; his intellectual escape from unpleasant truths must be regarded as a literary equivalent to his flight from all associations of their shared life, just after Marian's suicide.

If, as Henry Adams claimed, the *History* was a less personal testimony than *Esther*, its publication (from 1889 to 1891) nevertheless set a new standard for high achievement by the author.[23] Although nothing in Adams's earlier writing showed substantial promise of its greatness, the *History*, in its richness and variety, brought together for the first time all of the authorial skills displayed in the essays, novels, and biographies that preceded it.[24] To a combination of techniques for characterization and narration, the author added subtle interpretation and didacticism, careful overall organization, and a largeness of method and mind unparalleled in his other works. If Henry Adams had never written anything after the *History*, his reputation as an important American historian should still have been secure. Yet, although he never again attempted a study on the scale of the *History*, he did go on to conceive and execute those unique historical works *Mont-Saint-Michel and Chartres* and *The Education of Henry Adams* as well as some late essays on scientific history—writings that now make impossible any fair judgment of Adams on the basis of the *History* alone.

For his contemporaries, an overall evaluation of Adams's *History* proved to be difficult for another reason. From 1889 on, the work was published in segments, usually two volumes at a time, thus giving separate treatment to each Presidential term of Thomas Jefferson and James Madison.[25] Reviewers naturally found it difficult to do justice to the larger themes of the *History*, although by 1880 some reviewers were considering Adams's account of the entire eight years of Jefferson's Presidency, and by 1892, the following eight years of Madison's, sometimes in the context of the earlier volumes on Jefferson. Yet their partial and fortuitous nature makes the reviews themselves difficult to evaluate fairly, since reviews appearing at the same time often considered different portions of the *History*. But Adams must have read any and all of them—beginning with the earliest in 1889, which considered his first two volumes only—with some conception of the entire study already complete in his own mind.

An anonymous reviewer for the influential *New York Times* understood at least something of this larger conception, as he judged the first two volumes of the *History* to be the beginnings of a historical work "of great importance."[26] He went on to praise Adams's style, while noting a certain coldness in the overall treatment of Jefferson. Two months later, the *Nation* printed a two-part review that called for a fuller treatment of Jefferson's political differences with the Federalists, while it praised the author's thorough explanation of the development of Jeffersonian democracy and his skill in portraying historical personalities.[27] Unlike the reviewer, Adams might have ascribed part of his success with historical portraits to his fictional efforts in *Democracy* and *Esther*. In any case, he must have known that the first segment of the *History* to reach the public had been judged a clear improvement over both *Gallatin* and *John Randolph*.

The fullest measure of Adams's achievement in the *History* came from his critics in 1890, the year that offers a high-water mark in attention to the author during his lifetime. Serious if somewhat mixed reviews appeared in the *Critic*, the *Dial* of Chicago, the *English Historical Review*, *Harper's New Monthly Magazine*, the *New York Times*, the *London Critic*, and in four issues of the *Nation*.[28] In general reviewers found much more to praise in the volumes devoted to the eight years of Jefferson's Presidency than in the two (all as yet available) on Madison's first term, which were judged dull by comparison. The reviewer for the *Nation* found that Adams had distorted the historical figure of John Randolph, to make him function as a Greek "Tragic Chorus" during the Madison years, as a way of didactically underscoring the moral lessons of history.[29] From this and other reviews, Adams might have learned that when he left the great figure of Jefferson behind, his narrative declined in general interest and perhaps in historical and literary value as well.

By 1892, when reviews of the last three volumes appeared, the reputation of the *History* was already built on four years of piece-by-piece consideration—attention that failed to do justice to the values of the work as a whole. The critical record, moreover, showed such a mixture of petty prejudices and carefully qualified compliments that it must have aggravated the author's frustrations. His most vitriolic critic, "Housatonic" (later identified as William Henry Smith), treated the *History* as simply "A Case of Hereditary Bias." This personal attack on Henry Adams and his more famous ancestors asserted that the book was bad history and its author a bad historian.[30] At the other extreme, H. W. Thurston, writing in the Chicago *Dial*, told the author what he longed to hear: "Mr. Adams has done his work well, so well that there will be no need to do it again."[31]

If he kept score, Adams must have recognized that on balance his *History* drew more praise than adverse criticism from the press. While many critics found some parts to be dull and tedious, others praised the humor and freshness of his overall treatment. Yet the objective or "scientific" possibilities of his method seem not to have been comprehended by any of his reviewers, even those who felt the forceful impact of his volumes. As one anonymous critic wrote, "No works in American historical literature . . . combine so many merits and display such power."[32] Perhaps these words appearing in the London press helped to erase the unpleasant memories of "A Visit to Manchester." Certainly later critics, using the advantage of viewing the work whole and not in its parts, have agreed that the *History* is a classic of American historiography. But in his own day, the author never quite forgave the reading public or the representatives of the press for their lack of understanding and appreciation of all that he had accomplished. With a typical sense of ironic exaggeration, his *Education* treats the *History* as further evidence of failure: "As far as Adams knew, he had but three serious readers. . . . "[33] The truth, as the author well knew, was something else.

Moreover, if Adams was seriously disappointed with the reception given to the *History*, his disappointment did not turn him away entirely from historical writing. His signed essays "The Tendency of History" (1894), "Count Edward de Crillon" (1895), and *A Letter to American Teachers of History* (1910) added their lighter weights to the accumulation of evidence that documented his claim for recognition as a serious historian.[34] Yet every substantial, book-length work written by Adams after the *History* was printed privately, sometimes (as with the two versions of *Memoirs of Marau Taaroa Last Queen of Tahiti*, 1893 and 1901) with the authorship specially masked by spurious attribution. Adams's sensitivity and reticence, already evident in his earlier career as an author, became an increasingly complex part of the literary game that he insisted on playing from the time of the *History* until his death. The two major public statements which Henry Adams allowed during those years, 1892–1918, *Mont-Saint Michel and Chartres*, (first privately printed in 1904 but published in 1913) and *The Education of Henry Adams* (privately printed in 1907, published in 1918) were made public only after the author had been coaxed by readers who admired the work in its private form. Henry Adams, like a social wallflower, found a way to sit out the usual literary dance of author and critic until his confidence had been built by a private preview of what might be expected when he went public.

Of these two major works only *Chartres* actually produced a record of critical response that might have influenced the author's attitudes before his death. Because of its curious publication history, moreover, some of the important critics of the 1913 printing had become familiar with the book much earlier in one of its two private printings. Thus, the reception of the book among the selected readers of these private printings undoubtedly influenced the favorable consensus reached in the reviews of *Chartres* that appeared in 1913 and 1914. Henry Osborne Taylor, for example, admired the work in its earliest form, and he had an unusual opportunity to study the book thoughtfully for nine years before he took up the task of reviewing *Chartres* in the *American Historical Review*. Writing then largely for an audience of professional historians, Taylor insisted that readers of *Chartres* should be careful to distinguish between the historical realities of the Middle Ages and Adams's personal response to the architecture and religion of the period. With an acute perception that must have served readers of the *Education* as much as those of *Chartres*, Taylor warned that after reading we "are left in doubt whether we have gone the round of the twelfth and thirteenth centuries, or the round of the mind of Henry Adams."[35] Other reviewers were easier to please, like the anonymous critic for the *Booklist*; he termed *Chartres* "a careful and loving study," and unlike Taylor, "a work by a scholar, primarily for scholars."[36] Overall, Adams's first important public performance since the *History* was welcomed as a beautiful testimony of his love for the Medieval period, even though questions concerning its historical accuracy remained.

By the time the most significant reviews of *Chartres* appeared in 1913 and 1914, Adams had privately printed *The Education of Henry Adams* for a selected readership of fewer than 100 persons. Thus, while the printed reviews of *Chartres* did not influence the composition of the *Education*, they may well have encouraged Adams in his final decision to allow the general publication of his book only after his death.[37] In this way, at the least, he would not have to read what critics might say in the public press about the values of his self-history or the successes and failures of his private life. With the press, Adams took his leave a winner, as the popular author of *Chartres* and the historian of Europe and America. By keeping the *Education* out of the hands of reviewers and critics, Henry Adams managed to avoid in his lifetime the most painful "strife" that he could imagine.

Publication of *The Education of Henry Adams*, six months after Adams's death, ended the truce between the critics and the author. Newspapers and literary journals simply could not ignore so popular a book, and Adams's "lack of recognition" by "his country" (as noted by Taylor) soon turned into public notoriety, something that he had always professed to detest as unworthy of a gentleman. But with his death, of course, he lost control of the literary game, and the result was an unusual posthumous fame accorded to a bestselling author who had used the materials of his own life to fashion the instrument of his greatest success. His *Education* turned the course of criticism in another direction and made Adams first the subject of gossip, eulogy, biography—and only much later, a proper literary study as historian and writer. But that later extension of his reputation, Adams did not live to see or to reflect upon. What he had read of his critics during his life, however, he judged in 1915: "In general, one may say that in America an author never gets profit from printed comments on his work. What help he gets is from private inquiry or conversation—and very little of that."[38] Like so many judgments expressed by Henry Adams, this final claim against the critics of his time offers us something less than the complete truth.

More than half a century has passed since the death of Henry Adams and the publication of *The Education of Henry Adams*. Rightly or wrongly, that single work has now established itself as the central pillar in the author's popular reputation and as a kind of acid test for every broad consideration of Adams as thinker or writer. T. S. Eliot, in a review that appeared in the *Athenaeum* for 23 May 1919, recognized something of the modern fascination with the *Education* that has continued to the present: "The really impressive interest is in the mind of the author, and in the American mind, or that fragment of it, which he represents." But Eliot also sounded a warning which all too few of Adams's readers have taken seriously enough: "It is doubtful whether the book ought to be called an autobiography, for there is too little of the author in it." The rest, of course, is art.

Since 1919, the twin roots of Adams's life and art have nourished a rich growth of biographical and critical inquiry, the chief examples of which make a continuing claim for our attention. In fact, the complex relationship between the man and his work has proved especially interesting to the best of Henry Adams's many critics, as the essays selected for reprinting here will testify. In other ways, these essays cannot be easily categorized; nor do they demonstrate any single scholarly persuasion or style. Instead, this collection shows the variety of ideas to be found in the best writing about Henry Adams, a variety that this fascinating subject not only justifies but also requires.

Earl N. Harbert

Notes

1. See Ernest Samuels, *Henry Adams: The Major Phase*. (Cambridge: Harvard Univ. Press, 1964), pp. 332–39.

2. Taylor, p. 484.

3. Taylor, pp. 485, 490.

4. Taylor, p. 491.

5. For an attempt to evaulate the influence of the earlier members of the Adams family on the writings of Henry Adams, see my book, *The Force So Much Closer Home: Henry Adams and the Adams Family* (New York: New York Univ. Press, 1977).

6. 21 May, *Letters of Henry Adams (1858–1891)*, ed. Worthington Chauncey Ford (Boston: Houghton Mifflin, 1930), p. 160.

7. The best short summary of Adams's changing attitudes toward England and the English is William Dusinberre, "Henry Adams in England," *The Journal of American Studies*, 11 (August, 1977), 163–86. For a comprehensive treatment, see Dusinberre, *Henry Adams: The Myth of Failure* (Charlottesville: Univ. Press of Virginia, 1980).

8. Letters to J. G. Palfrey, 12 February and 20 March 1862, *Henry Adams and His Friends: A Collection of His Unpublished Letters*, compiled by Harold Dean Carter (Boston: Houghton Mifflin, 1947), pp. 14–15.

9. Ernest Samuels, *The Young Henry Adams* (Cambridge: Harvard Univ. Press, 1948), p. 118.

10. (Philadelphia: Lippincott, 1879).

11. Pp. 128–29, 144–45.

12. For the attribution to Charles Francis Adams, Jr., see Evelyn Page, " 'The Man Around the Corner': An Episode in the Career of Henry Adams," *New England Quarterly*, 23 (September, 1950), 401–03.

13. 20 October 1882.

14. (New York: Henry Holt, 1880).

15. Both reviews were anonymous. They first appeared in the *Academy* No. 503 (July, 1882), p. 5; the second in the *New York Semi-Weekly Tribune* for August 1, 1882 (n.p.).

16. 38 (1 July 1882), 78–93. "Civil Service Reform" first appeared in the *North American Review*, 109 (October, 1869), 443–76, and later as a separate pamphlet (1869).

17. Anon., *Saturday Review* (2 February 1884), pp. 154–55.

18. 30 (22 April 1880), 312. For the attribution, see Ernest Samuels, *Henry Adams: The Middle Years* (Cambridge: Harvard Univ. Press, 1958), p. 97.

19. (New York: Henry Holt, 1884).

20. For the effect of Mrs. Adams's suicide and other circumstances surrounding the publication and reception of *Esther*, see Samuels, *Middle Years*, pp. 222–25.

21. Anon., *Athenaeum* (25 July 1885), pp. 107–08.

22. Letter to Elizabeth Cameron, 6 February 1891, Ford, *Letters*, p. 468.

23. 9 Vols. (New York: Charles Scribner's Sons, 1889–1891).

24. See *The Force So Much Closer Home*, pp. 88–143.

25. The final three volumes, however, concerned with the second administration of James Madison, were issued together. For details of publication, see Samuels, *Middle Years*, pp. 424–26.

26. 27 October 1889, p. 19.

27. 12 and 19 December 1889, pp. 480–83, 504–06.

28. For specific bibliographical citations, see my *Henry Adams: A Reference Guide* (Boston: G.K. Hall, 1978) pp. 5–6. A useful account of the reception of the *History* may be found in Samuels, *Middle Years*, pp. 410–13.

29. *Nation*, 51 (27 November 1890), 424–26.

30. New York *Tribune*, 15 September, 15 December, 1890; later reprinted as *A Case of Hereditary Bias* (New York, 1891).

31. 11 (June, 1890), 33–35.

32. London *Critic*, 15 (28 February 1891), 106.

33. *The Education of Henry Adams*, ed. Ernest Samuels (Boston: Houghton Mifflin, 1973), p. 327. See also note 26, p. 632.

34. For a summary of the writings of Adams after 1892, including the particulars of publication, see Samuels, *Major Phase*, pp. 591–94.

35. 19 (April, 1914), 592–94.

36. 10 February 1913, p. 215. A brief discussion of other reviews may be found in Samuels, *Major Phase*, pp. 541–42.

37. The best discussion of Adams's decision may be found in Samuels, *Major Phase*, pp. 563, 566–71.

38. Letter to William Roscoe Thayer, 17 December 1915; *Letters of Henry Adams* (1892–1918), ed. Worthington Chauncey Ford (Boston: Houghton Mifflin, 1938), p. 635.

BIBLIOGRAPHICAL NOTE

Henry Adams is included in volume I of Jacob Blanck's *Bibliography of American Literature;* the most useful listing of "The Writings of Henry Adams" may be found in an appendix to each volume of Ernest Samuels's standard biography. The criticism on Adams has been surveyed by Charles Vandersee in two essays, both of which appeared in *American Literary Realism, 1870–1910,* Vol. II (1969), 90–119 and Vol. VIII (1975), 18–34; Vol. VIII of *ALR* (p. 180–88) also contains "Henry Adams" by Barrie Hayne and Katherine Morrison, a discussion of unpublished Ph.D. dissertations written to that date. My chapter, "Henry Adams," in *Fifteen American Authors Before 1900: Bibliographical Essays on Research and Criticism,* ed. Robert A. Rees and Earl N. Harbert (Madison: University of Wisconsin Press, 1971, 1974), pp. 3–36, identifies the chief contributions under five headings: bibliography, editions, manuscripts and letters, biography, and criticism. These discussions may be supplemented with the more selective *Henry Adams: A Reference Guide* by Earl N. Harbert (Boston: G.K. Hall and Co., 1978), which includes a brief historical "Introduction."

REVIEWS AND ESSAYS

"Democracy: An American Novel"

Mary A. [Mrs. Humphry] Ward[*]

About this time last year a small book began to be handed about in London. It was popularly reported that there were exactly three copies in England, each of which belonged to a distinguished American owner, that the book had made a great hit in America, that the authorship of it was a profound secret, and yet not so profound but that English people acquainted with such leading Americans as have visited this country of late years could make certain shrewd guesses at the authorship. The novel itself never failed to interest anybody who was fortunate enough to borrow or steal it—for the ownership of the three copies became in the end one of the most complicated problems—and combining merit as it did with the attractiveness of mystery, an English success seemed assured. But the supply was tardy; the novel was political, and American politics are not a strong point with the majority of us; and last, but not least, a far more imposing luminary rose almost at the same moment above the horizon. *John Inglesant* employed us for the winter. No one can accuse Mr. Shorthouse of having told his story with unbecoming brevity. On the contrary, he gave us a great deal to discuss, and the world was very glad to discuss it, especially as "even the youngest among us" at the present day has views as to the relations of religion to knowledge, as to the true field of the Church in human life. The admirers of *Democracy* for the moment forgot their cult. They were but few, and the *John Inglesant* current was irresistible. So absorbed have we all been in the Platonism of Father St. Clair, in the problems of Inglesant's conscience, in the subtleties of cardinals, and the luxuries of Renaissance palaces, that to call the public attention from these high things to a novel of three hundred and fifty pages intended to show the demoralising effects of the "spoils" system on American public life would have seemed too bold.

Democracy is a political novel, and, as such, sharply distinguished from the majority of its kinsfolk; for as a rule the American novelist makes it a point of honour to eschew politics, just as Boston society, or whatever Boston society stands for in America, eschews it in social life. Mr. Henry

*Reprinted from *The Fortnightly Review*, 38 (July 1, 1882), 78–93.

James's airy coteries, Mr. Howell's sensitive and delicately-drawn heroes and heroines, represent an art altogether removed from the art of this barely-outlined book, with its definite moral and its work-a-day incident. To our mind, however, it solves the question as to whether a political novel is a legitimate performance; for Mr. Trollope's parliamentary novels, with all their charm, and deeply as we were interested in the Duchess, left us undecided on the point. Treated as they are from the point of view of an Englishman, who naturally finds his own House of Commons a deeply interesting institution, and easily accepts the persons and associations connected with it as fit material for a novel, it was difficult to conceive these books attracting any but an English audience. Would a Frenchman, who cannot be expected to sympathize with Mr. Trollope's sense of the mysterious charm which lurks around the House of Commons, of the paradise behind, and the unimportant wilderness outside that magic door which admits the member of Parliament to his haven of unrest—would a Frenchman find Mr. Bonteen, and Mr. Monk, and Mr. Quintus Slide entertaining? And ought not a novel, as a work of art, to aim at an impression independent of such very limited conditions? Nor were our scruples laid at rest by *Numa Roumestan*, however piquant the Parisian world might find the damaging analysis of M. Gambetta's character with which it delighted to credit M. Daudet, or however graphic might be the portraiture, as one was told to consider it, of the great orator's first successes at the Café Malmus. French fiction, indeed, has a note of universality and brilliancy which has often carried off heavier subjects than politics. Still it remained true that most readers equipped with French knowledge, French sympathies, and French party spirit, were inclined to think *Numa Roumestan* a fascinating book, while, without these conditions, it was very possible to see nothing in it beyond a finished piece of writing devoted to a theme in reality quite uninteresting, a novel in which, when politics and style had been excluded as factors from the reader's judgment, nothing remained to discuss. Neither Mr. Trollope's novels, however, nor M. Daudet's satire, offer such good materials for comparison with *Democracy* as *Coningsby* or *Sybil*. It is always an evidence of rashness on the part of a reviewer to attempt to raise a new-comer to the level of the older accepted potentates. Still, when all allowances have been made for differences of scope—for the mere great difference of length—it is not, perhaps, too venturesome to say that *Democracy* has nothing to fear from a comparison with any of Disraeli's political novels. *Coningsby* and *Sybil* have probably an enduring place in English literature, if it were only for their connection with English history. The interest of the political judgments, the wit of the political conversations, will not nowaday be denied. But important and stimulating as they were politically, they suffered from that subordination of the characters to the subjects discussed, of the persons described to the criticisms of life they were employed to deliver, which ultimately reduced *Lothair* and *Endymion* to a string of sharp sayings and luxuriant descriptions, distributed among a number of clever puppets with high-sounding names. In *Democracy*, on the other hand, we have a novel written with a distinct political purpose, and yet so deftly managed that, while the political purpose is admirably served, the book is at the same time excellent as a work of art—that is to say, as an imaginative study of human life. It has for its theme one of the most tangled and viscid of all political situations, one presenting at every step hideous temptations to provinciality, to wearisomeness, to over-elaboration. And yet all these pitfalls have been safely passed. A certain central spot in American political society stands revealed by a kind of lightning-flash; but at the same time the particular figures chosen by the artist to give voice and meaning to his picture have a dainty individual grace or distinctness which entirely prevents your regarding them as mere properties and appurtenances. When you close the book two impressions about equally strong remain in your mind—the impression of patriotic rage and disgust with corruption which was in the author's mind as he wrote, and the personal impression of Madeleine and Sybil. "An accursed system!" one finds oneself saying. "How is America to go on if things are really so bad as this?" and in the same breath, "What a delightful girl! What strength in Madeleine! What true dignity in Carrington!"

Democracy opens with the picture of Madeleine Lee, a young widow of thirty, who, since her husband's death five years before the story opens, has exhausted all the resources of New York against *ennui*, and is now fleeing to Washington as a last refugee from that enemy of the unfettered rich:—

"In her despair she had resorted to desperate measures. She had read philosophy in the original German, and the more she read the more she was disheartened that so much culture should lead to nothing—nothing. After talking of Herbert Spencer for an entire evening with a very literary transcendental commission merchant, she could not see that her time had been better employed than when in former days she had passed it in flirting with a very agreeable young stockbroker; indeed there was an evident proof to the contrary, for the flirtation might lead to something—had, in fact, led to marriage—while the philosophy could lead to nothing, unless it were perhaps to another evening of the same kind, because transcendental philosophers were mostly married men, usually married, and when engaged in business somewhat apt to be sleepy towards evening. Nevertheless, Mrs. Lee did her best to turn her study to practical use. She plunged into philanthropy, visited prisons, inspected hospitals, read the literature of pauperism and crime, saturated herself with the statistics of crime until her mind had nearly lost sight of virtue. At last it rose in rebellion against her, and she came to the limit of her strength.

This path, too, seemed to lead nowhere. She declared that she had lost the sense of duty, and that, so far as concerned her, all the paupers and criminals in New York might henceforward rise in their majesty and manage every railway on the continent."

Europe she had already exhausted, and, besides, "she was American to the tips of her fingers." She neither knew or greatly cared whether Europe or America were best to live in. Her purpose was "to get all that American life had to offer, good or bad," and all that New York could give she had already devoured. In New York there are but two kinds of eminence—wealth and philanthropy. Madeleine found that wealth beyond a certain point becomes uninteresting. Society provides practically no means for bringing it into play; and philanthropy leads you only too soon into problems past human solving.

"She never had been able, since she became a widow, to accept the Brobdingnagian doctrine that he who made two blades of grass grow where only one grew before deserved better of mankind than the whole race of politicians. She would not find fault with the philosopher had he required that the grass should be of an improved quality, but said she, 'I cannot honestly pretend that I should be pleased to see two New York men where I now see one; the idea is too ridiculous.' "

Education and art had been alike tried and found wanting. Intellect abounded at Boston, so at least said tradition, but not even at Boston could she discover any real eminence, anything "that cast a shadow." She wanted to get at the heart of things.

"It was the feeling of a passenger on an ocean steamer, whose mind will not give him rest until he has been in the engine-room and talked with the engineer. She wanted to see with her own eyes the action of primary forces; to touch with her own hand the massive machinery of society; to measure with her own mind the capacity of the motive power. She was bent upon getting to the heart of the great American mystery of democracy and government."

Amusement she thought she was certain to get out of the political game, possibly instruction. And, if the worst came to the worst, and Washington society were really as bad as her friends told her, "she would have gained all she wanted, for it would be a pleasure to return—precisely the feeling she longed for." The decision was no sooner taken than executed. Mrs. Lee found a house in Lafayette Square, and, after a life-and-death struggle with the "curious barbarism" of the curtains and wall-papers, she and her sister, Sybil Ross, slipped into their places at Washington. While Madeleine carried about with her "an atmosphere indescribable as the after-glow, and impalpable as an Indian summer mist,"

Sybil was the most straightforward, gay, sympathetic, shallow, warm-hearted, and sternly practical of young women. Madeleine was unconventional, and had a natural aversion to churches and clergymen; Sybil bowed her white shoulders to the decrees of M. Worth, and was, besides, a Ritualist of the purest water. Whilst Sybil amused herself, Mrs. Lee began her apprenticeship to politics. Her first experiments, however, were not very successful. For a fortnight, indeed, she was indefatigable in her attendance on the debates. And even when her first fervour slackened, for a long time if she did not hear the speeches she read them. But a day arrived at last when she became pusillanimously content to take her countrymen's oratorical powers for granted, except on those rare occasions when some "star" performed, and it became evident that some more excellent way to the heart of the American mystery must be discovered. Meanwhile a circle of all that was brightest and most distinguished in Washington gathered round the sisters. Most welcome of all, perhaps, was John Carrington, a Washington lawyer and a connection of Mrs. Lee's. A Virginian by birth, he had borne arms for the South in the war, and at its close, leaving his mother and sisters to manage the ruins of the family estate, he had come up to Washington, where he was making a brave struggle with unkindly fortune. Sybil thought him dull, and not even fighting had been able to kindle his naturally depressed temperament into enthusiasm; but he was as true as steel, and "Mrs. Lee trusted him by instinct." Next to him ranked Lord Skye, the British Minister.

> "Tall, slender, bald-headed, awkward, and stammering with his elaborate British stammer whenever it suited his convenience to do so; a sharp observer who had wit, which he commonly concealed; a humourist who was satisfied to laugh silently at his own humour; a diplomatist who used the mail of frankness with great effect, Lord Skye was one of the most popular men in Washington. Everyone knew that he was a ruthless critic of American manners, but he had the art to combine ridicule with good-humour, and he was all the more popular accordingly. He was an outspoken adviser of American women in everything except their voices, and he did not even shrink from occasionally quizzing a little the national peculiarities of his own countrywomen—a sure piece of flattery to their American cousins."

Sybil's chief friend was "little Miss Dare," a dangerous piece of yellow-haired mischief who was "always absorbed in some flirtation with a Secretary of Legation," and while "apparently devoted to men in reality cared nothing about them, but found her happiness only in violating rules." Among the outer circle of visitors was Baron Jacobi, the Austrian *chargé d'affaires*, a witty, cynical, broken-down Parisian *roué*, whose mind was a magazine of amusing information, and who "believed in everything that was perverse and wicked, though he accepted the prejudices of Anglo-Saxon society, and was too clever to intrude his opinions upon others;" his friend Popoff, "an intelligent and vivacious Russian;" and Mr. French, the young Member of Congress from Connecticut, "who aspired to act the part of the educated gentleman in politics, and to purify the public tone," but who had an exasperating turn for what he called "badinaige," which alienated Sybil, while Madeleine was driven into revolt by his raw sententiousness on serious subjects. Mr. Gore, poet and historian, in pursuit of the Madrid Embassy; the innocent Irish peer, Lord Dunbeg, to whom Victoria Dare was soon engaged in showing the "phases" of American society, and a few more supernumeraries complete the list.

These, however, are but the chorus to the principal figures. The dramatic interest of *Democracy* lies in the clash of two relations—the relation of Madeleine to Senator Silas P. Ratcliffe, and the relation of Carrington to Madeleine through Sybil. As it was for the sake of drawing Ratcliffe that the book was mainly written, it will be well to examine his *rôle* with some care. Madeleine first notices him in the Senate, whither Carrington had taken her to hear him speak.

> " 'You will have a chance of hearing to-day what may be the last great speech of our greatest statesman,' said he; 'you should come.'
> " 'A splendid sample of our na—tive raw material, sir?' asked she, fresh from a reading of Dickens, and his famous picture of American statesmanship.
> " 'Precisely so,' said Carrington, 'the Prairie Giant of Peonia, the Favourite Son of Illinois; the man who came within three votes of getting the party nomination for the Presidency last spring, and was only defeated because ten small intriguers are sharper than one big one. The Honourable Silas P. Ratcliffe, Senator from Illinois; he will be run for the Presidency yet.'
> " 'What does the P. stand for?' asked Sybil.
> " 'I don't remember ever to have heard his middle name,' said Carrington. 'Perhaps it is Peonia or Prairie, I can't say.'
> " 'He is the man whose appearance struck me so much when we were in the Senate last week, is he not? A great ponderous man, over six feet high, very senatorial and digni-fied, with a large head and rather good features?' inquired Mrs. Lee.
> " 'The same,' replied Carrington. 'By all means hear him speak. He is the stumbling-block of the new President, who is to be allowed no peace unless he makes terms with Ratcliffe; and so everyone thinks that the Prairie Giant of Peonia will have the choice of the State or Treasury Department. If he takes either it will be the Treasury, for he is a desperate political manager, and will want the patronage for the next national convention.' "

Thus prepared, Madeleine goes to hear Ratcliffe, discovers in his speech the power of which she is in search, and instantly determines to know him. She carries out her intention at a dinner-party where she sits next to him, and where her wholesale flattery of him makes up the one thoroughly vulgar passage in the book. It is impossible that the Madeleine of the rest of the story should have condescended so far; the scene, therefore, is a shock to the reader's sense of probability and continuity. Ratcliffe, however, makes no difficulty about swallowing the bait dangled before him by Mrs. Lee. He had begun his dinner in sulky silence, "wishing he understood why the British Minister had worn no gloves," while he himself was uncomfortably conscious of the largest and whitest French kids to be bought in Pennsylvania Avenue.

> "There was a little touch of mortification in the idea that he was not quite at home among fashionable people, and at this instant he felt that true happiness was only to be found among the simple and honest sons and daughters of toil. A certain secret jealousy of the British Minister is always lurking in the breast of every American Senator, if he is truly democratic; for democracy, rightly understood, is the government of the people, by the people, for the benefit of Senators, and there is always a danger that the British Minister may not understand this political principle as he should."

At the second course, however, Mrs. Lee swoops upon him, and so liberal is her homage, so childlike her desire for knowledge, that in ten minutes she has this giant of politics at her feet. Silas P. Ratcliffe surrenders to her charm, and the play is fairly launched.

> "To her eyes he was the high-priest of American politics; he was charged with the meaning of the mysteries, the clue to political hieroglyphics. Through him she hoped to sound the depths of statesmanship and to bring up from its oozy bed that pearl of which she was in search; the mysterious gem which must lie hidden somewhere in politics. She wanted to understand this man; to turn him inside out; to experiment on him and use him as young physiologists use frogs and kittens. If there was good or bad in him, she meant to find its meaning.
> "And he was a western widower of fifty; his quarters in Washington were in gaunt boarding-house rooms, furnished only with public documents and enlivened by western politicians and office-seekers. In the summer he retired to a solitary, white farmhouse with green blinds, surrounded by a few feet of uncared-for grass and a white fence; its interior more dreary still, with iron stoves, oil-cloth carpets, cold white walls, and one large engraving of Abraham Lincoln in the parlour; all in Peonia, Illinois! What equality was there between these two combatants? what hope for him? what risk for her? And yet Madeleine Lee had fully her match in Mr. Silas P. Ratcliffe."

It was not very long before Ratcliffe had established himself as a familiar visitor in Mrs. Lee's parlour. He was not particularly welcome to anybody there, except its mistress. Carrington had his own good reasons for thinking ill of Mrs. Lee's latest conquest; Sybil detested him; Mr. French fell clumsily foul of him on the question of Civil Service Reform; and old Jacobi "despised and loathed an American Senator as the type which, to his bleared European eyes, combined the utmost pragmatical self-assurance and overbearing temper with the narrowest education and the meanest personal experience that ever existed in any considerable government." Ratcliffe, however, took small heed of the hostility of Mrs. Lee's friends. He was determined to make himself agreeable to her, and the more critical his political affairs became, the more Madeleine's fascination grew upon him. Washington, indeed, was at that moment passing through one of its periodical crises of political bargaining. A new President was expected, of whom the official world knew next to nothing. His election had been an accident, and all that even his party knew of him was that "he was a plain Indiana farmer, whose political experience was limited to stump-speaking in his native State and to one term as Governor." He belonged to the opposite section to that headed by Ratcliffe, and it was well known that his feelings towards the Prairie Giant were by no means friendly. "His cardinal principle in politics was hostility to Ratcliffe, yet he was not vindictive. He came to Washington determined to be the Father of his country; to gain a proud immortality—and a re-election." Ratcliffe's object is of course to make it impossible for the President to do without him, and at the same time to reap the harvest of offices for his dependents and friends, from which it was rumoured the President had sworn to cut him off. The details of Ratcliffe's intrigues, by which the more clumsily-witted President is finally ensnared and made to run tamely at Ratcliffe's heels, have been perhaps more quoted than anything else in *Democracy*. The author had a special reason for describing them at length, for, as we shall show some cause for believing, the book probably sprang from the conviction that so long as Presidents are weak and public opinion apathetic, corruption in America will go on, and that the essential conditions of any reform in public morality are, first, a strong President; secondly, a roused and indignant public opinion. But, clever as it is, the whole description suffers from caricature and what looks at times like the haste of the 'prentice hand, and is to our mind inferior to much else in the work. The President himself may very possibly have been violently overcoloured in order that it might be difficult for the reader to make any personal application of the sketch. After all, there have been only some twenty Presidents since America began, and it is therefore much less easy to satirise the weak points of Presidents as a class so as to be effective and yet decently impersonal than it is to perform the operation for the more numerous class of senators. And when all objections are made, Ratcliffe's negotiations with the "Hoosier Quarryman" are lively reading.

The Senator's political complications have a considerable effect upon his relations to Madeleine, for he is clever enough to enlist her sympathies with him as the victim of Presidential crookedness, and to make her, against her will, arbiter of as much of his cause as he chooses to reveal to her.

In this way the game goes on. Madeleine's friends, especially Carrington, begin to grow anxious. They see Ratcliffe's increasing influence with Mrs. Lee, and they find themselves powerless to stop it. They try in vain to make the man betray himself before her. He pretends to no superior virtue in her presence; he candidly confesses that if virtue will not serve him in politics he has no scruple against using vice. But at the same time he succeeds in preserving his largeness of outline in her eyes. She sees in him the victim of a corrupt system, and is not at all sure that it is not her duty to help him reform it. Carrington at last becomes desperate, and bethinks himself of fresh weapons. He happens to have in his possession certain secrets extremely damaging to Ratcliffe's character, for which the evidence, though strong enough to convince Mrs. Lee if it were put before her, is yet legally imperfect. He gives Ratcliffe one or two intimations that he possesses this knowledge. Ratcliffe takes the hint, and only resolves to get Carrington out of the way. A direct bribe in the shape of an appointment having been indignantly rejected by Carrington, who is thus made to appear vindictive and prejudiced in the eyes of Mrs. Lee, with whom he is all the time hopelessly in love, Ratcliffe uses his power as Secretary of the Treasury to find the means of making Carrington accept an appointment in Mexico, and triumphantly calculates upon getting his rival safely out of the way before he proposes to Madeleine. Carrington is miserable. He suspects Ratcliffe's agency in the appointment, carefully as it has been disguised. But there is no proving it, and on the other hand there are poverty and family claims urging him to accept. What is to be done? In his extremity, however, he discovers that one other person is as anxious as himself, and that Sybil is as desperate as he is at the thought of Madeleine's marriage with Ratcliffe. The two combine against the enemy, and in their last ride together a plan of campaign is matured.

It ends in Carrington giving Sybil a letter only to be made use of in case Ratcliffe proposes and Madeleine should incline to accept him, and he then goes off, torn with hopes and fears, to Mexico. With his departure the plot rapidly developes. Ratcliffe, whose manners are improving fast under the influence of his passion for Madeleine, becomes more and more dangerous; and Sybil, half in love with Carrington, and miserably anxious about her sister, gives a wholly new turn to the situation by arousing the suspicion in Madeleine's mind that she is consumed with a hopeless passion for Carrington. Madeleine at once jumps to the conclusion that if only she were out of the way Sybil's affection might stand a chance of being returned, and the idea determines her to sacrifice herself to Ratcliffe for the sake of Sybil first, and, secondly, for the sake of those wild dreams of power to be used in reforming political life inspired in her by her connection with him. At a ball given by Lord Skye matters come to a climax, and nothing but a convenient fainting-fit of Sybil's interferes between Ratcliffe's proposal and Mrs. Lee's "Yes." An exciting interview between the sisters follows. Madeleine, sure that she is doing her best for Sybil and society, declares that she means to marry Mr. Ratcliffe. So there is no help for it, and Sybil, driven to bay, produces Mr. Carrington's letter, and stands over her sister while she reads it.

The letter contains nothing but a very plain and matter-of-fact account of the manner in which Ratcliffe had been induced some years before to withdraw his opposition in the Senate to a certain steam-ship company concession in return for the round sum of 100,000 dollars, paid into his hands by a man well known to Carrington, and among whose papers Carrington had found a memorandum of the whole transaction. The affair was bad enough, although mild compared to many of the records of discovered or suspected frauds with which American political literature can furnish the inquiring mind. At any rate it is enough for Madeleine. She has never been in love with Ratcliffe. She has been in love with a shadow raised by her own vanity, and Carrington's well-aimed blow sweeps it for ever from her path.

Madeleine's final interview with Ratcliffe, which follows, is one of the most powerful scenes in modern fiction. The effrontery with which he meets Carrington's charge, the defence by which he makes bad worse, the growing wonder in Madeleine's mind as to how she could ever have let this man approach her so nearly, are drawn with passionate power. At the last moment, when Ratcliffe, feeling that the game is up, and that he has been checkmated, turns upon her with brutal violence, Madeleine pronounces a sentence upon him which reads like the sentence of American conscience on the corrupt political world exposed in *Democracy*.

> "Mrs. Lee's temper, too, was naturally a high one. At this moment she, too, was flaming with anger, and wild with a passionate impulse to annihilate this man. Conscious that the mastery was in her own hands, she could the more easily control her voice, and with an expression of unutterable contempt she spoke her last words to him, words which had been ringing all day in her ears:
>
> " 'Mr. Ratcliffe! I have listened to you with a great deal more patience and respect than you deserve. For one long hour I have degraded myself by discussing with you the question whether I should marry a man who by his own confession has betrayed the highest trusts that could be placed in him, who has taken money for his votes as a Senator, and who is now in

public office by means of a successful fraud of his own, when in justice he should be in a State's prison. I will have no more of this. Understand, once for all, that there is an impassable gulf between your life and mine. I do not doubt that you will make yourself President, but whatever or wherever you are, never speak to me or recognize me again!' "

"He glared a moment into her face with a sort of blind rage, and seemed about to say more, when she swept past him, and before he realised it he was alone.

"Overmastered by passion, but conscious that he was powerless, Ratcliffe, after a moment's hesitation, left the room and the house. He let himself out, shutting the front door behind him, and as he stood on the pavement old Baron Jacobi, who had special reasons for wishing to know how Mrs. Lee had recovered from the fatigue and excitements of the ball, came up to the spot. A single glance at Ratcliffe showed him that something had gone wrong in the career of that great man, whose fortunes he always followed with so bitter a sneer of contempt. Impelled by the spirit of evil always at his elbow, the Baron seized this moment to sound the depth of his friend's wound. They met at the door so closely that recognition was inevitable, and Jacobi, with his worst smile, held out his hand, saying at the same moment with diabolic malignity:—

" 'I hope I may offer my felicitations to your Excellency!'

" 'Ratcliffe was glad to find some victim on whom he could vent his rage. He had a long score of humiliations to repay this man, whose last insult was beyond all endurance. With an oath he dashed Jacobi's hand aside, and, grasping his shoulder, thrust him out of the path. The Baron, among whose weaknesses the want of high temper and personal courage were not recorded, had no mind to tolerate such an insult from such a man. Even while Ratcliffe's hand was still on his shoulder he had raised his cane, and before the Secretary saw what was coming, the old man had struck him with all his force full in the face. For a moment Ratcliffe staggered back and grew pale, but the shock sobered him. He hesitated a single instant whether to crush his assailant with a blow, but he felt that for one of his youth and strength to attack an infirm diplomatist in a public street would be a fatal blunder, and while jacobi stood, violently excited with his cane raised and ready to strike another blow, Mr. Ratcliffe suddenly turned his back and without a word, hastened away.

"When Sybil returned, not long afterwards, she found no one in the parlour. On going to her sister's room she discovered Madeleine lying on the couch, looking worn and pale, but with a slight smile and a peaceful expression on her face, as though she had done some act which her conscience approved. She called Sybil to her side, and, taking her hand, said:

" 'Sybil, dearest, will you go abroad with me again?'

> " 'Of course I will,' said Sybil: 'I will go to the end of the world with you.'
>
> " 'I want to go to Egypt,' said Madeleine, still smiling faintly; 'democracy has shaken my nerves to pieces. Oh, what rest it would be to live in the Great Pyramid and look out for ever at the polar star!' "

It is as if the author, but half content with Mrs. Lee's punishment, were fiercely adding to it Baron Jacobi's cane, as the only last impression worth connecting with ignominy like Ratcliffe's.

It must not be supposed, however, that the material of democracy is all of this sombre and painful quality. The characters of Carrington and Sybil form an admirable foil to those of Ratcliffe and Mrs. Lee. Carrington is everything that Ratcliffe is not. In life generally he has been on the losing side. He fought in the ranks of the South, not for slavery, but for independence and Virginia, and in love he fights Ratcliffe, not for himself, for "he habitually loses sight of himself," but for Madeleine and her freedom. Nothing can exceed the delicacy with which the ripening friendship between himself and Sybil is described. The common need of both, Madeleine's salvation, draws them together, and under the influence of their grand alliance his melancholy relaxes and her flippant gaiety grows softer. In one of their rides together "he told her all his private circumstances."

> " 'You say that love is nonsense, Miss Ross. I tell you it is no such thing. For weeks and months it is a steady physical pain, an ache about the heart, never leaving one, by night or by day; a long strain on one's nerves like toothache or rheumatism, not intolerable at any one instant, but exhausting by its steady drain on the strength. It is a disease to be borne with patience, like any other nervous complaint, and to be treated with counter-irritants. My trip to Mexico will be good for it, but that is not the reason why I must go.'
>
> "Then he told her all his private circumstances; the ruin which the war had brought on him and his family; how, of his two brothers, one had survived the war only to die at home, a mere wreck of disease, privation, and wounds; the other had been shot at his side, and bled slowly to death in his arms during the awful carnage in the Wilderness; how his mother and two sisters were struggling for a bare subsistence on a wretched Virginian farm, and how all his exertions barely kept them from beggary.
>
> " 'You have no conception of the poverty to which our Southern women are reduced since the war,' said he; 'they are many of them literally without clothes or bread.' The fee he should earn by going to Mexico would double his income this year. Could he refuse? Had he a right to refuse? And poor Carrington added, with a groan, that if he alone were in question, he would sooner be shot than go.

"Sybil listened wtih tears in her eyes. She never before had seen a man show suffering. The misery she had known in life had been more or less veiled to her and softened by falling on older and friendly shoulders. She now got for the first time a clear view of Carrington, apart from the quiet exterior in which the man was hidden. She felt quite sure, by a sudden flash of feminine inspiration, that the curious look of patient endurance on his face was the work of a single night when he had held his brother in his arms, and knew that the blood was draining drop by drop from his side, in the dense, tangled woods, beyond the reach of help, hour after hour, till the voice failed and the limbs grew stiff and cold. When he had finished his story, she was afraid to speak. She did not know how to show her sympathy, and she could not bear to seem unsympathetic. In her embarrassment she fairly broke down and could only dry her eyes in silence."

Sybil, however, repays his confidences on the subject of his passion for Madeleine with a mixture of encouragement and ridicule. In her eyes it is absurd that men should make such a fuss about women, and she altogether refuses to believe that the world will come to an end should Madeleine, after all, refuse to marry him.

There are one or two things that must be said about the political side of *Democracy*, but it may be as well here to sum up one's impressions of the story from the literary point of view. The inference may be an entirely wrong one, but the book strikes us as the first book, at any rate as the first novel of its author. There are signs in it of want of finish, there is an amount of caricature which, balanced against the brilliant ability and the imaginative power shown in it as a whole, persuade us that *Democracy* is the rapid work of a writer unaccustomed to throw his thoughts into this shape, and acquiring, as he writes, more and more dexterity in the use of his new tools. It is the novel-form only which is unfamiliar, for it would be hard to convince us that the author was in any other sense a literary novice. At the same time, the ease and rapidity of the story-telling is very great, and the dialogue, although not exactly of the same quality as that which delights us in Mr. James or Mr. Howells, has the true American sparkle and suggestiveness. This American dialogue, in the main the creation of Mr. James and his followers, has a stamp altogether its own. In an ordinary English novel the dialogue is used simply and solely for the purpose of developing the action. The story is told in it, and for the most part very baldly told. In his best novels, dialogue and conversation are principally used for the purpose of developing character, and there is no need to dwell on the delicacy and force with which our great novelists have employed both. With the dialogue used for airing social or philosophical "views" we are all well acquainted. But this American dialogue is like some bright many-coloured plaything. It tends to purposes of pure pleasure, and while the duty of unfolding character is, of course, often necessarily entrusted to it, it constantly aims at nothing more than exciting in the reader the same exhilaration which we get in real life out of such dainty tossing of the shuttlecock of speech. The author of *Democracy* shows no such perfection in the art as others have attained. The scantiness of his canvas perhaps forbade it, and his purpose was best reached by methods more swift and telling than those which delight us on the deck of the *Aroostook*, where all the change allowed is from a *tête-à-tête* with Dunham, sitting, to a *tête-à-tête* with Staniford, walking. Still at those rare points where the story loiters to let the author take his pleasure with his characters, the peculiar American ideal of conversation makes itself felt, and we are made to realise all the charms of Madeleine's cleverness and all the good spirits of Sybil's chatter. And throughout the dialogue is full of sharp sayings and epigrammatic turns of expression, while both in it and in the general management of the story, with a few slight exceptions, the writer shows admirable self-control. Too much might so easily have been attempted in the drawing of Ratcliffe or in the description of Washington society. Too much perhaps has been attempted in the picture of the President. But Ratcliffe's points are broadly handled, and for the rest a few touches and the thing is done. Lord Skye and his ball, the house at Mount Vernon, Sybil's ball-dress and Sybil's triumphs, they are there and done with in a few pages or a few sentences, of which in a first reading one may very well miss the significance, so rapid is the touch. The book has faults, but there is not a dull page in it to those who care for life as well as lovemaking, from the moment of Madeleine's entry upon Washington society to the moment when Ratcliffe's evil nature measures itself in powerless fury against a woman's soft inexorable resistance.

Politically, the moral of the book is easy to read. The pith of it lies in a speech of Baron Jacobi's. Madeleine has been appealing to Ratcliffe to know, "What is to become of us if corruption is allowed to go unchecked?"

" 'And may I venture to ask permission to hear Mr. Ratcliffe's reply?' asked the baron.

" 'My reply,' said Ratcliffe, 'is that no representative government can long be much better or much worse than the society it represents. Purify society and you purify the government. But try to purify the government artificially and you only aggravate failure.'

" 'A very statesmanlike reply,' said Baron Jacobi, with a formal bow, but his tone had a shade of mockery. Carrington, who had listened with a darkening face, suddenly turned to the baron and asked him what conclusion he drew from the reply.

" 'Ah!' exclaimed the baron, with his wickedest leer, 'what for is my conclusion good? You Americans believe yourselves to be excepted from the operation of general laws.

You care not for experience. I have lived seventy-five years, and all that time in the midst of corruption. I am corrupt myself, only I do have courage to proclaim it, and you others have it not. Rome, Paris, Vienna, Petersburg, London, all are corrupt; only Washington is pure! Well, I declare to you that in all my experience I have found no society which has had elements of corruption like the United States. The children in the street are corrupt, and know how to cheat me. The cities are all corrupt and also the towns and the counties and the States' legislatures and the judges. Everywhere men betray trusts both public and private, steal money, run away with public funds. Only the Senate men take no money. And you gentlemen in the Senate very well declare that your great United States, which is the head of the civilised world, can never learn anything from the example of corrupt Europe. You are right—quite right! The great United States needs not an example. I do much regret that I have not yet one hundred years to live. If I could then come back to this city, I should find myself very content—much more than now. I am always content where there is much corruption, and *ma parole d'honneur!'* broke out the old man with fire and gesture, 'the United States will then be more corrupt than Rome under Caligula; more corrupt than the Church under Leo X.; more corrupt than France under the Regent!' "

And this corruption we are given to understand depends upon the "spoils" system. It is this which has demoralized American public life to such an extent that the American Senator is no longer content with the corrupt distribution of patronage; he buys other people's votes by office, but he sells his own for money. It is a terrible charge; and one may well ask, in the face of the knowledge and the passion with which it is pressed home in *Democracy*, how near it comes to the truth. Any one who chooses may find it supported by many facts and much strong writing in Mr. Parton's famous article in the *North American Review*, for last July. "In the ninety-fifth year of the Constitution," said Mr. Parton, "we are face to face with a state of politics of extreme simplicity, of which money is the motive, the means, and the end." The men who provide and receive this money are the office-holders of the country, so that Government tends more and more to become "rather an appendage to a circle of wealthy operators than a restraint upon them." The scandals of 1875, which were the partial cause of the temporary Democratic revival of that year, throw Ratcliffe's performances into the shade, and although the *Nation* in reviewing *Democracy* protested against the sketch as over-coloured, its own pages contained a few weeks later a review of a case in which a prominent Senator played a part by no means unlike the transaction which cost Ratcliffe his suit, and in an article on Civil Service Reform about the same date, it admits that "the account given in *Democracy* of the feelings with which Senator Ratcliffe regarded Mr. French, the Connecticut Congressman, who ventured to broach the subject (of Reform) in his presence, is but a faint picture of the way one of its advocates would be regarded by a Republican boss and a party of henchmen in an hotel parlour. The mixture of loathing, contempt, and amusement he would excite in them would make all discussion with them impossible." Since 1861, in fact, American newspapers and magazines have teemed with discussion of this same unsavoury subject of political corruption, till at last the national conscience shows signs of having been roused, and we seem to be witnessing the beginning of what may prove to be a great popular reaction. It was to such a kindling of public opinion that all patriotic persons were long ago summoned to lend their aid by a remarkable article on Civil Service Reform in the *North American Review* for 1869. Are we misled by mere fancy in connecting it with *Democracy*? At least the writer of the novel seems to have almost exactly followed the lines laid down in that essay. In it the author, Mr. Henry Brook Adams, a name honourably known both here and in America, described the state of things which followed President Grant's accession to office in 1868. The President's original determination to oppose the "spoils" system, the vigour with which the disappointed office-seekers flung themselves on the White House, the struggle which followed, and the final surrender of the President, are drawn with a force, and at times with a humour, which constantly recall the scenes of *Democracy*. Moreover, as we have already pointed out, the author of the novel has sacrificed literary proportion for the sake of drawing the worst possible President—a man weak in knowledge, weak in manners, weak in will, and weak above all in his social surroundings. Given a President ever so little superior to Ratcliffe, he seems to say, and Ratcliffe's game would have been impossible. It is curious that the one conclusion drawn by Mr. Adams from the events of 1868 is that two things, and two things only, are wanted for political reform in America, a strong President, and at his back a strong public opinion.

> "If the President is weak," Mr. Adams continued, "it is merely because public opinion is silent and support is not to be found. Whenever public opinion has once declared itself in favour of Civil Service reform and against the corrupt use of patronage by politicians, the evil will cease, nor need any anxiety be thrown away in regard to resistance by the Senate, since such factious opposition would only give to the people the opportunity of striking at the agents of corruption, an opportunity which may one day be used with effect so soon as old political issues can be finally disposed of. But before this time arrives the public must be convinced that reform is a vital question, that the evils and dangers are real and not mere inventions of a lively fancy. To effect this, there is no way but to

attack corruption in all its holes, to drag it before the public eye, to dissect it and hold the diseased members up to popular disgust, to give the nation's conscience no rest or peace until mere vehemence of passion overcomes the sluggishness of the public mind."

It is clear that *Democracy*, whether Mr. Adams had a hand in it or not, represents just such an appeal to the people, just such an attempt to strike the popular imagination and to "overcome the sluggishness of the public mind." Strange that little more than a year after the appearance of the book there should arise the struggle over the collectorship of New York, and that public sympathy should have been, at least for the time, overwhelmingly enlisted on the side of the President in his conflict with a system which threatens to swamp the executive power altogether, by the sufferings and the courage of General Garfield. The tragedy of last summer purified for the moment all the associations of the Presidential office, and the memory of that death-bed, that domestic life, that poverty, may well bid us hope when *Democracy* has forced us to despair.

The book we have been describing has been freely used as a text for fluent denunciations of all things American and democratic. To those inclined to employ it in this way we would recommend the perusal of certain official reports issued last year, in which the veil was drawn from the administrative corruption which darkened the last days of Alexander II of Russia. The truth is, that neither empire nor republic, as such, has any monopoly of political greed and selfishness. In the younger community it is very possibly an inevitable incident of growth, of the extraordinarily rapid expansion of a heterogeneous society formed out of the broken materials of old and complex civilisations. But whether it be so or no, and whether the critics of America succeed or not in establishing a necessary connection between a republic and political demoralisation, the lesson of history and the signs of the future remain unaltered. For the future is with the masses, with equality, with democracy. We may resist and bewail ourselves, if we will, but the nobler part is to hope; the more courageous part is to throw ourselves into the stream of our time with something of the devotion expressed by one of the characters in this disquieting book—

"I believe in democracy. I accept it. I will faithfully serve and defend it. I grant it is an experiment, but it is the only direction society can take that is worth its taking; the only conception of its duty large enough to satisfy its instincts; the only result that is worth an effort or a risk. Let us be true to our time! If our age is to be beaten, let us die in the ranks. If it is to be victorious, let us be first to lead the column."

"The Expense of Greatness: Three Emphases on Henry Adams"

R. P. Blackmur*

Where your small man is a knoll to be smoothed away, Henry Adams is a mountain to be mined on all flanks for pure samples of human imagination without loss of size or value. That is the double test of greatness, that it show an attractive force, massive and inexhaustible, and a disseminative force which is the inexhaustible spring or constant declaration of value. As we elucidate our reaction to the two forces we measure the greatness.

In Adams the attractive force is in the immediate relevance that his life and works have for our own. The problems he posed of human energy and human society are felt at once to be special and emphatic articulations of our own problems. The disseminative, central force, which we find objectified in his works, may be felt and seen as the incandescence of the open, enquiring, sensitive, and sceptical intelligence, restless but attentive, saltatory but serial, provisional in every position yet fixed upon a theme: the theme of thought or imagination conceived as the form of human energy. We feel the incandescence in the human values and aspirations that were fused by it, from time to time, in persuasive form; and the cumulus of his life and works makes a focus, different as differently felt, whereby the particular values actually rendered shine concentrated as it were in their own best light. We make the man focus upon himself, make him achieve—as he never could for himself in the flux and flexion of life—his own most persuasive form. To make such a focus is the labour and the use of critical appreciation.

The approaches to such a labour are varied and must be constantly renewed and often revised. No single approach is omniscient or even sufficient. Here, in this essay, I want to take Henry Adams in a single perspective and submit it to three related emphases. I want to regard him as he often chose to regard himself, as a representative example of education:

but education pushed to the point of failure as contrasted with ordinary education which stops at the formula of success.

The perspective is worth a preliminary emphasis of its own. It was as failure both in perspective and lesson by lesson that Adams himself saw his education. Success is not the propitious term for education unless the lesson wanted is futile. Education has no term and if arrested at all is only arrested by impassable failure. Surely the dominant emotion of an education, when its inherent possibilities are compared with those it achieved, must strike the honest heart as the emotion of failure. The failure is not of knowledge or of feeling. It is the failure of the ability to react correctly or even intelligently to more than an abbreviated version of knowledge and feeling: failure in the radical sense that we cannot consciously react to more than a minor fraction of the life we yet deeply know and endure and die. It is the failure the mind comes to ultimately and all along when it is compelled to measure its knowledge in terms of its ignorance.

Most failures we have the tact to ignore or give a kinder name. That is because we know by instinct at what a heavy discount to put most proffered examples of failure. There was no effort of imagination in them and only private agony, where for great failure we want the utmost unrelenting imagination and the impersonal agony of knowledge searching the haven of objective form. Most failures come too easily, take too little stock of the life and forces around them: like the ordinary failure in marriage, or business, or dying; and so too much resemble the ordinary success—too solemn and scant and zestless for realisation. A genuine failure comes hard and slow, and, as in a tragedy, is only fully realised at the end. A man's success is in society, precarious and fatal; his failure is both in spite and because of society—as he witnesses its radical imperfection and is himself produced by it, its ultimate expression. Thus in a great man we often find inextricably combined the success which was his alone, though posthumously recognised, with the failure which as we feel it is also our own in prospect.

Let us take for our first emphasis Adams as a failure in society. If we assume that an education means the acquisition of skills and the mastery of tools designed for intelligent reaction in a given context, it will appear that Adams' failure in American political society after the Civil War was a failure in education. Society was bound for quick success and cared only for enough intelligence to go on with. It cared nothing for political mastery, and commonly refused to admit it had a purpose beyond the aggregation of force in the form of wealth. The effect on Adams as a young man was immediate but took time to recognize. If *vis inertiae* was enough for society, any education was too much; and an Adams—with the finest education of his times—was clearly useless. The question was perhaps not initially Adams' failure but of society's inability to make use of him: its inability to furnish a free field for intelligent political action. Washington was full of wasted talent—of able young men desperately anxious to be of use—as it is now; but no one knows what talent might accomplish, then or now, because talent has never been given a chance without being at the same moment brutally hamstrung.

The discovery—that he was to be wasted whether he was any good or not—was all the bitterer to Henry Adams because he had three generations of conspicuous ability and conspicuous failure behind him. Every Adams had ended as a failure after a lifetime of effort—marked by occasional and transitory success—to handle political power intelligently. Their intelligence they had kept; none had ever succumbed to the criminal satisfaction of power on its lower terms—whether power for interest, or, worst of all, power for its own sake: the absolute corruption, as it seems to a scrupulous mind, of giving in; but all equally had failed at the height of their abilities. If times had changed for Henry it was for the worse. Where his ancestors found in a combination of scruple and temper an effective termination of useful public careers, Henry found his scruple alone enough to preclude a public career altogether. Scruple is sometimes only a name for snobbery, stiffness, or even an inner coldness—all, forms of disability; but in an Adams scruple was the mark of ability itself, and its limit, as it made intelligence acute, responsible, and infinitely resourceful, but a little purblind to the advantage of indirection. An Adams could meet an issue, accept facts, and demonstrate a policy, but he could never gamble with a public matter. Jefferson's epitaph for John applied to them all: as disinterested as his maker. If the odds grew heavy against an Adams he resorted to an access of will—or, if you choose to call it, a wall of stubbornness, which is merely will grown hysterical. But acts of will or stubbornness are merely the last resorts of minds compelled to act scrupulously against the unintelligent or the unintelligible.

Thus it is that many great men, if seen as examples of intellectual biography, seem either sports or parasites upon the society that produced them. They were compelled to act against or outside it; and our sense of radical connection and expressive identity is only re-established in the examples of their works aside from their lives. Certainly something of the sort is true, with different emphases, of Whitman, Mark Twain, Henry James, Melville, and in our own day of Hart Crane and George Santayana. They stand out too much from their native society: all outsiders from the life they expressed and upon which they fed. If all knew the ignominy of applause, applause from the wrong people, for the wrong thing, or for something not performed at all, it only accented their own sense of eccentricity and loneliness. That is how Adams stood out, but without much applause ignominious or otherwise, eccentric and lonely; but within him, as within the others in their degrees, was an intelligence whose actions were direct, naked, and at their best terrifyingly sane.

If, as I think, it was the scruple of his mind that made Adams an outsider and that at the same time gave precise value to his eccentricity, then the scruple should be defined both for itself and in terms of Adams. It is what I have been deviously leading up to: as it represents the single heroic and admirable quality of the modern and sceptical mind as such; and a quality not called for by the occasion but crowning it, even when disastrously.

Scruple, generally speaking, is the agent of integrity, what keeps action honest on the level of affairs, or on the level of imagination when actuality or truth is the object. The etymology of the word refreshes the meaning I emphasise, where we have the Latin *scrupulus*, a small sharp stone, a stone in one's shoe, an uneasiness, difficulty, small trouble, or doubt. Scruples differ with the type of mind and education. Most men either get rid of them or show pride in their calluses. In either case the process of thought is made easy and reaction insensitive; you give in, you are practically carried along, but you get nowhere except where you are taken, and you know nothing at all of what you have been through, or of its meaning.

Specifically, with Henry Adams, scruple of thinking and thence of action was the whole point of his education for public life. Men without scruples either victimised power or succumbed to it; and if you had the wrong scruples you succumbed, like Grant, without knowing it. Political education was meant to supply the right scruples at the start, to teach sensitiveness to new ones as they came up, and to ingrain a habit of feeling for them if not apparent. It is scruples that compel attention to detail and subordinate the detail to an end. When excess atrophies the mind, whether of scruples or the lack of them, it is because either an impossible end or no end was in view. In science the adjudication of scruples is called method and taken for granted; but the whole test of the democratic process is whether or not the seat of power attracts the scrupulous intelligence and gives it rein. Here we may conceive Henry Adams as a provisional focus for that test.

In a sense no test is possible. Adams never held office. He only made himself embarrassingly available in the near background of Grant's Washington. Power was what he wanted, but on his own terms: the terms of his training. Perhaps he offered too much; perhaps his offers seemed too much like demands; at any rate he got nothing. But if we take him as a type—whether of 1868 or 1932—we can see that he was in the predicament of all young men whose abilities seem to lie in public life but who refuse waste motion. Society has no use for them as they are, and the concessions it requires are fatal to self-respect and taste, and lead either to futility, the treason of submission, or an aching combination of the two.

Both Adams and society saw politics was a game, but the difference in their angles of vision made their views irreconcilable. Adams saw the game as played impersonally with, as ultimate stake, the responsible control of social energy. Since ultimate value was never sure, every move ought to be made with the maximum intelligence and subject to every criticism your experience provided. If you stuck scrupulously to your intelligence you had the chance to come out right in the end under any scruples, democratic or not. You had a chance to put your society in control of itself at the centre of its being. That was Adams' idea of the game, the idea of any honest young man.

Society played differently. The stake was immediate power, the values were those of personal interest. Thus the actual stake—control of social energy—was left for the ventures of interests irresponsible to the government meant to control them. Society in its political aspect cared more for chaos than unity; and the democratic process was an unconfessed failure, obliviously committing itself to social anarchy. Yet the failure remained unconfessed; the society lived and gathered energy; it was omnivorous, rash, and stupid; it threatened to become uncontrollably leviathan; it seemed occasionally on the point of committing suicide in the full flush of life. Always it had been saved, so far, by its vitality, its prodigious capacity for successive ruination, or by the discovery of a new and available source of power.

There was the young man's predicament. Should he assume that society was no field for intelligence and that its own momentum was sufficient to its needs? Should he rather enter the field, outwardly playing society's version of the game, while inwardly playing his own as best he could? Or should he work on society from the outside, accepting his final defeat at the start, and express the society rather than attempt to control it?

The first choice is the hardest; taken mostly by weak minds, it resembles more the dullness of indifference than disconsolate impartiality. Most men of ability, fortunately, make the second choice; it is they that make the administration of society possible and intermittently tolerable. Individually, most of them disappear, either lose office or succumb to it; but the class is constantly replenished from the bottom. A few survive the struggle in their own identity, and these are the ideals the young men hope to cap. J. Q. Adams was one of these, Gallatin and Schurz are clearly two more, as Senators Walsh and Norris make two examples for our own day. Men like Cleveland and Theodore Roosevelt are partial survivals. Adams thought his friend John Hay not only survived but succeeded in establishing a sound foreign policy; history is a harsher judge than friendship. As a general thing promise in politics not only dies early but is resurrected in the corruption of party or unwitting interest, which is what happened to Adams' friend Lodge. For the most part Adams' reiterated sentiment remains apt: "A friend in power is a friend lost." Small men might pass unnoticed to honourable graves but the great were lost.

Henry Adams lacked the dimensions suitable to a small man in public life and lacked the coarseness of will and ability to dissimulate to seize the larger opportunity, had it offered. Hence he made gradually the third choice, and brought the pressure of all the education he could muster upon society from the outside. It took him seven to ten years to make the choice complete. The first form of pressure he exerted was that of practical political journalism, of which the principal remaining results are the essays on "The New York Gold Conspiracy," "The Session, 1869-1870," and the essay on American financial policy called "The Legal-Tender Act." The second form of pressure was also practical, and combined the teaching of history at Harvard with the editorship of *The North American Review*. Already, however, the emphasis of his mind was becoming imaginative and speculative. Seven years in Cambridge taught him the impossibility of affecting society to any practical extent through the quarterly press, or through any press at all. Two of his essays were made campaign documents by the Democrats—their import reduced to the level of vituperative rhetoric—and then forgotten; so that by the test of the widest publication possible their practical effect was nil. There remained a third form of pressure not so much indirect as remote, and that was pressure by the imaginative expression, through history and fiction and philosophy, of social character and direction; and the aim was to seize the meaning of human energy by defining its forms and to achieve, thus, if it was possible, a sense of unity both for oneself and one's society.

Expression is a form of education, and the form that was to occupy the rest of Adams' life, the subject of our second emphasis. Put another way, society had failed to attract Adams to its centre, and Adams undertook to see whether or not he could express a centre for it. Unity or chaos became the alternative lesson of every effort. Here we have gone over or climbed up to a second level of failure, which is the failure of the human mind, pushed to one of its limits, to solve the problem of the meaning, the use, or the value of its own energy: in short the failure to find God or unity. What differentiates Adams' mind from other minds engaged in the same effort is his own intense and progressive recognition of his failure; and that recognition springs from the same overload of scruples that made him eccentric to the society that produced him. What he did not recognise was the ironical consolation that the form his work took as a whole was itself as near the actual representative of unity as the individual mind can come; which is what we have now to show.

Henry Adams' mind acquired, as his work stretched out, a singular unity of conception and a striking definiteness of form. It was the idiosyncrasy of his genius to posit unity in multiplicity, and by exploring different aspects of the multiplicity to give the effect, known to be false or specious but felt as true, of apprehending the unity. In reading *The Life of Albert Gallatin*, so successfully is the effect of Gallatin's career composed, we have to think twice before realising that it is meant to show one aspect in the story of the failure of the democratic process to unite American society. Published in 1879, when Adams was forty-one, it so well struck the theme of Adams' whole career that it can be bracketed with Adams' own autobiography and be called "The Education of Albert Gallatin."

As important here, striking his theme gave Adams his first mature prose. The previous essays had been comparatively metallic, brittle, and rhetorical, and carried a tone of intermittent assertiveness rather than of cumulative authority. It was the subject perhaps that matured the style: Gallatin was the best in character, ability, and attainment that American history had to offer. At any rate, the biography of John Randolph, which came in 1882 and portrayed the worst waste in ability and personal disintegration in American history, showed a reversion to the earlier immature style. If Adams was, as Hay said, half angel and half porcupine, then it was altogether the porcupine that got into this book. The tragedy of Randolph was personal eccentricity, his constant resorts to hysteria and violence, and Adams brought those elements over into his own style. Later, in his History, Adams repaired his injustice and treated him with charity of understanding, as an energetic sample of his times.

Meanwhile and just afterwards, in 1880 and 1884, Adams published his two novels, *Democracy* and *Esther*. These suffer about equally from Adams' incompetence as a novelist, and the reader can take them best as brilliant documentary evidence of Adams' insights and pre-occupations. To intrude the standards of the art of fiction would be to obviate the burden the books actually carry. *Democracy* exhibits a political society full of corruption, irresponsible ambition, and stupidity, against the foil of a woman's taste and intelligence. So brilliant and light is Adams' execution, it is hard to decide which vice is worst of the three.

Madeleine Lee, Adams' foil, is struck a heavy blow in the face by her first and only presidential reception. She stands fascinated and aghast at the endless wooden procession. "What a horrid warning to ambition! And in all that crowd there was no one beside herself who felt the mockery of this exhibition. To all the others this task was a regular part of the President's duty, and there was nothing ridiculous about it." It was Adams, not Mrs. Lee, who felt the full force of the blow. He remembered what he had seen at Devonshire House a few years back when Mme. de Castiglione, the famous beauty of the Second Empire, entered.

> How beautiful she may have been, or indeed what sort of beauty she was, Adams never knew, because the company, consisting of the most refined and aristocratic society in the world, instantly formed a lane, and stood in ranks to stare at her, while those behind mounted on chairs to look over their neighbors' heads; so that the lady walked through the polite mob, stared completely out of countenance, and fled the house.

In *Democracy*, Mrs. Lee received a second blow, which we may obscurely feel as a consequence of the first, when, after his corruption is discovered to her and she taxes him with it, her suitor, Secretary of the Treasury Ratcliffe, defends himself by minimising his offence, passing it off as commonplace, and asks her to purify American politics through marriage to him and with his aid.

> The audacity of the man would have seemed sublime if she had felt sure that he knew the difference between good and evil, between a lie and the truth; but the more she saw of him, the surer she was that his courage was mere moral paralysis, and that he talked about virtue and vice as a man who is colour-blind talks about red and green; he did not see them as she saw them; if left to choose for himself he would have nothing to guide him.

Which blow was the harder to bear? Was corruption, like stupidity, only an atrophied form of intelligence? Given the system and the society, did not the practice of politics necessarily produce one form or the other?

Adams himself did not feel the full force of the second blow until twenty years later when Theodore Roosevelt inherited office from McKinley. Secretary Ratcliffe in *Democracy* was the archetype of all he hated and Roosevelt represented an approximation of a good deal he admired. Ratcliffe was about the worst you got and Roosevelt was the best you could expect. But the lesson the two men taught about the disease of power was much the same, however they taught it on different levels. At hear Roosevelt, as a type, was more source of despair than Ratcliffe.

> Power is poison. Its effects on Presidents had always been tragic, chiefly as an almost insane excitement at first, and a worse reaction afterwards; but also because no mind is so well balanced as to bear the strain of seizing unlimited force without habit or knowledge of it; and finding it disputed with him by hungry packs of wolves and hounds whose lives depend on snatching the carrion. Roosevelt enjoyed a singularly direct nature and honest intent, but he lived naturally in restless agitation that would have worn out most tempers in a month, and his first year of Presidency showed chronic excitement that made a friend tremble. The effect of unlimited power on limited mind is worth noting in Presidents because it must represent the same process in society, and the power of self-control must have limit somewhere in face of the control of the infinite.

"Here," Adams goes on, "education seemed to see its first and last lesson." Certainly it is part of the lesson of the second Roosevelt as well as of the first; and certainly it is a lesson that in one form or another can be drawn not only from Presidents, but from every concentration of power in single hands. Power is greater than the hands that hold it and compels action beyond any tolerable volition. No wonder men make a game of it, as they make mathematics of time and space, since it is only as converted into a game that the experience of fatal struggles is commonly found tolerable.

But the lesson had other forms, as the energy it attempted to express took other forms than the political. There is the well of character, the abyss of science, and the aspiring form of religion, all expressions of human energy, and a wakened and scrupulous mind was compelled to respond to them all. Experience is only separated into its elements in the *tour de force* of expression, and as in *Democracy* Adams separated the bottom level of political experience, in *Esther* he separated the highest level of religious experience he could find in America and measured it against the response of a woman's intelligence. The question asked and the lesson to be learned were simple and fundamental and desperate. Assuming the Christian insight in its highest contemporary form, could the Church supply a sense of unity, of ultimate relation with God or the sum of energy, to which intelligence could respond? If the Church couldn't—and the Church had no other motive for being—nothing else could, and the soul was left on its own and homeless. Or so it seemed to Adams; hence the desperateness of the question; and hence the dispropor- tionate importance relative to its achievement that Adams himself as- signed to the book. Writing to John Hay from Japan in 1886, he suggests that it was written in his heart's blood, and again to Elizabeth Cameron from Papeete five years later, he says: "I care more for one chapter, or any dozen pages of 'Esther' than for the whole history, including maps and in- dexes." The nine-volume history represented the predicament of the soci- ety he had abandoned, and *Esther* represented his own predicament in relation to that God or unity the hope of which he could never in his heart altogether abandon. Like Spinoza, Adams was god-intoxicated, like Pascal god-ridden. His heart's hope was his soul's despair.

That the responding intelligence in *Esther* as in *Democracy* should have been a woman's, only reflects a major bias of Adams' imagination. Women, for Adams, had instinct and emotion and could move from the promptings of the one to the actualities of the other without becoming lost or distraught in the midway bog of logic and fact. Impulse proceeded im- mediately to form without loss of character or movement. More than that, women had taste; taste was what held things together, showing each at its best, and making each contribute to a single effect. Thus the argu- ment of a woman's taste dissipated every objection of logic, and at its highest moments made illogicality itself part of its natural charm. Taste was the only form of energy sure enough of itself—as all non-human energies may be—to afford beauty; elsewhere the rashest extravagance.

Thus Adams tried everywhere to answer great questions in terms of a woman's taste and intelligence. Who else but Esther Dudley could form the centre of the book she named? Only the strength of her instinct could accept the Church if it showed itself alive, and only the courage of her taste could reject it if it proved dead or a shell. That she might be confused in instinct and unconscious of her taste, only made the drama more vivid and its outcome more desperate. The problem was hers, but an artist could help her solve it, and perhaps a scientist, too, if he felt the struggle as an artist feels it. So Wharton, the artist, puts the question to her and answers it. "It all comes to this: is religion a struggle or a joy? To me it is a terrible battle, to be won or lost." The object of the battle is Nirvana or paradise. "It is eternal life, which, my poet says, consists in seeing God." The poet is Petrarch, and his words: *Siccome eterna vita è veder dio.* Strong, the scientist, for his part tells her: "There is no science that does not begin by requiring you to believe the incredible. I tell you the solemn truth that the doctrine of the Trinity is not so difficult to accept for a working proposition as any one of the axioms of physics." Between them—between art as it aspires to religion and science that springs from the same occult source—Esther might have been able to accept religion as that great form of poetry which is the aspiration of instinct and informs the whole of taste; but the Church itself, in the person of the Reverend Mr. Hazard, her lover, failed her both in persuasiveness and light. Power in politics and pride in the Church were much alike.

> The strain of standing in a pulpit is great. No human being ever yet constructed was strong enough to offer himself long as a light to humanity without showing the effect on his constitution. Buddhist saints stand for years silent, on one leg, or with arms raised above their heads, but the limbs shrivel, and the mind shrivels with the limbs.

There is a kind of corruption in the best as well as the worst exemplars of each—which I suppose the Church would admit sooner than the state; a corruption in each case that makes for the self-falsifying effort of fanaticism. Hazard in his last argument appeals neither to instinct, intelligence, nor taste; he appeals to Esther's personal desperation and fear and so shows the ruination of emptiness within him. Esther can only answer him from the depth of revolted taste. "Why must the church always appeal to my weakness and never to my strength! I ask for spiritual life and you send me back to my flesh and blood as though I were a tigress you were sending back to her cubs." Although she loves him, the inadequacy of his church to its own purpose compels her to dismiss him, but neither for science nor for art, but for despair. That is the blood in which the book was written.

As *Democracy* foreshadowed the major theme of the *Education*, the theme of *Esther* is given deeper expression throughout *Mont-Saint-Michel*, and, as well, in at least one place in the *Education*. *Esther* is a representation of the failure in fact of American society to find God in religion. As he grew older, especially after the tragic death of his wife, and felt more and more that society had abandoned him, Adams grew more preoccupied with the ultimate failure of imagination itself, as illustrated in every faculty of the mind, than with the mere indicative failure of fact. Not facts which could be met but their meanings which could not be escaped were his meat. The meaning of *Esther* is intensified and made an object of inexhaustible meditation in the meanings Adams found in the monument Saint Gaudens made for his wife in Rock Creek Cemetery. Part of the meaning lay in its meaninglessness to most of those who saw it, and part in the horror of the clergy who saw in it their defeat instead of their salvation. In a letter, Adams gave the monument the same motto he had embedded in *Esther: Siccome eterna vita è veder dio*; you could, in a gravestone, if you had the will, see what life needed but never provided. In the *Education* Adams suggests that the monument mirrors to the beholder whatever faith he has.

In *Mont-Saint-Michel and Chartres* the problem of *Esther* is made at once more universal and more personal. There Adams made an imaginative mirror of his own effort towards faith in terms of the highest point of faith—that is, of effective unity—the world had ever seen: the Christianity of the great cathedrals and the great intellectual architecture of the schools. The Virgin dominated the cathedrals as a matter of course; and Saint Thomas dominated the schools by an effort of will; but without the Virgin the schools would merely have paltered, as the cathedrals would never have been built. The Virgin was pure energy and pure taste, as her spires and roses were pure aspiration. Adams' book is the story of her tragedy; not that she was destroyed or even denied, but that men no longer knew and loved her, so lost their aspiration with the benefit of her taste, and no longer felt any unity whatsoever. The Virgin herself is still there, "but looking down from a deserted heaven, into an empty church, on a dead faith." She no longer gave orders or answered questions, and without her the orders and answers of Saint Thomas were useless; and similarly, for Adams, the orders and answers of all later authorities.

Thus the education that led Adams to the Virgin was the greatest failure of all; the highest form of unity was, in effect, for the modern man, only the most impossible to recapture. Where Esther had very simply repulsed the church because it appealed only to her weakness, Adams was in the worse ail of having no strength with which to seize it when it called for all the strength there was: he had no faith, but only the need of it. The Virgin's orders were the best ever given; obeyed, they made life contribute to great art and shine in it; but he had nothing with which to accept her administration. Her answers to his problems were final; she was herself the cumulus and unity of energy, and she removed, by absorbing, all the contradictions of experience; but seven centuries of time had made life too complicated for the old answers to fit. The same energy would need a new form to give the same meaning.

The failure of education was the failure of the unity which it grasped; the pupil was left with a terrible and weary apprehension of ignorance. Thinking of the Virgin and of the Dynamo as equally inexplicable concentrations of energy, Adams was led into the last phase of his education in the application of the mechanical theory of the inevitable change of all energy from higher to lower forms. What he wrote may be found in the later chapters of the *Education*, and in his two essays "A Letter to Teachers" and "The Rule of Phase Applied to History." It was, I think, the theory of a desperate, weary mind, still scrupulous in desperation and passionately eager in weariness, in its last effort to feel—this time in nature herself—the mystery in energy that keeps things going. It was the religious mind applying to physics on exactly the same terms and with exactly the same honest piety that it applied to the Virgin.

The nexus between the two was shown in the need for either in that fundamental condition of the mind known as *ennui*; and Adams quotes Pascal, the great scrupulous mind of the seventeenth century.

> "I have often said that all the troubles of man come from his not knowing how to sit still." Mere restlessness forces action. "So passes the whole of life. We combat obstacles in order to get repose, and, when got, the repose is insupportable; for we think either of the troubles we have, or of those that threaten us; and even if we felt safe on every side, *ennui* would of its own accord spring up from the depths of the heart where it is rooted by nature, and would fill the mind with its venom."

Nature was full of *ennui* too, from star to atom. What drove it? What made energy change form in *this* direction and not that? Adams tried to find the answer in the second law of thermodynamics—the law that assumes the degradation of energy; the law which sees infinite energy becoming infinitely unavailable; and he tried hard to *feel* that law as accounting for change in human society. The attempt only put his ignorance on a new basis. As analogues, the laws of physics only made the human predicament less soluble because less tangible. You might learn a direction, but physics prevented you from feeling what moved.

Reason, in science, as Adams had discovered earlier in *Esther*, deserted you rather sooner than in religion; and the need of faith was more critical. Had Adams had the advantage of the development of the quantum theory from the thermal field to the whole field of physics, had he known that all change was to come to seem discontinuous and that nature was to reveal a new and profoundly irrational face, he would have given up his last effort before he began it. A *discontinuous* multiplicity cannot be transformed into unity except by emotional vision. Adams had earlier said it himself. "Unity is vision; it must have been part of the process of learning to see. The older the mind, the older its complexities, and the further it looks, the more it sees, until even the stars resolve themselves into multiples; yet the child will always see but one." In 1915 Adams wrote to Henry Osborn Taylor that "Faith not Reason goes beyond" the failure of knowledge, and added that he felt himself "in near peril of turning Christian, and rolling in the mud in an agony of human mortification." But he had not the faith; only the apprehension of its need which made him struggle towards it all his life.

Failure is the appropriate end to the type of mind of which Adams is a pre-eminent example: the type which attempts through imagination to find the meaning or source of unity aside from the experience which it unites. Some artists can be content with experience as it comes, content to express it in the best form at hand. Adams gives LaFarge as an instance. "His thought ran as a stream runs through grass, hidden perhaps but always there; and one felt often uncertain in what direction it flowed, for even a contradiction was to him only a shade of difference, a complementary color, about which no intelligent artist would dispute." Shakespeare is another instance. In such artists failure is incidental, a part of the experience expressed. But Adams, by attempting to justify experience and so to pass beyond it had like Milton and Dante to push his mind to the limit of reason and his feeling to the limit of faith. Failure, far from incidental, is integral to that attempt, and becomes apparent just so soon as reason falters and becomes abstract, or faith fails and pretends to be absolute. Aside from the question of magnitude, one difference between Adams and his prototypes is, to repeat once more, just this: that his scrupulous sophistication made him emphatically aware of his own failure; and this awareness is the great drive of his work.

Here is our third emphasis. The failure of Adams in society—or society's failure to use Adams—was perhaps self-evident when stated. The singular unity of Adams' subsequent efforts to express the unity he felt has, I hope, been indicated. There remains the question of Adams' special value in the light of his avowed failure. The value is double.

The greatness of the mind of Adams himself is in the imaginative reach of the effort to solve the problem of the meaning, the use, or the value of its own energy. The greatness is in the effort itself, in variety of response deliberately made to every possible level of experience. It is in the acceptance, with all piety, of ignorance as the humbled form of knowledge; in the pursuit of divers shapes of knowledge—the scientific, the religious, the political, the social and trivial—to the point where they add to ignorance, when the best response is silence itself. That is the greatness of Adams as a type of mind. As it is a condition of life to die, it is a condition of thought, in the end, to fail. Death is the expense of life and failure is the expense of greatness.

If there is a paradox here, or an irony hard to digest, it is not in the life experienced or the failure won, but in the forms through which they are conceived, in the very duplicity of language itself, in the necessarily equivocal character, earned by long use, of every significant word.

Thought asks too much and words tell too much; because to ask anything is to ask everything, and to say anything is to ask more. It is the radical defect of thought that it leaves us discontented with what we actually feel—with what we know and do not know—as we know sunlight and surfeit and terror, all at once perhaps, and yet know nothing of them. Thought requires of us that we make a form for our knowledge which is personal, declarative, and abstract at the same time that we construe it as impersonal, expressive, and concrete. It is this knowledge that leads to the conviction of ignorance—to the positive ignorance which is the final form of contradictory knowledge; but it is the triumph of failure that in the process it snares all that can be snared of what we know.

The true paradox is that in securing its own ends thought cannot help defeating itself at every crisis. To think straight you must overshoot your mark. Orthodoxy of the human mind—the energy of society in its highest stable form—is only maintained through the absorption into it of a series of heresies; and the great heresy, surely, is the gospel of unity, whether it is asserted as a prime mover, as God, or, as in art, as the mere imposed unity of specious form. In adopting it for his own, Adams knew it for a heresy. Again and again he describes unifying conceptions as working principles; without them no work could be done; with them, even at the expense of final failure, every value could be provisionally ascertained. That is the value of Adams for us: the double value of his scrupulous attitude towards his unifying notions and of the human aspirations he was able to express under them. To feel that value as education is a profound deliverance: the same deliverance Adams felt in the Gothic Cathedral. "The delight of its aspiration is flung up to the sky. The pathos of its self-distrust and anguish of doubt is buried in the earth as its last secret." The principles asserted are nothing, though desperate and necessary; the values expressed because of the principles are everything. For Adams, as for everyone, the principle of unity carried to failure showed the most value by the way, and the value was worth the expense.

"Henry Adams"

Henry Steele Commager*

"It would be fun to send you some of my examination papers," wrote Professor Adams to his friend Charles Milnes Gaskell. "My rule in making them up is to ask questions which I can't myself answer."[1] It was a report and a prophecy. All his life Henry Adams made it a rule to ask questions which he couldn't answer—questions which were, perhaps, quite unanswerable. In the beginning, when Adams was merely a teacher, there was something whimsical about it, and faintly perverse. Later on, it became part of a literary technique, an inverse method of stating a fact or suggesting an idea. In the end, it was a serious business, a desperately serious business. In the end he asked questions because he wanted answers—because, indeed, "a historical formula that should satisfy the conditions of the stellar universe weighed heavily on his mind."[2] But his true function was to ask questions, not to answer them; his true function was to provoke speculation, not to satisfy it.

What Adams did, then, was relatively unimportant; but what he signified was immensely important. At Harvard the teacher was more interesting than the subject; in his Washington study the author was more interesting than the books. In the end Adams abandoned the effort to eliminate the personal equation and recognized that, in so far as he was concerned, in so far as his generation was concerned, the Education of Henry Adams was the crucial question. He recognized that no questions which Adams could ask were quite as interesting as the questions which he inspired, that no facts summoned from the historical past were quite as illuminating as the facts of his own intellectual history. He recognized, quite impersonally, that if the historian expected to find a formula that would explain American character, if he expected to find a formula that would reduce history to a science, if he expected to find a formula that would satisfy the conditions of a stellar universe, he must find a formula to explain Henry Adams.

Obviously, then, it is not as a teacher or as a historian, or even as a philosopher, that Adams is chiefly significant, but as a symbol. Adams

* Reprinted from *The Marcus W. Jernegan Essays in American Historiography*, ed. William T. Hutchinson (Chicago: Univ. of Chicago Press, 1937, Pp. 191–206) by permission of the University of Chicago Press.

50

himself regarded his teaching experience as a failure, his historical work as negligible, and his philosophical speculations as suggestive rather than final; and Adams' critical acumen was so sharp, his judgment so sound, and his sincerity so unimpeachable that it would be insolent to differ with him. And Adams was very positive about this matter. Lodge and Laughlin and Taylor and half a dozen others might recall that he was the most inspiring of teachers, that his learning was prodigious and his interpretation profound; but he himself "was content neither with what he had taught nor with the way he had taught it"; and he was sure that Harvard University, "as far as it was represented by Henry Adams—produced at great waste of time and money results not worth reaching."[3] Nor was he less dogmatic about the value of his books—he who was so rarely dogmatic. Adams "had even published a dozen volumes of American history," he confessed,

> for no other purpose than to satisfy himself whether, by the severest process of stating, with the least possible comment, such facts as seemed sure, in such order as seemed rigorously consequent, he could fix for a familiar moment a necessary sequence of human movement. The result had satisfied him as little as at Harvard College. Where he saw sequence, other men saw something quite different, and no one saw the same unit of measure.[4]

Nor was this the perversity of old age or an effort to outwit criticism. Even as he was publishing the stately volumes of his *History*, he wrote to Elizabeth Cameron:

> There are not nine pages in the nine volumes that now express anything of my interests or feelings; unless perhaps some of my disillusionments. So you must not blame me if I feel, or seem to feel, morbid on the subject of the history. I care more for one chapter, or any dozen pages of *Esther* than for the whole history,[5]

and to Dr. J. F. Jameson he confessed: "I would much rather wipe out all I have ever said than go on with more."[6] And as for the dynamic theory of history, the rule of phase applied to history, the law of entropy, and the law of acceleration, Adams was too good a historian not to see the fallacy of analogies from science to society, too good a scientist not to know that the science of today is the superstition of tomorrow. He was concerned indeed—the conclusion seems inescapable—with urging the necessity of formulating some philosophy of history, some science of society; he was concerned with asking questions and pointing to the consequences of all conceivable answers.[7]

Adams dismissed his own historical labors in a paragraph, and it would perhaps be discourteous for us to insist that they deserve more than this inattention. But even if we should agree that Adams' teaching was futile and his historical writing irrelevant, we would still be eager to discover the cause of that futility, the meaning of that irrelevancy; we would still be inclined to ask questions. Here are the volumes, standing soberly on our shelves, eloquent witnesses to the unwilling conformity of an Adams: *The Writings of Albert Gallatin*,[8] *The Life of Albert Gallatin*,[9] *John Randolph*,[10] *The History of the United States of America during the Administrations of Jefferson and Madison*.[11] Why, it may be asked, did Adams write these books? Why did he write them in conventional, what he called "old-school," form? Why, having written them, did he profess to think them worthless? Adams himself could not answer these questions in any satisfactory way, and it is not to be supposed that we can do better than he was able to do. We could say that he wrote them because he could think of nothing better to do, but that would be to adopt consciously the paradox that is pointless if deliberate. We could say that he wrote them to satisfy his own curiosity about the Adams family and the role it played in the evolution of the American nation; and Adams, who was never unconscious of his family, would readily accept this explanation. Certainly he felt that the history of the Adams family was central to the history of the American people, and that the problem presented by the victory of Jefferson over John Adams and of Jackson over John Quincy Adams was as fascinating as any problem in history. We could say that he wrote them in order to clarify in his own mind the meaning of American history, in order to prepare the way for the formulation of historical laws. He observed:

> The scientific interest of American history centered in national character, and in the workings of a society destined to become vast, in which individuals were important chiefly as types. Although this kind of interest was different from that of European history, it was at least as important to the world. Should history ever become a true science, it must expect to establish its laws, not from the complicated story of rival European nationalities, but from the economical evolution of a great democracy. North America was the most favorable field on the globe for the spread of a society so large, uniform, and isolated as to answer the purposes of science. . . . . The interest of such a subject exceeded that of any other branch of science, for it brought mankind within sight of its own end.[12]

These histories and biographies conformed to a pattern, and the pattern was not without either beauty or symmetry. They satisfied certain requirements both of form and of substance; they were thorough, accurate, scholarly, critical, impartial; they were distinguished in thought and in style. It is not an exaggeration, indeed, to insist that the *Gallatin* is the best political biography, the *Administrations of Jefferson and Madison* the finest piece of historical writing, in our literature. They stated "such facts as seemed sure, in such order as seemed rigorously consequent"; they "fixed for a familiar moment" a sequence of human movement. But the result, we must remember, satisfied Adams as little as had teaching. The history was good history—better history had not been written. Everyone agreed that it was good history; but no one, least of all Adams, knew what it was good for. It was good for facts, of course; but Adams himself confessed that "I never loved or taught facts, if I could help it, having that antipathy to facts which only idiots and philosophers attain."[13] It was good for what it told of American character, for what it prophesied of American democracy; but the character changed and the prophecies were invalid, for Adams' ideal ploughboy was less likely in 1900 than in 1800 to "figure out in quaternions the relations of his furrows." It was good for the purposes of philosophy, in so far as it "fixed a sequence of human movement"; but Adams came to doubt that it was a necessary sequence and was satisfied that "the sequence of men led to nothing, and that the sequence of their society could lead no further, while the mere sequence of time was artificial, and the sequence of thought was chaos."[14]

But if, by his own valuation, Adams' historical labors contributed nothing to history, we can turn perhaps to his philosophy with hope of more satisfactory results. It is something to say that Adams is the only American historian who has ever seriously attempted to formulate a philosophy of history. He was not unaware of the difficulties; but no Adams had ever been frightened by difficulties, and Henry Adams, certainly, had nothing to lose. So in 1894, three years after he had published the last volume of that history which he regarded with such indifference, he addressed a letter to his colleagues in the American Historical Association on the tendency of history to become a science:

> That the effort to make history a science may fail is possible, and perhaps probable; but that it should cease, unless for reasons that would cause all science to cease, is not within the range of experience. Historians will not, and even if they would they can not, abandon the attempt. Science itself would admit its own failure if it admitted that man, the most important of all its subjects, could not be brought within its range.[15]

But alas, the generation of Comte and Buckle was past, and historians did not even undertake the attempt which Adams had announced as inevitable.

But, however derelict his professional colleagues, Adams would not be derelict. Years earlier, in drawing the brilliant Mrs. Lightfoot Lee, he had written sympathetically of the intellectual curiosity that looked for first causes:

> Here, then, was the explanation of her restlessness, discontent, ambition,—call it what you will. It was the feeling of a passenger on an ocean steamer whose mind will not give

him rest until he has been in the engine-room and talked with
the engineer. She wanted to see with her own eyes the action of
primary forces; to touch with her own hand the massive
machinery of society; to measure with her own mind the
capacity of the motive power.[16]

Adams experienced the same discontent, the same restlessness in the face
of the riddles of history. "To the tired student, the idea that he must give
it up seemed sheer senility. . . . Every man with self-respect enough to
become effective, if only as a machine, has had to account to himself for
himself somehow, and to invent a formula of his own for his own
universe, if the standard formulas fail."[17] That the standard formulas had
failed, none would deny; and Adams invented one of his own.

The result of Adams' speculations can be read in the concluding
chapters of the *Education*, in the "Letter to American Teachers of
History"[18] and in the essay on the "Rule of Phase Applied to History." "If
history ever meant to correct the errors she made in detail," he had written, "she must agree on a scale for the whole";[19] and these essays con-
stituted an attempt to formulate a scale for the whole. The scale was to be
large enough to be inclusive. The problem was to bring human history in
harmony with the organic laws of the universe, and the formula that
Adams hit upon was the Law of the Dissipation of Energy.

The formula had many ramifications and was supported by an impressive array of scientific data; for from those early years, when he had
hobnobbed with Sir Charles Lyell and with the *Pteraspis*, Adams had
prided himself on his knowledge of science. Those who will, can read the
evidence and ponder the conclusions; the argument, for all its bewilder-
ing mathematical formulas, is simple enough. The Second Law of
Thermodynamics announced that energy was constantly being expended
without being replaced. The idea of progress, therefore, was a delusion;
and the evidence customarily adduced to substantiate the idea sustained,
instead, a very different conclusion. Civilization itself had been brought
about by the operation of the Law of Entropy—the law of the dissipation
of energy by the constant degradation of its vital power, rather than the
reverse. Society, as an organism, is subject to the law of degradation
precisely like any other organism, and faces therefore the prospect of running down indefinitely until at last total stagnation is reached. And the
period of stagnation, Adams continued, is not in some remote future but
in the present. In the first quarter of the twentieth century, thought
"would reach the limit of its possibilities," and the honest historian might
logically "treat the history of modern Europe and America as a typical example of energies indicating degradation with 'headlong rapidity'
towards 'inevitable death.' " "Already," Adams concluded desperately,
"History and Sociology gasp for breath."[20] We are not concerned, here,
with the validity of this argument except in so far as it constitutes Adams'
contribution to the philosophy of history, and Adams himself has fur-

nished us the most pertinent comment on that contribution. "Historians," he observed, "have got into far too much trouble by following schools of theology in their efforts to enlarge their synthesis, that they should willingly repeat the process in science. For human purposes a point must always be soon reached where larger synthesis is suicide."[21] In this case, certainly, the larger synthesis was suicide. Suggestive, provocative, brilliant, and profound the dynamic theory of history indubitably was; but the most interesting thing about it was that Adams should have advanced it.

But if Adams had damned his formal contributions to history as insignificant and characterized his historical synthesis as intellectual suicide, we are left with only one alternative. If we can consider neither the history nor the philosophy, we must fall back on a consideration of Adams himself. Such an approach has, fortunately, the warrant of excellent precedent; for it is precisely what Adams himself did in the circumstances. "One sought," he tells us, "no absolute truth. One sought only a spool on which to wind the thread of history without breaking it. Among indefinite possible orbits, one sought the orbit which would best satisfy the observed movement of the runaway star Groombridge, 1838, commonly called Henry Adams."[22]

And there is no more convenient spool upon which to wind the thread of history than Henry Adams. For Adams was not only a historian: he was himself a historical fact—he was, indeed, to use a term too often used, a significant fact. Of Adams alone, among the major historians, can it be said that what he was is more significant than what he wrote. Of Adams alone can it be said that, given a choice between what he wrote and what he was, we should inevitably choose the latter. For it is no merely capricious judgment that has preferred the *Mont Saint Michel and Chartres*[23] and the *Education* to the "History" or the biographies; and as for Adams' philosophical speculations, the most thoughtful of American historians has justly observed that "Adams was worth a wilderness of philosophies."[24]

It is an exaggeration, of course, to suggest that we can interpret the whole of American history in the person of Henry Adams, but it is no very shocking exaggeration to insist that to the student of American history the contemplation of Adams is the beginning of wisdom. For whether we confine ourselves to the mere outward aspects of Adams' career or embrace the history of the entire family which he recapitulated, or penetrate to his own intellectual and psychological reactions to his generation, we will find that Adams illuminates, better than any of his contemporaries, the course of American history.

He explains for us the shift in political power from New England to the West, from agriculture to industry, from the individual to the mass, and the change in the nature of political power from intelligence to instinct, from reason to force. He reveals the decline of the intellectually aristocratic tradition and of the family tradition, the futility of intellectual discipline, the impotence of moral integrity, and the irrelevance of fastidiousness, in politics. He emphasizes what Brooks Adams called the "degradation of the democratic dogma" and the failure of eighteenth-century concepts of democracy to effect a compromise with nineteenth-century society. Intellectually he represents the transition from transcendental faith to pragmatic acquiescence, from evolutionary optimism to mechanistic pessimism, from unity to multiplicity, from order to chaos. He illustrates the rejection of the Victorian idea of progress for the idea of entropy, the rejection of a teleological universe for a mechanistic universe, the substitution of science for philosophy, of the machine for man, of force for faith, of the dynamo for the Virgin, and, at the same time, the convulsive effort to discover a philosophy that would satisfy the requirements of both instinct and reason. And he was never unaware of his significance as a symbol and as an experiment, never unconscious of the larger meaning that could be read out of his intellectual and spiritual biography, and never unwilling to undertake himself the task of interpretation.

No one who has ever turned the leaves of the *Education* will forget Adams' description of the Grant administration,[25] no one who has ever read the scintillating pages of *Democracy* will fail to remember the picture of political corruption in the Washington of the seventies.[26] Anonymity could not conceal, or objectiveness disguise, the intensely personal character of these reflections. But it is a singular distinction of Adams that where he was most personal he was most general. The failure of Henry Adams to adjust himself to the politics of the Grant administration illustrated the failure of eighteenth-century democracy, of the democracy of Gallatin and John Quincy Adams, to effect such an adjustment. The indifference of the politicians of post-war America to the talents and the ideals of Adams represented the indifference of a new, industrialized America to the discipline and the ideals of the past. Adams was at pains, here, to account for his own failure; but had that been the whole of the matter, he would have dismissed the experience as cavalierly as he had dismissed Harvard College or the *North American Review*. It was because he understood the pertinence of his own experience to the experience of the American people, because he appreciated the moral implicit in his story, that he dignified this episode in his life with elaborate analysis and interpretation. So, too, with *Democracy*, that sprightly commentary on American politics and society in the gilded age. As a novel it is thin, and as an analysis of the forces behind American political corruption it is thinner still; but even its brittle thinness, its dilettantism and exoticism, may be taken to reflect certain qualities in the American mind.

Adams himself furnished the best criticism of *Democracy*. The authorship of the book had been well concealed, and it amused Adams to impute it to his friend John Hay. He wrote to the long-suffering Hay:

> I repeat that your novel . . . . is a failure because it
> undertook to describe the workings of a power in this city, and
> spoiled a great tragic subject such as Aeschylus might have
> made what it should be. . . . . The tragic element, if accepted
> as real, is bigger here than ever on this earth before. I hate to
> see it mangled à la Daudet, in a tame-cat way. Men don't
> know tragedy when they see it.[27]

Could anything better illustrate the futile liberalism of the postwar years
than this confession that a great tragic subject had been treated,
deliberately, as a joke, or, what was worse, as an essay in cynicism? It is
suggestive that the author of the *Gallatin*, of the *Jefferson and Madison
Administrations*, should also be the author of *Democracy*; suggestive that
the historian of democratic idealism should be the critic of the degradation of the democratic dogma. It is even more suggestive that that mind
which had celebrated so magnanimously the idealism of Jefferson should
be reduced by Blaine and Conkling to a cynicism that was frivolous and a
satire that was frustrated. It was personal perhaps, but no one who recalls
the impotence of the genteel tradition as represented by Godkin and
Gilder and Curtis can doubt that it was more than personal.

Yet, it would be unjust to imply that Adams and his generation of
liberals were defeated by the political pigmies who strut and fret their
way through the pages of the *Education* or *Democracy*. Nothing as trivial
as a phalanx of Blaines, Conklings, Camerons, and Butlers could account
for the failure of an Adams. These men, after all, were the proper objects
of satire and, where they did not render even satire ridiculous, could be
disposed of easily enough. Nor was it even the more powerful Goulds and
Vanderbilts and Whitneys and Morgans who made the existence of Adams
irrelevant, if not impertinent. These were but the instruments of larger
forces—objects, as Adams showed, of scientific study, not of moral indignation. What silenced Adams was precisely the realization that
"modern politics is, at bottom, a struggle not of men but of forces. The
men become every year more and more creatures of force, massed about
central powerhouses. The conflict is no longer between the men, but between the motors that drive the men, and men tend to succumb to their
own motive forces."[28] It took, after all, cosmic forces to account for the
tragedy of John and John Quincy Adams, and the indifference of a
modern world to the existence of a Henry Adams was less humiliating
when it was seen to be the inevitable consequence of scientific forces over
whose operation man exercised no control. The failure of Henry Adams to
achieve his education was indeed a failure of so cataclysmic a character
that it was necessary to invoke the whole of science and philosophy in
order to explain it.

But here, again, the experience of Adams was the experience of his
generation, though Adams alone seemed to appreciate it. For when
Adams began that long pilgrimage which was to end, so curiously, before

the altar of Chartres, he had no need of faith other than faith in the beneficient workings of the laws of the universe. Darwin and Lyell had taught him evolution, and every one knew that evolution meant progress. Science and sociology joined hands to justify the findings of the historian; and it was clear that the dreams of Rousseau and Condorcet, of Jefferson and Gallatin, fell short of realities, and that the intuitive truths of transcendentalism were to be justified by the experimental truths of the laboratory. "Then he had entered gaily the door of the glacial epoch, and had surveyed a universe of unities and uniformities."[29] But science was a slut, and treated Adams as shamefully as she had treated his grandfather, John Quincy Adams. Parrington says:

> In the nineties the clouds drew over the brilliant Victorian skies. With the substitution of physics for biology came a more somber mood that was to put away the genial romanticism of Victorian evolution, substitute a mechanistic conception for the earlier teleological progress, and reshape its philosophy in harmony with a deterministic pessimism that denied purpose or plan in the changing universe of matter.[30]

Of all Americans, Adams most fully comprehended the change, and he most fully illustrated it. Not for him the heavenly vision of truth that was revealed to John Fiske in his youth: "When we have come to a true philosophy, and make *that* our standpoint, all things become clear. We know what things to learn, and what, in the infinite mass of things to leave unlearned—and then the Universe becomes clear and harmonious."[31] Alas for Adams, his true philosophy taught him only infinite confusion and chaos and left him naked and defenseless in a world that had "neither joy, nor love, nor light, nor certitude, nor peace, nor help for pain."

It would be misleading, of course, to interpret this tragedy as intellectual merely. Indeed, it might almost be said that the whole of Adams' intellectual career was an effort to find some impersonal meaning in the tragedy that had shattered his life. For when he returned home that bleak December morning to find Marian Hooper dead, he entered the waste lands; and for twenty years he walked in desolation until at last he had convinced himself that the universe was but desolation.

To an intimate, he might reveal his anguish; and to Elizabeth Cameron he confessed: "The light has gone out. I am not to blame. As long as I could make life work, I stood by it, and swore by it as though it was my God, as indeed it was."[32] But in his more formal writing he preserved his immaculate impersonality:

> The child born in 1900 . . . . found himself in a land where no one had ever penetrated before; where order was an accidental relation obnoxious to nature; artificial compulsion imposed on motion; against which every free energy of the

universe revolted; and which, being merely occasional, resolved itself back into anarchy at last. He could not deny that
the law of the new universe explained much that had been
most obscure, especially the persistently fiendish treatment of
man by man; the perpetual effort of society to establish law,
and the perpetual revolt of society against the law it had established; the perpetual building up of authority by force, and the
perpetual appeal to force to overthrow it; the perpetual symbolism of a higher law, and the perpetual relapse to a lower
one; the perpetual victory of the principles of freedom, and
their perpetual conversion into principles of power; but the
staggering problem was the outlook ahead into the despotism
of artificial order which nature abhorred. . . . .

All that a historian won was a vehement wish to escape.
He saw his education complete, and was sorry he ever began it.
As a matter of taste, he greatly preferred his eighteenth-
century education when God was a father and nature a
mother, and all was for the best in a scientific universe.[33]

Adams was right, of course, in generalizing his own tragedy; that
tragedy was more immediate, more catastrophic even, than the tragedy
of others who wandered in the waste lands of the new century; but that it
was universal, rather than merely personal, no one can doubt. Twentieth-
century America was a nation adrift from its moorings, skeptical of its
past, uncertain of its future, The old faiths were gone, the muscular
Calvinism of the seventeenth century, the enlightened deism of the
eighteenth, the romantic and buoyant transcendentalism of the nineteenth. Pragmatism was a sorry substitute for faith, and the drift from
Jefferson to Emerson and from Emerson to Dewey was as heartbreaking
as the drift from Newton to Darwin and from Darwin to Haeckel.

No one better illustrated this drift than did Adams himself, and no
one was more sensitive to its significance. To Jefferson and his followers
the destiny of America, the destiny of mankind, was plain, and they did
not doubt the ability of man to control that destiny; but Adams knew that
he was the creature, the victim, of forces that he but faintly understood
and over which he could exercise no control, and he knew that he was
unique only in the extent to which he understood his impotence.
Intellectually Adams recognized the chaos, the multiplicity, of the twentieth century; and he even went so far as to furnish us with the most illuminating study of that multiplicity in our literature. But intellectually
he had recognized, too, the inevitable defeat of "his eighteenth century,
his Constitution of 1789, his George Washington, his Harvard College,
his Quincy, and his Plymouth Pilgrims. . . . . He had hugged his anti-
quated dislike of bankers and capitalistic society until he had become little better than a crank. . . . . He had known for years that he must accept
the régime, but he had known a great many other disagreeable certain-

ties—like age, senility, and death—against which one made what little resistance one could."[34] Recognition and acquiescence were very different matters, and there was rebel blood in the Adams veins. "The soul," he wrote, "has always refused to live in peace with the body. The angels, too, were always in rebellion." As a matter of taste, he had said, he much preferred a philosophy in which "God was a father and nature a mother, and all was for the best in a scientific universe."[35]

His revolt against the chaos of modern science threw him back on the unity of the church. It was not a matter of taste merely. Force for force, as he never tired of observing, the Virgin was as intelligible as the dynamo, and as powerful. So Adams, "happy in the thought that at last he had found a mistress who could see no difference in the age of her lovers,"[36] turned to the adoration of the Virgin. It was in part an emotional reaction, an act of faith; but Adams could not be satisfied with a reaction merely emotional: he had to rationalize his faith in the power and the grace of the Virgin as John Quincy Adams had rationalized his faith in a democracy. He who had lived, passionately, the life of reason, who had inherited from generations of Adams' a reverent respect for reason, made this gesture of faith an exercise in historical logic.

Abélard had been silenced, and St. Thomas had formulated a philosophy which explained the universe as a unity; but Adams found unity not as the conclusion of a syllogism, though he was fascinated by the syllogism, but in the life and thought and emotion of generations of men. He was persuaded not by the *Summa theologiae* but by the Merveille of the cathedral of St. Michel, by the rose window of Chartres, by the *Chanson de Roland*, and by the miracles of the Virgin.

The Virgin was not rational, but she was the most rational thing in an irrational universe. Faith was above law and scorned logic; and Adams, who had discovered that law was chance and logic bankrupt, preferred to take his chances with the Virgin rather than with science.

> Mary concentrated in herself the whole rebellion of man against fate; the whole protest against divine law; the whole contempt for human law as its outcome; the whole unutterable fury of human nature beating itself against the walls of its prisonhouse, and suddenly seized by a hope that in the Virgin man had found a door of escape. She was above law; she took feminine pleasure in turning Hell into an ornament; she delighted in trampling on every social distinction in this world and the next. She knew that the universe was as unintelligible to her, on any theory of morals, as it was to her worshippers, and she felt, like them, no sure conviction that it was any more intelligible to the Creator of it.[37]

Uprooted and demoralized, his life a broken arch, his past without meaning and his future without hope, tortured by a restlessness that found no repose in thought and no purpose in action, resigned to the bankruptcy of reason and the futility of knowledge, disillusioned of progress and of evolution, reconciled to the degradation of energy, the exhaustion of society, and the fall of man, lost in a universe that was mechanistic and chaotic, Adams turned in desperation to the one symbol of unity that seemed to have meaning, and found there such solace as he could. "Her pity," he knew, "had no limit";[38] and it was not only Adams but his generation that needed limitless pity.

Notes

1. Worthington C. Ford (ed.), *Letters of Henry Adams, 1858–1891* (Boston, 1930), p. 211.

2. H. Adams, *The Education of Henry Adams: An Autobiography* (Boston, 1930), p. 376. The first edition of this work appeared in 1918.

3. *Ibid.*, p. 304.

4. *Ibid.*, p. 382.

5. *Letters of Henry Adams*, Feb. 13, 1891, p. 468.

6. *American Historical Review*, XXVI, p. 9. See also *The Education of Henry Adams*, p. 325.

7. *The Education of Henry Adams*, pp. 474–98.

8. 3 vols.; Philadelphia, 1879.

9. Philadelphia, 1880.

10. Boston, 1882.

11. 9 vols.; New York, 1889–91.

12. Adams, *History* (edition of 1930), Book IX, pp. 222, 225.

13. Letter from H. Adams to H. O. Taylor in 1915, quoted by J. T. Adams on pp. 340, 348, of his *The Adams Family* (New York, 1930). *The Education of Henry Adams*, pp. 37, 301–2.

14. *The Education of Henry Adams*, p. 382.

15. "The Tendency of History," American Historical Association *Annual Report, 1894* (Washington, 1895), p. 18.

16. H. Adams, *Democracy, an American Novel* (New York, 1880), p. 10.

17. *The Education of Henry Adams*, p. 472.

18. Henry Adams, with an introduction by Brooks Adams, *The Degradation of the Democratic Dogma* (New York, 1919), pp. 137–209.

19. *Ibid.*, pp. 267–311; *The Education of Henry Adams*, p. 434.

20. *The Degradation of Democratic Dogma*, pp. 243, 261. See also pp. 142, 154, 308.

21. *The Education of Henry Adams*, pp. 401–2.

22. *Ibid.*, p. 472.

23. Washington, 1904.

24. Carl L. Becker, *Everyman His Own Historian: Essays on History and Politics* (New York, 1935), p. 156.

25. *The Education of Henry Adams*, chaps. xvii and xviii.

26. *Democracy, an American Novel, passim.*

27. *Letters of Henry Adams*, Mar. 4, 1883, p. 348.

28. *The Education of Henry Adams*, pp. 421–22.

29. *Ibid.*, p. 400.

30. V. L. Parrington, *The Beginnings of Critical Realism in America* (New York, 1930), pp. 190–91.

31. Quoted by John S. Clark in his *The Life and Letters of John Fiske* (2 vols.; Boston and New York, 1917), I, 255.

32. *Letters of Henry Adams*, Jan. 2, 1891, p. 458.

33. *The Education of Henry Adams*, pp. 457–58.

34. *Ibid.*, pp. 343–44.

35. *Ibid.*, p. 458.

36. *Ibid.*, p. 470.

37. *Mont Saint Michel and Chartres*, p. 241; see also p. 286.

38. *Ibid.*, pp. 83, 244.

"Augustine's *Confessions* And *The Education Of Henry Adams*"

Gene H. Koretz*

That Henry Adams read Augustine and was familiar with the *Confessions* is indicated by frequent mention in his published letters. Between 1908 and 1915 Augustine's name appears eight times, five times in connection with the *Confessions* and the *Education*.[1] Most of the letters having references to Augustine were written in the key year of 1908, when Adams sent privately printed copies of the *Education* to his friends and acquaintances for the correction of any factual errors which might have escaped his attention and for suggestions for improvement. Such a request naturally resulted in queries from his friendly critics in regard to the intention of the book and the author's own sentiments concerning its virtues and shortcomings. The following letter written to Edith Morton Eustis in February 1908, after she had returned a copy of the *Education* which Adams had sent her, is especially revealing for the purposes of this paper:

> Between artists or people trying to be artists the sole interest is that of form . . . The arrangement, the construction, the composition, the art of climax, are our only serious study. Now that I have the stuff before me—in clay—I can see where the form fails; but I cannot see how to correct the failures. I believe the scheme impossible.
>
> If you are curious to study the literary problem, send for the *Confessions* of St. Augustine, my literary model, and ask him why he failed too, as artist.[2]

This reference to Augustine's *Confessions* as the model for the book is the only explicit and definite statement in the letters or elsewhere concerning Adams' literary sources. Such writers as Rousseau, Franklin, and Cellini have been frequently mentioned as possible literary precedents, and no complete investigation of the problem of the *Education* can afford to ignore their possible influence; but it is clear that Adams regarded *The Confessions of St. Augustine* as the prototype of the kind of thing he had in mind in writing the *Education*. In the so-called "Editor's Preface" to

*Reprinted by permission from *Comparative Literature*, 12 (1960), 193–206.

the *Education*, which first appeared after Adams' death over the signature of Henry Cabot Lodge, Adams compared himself to St. Augustine and his book to the *Confessions*. Speaking of himself from behind the mask of a friend's name, he wrote:

> . . . he used to say, half in jest, that his great ambition was to complete St. Augustine's "Confessions," but that St. Augustine, like a great artist, had worked from multiplicity to unity, while, he, like a small one, had to reverse the method and work back from unity to multiplicity.[3]

In 1915 in reply to a request that he allow the volume to be published Adams declared:

> The book is . . . not in a condition to appear as a work of mine. My idea of what it should be proved beyond my powers. Only St. Augustine ever realized it.[4]

To William James some seven years earlier Adams had expressed himself more fully concerning the relationship between the *Confessions* and the *Education*:

> Did you ever read the Confessions of St. Augustine, or of Cardinal de Retz, or of Rousseau, or of Benvenuto Cellini, or even of my dear Gibbon? Of all of them, I think St. Augustine alone had any idea of literary form,—a notion of writing a story with an end and object, not for the sake of the object, but the form, like a romance.[5]

What Adams admired most of all in Augustine was his consummate craftsmanship. He recognized in the *Confessions* a book which was at least quasi-literary in intention and which had been molded and pressed into significant form, so that to a large extent it transcended the limitations of its immediate purpose. The *Confessions* had been conceived under the stimulus of an emotion which, as Adams tells us in both the *Education* and *Mont-Saint-Michel*, had gradually deteriorated in strength as the forces of society became more diversified. It survived for the citizen of the modern multiverse only through its expression in the great churches and cathedrals of mediaeval France or in literary achievements such as Augustine's *Confessions*. In seeking to do for his own society what Augustine had done for fifth-century Rome—to forge a work of art which is drawn from the life and tenor of the times—Adams hoped to prove that at least one vital instinct of man, the capacity for aesthetic expression and appreciation, was still alive and capable of growth. He also hoped to provide, as Augustine had, some plan of action for his contemporaries beset by the perplexities and disturbances of their world. Perhaps the most revealing commentary on his literary problems and intentions in writing the *Education* is to be found in a letter written to Barrett Wendell, one of his old students at Harvard, in 1909:

When I read St. Augustine's Confessions, or Rousseau's, I feel certain that their faults as literary artists are worse than mine. We have all three undertaken to do what cannot be successfully done—mix narrative and didactic purpose and style . . . St. Augustine's narrative subsides at last into the dry sands of metaphysical theology. Rousseau's narrative fails wholly in didactic result; it subsides into still less artistic egoism . . . My experiment of trying to find the exact point of equilibrium where the two motives would be held in contact was bound to be a failure, but it was very amusing to carry out; and I still maintain that, if I could have had a dramatic setting like St. Augustine . . . I could have made it a success.[6]

The central problem which faced Adams in the *Education* was to combine successfully two seemingly irreconcilable modes of literary composition, to "mix narrative and didactic purpose and style," to write a philosophical treatise in the act of writing a personal spiritual biography. To find a guide for his projected "autobiography" Adams turned to the past examples of Rousseau and St. Augustine. Rousseau's essay in the art of confessions proved to be ill-adapted to both his temperament and his purpose. The bold frankness and egoism of the French philosopher were inimical to the inhibiting traits of Adams' New England conscience. More important than this, "Rousseau's narrative fails wholly in didactic result." Properly speaking, Adams was not seeking to write an autobiography at all, if what is meant by that term is a detailed and factual account of a person's life, written by him in order to shed some light on his own peculiar experiences and personality. Rather he desired to treat only those aspects of his personal history from which lessons of universal applicability could be drawn. It was his intention to examine in retrospect the tangled threads of his existence and to extract whatever general meaning they might possess for his audience. Of all those who had attempted to perform such a task in the past, only Augustine seemed to have achieved some modicum of success, to have used his own life as a springboard toward some philosophical truth, without sacrificing either the narrative form or the didactic object.

Barring the discovery of notes he may have made while working on the *Education*, the exact nature of Adams' debt to the *Confessions* can never be definitely ascertained. In many ways it is difficult to think of two books so dissimilar. Augustine records the history of a passionate and violent nature, driven by impulses which it was powerless to control, and obsessed by an overwhelming sense of sin. The Henry Adams of the *Education* is a temperate and sober individual who exhibits little emotional or intellectual intensity, and who acts less than he is acted upon. Augustine finds his salvation in a complete affirmation of Godhead. Adams' solution is a guarded and limited one, thrown out by suggestion rather than explicitly stated. Yet, despite their obvious differences, the

Education and the *Confessions* possess many characteristics in common, and a close inspection of both yields analogies which are more than fortuitous.

In the second book of the *Confessions* Augustine defines his reasons for writing:

> To whom tell I this? not to Thee, my God; but before Thee to mine own kind, even to that small portion of mankind as may light upon these writings of mine. And to what purpose? that whosoever reads this, may think out of what depths we are to cry unto Thee. For what is nearer to Thine ears than a confessing heart, and a life of faith?[7]

The form of the *Confessions* is that of a public acknowledgment of sinfulness and profession of faith. The object is twofold: to please God by the spectacle of a penitent sinner, and to stimulate others to draw closer to God. Augustine was writing in an era of religious and political turmoil in which Christianity was engaged in a deadly struggle with pagan religions to win the allegiance of the people. By recounting his own tortuous search for truth, he hoped to influence others in the way of righteousness and salvation. Thus the *Confessions* is primarily a spiritual biography, concerned not so much with what Augustine did as with what he thought. Since during his lifetime he had wrestled with the same problems which were plaguing his contemporaries, such as the Christian-pagan controversy, he could legitimately include a refutation of heretical doctrines in the story of his life.

But while the *Confessions* does trace the progressive evolution of Augustine's thought, the author does not restrict himself to a mere narration of his experiences as they occurred. This would have risked excessive emphasis upon his personal drama at the expense of its moral implications. As a manifestation of earthly pride, the spectre of the ego was no less repugnant to Augustine than it was to Adams; he exorcised it by relating his own existence to its source in God. Although the thread which binds the *Confessions* together is that of chronological sequence, the real order is that of a meditation in which Augustine expounds theology. The descriptions or the experiences of the young and sinful Augustine are alternated with apostrophes to God in which Augustine the convert analyzes his life in terms of Christian doctrine. The effect is similar to that of the alternating roles of the actors and the chorus in Greek drama. There is a relieving of tension as the physical action releases a flow of comment which becomes the embodiment of the intrinsic meaning. The finite and transient is linked through the consciousness of the narrator to the eternal and infinite which is truth and God. By this device Augustine both foreshadows imaginatively the discussions of memory and the immaterial nature of the soul in the later books of the *Confessions* and keep his main theme clearly in his readers' minds [sic].

In the *Education* Adams employs a similar technique, with certain significant differences. Augustine had used his own life to exemplify the Christian conception of the relation of the individual to God. In the same way, Adams uses himself as a "model" or type, a point of reference from which to establish the relationship of the individual to the twentieth-century multiverse. He states this explicitly in the preface to the *Education*:

> As educator, Jean Jacques was, in one respect, easily first; he erected a monument of warning against the Ego. Since his time, and largely thanks to him, the Ego has steadily tended to efface itself, and, for purposes of model, to become a manikin on which the toilet of education is to be draped in order to show the fit or misfit of the clothes. The object of study is the garment, not the figure . . . The manikin . . . has the same value as any other geometrical figure of three or more dimensions, which is used for the study of relation. For that purpose it cannot be spared; it is the only measure of motion, of proportion, of human condition.[8]

In his "Study of Twentieth-Century Multiplicity" Adams treats himself as a representative figure of his age whose adventures provide convenient opportunities for philosophical exposition. To guard against the intrusion of the ego, an emphasis which might qualify his theoretical assertions and convert the work into a mere memoir, he employs two stylistic devices. He tells his story in the third person and thus secures an effect of objectivity and detachment. And he cultivates an ironic tone which permits him to disparage the significance of the persona Henry Adams in the narrative.[9] (We recall that Augustine solved the same problem by making God the hidden actor in his personal drama, to whose influence he attributed all of his actions which were just and admirable.) Gerrit H. Roelofs has gone so far as to suggest that the Henry Adams of the *Education* is primarily a literary device, a dramatically conceived character or "masque" whose resemblance to the writer is only a nominal one.[10] Lending support to this interpretation is the evidence cited by Ernest Samuels that Adams consistently and deliberately distorts the facts concerning his personal history in the *Education*. Samuels shows, for instance, that Adams' deprecatory account of his Harvard education is a radical misrepresentation of the facts.[11]

A closer parallel may be found in the principle governing the selection of narrative material in the two works. In each case the didactic intent determines the nature of the experiences related by the narrator, and situations or people who would receive detailed consideration in an authentic biography are either passed over lightly or entirely omitted. Thus we hear relatively little of Augustine's father in the *Confessions*, while his mother has become one of the most memorable figures in all literature. Augustine's reason for taking up his pen was propagation of the faith, and he sought to accomplish this by recounting the story of his own conversion from paganism to Christianity. His father played a negative role in this drama; his mother was a motivating force behind his conversion. Consequently she is treated at length.

Critics have commented upon the brevity of Augustine's description of his parting with his mistress. When he became engaged to marry a young girl, it was held necessary that he should break from his mistress. "My concubine," he writes, "being torn from my side as a hindrance to my marriage, my heart which clave unto her was torn and wounded and bleeding. And she returned to Africa [Augustine was at this time in Milan], vowing unto Thee never to know any other man, leaving with me my son by her."[12] These are the only lines in the *Confessions* in which Augustine speaks of his mistress as anything but the object of his carnal desires. They are followed by an account of how he immediately secured another mistress to take her place. The fact that Augustine could have so callously dismissed a relationship with a woman whom he had lived for many years and who had borne him a son is shocking, but even more offensive is the casual way in which Augustine alludes to the episode. Does not this woman, who loved him faithfully and whom he also professes to have loved, deserve more than the slight attention she receives in the *Confessions*? The answer is that Augustine felt that a more thorough description of this relationship would disrupt the total unity of the work. His subject was the relation of the individual to God, and shifting his focus to a romantic situation would weaken the religious emphasis.

In the *Education* too, we find a significant paucity of comment about certain matters which we would expect to receive fuller coverage in a life story. For example between Chapters XX and XXI there is an abrupt leap of twenty years in the chronology, which has been held by many critics to be a major structural flaw in the book. We know that the period which Adams omitted spans the course of his ill-fated marriage; no doubt his primary reason for the omission was that it was too intimate a chapter of his life to exhibit before the public. However, it would be a mistake to ascribe the omission entirely to personal reticence. Adams' thesis in the *Education* is largely a historical one concerned with the growing complexity of modern life, particularly in the spheres of politics, economics, and science. Clearly, a love story would be as out of place within this context as it would be in the *Confessions*. It is true that what Adams' critics have labeled the "feminine principle," the generative and emotive force he attributed to women, plays a part, though a relatively insignificant one, in the thematic structure of the book; the concept is, however, much more crucially related to the design of *Chartres* than to the design of the *Education*.

Another technique which Adams appears to have borrowed from Augustine is the habit of converting a particular incident or situation into symbol, of loading what often seems to be an entirely innocuous or trivial occurrence with as much discursive meaning as it can possibly bear. Augustine's symbolizing technique is obviously related to the tradition of allegorical Biblical interpretation established by the early Church Fathers. The most striking example in the *Confessions* is the account in Book II of a boyish prank in which Augustine and some companions despoiled a neighbor's pear tree, although they were neither hungry nor desired the fruit for any other purpose. The narrator analyzes this act from all possible angles. It takes on a potent symbolic significance, since Augustine regards it as containing a key to one of the most perplexing problems in the *Confessions*, the source of evil. Another example of his symbolizing technique is Augustine's description of a chance encounter with a joyous beggar on the streets of Milan who had been drinking heavily. This incident gives rise to an exhaustive discussion of the nature of true happiness, and the figure of the drunken beggar emerges as a kind of symbol of the ephemeral and superficial nature of all joy without God.

Similar symbolic episodes occur in the *Education*, and it is apparent that Adams was aware of the potentialities of this technique to a far greater extent than Augustine. Symbolization so thoroughly pervades the *Education* that one critic has suggested that Adams was endeavoring to perfect a "new sort of epic or symbolic form."[13] The central symbol of the book is, of course, the dynamo which Adams saw at the Paris Exposition of 1900, and which he began to feel "as a moral force, much as the early Christians felt the Cross."[14] As a modern scientific image representing ultimate energy and infinite force, it balances the religious symbol of the Virgin in *Chartres*. But the dynamo is only one thread, albeit the most important, in a vast network of symbolic elements in the *Education*.

In the first chapter, for example, mention is made of two family residences of the Adamses, Quincy and Boston. It is soon made clear that they are cited, not to enlighten the reader concerning the living habits of the Adams clan, but to contrast two different and conflicting ways of life. Quincy is eighteenth century; it stands for a simple world with simple virtues, for the Newtonian universe of balance, harmony, and order, for a republican theory of government which stresses moral principles in politics, for a life based upon "abstract ideals" and "ancestral prejudices." Opposed to it is Boston, which represents the social and philosophical currents of the coming age in which unity and order have been destroyed. It is an age of scientific advancement and rapidly accelerating industrialism, of power politics and bankers, an age in which practical considerations and the desire for personal gain provide the only acceptable motives for action. In their symbolic functions Quincy and Boston prefigure one of the basic themes of the *Education*, the transition from the unified world of eighteenth-century rationalism to the multiverse of twentieth-century science.

There are many other instances in which narrative elements are made to do double duty as symbols. Towards the middle of the *Education*

Adams describes his investigation of the theories of Darwin and his discovery of certain data which seemed to contradict Darwin's conclusions. The information that the first known fossil vertebrate was a fish named *Pteraspis* is particularly disturbing to him, and he regards this fact as a valid refutation of Darwinism. *Pteraspis* becomes a symbol of the deficiencies of human knowledge and reappears throughout the rest of the book as a metaphorical leitmotif. A possible analogue for the beggar episode in the *Confessions* is Adams' account of his meeting with Garibaldi at Palermo, which taught him the lesson of "the extreme complexity of extreme simplicity."[15] One could go on indefinitely illustrating Adams' symbolic technique, but one more example will suffice. One of the most dramatic and moving moments in the *Education* is Adams' description in Chapter XIX of his reaction to the death of his sister from an infection she had received as the result of a cab accident. Jolted out of his sense of security and purpose in life, the world became for Adams a chaos of anarchic and purposeless forces:

> Impressions like these are not reasoned or catalogued in the mind; they are felt as a part of violent emotion; and the mind that feels them is a different one from that which reasons; it is thought of a different power and a different person. The first serious consciousness of Nature's gesture—her attitude towards life—took form then as a phantasm, a nightmare, an insanity of force. For the first time, the stage-scenery of the senses collapsed; the human mind finds itself stripped naked, vibrating in a void of shapeless energies, with resistless mass, colliding, crushing, wasting, and destroying what these same energies had created and labored from eternity to perfect. Society became fantastic, a vision of pantomime with a mechanical motion; and its so-called thought merged in the mere sense of life, and pleasure in the sense. The usual anodyne of social medicine became evident artifice. Stoicism was perhaps the best; religion was the most human; but the idea that any personal deity could find pleasure or profit in torturing a poor woman, by accident, with a fiendish cruelty known to man only in perverted and insane temperaments, could not be held for a moment. For pure blasphemy, it made pure atheism a comfort. God might be, as the Church said, a Substance, but He could not be a Person.[16]

A similar incident is the object of Augustine's attention in Book IV of the *Confessions*. In relating the life of his youth, he describes his grief at the death of a childhood friend:

> At this grief my heart was utterly darkened; and whatever I beheld was death. My native country was a torment to me, and my father's house a strange unhappiness; and whatever I had shared with him, wanting him, became a distracting tor-

ture. Mine eyes sought him every where, but he was not granted them; and I hated all places, for that they had not him; nor could they now tell me, "he is coming," as when he was alive and absent . . . Wretched I was; and wretched is every soul bound by the friendship of perishable things; he is torn asunder when he loses them, and then he feels the wretchedness, which he had, ere yet he lost them.[17]

Both passages are crucial to the dramatic and discursive development of the works in which they appear. In each case the death of someone close to the narrator acquires an aura of symbolic meaning which adumbrates the philosophical or didactic intention of the work. To Augustine, for whom unity transcended earthly experience, it illustrated the folly of directing one's love towards a lesser object than God. For Adams, for whom unity must arise from the essential nature of experience itself, its moral was that "Chaos was the law of nature; Order was the dream of man."[18]

The most obvious resemblance which the *Education* bears to the *Confessions* lies in the general structural organization of the two books; and, if direct influence may anywhere be safely predicated, it is here. In each book a narrative exposition of the author's life is developed through the work and lends to it a formal coherence of chronological order. And in each there is an introduction of abstract and theoretical material at the end, almost in the position of an appendix. Although Adams wrote in one letter that the *Confessions* was flawed because the "narrative subsides . . . into the dry sands of theology," elsewhere he expressed the opinion that Augustine had succeeded magnificently in creating a balanced work of art.[19] It appears extremely probable that Adams relied upon the example of Augustine in shifting the final emphasis of the *Education* from a personal and dramatic mode to a discursive one.

Because of its theoretical nature, many readers have misunderstood the function of the final section of the *Confessions* (concerned with Biblical exegesis and a disquisition upon the nature of time) and have failed to perceive its relation to the body of the work.[20] Actually it balances and fulfills the dramatic climax of the book in which Augustine recounts the circumstances of his conversion. The *Confessions* is the record of a soul searching for ultimate truth. According to Augustine's epistemology, this truth resides in God and it can only be grasped through his infinite mercy. Although indispensable within the Christian scheme, reason alone is not sufficient to arrive at knowledge of God and His works; reason must be preceded or supplemented by a will to believe which is the gift of God's grace. The attainment of grace is illustrated by the mysterious incident in the garden at Milan in which Augustine is suddenly granted the sustaining power of faith. Once he has experienced divine illumination (to give it its traditional name), he is able to comprehend the mystery of God and the complex relations of the creation, and it is this culminating act which the last three books of the *Confessions* carry out. Long regarded as a mere superfluous appendix, they are in fact an integral part of the whole and a fitting consummation of the quest which lies at the center of the narration. Étienne Gilson has rightfully declared that these books are "the most splendid part of the *Confessions*."[21]

Similar objections have been leveled at the final chapters of the *Education*, in which the "Dynamic Theory of History" and the "Law of Acceleration" are expounded. Nathalia Wright, writing in the *New England Quarterly*, argues that these chapters are included in the *Education* because Adams' puritan caste of mind would not sanction an expenditure of time writing a mere autobiography.[22] He must turn his energies to some moral and intellectual purpose such as the formulation of a theory of history. As an insight into Adams' character, Miss Wright's remarks may possess some validity, but they are not valid as a criticism of the *Education*. Miss Wright implies a clear disjunction in the book between a portion which is essentially personal and biographical and a theoretical addendum which the writer's conscience forced him to tack on before allowing the book to go to press. The evidence indicates that the book was neither meant to be, nor can be considered, a sincere and truthful statement of the author's life. Furthermore, the early part of the *Education* clearly foreshadows the contents of the final chapters, as any study of the imagery (Adams' frequent recourse to metaphors of force and energy) and symbolism will show.[23] The discursive or didactic elements are not in conflict with or disjoined from the narrative, but, as is the case with the *Confessions*, actually grow from and complete the dramatic action. The device of the persona Henry Adams is retained to the very last line. The historical theories are tentative and suggestive rather than conclusive and final. Clearly the notion that the structure of the *Education* is seriously impaired by the sudden and unprepared-for introduction of a scientific treatise is not borne out by the facts.

To understand the function of the "Dynamic Theory of History" in the *Education*, it is necessary to recall that there are in a sense two subjects in the book. As a whole it may be conceived as a panoramic study of the nineteenth century, a survey of historical trends with the purpose of discovering the basic laws of history and determining the direction of human activities in the future. The objective historical argument of the *Education* may be briefly summarized as follows: In the nineteenth century there occurred what amounted to a revolution in the nature of society and man's place within society. The Newtonian universe of the eighteenth century, in which the individual had a significant and vital role, was suddenly replaced by a world of exploding forces and shifting values, a world which for sheer complexity and accelerating energy far surpassed the wildest premonitions of any previous age. Materialistic and scientific advances made themselves felt in every sphere of human activity. Traditional systems of ethics, politics, science, and philosophy were suddenly relegated to the realm of fairy tales, and man found himself a limited and insignificant creature, an ironic victim of brute forces which he had helped to unleash but was powerless to control. The ultimate effect of this new chaotic supersensual multiverse upon the future of the human race was uncertain. One thing was obvious—the old implements of thought were inadequate to cope with the new forces. A new start would have to be made, and the outmoded forms of education would have to be discarded. Unless man could come to terms with his world and could learn to regulate to some extent its diverse energies, disaster and self-destruction would be the probable result.

Dramatizing and representing concretely this historical framework is the second subject of the book, the personal drama of the protagonist Henry Adams, whose problem is to adjust to his complex environment, to find his own place in the world of multiplicity. He solves it by formulating the "Dynamic Theory of History," for it is only by attempting to synthesize one's experience of the world into some sort of unified system that one can hope to act with purpose and economy. At the same time, the "Dynamic Theory" functions as the solution to the historical problem of the *Education;* it attempts to define the laws of history which are responsible for the phenomenon of multiplicity in the twentieth century. Just as Adams' account of his growing awareness of the dynamo at the Paris Exposition of 1900 as the symbol of a world dominated by naked force parallels the dramatic rendering of Augustine's conversation in the garden at Milan, so the formulation of the "Dynamic Theory of History" in the *Education* is the equivalent of the final philosophical epiphany in the *Confessions.*

It has been demonstrated that Adams' debt to Augustine is of a general rather than a specific nature. Adams saw in the *Confessions* a model for the kind of thing he had in mind in the *Education,* a work which balanced and harmonized aesthetic and didactic motives. In making the main action of his book a quest for knowledge and truth, in adhering to a strict principle of selectivity, in employing symbolic episodes to augment his theme, and in concluding his book with a theoretical exposition, he relied upon the example of Augustine. But he was no slavish imitator, and the form which he finally achieved drew its distinctive qualities out of the material which it embodied. In the *Education* Adams writes of his method of composition:

> The pen works for itself, and acts like a hand, modelling the plastic material over and over again to the form that suits it best. The form is never arbitrary, but is a sort of growth like crystallization, as any artist knows too well.[24]

It is a tribute to Adams' originality that his debt to St. Augustine cannot be more specifically determined.

Notes

1. *Henry Adams and His Friends: A Collection of Hitherto Unpublished Letters*, ed. Harold Dean Cater (Boston, 1947), p. 615: *The Letters of Henry Adams (1858–1918)*, ed. Worthington C. Ford (Boston and New York, 1930–38), II, 490, 526, 635; *The Selected Letters of Henry Adams*, ed. Newton Arvin (New York, 1951), p. 255.

2. *Henry Adams and His Friends*, p. 615. Adams' estimation of Augustine's artistic success in the *Confessions* fluctuated considerably: see the letters quoted below. His statement here that he believed the *Education* to be a failure with respect to artistic form is apparently sincere, and there is no evidence that it is meant to be ironical or a defensive measure against astringent criticism. His friends universally acclaimed his book, most of them taking the liberty of retaining the copies he had sent them; yet he remained adamant in his refusal to allow it to be published during his lifetime. Adams' own admission of failure, however, is not a valid criterion, as some critics have supposed, for damning the book. It need hardly be stressed that it is the duty of the critic to judge a work of art solely on its own merits.

3. *The Education of Henry Adams: An Autobiography* (Boston and New York, 1918), pp. vii–viii. All quotations are from this edition.

4. *The Letters of Henry Adams*, II, 635.

5. *Ibid.*, p. 490.

6. *The Selected Letters of Henry Adams*, p. 255.

7. *The Confessions of St. Augustine*, tr. E. B. Pusey, Everyman's Library (London, 1907), p. 23. All quotations are from this edition.

8. *Education*, p. x.

9. For detailed consideration of Adams' style in the *Education* see the following: Joseph Warren Beach, "Henry Adams," in *The Outlook for American Prose* (New York, 1929), pp. 263–269; Yvor Winters, "Henry Adams, or the Creation of Confusion," in *The Anatomy of Nonsense* (Norfolk, Conn., 1943), pp. 23–87; Robert A. Hume, "The Style and Literary Background of Henry Adams," *American Literature*, XVI (1945), 296–315.

10. Gerrit H. Roelofs, "Henry Adams: Pessimism and the Intelligent Use of Doom," *ELH*, XVII (1950), 214–239.

11. Ernest Samuels, *The Young Henry Adams* (Cambridge, Mass., 1948), pp. 8–52.

12. *Confessions*, p. 116.

13. Robert E. Spiller, "Henry Adams," in *Literary History of the United States*, II (New York, 1948), 1103. In his recent book, *The Mind and Art of Henry Adams* (Cambridge, Mass., 1957), J. C. Levenson suggests that Adams carried this technique too far in the *Education:* "He made the mistake of thinking that almost anything which happened to him must have symbolic value" (p. 257).

14. *The Education*, p. 380.

15. *Ibid.*, p. 95.

16. *Ibid.*, pp. 288–289.

17. *Confessions*, pp. 50–57.

18. *The Education*, p. 451.

19. See the letters quoted above.

20. A convenient summary of the traditional controversy concerning the unity of the *Confessions* is given by P. Courcelle, *Recherches sur les Confessions de saint Augustin* (Paris, 1950), pp. 21 ff. For an earlier statement of the theory advanced above, see my note, "Augustine's *Confessions*," *The Explicator*, XII (1954), item 37. Recently I have become aware of John J. O'Meara's *The Young Augustine* (London, 1954). Professor O'Meara makes a distinction similar to my own: "If there is unity in the *Confessions* it lies . . . in the contrast

between the search for Truth under the guidance of Providence in the first part of the work, and the enjoyment of Truth in the Scriptures in the second part" (pp. 17–18).

21. Étienne Gilson, *The Spirit of Medieval Philosophy* (New York, 1936), p. 143.

22. Nathalia Wright, "Henry Adams' Theory of History: A Puritan Defense," *NEQ*, XVIII (1945), 204–210.

23. See Elizabeth Stevenson, *Henry Adams: A Biography* (New York, 1955), p. 348.

24. *The Education*, p. 389.

[Democracy and Esther: Two Novels by Henry Adams]

Ernest Samuels*

In the pages of Henry Adams's novels, *Democracy* and *Esther*, there comes into sharp focus a side of the American experience largely overlooked by our novelists: the Washington world of politics and society of the late seventies and early eighties of the nineteenth century, when the city was growing up into one of the important world capitals. Mark Twain in his sprawling first novel had aptly christened the period immediately after the Civil War "The Gilded Age," to symbolize the shallow morality and taste of the epoch presided over by President Ulysses S. Grant and ruled by political buccaneers who had been welcomed aboard the ship of state. Henry Adams took up permanent residence in Washington in 1877, at the age of thirty-nine, a few months after Grant gratefully surrendered the White House to Rutherford B. Hayes. With the help of congressional committees and grand juries the country was now beginning to figure up the cost of political incompetence and commercial fraud.

Adams brought a unique perspective to the turbulent scene. The city was rich in ancestral associations for him, and the atmosphere thick with history. His great-grandfather, John Adams, Washington's successor to the Presidency, had been one of the authentic Founding Fathers, a nation-maker among such fellow giants as Thomas Jefferson, Benjamin Franklin, and Alexander Hamilton. His grandfather, John Quincy Adams, the sixth President of the United States and a model of the philosophic statesman, had returned to Washington after Andrew Jackson's grassroots democracy wrecked his chance of a second term and had taken a place in the House of Representatives to carry on the fight against slavery until he dropped in harness at the age of eighty. Henry Adams's father, Charles Francis Adams, elected to Congress from the Quincy, Massachusetts, district had brought him to Washington as a private secretary during the secession winter of 1860, seasoned for the job by two years' study and travel in Europe following his graduation from

*Introduction reprinted from *Democracy and Esther* (Doubleday and Co., Garden City, 1961), ix–xix.

76

Harvard. At his father's elbow at the highest party councils he could almost grasp the "levers of power" in the strife-torn capital. Filial duty took him to London during the war years, where he studied international diplomacy at first hand as his father steered the legation through the crosscurrents of continental power politics. He "gravitated" to Washington again in 1868 to make a name in the press as a crusader for political and financial reform. Lured away from Washington journalism by the offer of an assistant professorship in history at Harvard and the editorship of the *North American Review*, Adams put his reforming zeal to work, to initiate advanced seminars, first in medieval history, and then in American history.

Seven years of "exile" proved more than sufficient. He was weary of teaching and he was at last convinced that a political career in Massachusetts was blocked by his two older brothers. Glad to escape from his native Boston and all its wintry constraints, he set up shop as a historian in Washington's Lafayette Square, opposite the White House. He and his witty and talented wife, Marian, a New England Brahmin like himself, soon established the most brilliant and exclusive salon of the town. Senators, congressmen, ambassadors, scientists, artists, and literary notables met at the five-o'clock tea table to anatomize their brilliant microcosm. From this privileged vantage point Adams cocked a philosophical eye upon a society roaring hopefully ahead to Eldorados of material and scientific progress, yet never free of anxiety about the true nature of the new economic and social forces that were transforming America. In the churning wake of Darwin's *Origin of Species* a flood of books and articles proclaimed the warfare between science and religion. The women's-rights question grew more alarming year by year. People took up Schopenhauer and Buddhism and denounced the rise of communism among the laboring classes. On the northwestern frontier the Sioux Indians still disputed the march of progress. In New York, Boss Tweed raided the public treasury with the loyal approval of the immigrant vote. As for the new South, left to itself in the backwash of Northern industrial expansion, it quietly unraveled the web of Reconstruction and equal rights. The West burgeoned with railroads, mortgage-laden farms, and town speculators. Every vibration of this dizzying postwar society came to Washington as to a central telephone exchange and loudly echoed in the "Cave of the Winds" on Capitol Hill.

In such a challenging environment Adams, an instinctive satirist, could hardly avoid turning to the novel to give free vent to his opinions on the passing scene in intervals stolen from biography and history. His massive biography of Albert Gallatin, Jefferson's Secretary of the Treasury, for which he had mined the archives of the State Department, was soon to be followed by a slashing biography of John Randolph, and all was to be capped in 1890 by the monumental nine-volume *History of the United States during the Administrations of Jefferson and Madison.*

This would be for reputation and posterity. And this was to be nearly all that posterity was to know of Henry Adams until after his death in 1918. His great classic on medieval life and art, *Mont-Saint-Michel and Chartres,* privately printed in 1904, was not published until 1913. The book that was to give him his widest audience, *The Education of Henry Adams,* privately printed in 1907, was not published until several months after his death.

The novels were never acknowledged by Adams except to a very few completely loyal intimates. The publisher, Henry Holt, finally put an end to speculation about the authorship of *Democracy* in 1921 and he placed Adams's name on the title page in the 1925 edition. Thayer, the biographer of John Hay, discovered the secret of the authorship of *Esther* but discreetly withheld public comment until August of 1918. Adams's letters, published in 1930, confirmed the fact.

Democracy, written in a burst of creative enthusiasm late in 1878, obviously served as a safety valve for all of Adams's accumulated disgusts with American politics under Grant and his successor in "respectable nullity," Hayes. His wife gaily urged him on and supplied a touch or two of the descriptions of the women's dresses at the presidential ball, where patriotic Americans could fawn upon visiting royalty. First issued in the United States in March 1880, it was quickly taken up in England, where the satire on the democratic process was hugely savored. One of Adams's English friends, the novelist Mrs. Humphry Ward, shrewdly nominated Adams as the author, pointing out that the novel "almost exactly followed the lines laid down" in Adams's "Civil Service Reform" in the *North American Review* of 1869. No one seconded the nomination. Adams and his wife could safely lean back and enjoy the fun as patriots and victims howled with rage. He had struck "a blow against democracy," against its pretensions and weaknesses, with the same therapeutic candor as in his days as a muckraking journalist and drew blood right and left. Only a few readers perceived the affirmative faith concealed by the satire. A dozen years later, for example, a writer in the English *Quarterly Review* drew this moral: " 'Democracy,' it has been remarked in a famous novel, 'asserts the fact that our masses are now raised to a higher intelligence than formerly; it means faith in human nature, faith in science, faith in the survival of the fittest.' "

For a few seasons the book reigned as a best seller in England and America, the London edition being published by Macmillan in May 1882. The 1908 printing, the last in Adams's lifetime, was the sixteenth. A French translation was hurried into print six months after the English edition. English critics rated the anonymous author as surpassing Disraeli and Trollope in blending politics and romance. They hailed him as a new luminary to shine alongside Henry James and William Dean Howells. His psychological insights recalled the French realist Alphonse Daudet. One London review gave the highest accolade: "A masterpiece." On this side the *Atlantic* thought there was "nothing in its way so good in our literature." Some of this enthusiasm may be written off on the score of the timeliness of the novel and the partisan feelings it aroused. But even those who resented it recognized a literary stylist of the first order.

One of the private dissenters was one of Adams's closest friends, the noted geologist Clarence King. He remarked to the third member of their triumvirate, John Hay, that the English reader would find "his cruelest suspicions about American institutions offered as truth, only garnished with a little local color and succulent with Henry's wit." For him, the heroine, Madeleine Lee, was Beacon Street incarnate. James Bryce, the English historian, publicly protested that America was no worse than England. He urged his countrymen not to be taken in by the exaggerations of the novel, advice that must have had a special piquancy to his good friend Henry Adams.

Several of the characters of the novel were so thinly disguised that for a few years identifying the originals who sat for their portraits was one of the liveliest parlor games in high political circles. With his ancestral "instinct for the jugular" Adams paid off most of his outstanding political scores, the chief one being of course his disappointment with the Grant administration. Twenty-five years later he was to write his definitive appraisal of the stone-age mentality of the man from Galena, Illinois, in the urbane epitaph of *The Education.* Here his President was recognizable to the politically sophisticated reviewers as a composite of Grant and Hayes, with a dash of Lincoln's social gaucherie thrown in for good measure. The train of association was easily spelled out: "career as a stone-cutter in a quarry"—"Old Granite"—Grant. Grant's political naïveté among the hard-bitten professionals of the party got short shrift from Adams's pen. Bewildered by the immensity of his responsibilities, Grant had gratefully shed them upon the willing shoulders of subordinates, such as his private secretary Babcock, who soon learned the cash value of his political influence in the service of the whisky-distillers' ring. Grant had bumblingly accepted the expert advice of Senator Roscoe Conkling of New York who had served as errand boy to Senator Morton and his clique to deliver orders to the White House. In one of the choicest episodes in *Democracy* the hapless President falls into the astute snares of his principal adviser, infinitely relieved to be rid of the patronage problem. The epitaph of his good intentions: "These are friends of mine; got to be looked after. Just stuff 'em in somewhere."

The most merciless satire was aimed at Senator James G. Blaine. He furnished the principal features of the egregious and masterful Senator Ratcliffe. Blaine's cynical pretense of interest in civil-service reform, finally exposed by his attack on Adams's idealistic friend Carl Schurz, made him a "pet enmity" with whom Adams and his wife would have no traffic even when he became Secretary of State under their friend Garfield. Blaine unknowingly returned the compliment by publicly cutting

Clarence King, believing him to be the author of the novel. The episode of Sam Baker's bribing of Ratcliffe was an unmistakable thrust at Blaine's unsavory role in the Mulligan-letters scandal, though Adams broadened the attack by blending in several other dubious transactions in which Blaine had figured. Nathan Gore was quickly identified as John Lothrop Motley, the minister to Madrid whom the roughhewn Grant had sacked because, as Secretary of State Fish told Adams, Motley "parted his hair in the middle." In the idealistic and gentlemanly Carrington, Adams paid tribute to James Lowndes, a Washington lawyer who had fought gallantly on the Rebel side. He was one of a contingent of Southerners who enlivened the talk at the Adams fireside, a group that included the courtly Senator Lucius Q. C. Lamar of Mississippi, General Richard Taylor, son of the late President Zachary Taylor, and the noted publicist William H. Trescott.

Society relished most the patent satire of President Hayes's wife, who had banned alcohol and low-cut dresses from the White House in an effort to reform the Roman depravity of the city by importing the simple virtues of Ohio. In the unconventional Victoria Dare, Adams limned one of his favorite Lafayette Square neighbors, the California heiress Emily Beale, whose artless satire made her the terror of vulnerable Congressmen. She was furious at, if flattered by, the portrait. The cynical Baron Jacobi gave back the worldly-wise traits of another frequenter of the Adams salon, the popular Turkish diplomat and journalist, Aristarchi Bey. For his heroine, Mrs. Lightfoot Lee, and her sister Sybil, Adams gracefully lifted the salient features of Mrs. Bigelow Lawrence, a society matron and summer neighbor of the Adamses at Beverly Farms, and her ravishing sister, Fanny Chapman, to whom Senator Blaine was a devoted courtier. But if in most cases Adams began with real-life models, he freely improvised on the originals to serve his artistic—and satiric—purposes. This is nowhere more evident than in the figure of the ambitious Mrs. Lee. Her inner consistency comes from Adams's own tastes and temperament. Her passion for power, her inveterate philosophizing, her love of elegance, her patriotism, and her unyielding moral integrity—all hold up the mirror to the ideals of the author. In her frankness and womanly independence one glimpses also the distinctive personality of Marian Adams.

One may read the conclusion of the novel as a renunciation and flight from the world—a reflection of one of Adams's own recurring fantasies—or one may take it, as a recent English critic has suggested, as a "temporary withdrawal," the kind of open end that Henry James sometimes employed, as in *The Portrait of a Lady*. Perhaps the inconclusiveness is organic to the conception, reflecting the "impasses" which Adams and his friends Hay and King saw on every hand. Certainly a Hamlet-like indecisiveness was to deepen with the years, an ambivalence and doubleness of vision that would flower in *The Education*. Undoubtedly the novel has a special interest as marking a stage in Adams's own Odyssey; its lasting appeal, however, rests on the vitality of the characterizations, the unfading authority of the political insights, the firm sense of structure, and on the grace of literary style.

For his second novel, *Esther*, Adams once more centered his gaze upon the figure of a charming and sophisticated woman. Woman, he could and did idealize; man, the American man especially, he was wont to say in later life was a "chump." In cynical moments he would agree with Clarence King that woman was a biological mistake of nature, but as a philosophical man of the world he regularly acknowledged that he owed everything to women. He trusted their intuition and their taste. He conceded their natural superiority. In *Democracy* a major theme is woman's role in politics, the problems which stem from her nature. The crisis comes when she faces the choice of marrying an unscrupulous politician or giving him up for the sake of her moral scruples. *Esther* poses a similar dilemma. The heroine must ultimately choose between adopting her fiancé's religion, he being a minister of a fashionable Episcopalian church, or adhering to her intellectual skepticism and denying her emotions. For the backdrop of the action Adams chose the then intense conflict between religion and science, a conflict which had created a chasm between orthodox and liberal religion.

The novel appeared in March 1884, under the pseudonym Frances Snow Compton. The writing of it marked an interval in Adams's protracted work on his *History*, a kind of celebration of his having passed the halfway mark. Always the iconoclast, Adams decided on a whimsical and yet serious experiment. Holt should issue the book without advertisement to test whether there was an active literary taste in the country, independent of publishers and their claques. Holt humored his friend, more willingly since Adams could easily afford to subsidize the odd venture. Of the edition of one thousand copies, five hundred were sold the first year. The remainder were ultimately bought up by the author and destroyed. The book was completely ignored by the press, despite its timeliness. For Adams this was failure, and it proved his pessimistic point. Bentley, the English publisher, placed a modest advertisement in the *Athenaeum*. The review copy drew comment: "*Esther* is, like many another American novel, clever and inconclusive. It gives the reader the impression that the writer's object is to show that she is up to the mark in art, science, religion, agnosticism, and society. The reader is therefore more ready to compliment Miss Compton than to thank her." One suspects that even if the book had been widely advertised it would have fared no better in that period of literary conformity, when the publishers of magazine serials lived in fear of Mrs. Grundy. Esther's advanced ideas smacked of all the horrid agitation for women's rights that increasingly disturbed the night's rest of the Victorian paterfamilias.

The secret of the authorship of *Esther* was even better kept than that of *Democracy*. There is some reason to believe that Marian Adams read it, though for nearly two years none of the others of their innermost circle, "The Five of Hearts," had any inkling of it. By then Adams's wife was dead, having taken her own life on December 6, 1885, after several months of severe nervous depression. The catastrophe suddenly gave the novel a new character in Adams's eyes. The heroine owed so much to Marian, to her personality and ideas, that Adams treasured it beyond anything else he had written and in his grief kept it as a private shrine. King and Hay were soon to read and admire it. Beyond them a favorite niece or two were admitted, and then the chapter was closed. The relation of Esther to her father paralleled in many ways that of Marian Adams to her indulgent parent. By an unlucky chance fate completed the parallel. In the book, Esther's father dies and she suffers a profound traumatic shock, for ever since the early death of her mother she had centered all her affection upon him. Esther survived the ordeal; Marian did not.

Adams found most of his characters in his own drawing room, so to speak, the novel providing a brilliant theater for the extension of their remarks. Admittedly the plot is even slighter than that of *Democracy*. There is little incident and no adventure. The drama is internal, cerebral. The psychological tensions arise from the collision of ideas and of wills. In a time when churchgoing was, if not more common, at any rate more deeply committed than now, the opposition of a clergyman and an agnostic had all the piquancy of situation in which Adams delighted. What would a woman like his own wife, militantly anticlerical and even agnostic as she was, have done if she had fallen in love with a devout clergyman like his cousin Phillips Brooks, the famous pastor of Boston's Trinity Church? Here was a challenging problem in psychological algebra. Brooks went into the equation. In also went John La Farge, who had painted the great murals in Trinity Church and, more recently, had worked on the decoration of St. Thomas Church in New York. As Wharton, he presents the claims of the world of art and intuition. The character of Strong drew heavily on Clarence King, scientist, art connoisseur, and cosmopolite, whose love of paradox was as keen as Adams's own. Strong comes nearest to being Adams's spokesman in the novel.

To balance the intellectual and strong-willed Esther is Catherine Brooks, a vessel of pure emotion. Vivacious and exquisitely lovely, she recalls Elizabeth Cameron, the young wife of Senator James Donald Cameron, whose beauty made Petrarchan poets of her middle-aged admirers. Adams was to follow in her train until the end of his life, worshiping the ideal which she represented. Significant of this opposition of feminine types is the fact that Esther tries to paint, an essentially masculine activity, whereas Catherine serves as a model, passively feminine. In the interplay of the sharply defined characters, Adams shows the consequences of such varied endowments tried by the dogmas of religion, by the creative demands of art, by the touchstone of poetry, by the challenge of materialist science, and by the passional demands of the heart.

Like its predecessor, the story ends in an impasse. Clarence King pointed out to Adams that he had left his heroine no alternative but suicide to escape the trap into which her intellectual scruples and her emotions had placed her. Her creator acknowledged that the point was well taken, but since he disliked being forced to ultimate conclusions he frankly evaded the issue.

Esther explored the role of woman in contemporary society with much more subtlety than the first novel. The student of Adams's later writings will readily see in it an anticipation of his major themes. The feminine ideal of which Esther and Catherine are complementary facets would find ultimate expression in the Virgin Mary of the *Mont-Saint-Michel and Chartres*. The contrast that Adams was to dramatize by the symbols of infinite power, the Virgin for the twelfth century, the Dynamo for the twentieth, had its beginnings in the two novels. They represent his first imaginative encounter with the centrifugal forces of modern life, the first intimations of the chaos and multiplicity of the twentieth century.

Seen against the fiction of their time, the two novels show an astonishing maturity of talent. The urbane yet trenchant satire of the Washington political scene stands alone in its time for wit and Swiftian point. In Senator Silas P. Ratcliffe, Adams created a memorable example of the political opportunist whose type is always with us and always to be feared. Able, daring, and unscrupulous, he stands as a lasting warning of the dangers of boss rule in party politics. Though no such Mephistophelean figure is evoked in *Esther*, its civilized heroine belongs in the small company of women figures who have permanently enriched American literature. In any collection of distinguished American novels, these minor classics have earned a rightful place. In now making them available in convenient and inexpensive format, the publishers recover for us a valuable portion of our literary heritage.

"Henry Adams: 1838–1918"

Ernest Samuels*

As a result of the revolution of taste that reduced the reputations of Longfellow, Dr. Holmes, and Lowell from Brahmin high priests to Saturday Club sentimentalists, it is now evident that much of the old authority passed into the hands of Henry Adams and Henry James, though they both abandoned Boston to escape such a destiny. Brought up to revere the keepers of the genteel tradition, each in turn rebelled against its narrow provinciality. Yet, ironically, it was to be a common bond of their lifelong intimacy that they carried with them into exile the quintessence of that tradition. The rebellion of Henry Adams against the Brahmin failure of nerve was all the deeper for his having been Boston born and bred, anchored by ancestral ties to its historic ground. A patrician to the marrow, Adams was fated to quarrel with his class, aware all the while that though he was a brand plucked from the burning he had been deeply scorched. From the time he left Boston in 1877, he wore his nativity like a hairshirt through all his wanderings, clinging with a certain guilty pride to the finicking tastes he owed to it. In one of his incomparable letters to Henry James he held up the mirror to their class: "God knows that we knew our want of knowledge! the self-distrust became introspection—nervous self-consciousness—irritable dislike of America, and antipathy to Boston."

Adams found no repose in the frictionless complacencies of Beacon Hill. His moral idealism vaulted a long half-century to draw its strength from the older and more austere Puritan ethos. His father's motto was "Work and Pray." It served as well for the restless son, though he learned to pray to strange gods—and goddesses. His brother Brooks once wrote a book to celebrate the emancipation of Massachusetts from the Puritan priests. Henry dissented from the harsh estimate. The Puritans may have been intolerant but they had the courage of their moral vision. As practical Calvinists they did not overrate the possibilities of average human nature.

Henry Adams was not a literary figure in the traditional sense. His closest friendships were not with novelists or poets. Socially he was on friendly terms with many writers, including Browning, Arnold, Kipling,

* From *Major Writers of America*, Volume II edited by Perry Miller, copyright © 1962 by Harcourt Brace Jovanovich, Inc. and reprinted with their permission.

Stevenson, James, Howells, S. Weir Mitchell, Richard Watson Gilder, Bret Harte, and Charles Warren Stoddard. He belonged to no literary school and generally avoided discussion of his books and his literary problems. He had no overmastering drive toward literary distinction. When his ambitious elder brother, Charles Francis Adams, Jr., prodded him to seek a literary career, he rejected the meanness of an existence devoted to feeding the monthly magazines as a popular literary entertainer. Even when he had begun to make a name for himself as a crusading Washington journalist for the *Nation* and the *North American Review*, he bristled like a porcupine to defend an inner ideal. "I will not go down into the rough-and-tumble," he told his brother,

> nor mix with the crowd, nor write anonymously, except for mere literary practice. . . . You like the strife of the world. I detest it and despise it. You work for power. I work for my own satisfaction. You like roughness and strength; I like taste and dexterity. For God's sake, let us go our own ways and not try to be like each other.

His was an Emersonian self-reliance; his heart vibrated to that iron string as he marched alone on "chaos and the dark." If he would not keep pace with his companions it was because, like Thoreau, he heard "a different drummer."

Adams belonged to the generation of Mark Twain and William Dean Howells. He did not begin to figure significantly in literary history until after his death on March 27, 1918, at the age of eighty. In academic circles he had been widely known as a leading historian, the author of the monumental nine-volume *History of the United States During the Administrations of Jefferson and Madison* and of two important political biographies—*Albert Gallatin*, a massively documented study of Jefferson's Secretary of the Treasury, and *John Randolph*, the fiery spokesman of the antebellum South. Elected president of the American Historical Association in 1894, he ended his one-year term with a characteristic gesture, flight from the public eye. He decamped to Mexico, leaving behind him his iconoclastic presidential address, "The Tendency of History." For years he lived in the shadow of his friend and neighbor, Secretary of State John Hay, as a political oracle at the service of high-ranking officials and diplomats. His career as a distinguished, if somewhat eccentric, litterateur came to light only by stages, reluctantly and after many importunities. That the dignified aristocrat, whose famous Romanesque house on Lafayette Square overlooked the White House, was a literary artist of the highest order was known only to a small circle of friends and a court of nieces who "matronized" at his famous twelve o'clock breakfasts. In 1913 the architect Ralph Adams Cram, a leading Gothic enthusiast, persuaded him to allow the publication of his *Mont-Saint-Michel and Chartres*. This masterly evocation of the art and thought of the Middle Ages in northern France had been privately printed in 1904 and distributed to friends and a few university libraries. In 1915 his poem "Buddha and Brahma," which had passed about in manuscript for twenty years, appeared in the *Yale Review*. Adams did not really come into his own until late in 1918 when his study of twentieth-century multiplicity, as he described his autobiography, *The Education of Henry Adams*, was posthumously published. It, too, had been privately printed and issued in 1907 to a select circle of readers who broadcast its brilliant paradoxes far and wide. The book excited a profound interest among war-weary intellectuals. Awarded the Pulitzer prize in 1919, it soon established itself as an American classic and one of the half-dozen great autobiographies of the world.

For more than forty years Adams's reputation has been dominated by that "wise and witty book," as Robert Spiller calls it, a dazzling enigma of a book, compounded of poetic feeling and scientific speculation. Its good-humored cynicism and Voltairean mockery captivated the generation of intellectuals who lost their ideals at Versailles. The incantatory symbols of the Virgin and the Dynamo marked the appearance of a Carlylean prophet in the modern wasteland. T. S. Eliot and Ezra Pound would soon echo his themes in their sardonic elegies. Few critics have been able to resist quoting the *Education* for its urbane epigrams, its inexhaustible ironies on things-in-general, and its vignettes of nineteenth-century history. To disillusioned idealists of the right and left, the book seemed the authentic swan song of an amoral acquisitive society. Adams's image of himself as a "weary Titan of Unity," an Ishmael of the spirit lost in the darkening chaos of the modern world, still exerts a hypnotic influence. In the long shadow of the radioactive mushroom cloud, his menacing vision of the future is as meaningful to our time as Melville's desperate thrusting through the mask of fate in *Moby-Dick* and Hawthorne's glimpses into the infernos of the human soul.

Nothing, perhaps, would have astonished Adams more than the perversity of fate that has placed him among the major American writers. It was hardly what he bargained for. When he sought fame and power, they eluded him. When he contemptuously turned his back on the public, fame hunted him out. It was enough to justify one's lifelong quarrel with the lack of order in human affairs. The question of fame and success haunted him more, perhaps, than it did any other American writer, until its ramifications overwhelmed him in philosophical quicksands. To an important degree the *Education* is a study in the philosophy of success. As a young man Adams had dreamed of "a national set of young men like ourselves or better, to start new influences not only in politics, but in literature, in law, in society, and throughout the whole social organization of the country—a national school of our own generation." In old age he felt himself to be a kind of John the Baptist, seeking a new Redeemer who would save the world from the irresponsible "Atom King."

The vision of the *Education* is romantic and grandiose. In its cosmic glare Adams's own life seems indeed an ordeal of frustration, no matter how much it may have surpassed that of his rivals in interest and achievement. Self-depreciation was his vice, he observed, and in the *Education* he indulged it to the full, though at the expense of his fellow men. The Olympian detachment reflected the doubleness of his nature, the incessant oscillation of his feelings between the life of action and the life of thought, of the participator and the bystander. He was like the heroine of his anonymous novel *Democracy*. He had a scientific curiosity about the workings of his own mind and would take off his "mental clothing" and study it as if "it belonged to someone else." In Ed Howe's salty phrase, he was "the only man in America who could sit on a fence and see himself go by." Political journalism attracted him because he could be at the center of power and yet remain calm on his high stool above the battle. In his diminishing phrase he saw himself as a "stable companion" of statesmen. Justice Oliver Wendell Holmes was one of the first to protest Adams's too exacting standards:

> I note in your *Education* you talk very absurdly as if your work has been futile. I for one have owed you more than you in the least suspect. And I have no doubt that there are many others not to be neglected who do the same. Of course you may reply that it is also futile—but that is the dogmatism that often is disguised under pessimism. . . . If a man has counted in the actual striving of his fellows he cannot pronounce it vain.

The debate on the worthwhileness of human exertion goes on with unquenchable liveliness as men continue to ask, Whither mankind? Adams captured in his candid lens the secret doubts of even the most convinced pragmatist—Are all human values in the timeless flux of things merely relative? He brought to light the hidden second thoughts of the philosophical idealists—Is the world in fact only a dream in the mind of man? Adams put the practical dilemma on the point of an aphorism: "Pessimists are social bores. Optimists are intellectual idiots." It all depended where one stood. Outraged by the dehumanizing of man in the new industrial society, Adams felt a prophet's share in the common guilt and despised himself for his complicity. The twentieth century swept in to the rumble of imperialist guns in China, the Philippines, and South Africa. The spectacle of Christian progress upset him as much as it did Mark Twain. "The little good I ever knew of my own century," he told a correspondent,

> quite disappears and is lost to my eyes in the dazzle of having, since the first year of my era—according to the Christians, 1838—won all my stakes, triumphed in all my interests, betrayed all my principles, lost all my self-respect, and been mistaken in every opinion I ever held. The consequence is that I am respected, sought, and if I live to be wholly, instead of

partially imbecile, shall be admired. Under these favorable circumstances I try not to be impatient of—other people's— cant or hypocrisy or lies.

The "sentimental pessimism"—Paul Elmer More's phrase—has long stood between Henry Adams and a just appreciation of his literary career. In the general eye he has been thought of as a man of one book. The world accepted the image he created. That image was the creature of the transforming power of time and memory. "The actual journey," he said of a boyhood visit to Washington, "may have been quite different, but the actual journey has no interest for education. The memory was all that mattered." The hero of the book was the double behind which an enormously sensitive temperament could hide itself from posterity or at least save a vestige of heroism. Only by careful study of his immense correspondence, by reascending the actual path of his career can we fully appreciate the artistry—and the artfulness—of the persona he created. Ridden by the urgency of his thesis, the need to master the chaotic new forces of science and technology, he obscured his career in a web of understatement. The whole middle section of his life, nearly twenty years of prolific writing and the period of his happy marriage, was consigned to limbo by the tyrannous scheme. One must disengage his career from the power nexus which obsessed his later life, free it from the exaggerated pessimism of the *fin de siècle*, unearth the buried life of his maturity to see the true stature of his achievement.

II

One of Adams's many private jokes was that he had been an average young man. Nothing was farther from the fact. Born with a silver spoon and a steel-nibbed pen, he soon learned that he stood apart from his fellows by birth and by virtue of family tradition. The Boston State House that cast its protective shadow over his boyhood home daily reminded him of his heritage. The history of Massachusetts and of the nation were a familiar part of the family record; genealogy and politics went hand in hand. The first Henry Adams had emigrated from Somersetshire in 1636 to settle in what is now Quincy, Massachusetts. For three generations the family multiplied with Biblical abundance in respectable obscurity. In the middle of the eighteenth century a member of the family suddenly made his entrance on the stage of history. The Boston authorities summoned thirty-year-old John Adams, then a part-time village lawyer and farmer, to argue the invalidity of the Stamp Act. For the next hundred years after that event, he and his descendants helped shape the destiny of the new nation. He became the second President of the United States. His eldest son, John Quincy Adams, followed in his footsteps as a lawyer and independent political leader, broke with the pro-British crowd of State

Street, and supported Thomas Jefferson's Embargo. Rising to Secretary of State under James Monroe, John Quincy was largely responsible for the issuance of the Monroe Doctrine. In 1825 he became the sixth President of the United States, a storm center of controversy like his father and like him a mixture of passionate ambition and unyielding moral principle. His third son, Charles Francis Adams, the father of Henry Adams, gravitated toward politics, became a congressman and then American minister to England. The family fortunes had been steadily rising but as a result of the marriage in 1829 of Charles Francis Adams to one of the daughters of Peter Chardon Brooks, the leading New England millionaire, for the first time an Adams was a rich man. Henry Adams of the *Education* was the third of four sons who grew to manhood. In spite of notable promise, none was able to win political eminence.

Henry Adams began life at an altitude that gave him a unique perspective of the terrain below where ordinary mortals shouldered their way to success or oblivion. The Quincy chapter of the *Education* wonderfully evokes the half-mythic character of a boyhood drenched in history, dominated by a sense of family mission. The young Henry steeped himself as his father had before him in the self-probing diaries of his forebears, so like the old Puritans' daily accounting of the ordeal of their souls. He took up the hereditary quarrels of the Adamses which eventually fell to his lot to settle at the bar of history: the malice of English statesmen like Canning and Perceval, the calumnies of the Federalists who had disowned them, the slanders of John Randolph, the enmities that had denied reelection to their presidents.

The noblest fighter of them all had been John Quincy Adams. Defeated by Jackson in the fierce campaign of 1828, he had swallowed his pride and gone back to the House of Representatives to carry on the fight against the Slave Power. As "Old Man Eloquent" he won his fight against the "Gag Rule," staying on to die at last in harness. There was Roman stoicism in his advice to his son, Charles: "Fortify your mind against disappointments . . . Keep up your courage, and go ahead." There was also bitterness. Looking back over his astonishing career, he could not "recollect a single instance of success in anything." His son, in like mood, after a distinguished career in diplomacy, wrote to a young friend, "When I was entering into life I was disposed to mount a high horse and challenge the world to disputation for prizes which now I would not cross the room to secure." The pattern of courage and disenchantment descended to the "Fourth Generation" of the line that first emerged with John Adams. In Henry Adams it was to be deepened by personal tragedy.

Adams's early career showed the vitality of the Brahmin ideal. A handsome, almost dapper little fellow, not more than five feet three, with dark wavy hair, he was the center of a coterie of convivial college mates at Harvard in the Class of 1858, a group of ninety young men. He was a serious and bookish student. He had a flair for the classics and carried a pocket Horace with him. His capacious memory became a concordance of literary allusions to Shakespeare, Byron, Voltaire, Carlyle, and scores of others whose apt phrases would leap to his pen. He was most at home in French in which his father had tutored him. He studied the Italian of Dante under Luigi Monti at Harvard. One of his favorite pastimes, many years later, was to translate a canto of the *Divine Comedy* or a sonnet from Petrarch. Thirty years after he left college he could still take pleasure, while resting on the beach at Tahiti, in translating the hexameters of Homer's *Iliad*. German came hard to his Gallic temperament, but in time he was able to worry his way through the most abstruse scientific treatises in that language. To prepare himself for a visit to Spain he taught himself the language by plowing through an array of plays and novels. At another time, anticipating a journey to China he set himself a stint of a thousand characters every two weeks. He even tried his hand at Tahitian in order to translate some of the oral literature.

In philosophy and economics the instruction at Harvard was safely conservative. Only much later did Adams encounter the *Communist Manifesto*. One of his most glaring slips of recollection in the *Education* reproached his teachers for not acquainting him with Karl Marx's *Capital*—the book did not appear until a dozen years after he left Harvard. The small faculty had uncommon distinction, especially in science. Charles Darwin admired Asa Gray and envied him the extraordinary set of colleagues. The two men who most influenced Adams were Louis Agassiz, one of the greatest geologists of the time, and James Russell Lowell. Within a few years Asa Gray became the defender of *The Origin of Species* and Agassiz its most severe critic. Lowell brought with him the aura of vast literary success. His *Bigelow Papers* were on every table. Adams contributed frequently to the *Harvard Magazine*, essays with a rather moralistic slant; he won a literary prize, and achieved glory as Class Day orator. A newspaper editor remembered the oration for its irony and cynicism, overlooking the intense moral idealism on which Adams based his attack on their materialistic society. In all the subsequent turns of his thought he remained faithful to this affirmation of the supremacy of spiritual values.

After Harvard he began his career as a world traveler that ultimately qualified him for the role of geopolitician to the American secretary of state. Unable to follow the lectures in civil law at Berlin, he doggedly studied the language among the youngsters in a German preparatory school. For two years he studied and traveled in Switzerland, Italy, and France. The Boston *Courier* published a series of his travel letters from Italy, his most notable coup being an interview with the victorious Garibaldi in Sicily. His plan to study law and follow the "family go-cart" fell by the wayside when he joined his father in Washington as private secretary during the secession winter of 1860. Henry acted as correspondent for the Boston *Advertiser* and did his youthful best to support his father's work as a leading peacemaker. Lincoln appointed the elder Adams to the Court of St. James's, disposing as well of Henry's fate. From a distance young Adams envied the military exploits of his classmates, but he soon accepted his fate as a private secretary and made the most of his opportunity to study at close range the course of power politics. For a year he contributed a weekly column to the New York *Times*, skillfully taking the pulse of British public opinion. The series ended abruptly when his identity was inadvertently disclosed by the proud editor of the Boston *Courier* as the author of a special report to that paper.

London was much more than a school of diplomacy to him. It gave him a postgraduate course in art appreciation, literature, science, and public affairs. His teachers were the best that England had to offer. He sat at the feet of liberal statesmen like Cobden, Bright, and Forster; argued with John Stuart Mill, the great Utilitarian and popularizer of Auguste Comte, the founder of scientific Positivism; attached himself to Charles Lyell, England's leading geologist and new champion of Darwin. Excited by the tremendous upsurge of discovery, Adams thought for a time of making a career in science. He bowed at Court before Queen Victoria, resplendent in knee breeches and sword. He dined out incessantly, became an inveterate clubman, and learned to be bored by small talk with dukes and duchesses. He liked best the medieval charm of the country house of his friend Charles Milnes Gaskell at Wenlock Abbey in Shropshire; they remained lifelong friends. The successful close of the Civil War made Adams impatient to begin an independent career, for time was running out as he neared thirty. His eldest brother, John Quincy II, plunged hopefully into politics; Charles aimed for the railroads and the scandals of the Erie as a free-lance journalist; Henry made his debut with a slashing article for the *North American Quarterly* debunking the patron saint of Virginia, Captain John Smith. He quickly followed this up with two able historical studies of British finance after the Napoleonic wars to warn Americans against inflationary nostrums during the postwar period. He next turned his versatile pen to a long and penetrating essay-review of Lyell's tenth edition of the *Principles of Geology*, the edition in which Lyell aligned himself with Darwin. To Adams the occasion offered a dramatic confrontation between his Harvard teacher Louis Agassiz and the Darwinians. Torn between two eminent parties, he characteristically suspended judgment on the theories.

Now known as a leading writer for the *North American*, Adams confidently headed for Washington in 1868, sure of an entree into the highest official circles. For two years he was one of the most active members of the press corps, dashing off articles for the recently founded reform weekly, the *Nation*, and the New York *Evening Post*, directing his gadfly attacks upon the spoils system and the mismanagement of government finances. His masterly analysis of Congressional incompetence in his annual "Session" articles and in one on civil service reform showed the birth of a powerful new writer. The most notable of his muckraking efforts was "The New York Gold Conspiracy," a devastating exposé of the efforts of Jim Fisk and Jay Gould to corner the gold market right under the nose of gullible President Grant.

At the height of Adams's success as a crusading journalist, family counsels again prevailed. As it was obvious that Grant would not reward so dangerous a critic, Henry was shunted off to Harvard to become an assistant professor of history and to help Charles William Eliot carry out his ambitious scheme of reforming instruction. The editorship of the *North American* went along with the offer. Determined not to vegetate in Cambridge, Adams made the quarterly a vehicle for the Liberal Republican movement, pooling efforts with his brother Charles and with his younger brother Brooks, who was just beginning his career as a lawyer and publicist. Adams recruited authorities in the most varied fields—politics, science, philosophy, literature, linguistics, history, economics—and himself reviewed more than a score of books, ranging from learned treatises like Sohm's *Lex Salica* to a Howells novel, *Their Wedding Journey*.

In the classroom he was a vigorously Socratic lecturer. His revolutionary premise was that education existed for the student; the professor existed to incite the student to work on his own. He borrowed the intensive research methods of German scholarship and in the seminars, which he initiated at Harvard, he taught the young men to go to the primary documents. Students responded with the greatest enthusiasm to his unconventional approach and embarrassed him by crowding his classes. Assigned first to medieval history, he soon mastered the subject, thanks to his incredible intellectual energy. He then branched off into American history where the full significance of his heritage opened up to him, and he began to dream of a magnum opus on the early years of the republic. His monument to his medieval studies was an enormously learned essay on Anglo-Saxon law, showing his adoption of the institutional approach to history, which he published with essays by his three doctoral students, the first to receive such degrees at Harvard. He had a lasting influence on the teaching of history. Among his scholars who rose to distinction were Edward Channing, Henry Osborn Taylor (the noted Medievalist), and James Lawrence Laughlin (the political economist). His protégé was Henry Cabot Lodge who went on from history into politics, rose to leadership in the United States Senate, and found his place in history as chief adversary of Woodrow Wilson.

Adams married in 1872 a bluestocking Boston heiress, Marian Hooper, an intimate friend of the young Henry James and a witty satirist in her own right. The marriage brought Adams into a wider circle of artists and writers. They spent a wedding year in Europe, renewing a host of acquaintances and establishing fresh intellectual alliances. On their return Cambridge and Boston grew more and more confining to the two rebels. Weary of teaching schoolboys and anxious to begin a new career as a professional historian, Adams decamped from Boston in 1877 for the genial freedom of Washington. His chance came when he accepted a commission to do a biography of Albert Gallatin, whose philosophical statesmanship was for Adams an American model.

The chapter of life that now opened was a brilliant idyl for the two happy expatriated Bostonians. Marian presided over their exclusive salon in Lafayette Square which quickly became the chief intellectual center of society. Cabinet members, ambassadors, senators, congressmen, bureau chiefs, and visiting notables made their rendezvous at the five o'clock tea table. Good talk, fine wines, and an imaginative cuisine delighted the intimate dinners of six and eight. Henry James, returning briefly from his own exile in London, thought his friends a little too severe in their standards of political and social propriety; their salon "left out on the whole, more people than it took in." What it took in was of the best. Here the repartee of Clarence King and John Hay crackled about the hearth; here Carl Schurz improvised on the piano; here the Congressional leader James A. Garfield planned strategy. William James came down full of the new psychology. Matthew Arnold renewed their London acquaintance. Whenever weather permitted, Henry and Marian rode out to Rock Creek and the Virginia countryside to enjoy the dogwood and the Judas tree. Summers they joined the quiet summer colony at Beverly Farms within sound of the Massachusetts surf.

The *Gallatin* came out in 1879, first fruit of Adams's efficient labors in the archives of the State Department. The biographical narrative was largely carried by quotations from original sources. This method, common to the "Life and Letters" biographies of the time made for a ponderous structure. For Adams it served as a trial run for the *History* in which he would refine the method into high art. The volume showed his assimilation of the grand style of his favorite historians, Gibbon and Macaulay, in many of its key passages. It established his authority as an important historian and was to remain the definitive study of Gallatin for nearly seventy-five years.

For many years Adams had toyed with the notion of writing a novel, for literary practice if for nothing else. The opportunity arrived when he finished the Gallatin manuscript late in 1878. He turned his now well-seasoned pen to a novel of his favorite city, a satire on the Washington which now lay like an open book before him, crying to be anatomized. The surgery was much too ruthless to be publicly acknowledged by a sober—and vulnerable—historian. Issued anonymously as *Democracy: An American Novel*, it made a sensational success in England and then became, by reflex action, a best seller in America. Critics praised the unknown author as the peer of Henry James and William Dean Howells and superior to Disraeli in the mixing of politics and Romance. Friends like Lord Bryce deplored the mischief it might do and Clarence King, who was in on the secret, started an abortive novel on aristocracy to answer it. The easily recognized victims accused various members of the Adams circle. One of them, Senator James G. Blaine, who figured prominently as the egregious Senator Ratcliffe, publicly snubbed King, believing him to be the author. The secret was perfectly kept by the Adams inner circle, "The Five of Hearts," and Adams's authorship remained almost unknown until the 1920's. A minor classic among political novels, it was frequently reprinted during Adams's lifetime, its psychological insight into the motives of politicians undimmed by the passage of time. Its heroine, Mrs. Lightfoot Lee, like her creator, hungered to touch the levers of power but shrank from the price which democracy seemed to exact for the privilege.

Adams went off to Europe again, as a scholar to whom archives magically opened. He mined away for his *History* in Paris, Madrid, and London, setting copyists to work after the lavish example of cousin George Bancroft, the dean of American historians. In the frequent intervals of work he settled down to being lionized a little in London and enjoying the constant companionship of Henry James. Among the new intellectual lights, he made the acquaintance of men like William Lecky (the historian of rationalism), John Richard Green, Herbert Spencer, and Ernest Renan.

Returning to Lafayette Square late in 1880, Adams briefly diverted himself with a popular biography of John Randolph for the American Statesmen series as a kind of outrider for the great work which was slowly taking shape. Unlike the massive *Gallatin*, the *Randolph* moves with a fine novelistic verve, sharply focused on the drama of Randolph's eccentric career. In this book Adams fully settled the family score against another traducer of John Quincy Adams. The tragic figure that stalks half-dementedly through Adams's pages still rankles in the hearts of loyal Virginians. Modern scholarship, however, has not substantially altered the portrait, still less matched the supple and vigorous prose. The success of the *Randolph* inspired Adams to dash off a similar study of Aaron Burr, the "Mephistopheles of politics," now chiefly remembered for having killed Alexander Hamilton in a duel. The publisher shied away from dignifying Burr as a statesman. Adams angrily suppressed the volume though his wife thought it even better than the *Randolph*. Much of the manuscript seems to have been incorporated in the *History*.

By 1884 Adams reached the halfway mark in his long labors and sought respite from historical scholarship in another novel, again choosing a woman for his central figure. *Esther* is an imaginative re-creation of the debates over religion and science and their relation to art and poetry in the world which had been overturned by Darwin, Spencer, and the new psychology, debates that regularly enlivened the Adams salon. What was an enlightened woman's role in such a world? Could the new woman fulfill herself in love and marriage? The book explored controversies that are still unsettled. As a psychological study of a woman's character it surpasses *Democracy*. Its philosophical themes foreshadow those of the *Mont-Saint-Michel and Chartres* and the *Education*. Adams persuaded his publisher, Henry Holt, to issue the book without advertising in order to test the responsiveness of public taste. He also affixed a pseudonym to the title page, "Frances Snow Compton." The critics, almost to a man, ignored the book which paid such little heed to the prevailing formulas of Romantic sentiment. It vanished from sight, confirming Adams's low opinion of the state of American culture.

A mixture of motives—pride, diffidence, an almost morbid sensitivity to criticism—led Adams to guard the secret of authorship even more carefully than that of *Democracy*. Its charming and cultivated heroine was closely modelled on his wife. His natural chivalry turned to a kind of panic dread in the following year. On December 6, 1885, Marian, who had become widely known as an amateur photographer, took her own life, using one of the chemicals of the darkroom. She had been unable to endure the recent loss of her father to whom she had been deeply attached since childhood when the death of her mother had made her entirely dependent on him. The heroine of *Esther* surmounted a similar ordeal; she could not, in spite of all of Adams's devoted care. The tragedy was front page news in Washington, New York, and Boston. The shock to Adams was appalling, as his life tumbled in ruins about him. It was made no easier to bear by the fact that their marriage had been childless. His life broken in half, he felt for a long time that he also had died, and he sometimes startled inquirers by insisting on the grim jest. He was humored in his morbid fancies by the sympathetic young matrons of their circle, especially by the wife of Senator James Donald Cameron whose beauty he had idealized in the character of Catherine Brooks in *Esther*. Henceforth, Adams withdrew as far as possible from public notice. Lonely and embittered, he made Mrs. Cameron his closest confidante and gradually condemned himself to hopeless adoration, a Chateaubriand, as he came to think of himself, to her Madame Recamier.

Life, even "posthumous" life, had to go on and Adams, shutting away his grief, the only outward sign of it being the enigmatic statue in Rock Creek cemetery sculptured by Augustus Saint-Gaudens, bent again to his work with his usual driving energy. The tragedy brought out all his latent restlessness. Marriage had made him quiet. Now his belated romantic attachment for Elizabeth Cameron made him a lovelorn wanderer who complained that he could not be happy in any one place more than three days. He made travel a fine art and his letters grew to be masterpieces of acute observation. The reticent Henry James marveled at his power to bare his soul. The more than thirty years of active existence remaining to him took him all over the globe. In 1886 he voyaged to Japan with the artist John La Farge, feeding his historical imagination on Japanese art and religion. In 1890, the nine volumes of the *History* finally in print, he escaped to the South Seas, again in the company of La Farge, sketching under his companion's tutelage, geologizing, and studying Polynesian folklore and history. He became interested in the fortunes of his Tahitian hosts, leaders of the dethroned Teva family, and wrote a touching historical memoir of the last queen, privately printing the book in 1893.

He finished his tour around the world late in 1891, after savagely sampling the decadence of Paris. He shared the common American opinion of its immorality but recognized it as the most civilized and intellectually alive place in the world. He became a connoisseur of World Fairs measuring the progress of civilization by their display of scientific marvels. The Far West was one of his earliest enthusiasms: first he traversed Wyoming and Colorado by pack train in the summer of 1870; there he first met the fabulous Clarence King, a geologist then with the United States Fortieth Parallel Survey. Later journeyings carried him from Canada to the Rio Grande. The exotic life of Cuba and the West Indies fascinated him. He was drawn in by King as an active partisan in the movement for Cuban independence. In Mexico, nearing sixty, he could still manage twenty miles a day on horseback. But Europe drew him most as the shadow of coming wars and revolutions added a dangerous charm to the sight of jostling cultures. Egypt had long been a familiar story. His interest in geopolitics deepened as he circled the Mediterranean basin in the late nineties, saturating himself in archaeology and art and pouring out his inspired commentary in essay-letters to his friends. Italy drew him again and again, especially Rome where he felt himself another Gibbon meditating on the steps of the church of Aracoeli above the Forum. One long deferred expedition took him in the company of the Lodges to Moscow. He then went on alone to Scandanavia and the North Cape to meditate like a new Teufelsdröckh on the coming struggle for power between Russian inertia and the dynamism of Western Europe.

Wherever Adams traveled he projected his lines back into the past and forward into the future. His most significant travel in time carried him back to the Middle Ages, to the birth of Gothic architecture. John Ruskin and the Pre-Raphaelite poets and artists of the medieval revival of the nineteenth century had already given an idealistic turn to his earlier study of medieval history and architecture. His brother Brooks had also "mapped out the lines and indicated the emotions," as Henry afterwards remembered. The terrible depression of 1893 revealed to him all the ugly tendencies of *laissez-faire* economics and the growing despotism of the "gold bug," the finance capitalist. Never did the remote past seem so winning and fair as he saw it one summer in 1895 in the Gothic cathedrals of Normandy, when he accompanied the Lodges in his favorite role of avuncular schoolmaster. His letters radiated his new intuitions as he worshiped before the great "glass gods" of Chartres whose stained glass is the wonder of Christendom. Suffused with a sense of history, he felt a return to spiritual fountains, experiencing a vaulting back in imagination to his Norman ancestors. "I can almost remember," he wrote John Hay,

> the faith that gave me energy and the sacred boldness that made my towers seem to me so daring. . . . Nearly eight hundred years have passed since I made the fatal mistake of going to England, and since then I have never done anything in the world to compare in the perfection of spirit and art with my cathedral of Coutances.

Thereafter, the Gothic renaissance of the twelfth century became his anchor in history and his symbol-haunted mind assimilated to it all the imagined virtues of archaic societies everywhere. To him it was filled with a primal moral vigor, a society whose art and poetry affirmed universal values, whose maternal women inspired their warrior husbands to selfless devotion and heroism. For the remaining twenty years of his life Adams steeped himself obsessively in the art and lore of medieval France, bringing to a focus on that period all his far ranging studies in archaeology, history, and science. He formed the almost invariable habit of spending his summers in France, dashing recklessly down the country roads in his Mercedes, learning the statuary and stained glass by heart. The other half of each year he spent in intense study of modern science, technology, and world politics, trying to predict the future course of human history.

The new drift of his thinking had emerged in his presidential address of 1894. History must become a science in spite of the resistance of such vested interests as the State, the Church, Capital, and Labor. His brother Brooks's recent *Law of Civilization and Decay* analyzed the discontents of the time in terms of the centralizing tendencies of capitalist society. The decline of the West was the logical result of the legitimation of usury. Brooks's "Bible of Hell" traced the process from Roman times to the present. For Henry, his favorite twelfth century was a doomed interlude in his brother's panorama of history, a moment of precious respite in the march of universal avarice. At the turn of the century he wrote the *Chartres* to wrest from history the secret of the movement that covered northern France with great cathedrals. His *History of the United States* had established a datum line in American history for future historians, a mark from which to measure progress—or failure. The *Chartres* did the same thing for the Western world. Against its background the chaos and anarchy of the twentieth century might stand etched in all its horror. Adams aimed at no mere historical analysis. The work was a means of esthetic identification, a lyrical evocation of the spirit of the age. Dubious as history, it triumphed as art.

He returned to the charge in the *Education*, proposing as a model for future historians a "Dynamic Theory of History," in which his emerging theory of all history as an onrushing deterministic system of interchangeable mechanical forces found first expression. He elaborated this conception in "The Rule of Phase Applied to History" (1909), not published until 1919, in the *Degradation of the Democratic Dogma.* The essay is based on a highly impressionistic reading of Willard Gibbs's phase rule formulas in physical chemistry concerning the "coexistence of phases in the equilibrium of heterogeneous substances." What Adams thought he had found was a scientific analogy to illustrate the *succession* of increasingly complex stages in modern civilization. Still tinkering with the impossibly difficult task of absorbing into an all-encompassing philosophy of history the latest developments in social psychology and atomic science, Adams next tried to utilize the second law of thermodynamics, the tendency of energy in a closed system to reach a maximum of equilibrium, to explain the apparent decline of social and psychic energy in modern society. Adams assumed that the cosmos was a vast heat machine that was running down. The resulting essay was *A Letter to American Teachers of History* which he issued privately in 1910 to historians and university librarians throughout the country. It remains a brilliant curiosity of pseudoscientific speculation.

With the death of his most intimate friend, John Hay, in 1905, at the height of his influence as Secretary of State, Adams's role as an unofficial elder statesman virtually came to an end. President Theodore Roosevelt admired his genius and continued to cultivate him but preferred the more aggressive imperialism of Brooks Adams. Henry prepared an edition of Hay's letters at the request of his widow, excessive diffidence preventing him from doing a biography which would entail the "obtrusion of a third person" between the reader and the subject. It may also be, as Herbert Croly suggests, that his high estimate of Hay's achievement rapidly declined. Knowing Hay as one of the best talkers of his time, Adams selected "everything that resembled conversation;—everything he said to me without literary purpose." His public career he left to history. "The result," he conceded, "was desperately muddled." Unfortunately, Mrs. Hay in bringing out the private edition deleted nearly all the names. Usable only with the "Key" which Adams prepared for his own use, the work remains little known. His lingering protest to Ambassador Whitelaw Reid illuminates his own early literary escapades:

My view is that we, who set up to be educated society, should stand up in our harness and should play our parts without awkward stage-fright of amateurs. . . . God knows, I have no love of notoriety, ' it I have never shrunk from it, if it seemed to be a proper and becoming part of social work.

Another duty of friendship fell upon him in 1910 after the sudden death, at thirty-six, of the poet George Cabot Lodge, who had been Adams's window on the literary Bohemia of Paris in the late nineties. Adams once again used his favorite device of letting the letters tell most of the story. Adams's scruple worked against the poet. As Edith Wharton said, Lodge was not meant for "an active task in letters" and his intellectual dependence on older men like Adams and Hay kept him in a state of "brilliant immaturity." Published in 1911 by Houghton Mifflin the book received little notice, for Adams had too accurately caught "the spirit of the man and his circle." It was reprinted in 1943 in Edmund Wilson's anthology of neglected classics, *The Shock of Recognition,* but even he felt a certain chill in its Rhadamanthine judgments.

With the declining years Adams became to his dismay a "benevolent sage" to the large circle of acquaintances who won the privilege of paying their court at the twelve o'clock breakfasts in Lafayette Square or in Adams's luxurious "garret" in the Avenue du Bois de Boulogne. Beneath the incorrigibly sardonic witticisms they recognized one of the most extraordinary intelligences of the time, an intellectual bystander who had attained Matthew Arnold's ideal of the highest culture. In his book-lined study surrounded by a favorite Corot or Turner, choice water colors, and rare objects of Oriental art, Adams maintained an impregnable island where the old Brahmin order stood up manfully to the despotisms of the new. Here in his final years, especially after a temporarily paralyzing stroke in 1912, Adams worked on in his Voltairean garden, listening to medieval music and old French chansons, hunting out forgotten chansons in French archives, and sometimes putting his hand to a translation from Old French or Latin, his marvelously precise script now flawed by age.

Despite the formidable authority of his manner, he continued to draw the ablest men to him and to hold their friendship with his superb letters. One of those whose judgment he specially prized was the art critic and connoisseur Bernard Berenson, who was creating at I Tatti in Florence a private refuge of culture like that of Adams in Washington. Adams cultivated still another interest in the work of Henri Hubert, a distinguished French archaeologist, and for a number of years he cheerfully subsidized Hubert's fruitless excavations near Les Eyzies. His political interests steadily changed. For a time in the nineties he backed Bryan against the Wall Street combine, then losing faith in the socialistic tendencies of the reform movement, disgusted by the bourgeois ambitions of the underdog, he proclaimed himself a "Conservative Christian Anarchist" with the right to call down a plague on all political houses.

Believing that the contradictions in modern industrial society must lead to an overwhelming collapse when the financial colossi began to prey upon each other in an economic Twilight of the Gods, Adams professed himself a "goldbug" Republican, justifying himself with the thought that he would thus help bring on the salutary collapse sooner. His anarchistic philosophy thus conspired to ally him with his politically conservative friends. This development was complicated, however, by his hereditary patriotism. Moral philosophy might demand the repudiation of contemporary society, but patriotism required that the United States achieve supremacy in the international jungle. Thus though he sided with the anti-imperialist minority during the Spanish-American War and likened the struggles of the Boers against England to the American War for Independence, he came round to the position that the United States must sustain England in order to block the imperial ambitions of Germany in the Pacific and elsewhere. Theodore Roosevelt's trustbusting seemed to him a mere defiance of inevitable economic processes and he deplored his crude diplomacy in Latin America. A born mugwump, he supported the regular Republican candidates, however reluctantly, chiefly because of his hysterical dread of political disorder. Once Woodrow Wilson was elected he refused to countenance indecent attacks upon him at his table. World War I confirmed all his geopolitical predictions. After forty years of close friendship with British diplomats and statesmen from Joseph Chamberlain to Cecil Spring Rice, his sympathies forbade any course but the rescue of England.

His opinions remained as peppery and picturesquely extravagant as ever. Democracy as an equalitarian shibboleth seemed now irrelevant in the onrushing era of vast social revolution. From the height of philosophic contemplation he looked on with sardonic pessimism at the working out of mysterious forces, insisting he had foretold it all in the final chapters of the *Education*. The cosmic forces which man had summoned out of nature were running away with him while man as a form of energy was steadily undergoing degradation, impoverishment, dissolution. This view led to utter skepticism and stoicism, and yet a close reading of his sulphurous letters leads one to conclude that the sustained hysteria that runs through them is that of an actor who became the captive of his role, who had played Hamlet so long that he became him. His role was to convince his high-placed fellow men that there were more things in heaven and earth than were dreamed of in their shallow philosophies. He expressed himself in a kind of philosophic shriek because most men were deaf to quiet persuasion and needed to be startled into an awareness of the tragic complexities of the human condition. If he spoke wildly of the end of the world, it was the cry of a sensitive soul outraged by the multiplying barbarisms of the world he had survived into.

III

Adams was a bundle of contradictions. His lifelong quest for unity was no more than his effort to answer the most overwhelming of personal questions: Who am I? What am I? He felt that Rousseau had disgraced the ego; yet few writers have had such a capacity for baring their souls. He repeatedly warned his correspondents that contradiction was unavoidable. It was the law of life. He could say with Whitman, "Do I contradict myself? / Very well then I contradict myself, / (I am large, I contain multitudes)." As Adams says in the *Education*, "Words are slippery and thought is viscous." Or in a different key, "Did he himself quite know what he meant? Certainly not! If he had known enough to state his problem, his education would have been complete at once." He felt his personality whirl among contending polarities. He loved order and decorum and created in his heretical image of the Virgin Mother the type of all rebellion against the status quo. He was prudish and finicking in his fastidiousness yet affirmed the fact of sex and fecundity as the most vital of social energies. He had a Byronic passion for solitude and would not travel without a companion. He scorned the pageant of a bleeding heart and for his intimates wore his own on his sleeve. He scorned bourgeois taste and the preoccupation with material things and wistfully envied the possessors of great wealth. High society repelled him with its inhibitions and artifice but he would associate only with those entitled to be of it. He complained of nerves and dyspepsia all his life, neurotically feared the loss of his mental powers, and lived "to dance on the graves" of practically all of his contemporaries. He was passionately addicted to scientific discovery and then turned science upside down to show its limitations. He despised business and prided himself on his business acumen.

As a biographer he saw his own contradictions mirrored in the men he analyzed. Reading Morley's *Gladstone*, he remarked, "Of course in him, as in most people, there were two or three or a dozen men; in these emotional, abnormal natures, there are never less than three." He applied this principle to his conception of character in all his writings. The psychological tensions of both of his novels arise from the inner warfare of the psyche. His great portraits in the biographies and the *History*—figures like Jefferson, Canning, Napoleon, Toussaint, Tecumseh—all illustrate it.

In fiction his power of invention was not great; he approached plot and character intellectually. His strength lay in dramatizing ideas, pursuing them to their ambiguous consequences. Men and women were more important—at any rate, more interesting—for what they thought than for what they did. For the serious writer only the ironic posture was possible. To think was to satirize. Satire expressed the ultimate self-awareness of the writer. As a literary stylist Adams worked toward a Swiftian directness of statement yet with a craftsman's knowledge of the infinite variety of English syntax. He had a Flaubertian zeal for adapting the style to the matter of his discourse. In historical exposition he relied mainly on a flexible and fluid prose with muscular nouns and verbs, but he knew also the value of modulation and color for his climaxes and the rolling arrest of balanced sentences. At first imitative of the great stylists of his craft, Gibbon and Macaulay, he adapted their medium to the developing character of American colloquial speech. He had a keen ear for slang and flavored his letters with the going idioms. His literary allusions please the reader with the repeated compliment to his taste. In the great works of Adams's literary maturity, the *Chartres* and the *Education*, he experienced the epiphany of the poet and the artist. He learned to apply to prose the lessons of color harmony taught him by John La Farge, to charge his terms with associations as an artist blends his colors on the palette. His use of image and symbol is thoroughly modern. So, the broken arch of the Gothic church supports a whole domain of aspiration. Like Emerson he saw words as symbols of things and things as symbols of spiritual truths. Philosophy comes to life in the dramatic confrontations of the *Chartres*. Abelard and Bernard argue the subtleties of essence and substance because life did depend on it, as in a later age men disputed about the atom because it held the secret of the common destiny.

In the *Education* Adams created his richest fabric of symbols. From the initial conception of the Carlylean mannikin upon whom he is to display the dress of education to the image of the comet-meteor for the acceleration of mind, Adams constantly surmounts the limitations of objective statement. The mind may be caught by argument but the image holds it. The image best hints at the polarity of things, the unity and multiplicity which define the limit of thought. Thus the Virgin and the Dynamo incarnate their ages as symbols of infinite power, the one centripetal, drawing the chaos of existence into patterns of order; the other, centrifugal, accelerating the flight toward chaos. The voyage toward multiplicity in which the old man found himself enmeshed rises to a heroic and even tragic quest in which the homunculus hero figures in a variety of guises—Ulysses and Tannhauser, Teufelsdröckh and Faust.

Adams's writings have aroused an enormous amount of interest among intellectuals, touching as they do upon almost every field of serious inquiry. He is abhorred as a cynical snob by those who are put off by his pose and his affectations. He is hailed as a realistic critic of democracy and the rare example of a fully civilized man. The great Jeffersonian partisan, Vernon Louis Parrington, saw him as a wholesome critic of the Hamiltonian tradition as well as a master stylist. To the conservative reaction of the 1950's he seemed a defender of the Burkean tradition in politics and society. He himself hoped to serve no faction. His *History* may have been overrated by Yvor Winters as the greatest work of its kind since Gibbon but it stands in any case as the high-water mark of American historiography. Perhaps the most unstinted praise has gone to the *Chartres*, whatever cavils it may deserve for its romantic distortions of life in the Middle Ages and for its highly unorthodox theology. The Virgin of his creation is undoubtedly one of the remarkable heroines of literature. The *Education* continues to have an almost topical vitality and will continue to have it so long as the age of crisis continues. Undeniably one of the most brilliant commentaries on the shaping forces of American culture since 1865, it stands in need of constant correction of its sardonic parallax, not so much for its facts as for its one-sided evaluations of men and events. The science of it cannot be taken seriously, yet Adams shows in his virtuosity in manipulating the new concepts that a new field of metaphor is available to the literary artist and that scientific reality can add a new idiom to poetry. His writings show the infinite capacity of the mind to feel, to be aware, and to respond to the full reach of experience. From the depths of his despair he affirms the boundless possibilities of the human spirit.

"Adams' *Esther*: The Morality of Taste"

Millicent Bell*

The extraordinary sensibility of Henry Adams, with its delicate and powerful response to history, to art, to human personality, would seem to demand expression in the art of fiction. Yet better novels than *Esther* have been written by men less curious about life and less informed, even by writers with a vastly inferior faculty of style. What Adams lacked, probably, was just the sense of vocation that so completely possessed his friend Henry James. He was a deliberate amateur.

Esther is thus too personal, too private. It is impossible to perceive the author's full intentions without considering the intimate material out of which it was fabricated. Inevitably, *Esther* requires some sort of annotation from the record of Adams' life. The haunting image of Marian Adams seems to hover over the story, as though we were in the presence of St. Gaudens' ambiguous memorial to her, at Rock Creek. And the ideas that are placed one against the other in the novel become distinct only after one considers their fuller expression in Adams' other writing. Consequently, the book lacks the public voice of art—that sense in which a great novel stands away from its creator and his conditions and exists outside of him by means of a completely exhibited statement.

It is, moreover, the exercise of a man who felt himself inadequately occupied with the toy of letters. It is certain that he would rather have been an actor in history, like his distinguished forebears, than a mere notetaker—historian, journalist, or novelist. He practiced a too-elaborate indifference to literary reputation, publishing privately or anonymously with the declaration: "I hate publishing and do not want reputation. There are not more than a score of people in America whose praise I want." What was really his natural audience was a private group of friends. His novels, like his deft and affectionate letters, seem to have been written for the diversion of these select companions—for whom a book like *Esther* would be the merest topic-outline of long-shared thought and experience.

It is so, by an effort of reconstruction, that *we* must read it. What

*Reprinted from *The New England Quarterly*, 35 (June, 1962), 147–61.

strikes one about *Esther* is not, indeed, that it is superficial, but that it is the representation of rather profound reflection by means of a story somehow too light and simple, and by characters whose motives would be obscure unless placed in a more intense, a more complicated atmosphere. This imperfect, too-slight piece of work becomes very interesting, on the other hand, if we bend ourselves to complete that part of the job the amateur novelist left unfinished, and reconstruct the moral and intellectual medium which a greater artist would have placed firmly within the book. This is easy to do once the work is regarded less as a finished piece of fiction than as a chart to a portion of Henry Adams. As a biographical document, it is closely related to the famous *Education*, and to *Mont-Saint-Michel and Chartres* and other writings.

When the ban of anonymity was lifted after Adams' death, William Roscoe Thayer wrote an enthusiastic "first review" in the Boston *Evening Transcript* in which he declared that the novels, now acknowledged to be Adams', gave their author claim to the title "the American Voltaire,"[1] equally adept at fiction or philosophy. *Esther* is no *Candide*, of course, but it is a reasonable draft for a novel of ideas.

Where *Democracy*, his earlier novel, had dealt with the conflict of conscience with contemporary political institutions, *Esther* was concerned with the more fundamental question of the relation of conscience to its traditional source—religion. In both books, it is a woman who makes this exploration; Mrs. Lightfoot Lee confronts her problem with only her innate sense of taste, and the uncomplicated surety of the imagination which Adams conceived of as essentially feminine. Thus, Esther, a woman of artistic taste and an instinctive moral delicacy, becomes engaged to marry the young rector of the fashionable Fifth Avenue Church of St. John. How and why she finds that she cannot accept his Church, cannot believe in either its dogmas or its social function, constitutes the chief tension of the story.

Now Adams was obsessed by the problem of choice. The *Education* is a long chronicle of choices and this autobiography so ironically titled seems in the end to come to rest in the realization that no choice had been possible. Thus young Adams pondered the question of State Street *vs.* Quincy. It was, he wrote, "a dilemma that might have puzzled an early Christian."[2] He knew that State Street was wrong—between the scramble for profits and "the moral principle" represented by his Quincy heritage, he made the only choice an Adams could make—he resisted the fatted calf. But he was to find himself powerless to do more than resist. There seemed to be no positive alternative to State Street which led to a career. His "moral principle" became less a guide to action than "the habit of doubt"[3] for which he compared himself to Hamlet.[4] Indeed, his Puritan gift for denying developed "to a degree that in the long run became positive and hostile," a negative impulse which swallowed up all possibility of understanding or justifying life.

Esther's dilemma seems to consist in the fact that she cannot marry Hazard because her scorn of his Church would leave her merely "half-married" and because she will not destroy his professional security by the scandal of her agnosticism. Yet she struggles to mount over these barriers—she even attempts to read the theologians and argues with her scientist cousin, the geologist George Strong—in an effort to find conviction. In the end her decision is one of flight and not of triumph; like Adams' choice of Quincy rather than State Street, it is an act of negativism, even despair. No wedding bells ring down the curtain on this novel of courtship as they would do on one of Jane Austen's stories. When George Strong, "who looked at churches very much as he would have looked at a layer of extinct oysters in a buried mud-bank,"[5] offers to marry her, Esther

> looked at him with an expression that would have been a smile
> if it had not been infinitely dreary and absent; then she said,
> simply and finally:
> "But George, I don't love you, I love him!"[6]

So the book ends. She cannot will herself into Hazard's faith, but neither can she respond to the cool unbelief of George Strong.

The reasons for Esther's choice are actually indicated only sketchily in the novel. Her aunt, Mrs. Murray, causes her to be aware of the purely practical argument against the match—Esther will ruin Hazard's career by marrying him as she is and thus will force him to choose between her and his work—a situation no woman can help finding intolerable. Catherine Brooks, the lovable, completely natural young visitor from Colorado, fails to see that one's husband's business activities should make the slightest difference in one's relation to him; "Why should you care what he preaches?"[7] she asks Esther. And when Esther and Strong discuss the relation of reason with faith, one is given the impression that mere rationalism causes her to reject the superstitions of religion.

But what seems to repel Esther herself is indicated in the opening chapter of the book. As she listens to Hazard preach in his handsome new church, she becomes aware of the demand of the pulpit for tyrannical sovereignty, and looking about her at her complacent fellow parishioners, of the substitution of formal habit for personal discrimination, in the pew. The sermon text was: "He that hath ears to hear, let him hear," and Mr. Hazard

> took possession of his flock with a general advertisement that
> he owned every sheep in it, white or black, and to show that
> there could be no doubt on the matter, he added a general
> claim to right of property in all mankind and the
> universe. . . . The sermon dealt with the relations of religion
> to society. It began by claiming that all being and all thought

rose by slow gradations to God,—ended in Him, for Him—existed only through Him and because of being His.

The form of act or thought mattered nothing. The hymns of David, the plays of Shakespeare, the metaphysics of Descartes, the crimes of Borgia, the virtues of Antonine, the atheism of yesterday and the materialism of today, were all emanations of divine thought, doing their appointed work. It was the duty of the church to deal with them all, not as though they existed through a power hostile to the deity, but as instruments of the deity to work out his unrevealed ends.[8]

Esther found that such authority corrupts by making religion an appeal to fear. Of the Reverend Stephen Hazard's will to dominate there can be no doubt. He had a "knack of fixing an influence wherever he went"[9] and "Esther found him a very charming fellow especially when he was allowed his own way without question or argument."[10] But this is a more than personal characterization. It is Adams' conception of the inevitable effect of a priest's rôle. It was Hazard's "lifelong faith that all human energies belonged to the church."[11] As his friend Strong remarked:

He sees nothing good in the world that he does not instantly covet for the glory of God and the church, and just a bit for his own pleasure. He saw Esther; she struck him as something out of his line, for he is used to young women who work altar-cloths; he found that Wharton and I liked her; he thought that such material was too good for heathen like us; so he fell in love with her himself and means to turn her into a candlestick of the church.[12]

Adams feared the effects of power in any form. He was wont to say that "a friend in office is a friend lost" and his observation of the effect of power on Theodore Roosevelt, a man he admired, confirmed his belief that "power is poison." As he observed in the *Education*, "The effect of unlimited power on limited mind is worth noting in Presidents because it must represent the same process in society, and the power of self-control must have limit somewhere in the face of the control of the infinite." In *Esther*, the effect of religious power is seen as equally menacing. Adams wrote of Hazard: "The strain of standing in the pulpit is great. No human being ever yet constructed was strong enough to offer himself long as a light to humanity without showing the effect on his constitution."[13]

Yet in Esther Hazard met a power superior to his own. Strong put his money on her:

He has done what he liked with us all his life. I have worked like a dog for him and his church because he was my friend. Now he will see whether he has met his match. I double you up all round on Esther.[14]

Not the mere worldliness of the church, but its absorption of the personal moral function, oppresses Esther. Her reasons for rejecting Hazard are profound. "Do you really believe in the resurrection of the body?" she asks Hazard at the last. "To me it seems a shocking idea. I despise and loathe myself, and yet you thrust self at me from every corner of the church as though I loved and admired it. All religion does nothing but pursue me with self, even into the next world."[15] The appeal of the Church, she recognizes, is not based on ideas at all—but on the childish notion of punishment and reward, and on the concern of men with their particular destinies. How poignant and heroic is her agonized cry, "Why must the church always appeal to my weakness and never to my strength?"[16]

Perhaps this is why Adams chose to call her Esther Dudley, after Old Esther Dudley in Hawthorne's fourth legend of the Province House. In Hawthorne's tale, Mistress Dudley is an aged, half-demented partisan of the king's cause who keeps watch for the return of a royal governor in the abandoned Province House, long after the last British troops have left. She keeps the keys ironically entrusted to her by the defeated Sir William Howe, keeps them year after year, unaware that the old order will never return. Finally, Governor Hancock comes to claim the Province House for the Republic and Esther Dudley falls at his feet, the keys slipping from her grasp. She had been faithful to the death. Is there perhaps a sense in which Adams' Esther Dudley is the keeper of a vanished authority, that of the Puritan conscience, which required the act of virtue without promise of salvation?

Esther seems to be a representative of an ethical instinct more refined than that of the Church—her conscience is the Protestant conscience severed from its support in theology and forced to operate by the rule of taste alone. Was not this exactly Adams' case? Yvor Winters has observed that Adams possessed the moral sense "in a very exasperated form"[17] but in his thinking Puritan fideism had finally reached its logical outcome. Winters points out that the Protestant tradition which Adams inherited contained its own destruction in the Ockhamist theory which justifies the universe by faith alone. He quotes Étienne Gilson's summary: "Instead of being an eternal source of . . . [the] concrete order of intelligibility and beauty, which we call nature, Ockham's God was expressly intended to relieve the world of the necessity of having any meaning of its own."

It is such voluntarism, in fact, that Hazard preached in the sermon from which we have quoted above. Its ultimate expression in New England was perhaps transcendentalism—which assumed a moral coherence in the world which was inaccessible to reason. Now only a single step separates an optimistic from a pessimistic view of life's unknowableness, as can be seen in the writing of Herman Melville, where it leads towards the disturbing suspicion that "perhaps there is no secret" and that the universe of discrete events may have no underlying unity at all. Henry Adams reached such a conviction very early—it is the major theme of the *Education* that it is really impossible to understand life. Adams discovered that it was impossible to understand character— Garibaldi's for example,[18] that it was surely impossible to write or teach history with any conviction of certainty, that all events were isolated and impenetrable. He even felt that aesthetic determinations, such as the relative excellence of the two towers of Chartres cathedral, were impossible.[19]

Even science, he found, contained mysteries as impenetrable as religion. In the *Education*, Adams records his confusion upon discovering that the biologists and the physicists saw no more reason in the non-human order of creation than he had been able to find in history, which he called "a tangled skein."[20] He heard Haeckel avow that "the proper essence of substance appeared to him more and more marvellous and enigmatic as he penetrated further into the knowledge of its attributes." In the novel *Esther*, George Strong confesses the same. "Mystery for mystery," he remarks to Mrs. Murray, "science beats religion hollow. I can't open my mouth in my lecture room without repeating ten times as many unintelligible formulas as ever Hazard is forced to do in his church."[21] He tells Esther, by way of offering her some comfort in her distress over her inability to believe the first principles of faith, "There is no science which does not begin by requiring you to believe the incredible."[22]

Like Melville, Adams was occupied all his life with the search for some "talismanic secret" which would explain the fantastic illogic of existence. The conviction that the universe was an allegory haunted both but neither felt satisfied that he had found the formula which would reveal a universal plan. Interestingly, both had a fearful vision of a Nature which was pure force—"the brute energies of existence," in Melville's phrase. Adams' first serious consideration of this idea—which was simple atheism—occurred after he had watched his beloved sister die in the agony of lockjaw one brilliant summer day in Italy, while outside her sickroom "the hills and vineyards of the Apennines seemed bursting with mid-summer blood."[23] It was then, in what he called "the last lesson—the sum and term of education—"[24] that "the first serious consciousness of Nature's gesture—her attitude towards life—took form then as a phantasm, a nightmare, an insanity of force."[25] "The idea that any personal deity could find pleasure or profit in torturing a poor woman by accident, with a fiendish cruelty known to man only in perverted and insane temperaments, could not be held for a moment. For pure blasphemy, it makes pure atheism a comfort,"[26] he wrote. So he went into the mountains to recover his nerve and met Nature at her most impersonal. He did not yet know it and he was twenty years in finding it out;

but he had need of all the beauty of the Lake below and of the Alps above, to restore the finite to its place. For the first time in his life, Mont Blanc for a moment looked to him what it was—a chaos of anarchic and purposeless forces—and he needed days to repose to see it clothe itself again with the illusions of his senses, the white purity of its snows, the splendor of its light, and the infinity of its heavenly peace.[27]

Something like such an experience seems to come to Esther herself, with the death of her father William Dudley. As Adams went to Mont Blanc for lessons about the place of the finite, Esther plays out her final little scene, and her rejection of Hazard, against the backdrop of Niagara Falls. As she combed her hair and looked at the Falls from her hotel window, she

knew they were telling her a different secret from any that Hazard could ever hear. "He will think it is the church talking!" Sad as she was, she smiled as she thought that it was Sunday morning, and a ludicrous contrast flashed on her mind between the decorations of St. John's, with its parterre of 19th century bonnets, and the huge church which was thundering its gospel under her eyes . . . Hazard spoke with no such authority; and Esther's next idea was one of wonder how, after listening here, any preacher could have the confidence to preach again. "What do they know about it?" she asked herself. "Which of them can tell a story like this, or a millionth part of it?"[28]

And from this point we may look forward to Adams' final desolating vision of a world moved purely by natural energy, his deification of the dynamo at the Great Exposition of 1900.

We know that Adams himself did not and could not rest with the concept of an impersonal universe, without "the illusions of the senses" or "the church talking." In this novel he has dignified above everything else the intuitive wisdom which was his only substitute for religious belief—and his refuge from logic—the wisdom of instinct and taste. Embodying all her creator's questions, Adams' heroine also supplies his answer. For who is Esther? In terms of mere autobiography, she is Marian Hooper Adams, just as George Strong, the geologist, may be identified with Clarence King, and Wharton, the artist in the book, with Adams' friend the painter John La Farge. The biographical parallel is quite precise as a matter of fact. Katherine Simonds has shown[29] that point-for-point correspondence exists between Esther's personal characteristics and family history and those of "Clover" Hooper—so much so indeed that Esther's anguish over the death of her father appears to have been a frightful anticipation of Mrs. Adams' breakdown following the death of *her* father less than a year after the book was published.

There seems certainly to be no question that Esther was a portrait. It is this fact that made the book of such singular preciousness to the bereaved Adams. In 1891, he wrote to Elizabeth Cameron from Papeete: "I care more for one chapter, or any dozen pages of Esther, than for the whole history, including maps and indexes; so much more, indeed, that I would not let anyone read the story for fear the reader should profane it."[30] Yet when the book was written, Adams had no thought of carving a memorial, and he thoughtlessly gave Esther many of his wife's characteristics because he wanted to use certain qualities in her personality to cast light upon the problems of belief. Thus, the artist Wharton was to consider the problem posed by Esther Dudley:

> I want to know what she can make of life. She gives one the idea of a lightly-sparred yacht in mid-ocean; unexpected; you ask yourself what the devil she is doing there. She sails gaily along, though there is no land in sight and plenty of rough weather coming. She never read a book, I believe, in her life. She tries to paint but she is only a second rate amateur and will never be anything more, though she has done one or two things which I give you my word I would like to have done myself. She picks up all she knows without an effort and knows nothing well, yet she seems to understand whatever is said.[31]

These qualities were feminine and endearing—Marian Adams had them to a very high degree. Reading her letters[32] one gets a vivid picture of the woman who posed for Esther Dudley—a mixture of frivolity and seriousness, sensitive and charming with a feeling for manners and clothes as well as for friendship, a woman who "laughed at being thought a blue"[33] and was yet capable of great love and great grief. Adams thought of these qualities as those of the eternal woman. He never wearied of responding to them in the women who were his friends, feeling somehow that woman had retained a human virtue which intellectual and authoritarian man had lost. His final portrait of these qualities was to be the Virgin of Chartres.

Intertwined with the story of Esther and Stephen Hazard is a second love story, that of Catherine Brooks and the artist Wharton. It serves to fill out the rather bare structure of Adams' novel in the way of a sub-plot; it also acts to clarify the themes of faith and passion with which the main narrative is concerned. Catherine Brooks, known to her friends as the Sage Hen, enters the circle of Esther's friends—Hazard, Strong, and Wharton—like a prairie breeze, all fresh and happy simplicity. Wharton declared of her that "she stood nearer nature than any woman he knew." It is she whom Esther uses as a model for a Saint Cecelia which she is painting under Wharton's direction on a wall of Hazard's church—the "new Madonna of the prairie."[34]

There is some important discussion over this painting. Hazard and Wharton want Esther to paint Catherine a mater dolorosa, or "a first century ascetic."[35] But Esther wants to paint her as she is—lovely and young and happy. Once, when Wharton, who sees religion as a struggle rather than a joy[36] redraws Esther's sketch, Esther declares: "This is a man's work . . . No woman would ever have done it."[37] For Wharton's image of Catherine gave her "an expression of passion subdued and heaven attained."[38] And Wharton admits, "I can't paint innocence without suggesting sin."[39]

But that is not Esther's way, as it is not the way Adams saw the Virgin of Chartres. The Virgin was "above law; she took feminine pleasure in turning hell into an ornament." If Niagara in the novel anticipates Adams' image of the dynamo, the faceless might of Nature made manifest, Esther Dudley anticipates Adams' portrait of Mary the Mother of God, who "was illogical, unreasonable and feminine"[40] and "had no very marked fancy for priests as such"[41] and "troubled herself little about theology."[42] The Virgin, like Esther, like Adams, preferred individual facts to logic. "She knew that the universe was as unintelligible to her, on any theory of morals, as it was to her worshippers . . . to her every suppliant was a world in itself, to be judged apart, on its own merits, by his love for her."[43]

Adams conceived of such a response to life as essentially feminine for he found it frequently in the women he liked—and hardly ever in men. In later life his best friends were often women.[44] Adams wrote in the *Education* that he "owed more to the American woman than to all the American men he had ever heard of."[45]

It seems to have appeared to Adams that women were still in touch with the primary sources of vitality, where men, by what they called civilization, law, institutions, and above all, by the exercise of power—had cut themselves away from these sources. He came to believe, however, that in one century of the human story, the twelfth, an age dedicated to the Virgin and the courtly mistress—man had achieved a greater flowering of emotion and expression than ever before or since.

Adams' use of women to represent an intuitive virtue in human personality is very much like that of the greater fictionist Henry James. In Adams' two novels, as in many of James's, woman, with her uncorrupted moral sensibility, is trapped within a man-made civilization. James's moral measure was also, moreover, the *American* woman, and one wonders if his observation that Mrs. Henry Adams seemed to him "the incarnation of my native land"[46] indicates that he, too, felt this virtue in the woman who inspired Esther.

What Adams celebrated, in fact, was an essential primitive quality in *all* human beings, something antecedent to reason. He came to like tropical and unsophisticated cultures, where the instinctive response still flourished. Whenever he was weary of life, he grabbed King or La Farge and made off for the Far East, or the Caribbean, or the South Seas where man seemed still to accept both life and death with equanimity. The attitude was identifiable, however, as far back as his undergraduate years at Harvard. He had felt even then that the college was "a negative force" and his best friends were not intellectual New Englanders like himself, but young Southerners like "Roony" Lee, who were handsome, genial, and "simple beyond analysis."

His deification of woman is thus of a piece with his feeling that reason was a form of energy which was "lower in tension" than religious and artistic emotion, and that "thought . . . appears in nature as an arrested—in other words, as a degraded,—physical action."[47] He exalted the imaginative against the logical, commenting to Brooks that when the first dominated you got "cobblers interested in angels," when the second appeared in ascendency, as in the nineteenth century, "every priest was a huckster."[48] He defined his own times as essentially depersonalizing, declaring that modern politics was a struggle not of men but of forces, of motors. Finally, he believed that the passive mind was the best medium for seeking truth. Such a mind was Esther's.

Notes

1. William Roscoe Thayer, "Henry Adams: Central in a Literary Discovery," Boston *Evening Transcript*, August 10, 1918.

2. *The Education of Henry Adams, an Autobiography* (Boston, 1918), 21.

3. *The Education* . . . , 6.

4. *The Education* . . . , 232.

5. Henry Adams, *Esther*, Scholars' Facsimiles and Reprints (New York, 1938), 219.

6. *Esther*, 302.

7. *Esther*, 174.

8. *Esther*, 6–7.

9. *Esther*, 61.

10. *Esther*, 100.

11. *Esther*, 209.

12. *Esther*, 184.

13. *Esther*, 91–92.

14. *Esther*, 184.

15. *Esther*, 298.

16. *Esther*, 299.

17. Yvor Winters, *In Defense of Reason* (New York, 1947), 388.

18. *The Education*, 95.

19. Henry Adams, *Mont-Saint-Michel and Chartres* (Boston, 1904), 63.

20. *The Education*, 302.

21. *Esther*, 191.

22. *Esther*, 199.

23. *The Education*, 288.

24. *The Education*, 287.

25. *The Education*, 288.

26. *The Education*, 289.

27. *The Education*, 289.

28. *Esther*, 259–260.

29. "The Tragedy of Mrs. Henry Adams," *New England Quarterly*, IX, 564–82, (1963).

30. *Letters of Henry Adams (1858–1891)*, edited by Worthington Chauncey Ford (Boston, 1930), 468.

31. *Esther*, 27.

32. *The Letters of Mrs. Henry Adams (1865–1883)*, edited by Ward Thoron (Boston, 1936).

33. Letter to Charles Milnes Gaskel, May 30, 1872, *Letters* (1858–1891), 227.

34. *Esther*, 74.

35. *Esther*, 85.

36. *Esther*, 120.

37. *Esther*, 78.

38. *Esther*, 79.

39. *Esther*, 129.

40. *Mont-Saint-Michel and Chartres*, 261.

41. *Mont-Saint-Michel and Chartres*, 101.

42. *Mont-Saint-Michel and Chartres*, 101.

43. *Mont-Saint-Michel and Chartres*, 276.

44. Elizabeth Cameron, Anna Cabot Mills Lodge or Rebecca Gilman Rae were closer to the aging Adams than their husbands who were his good friends. He had a small tribe of nieces actual and adopted—Mabel Hooper La Farge was an actual niece while Aileen Tone was an adopted one who nursed him in his last illness. Brooks reported: "Henry came rather to shun me, seeming to prefer women's society in which he could be amused and tranquilized."

45. *The Education*, 442.

46. *The Letters of Mrs. Henry Adams*, 384.

47. *Degradation of the Democratic Dogma* (New York, 1918), 192.

48. R. P. Blackmur, "Henry and Brooks Adams: Parallels in Two Generations," *Southern Review*, v, 311.

"Henry Adams, 1838–1918"

Charles R. Anderson*

Quest for form is the keynote of Adams' whole career as a writer. Because he had many things to say he experimented with many forms, always searching for the one that would embody the meaning he was trying to express in a particular work. But in spite of the variety of his writings there is one purpose underlying them all: to discover the meaning of history and man's place in it, or at least to chart its direction, since motion might be its only meaning and history itself might be something quite different from what it was traditionally supposed to be. His heritage as an Adams placed him at the center of his own country's history. His wide travel and study in Europe, later extended to the Orient, broadened his scope to a world view.

Naturally enough, then, he began as a professional historian, though hardly an orthodox one, first on the faculty at Harvard (1870–1877), afterward as an independent researcher and author of a dozen volumes that still occupy a prominent place in the American canon. This impressive achievement, to which he devoted twenty years of his prime, tended during his lifetime to put him in a category quite outside the bounds of a literary anthology. But his last two works, by which he set greatest store, are of a different sort entirely. They raise the question whether history was his real goal or merely one of several means toward a more ambitious end. These books, reaching a wide audience only after his death, have tended during the twentieth century to bring Adams into the fold of American literature as a major author, though there is still considerable uncertainty as to why he should be so classified. A brief survey of his whole shelf is essential to an understanding of the two volumes that form the capstone of his career.

One of the most striking things about Adams' historical writings is how closely related they are to his own family's role in American history, how personal they are compared to works like Prescott's *Conquest of Peru* and Motley's *Rise of the Dutch Republic*, at least in terms of the subjects chosen. His *magnum opus*, the nine-volume *History of the United States* (1891), is focused on the administrations of Jefferson and Madison, the in-

*Reprinted from *American Literary Masters* (Holt, Rinehart and Winston: New York, 1965), Vol. II, pp. 315–41. By permission of Charles R. Anderson.

terregnum of Virginia Democrats between the presidencies of two Adams Federalists from Massachusetts. John had tried to set the conservative tone for the new republic, and John Quincy had tried in vain to restore it before the liberal tendencies of Andrew Jackson swept away all the old foundations. Their descendant, feeling that these first decades of the nineteenth century were crucial to American history, sought to discover their meaning by a detailed chronicle of events. This was the newest and most approved method, following the "scientific" historian Ranke. But Adams was never satisfied with it because he was coming to think that history should be an art as well as a science, and he could not find any unified form in mere sequence. His central theme in the *History* is the inability of man to shape his own life or control the forces outside himself. Things happen because they must.

As offshoots from this major effort he turned to biographies, as a kind of test of Carlyle's theory of heroes, to see if the meaning of history could be found in the lives of great men. It is interesting that his chosen subjects were Albert Gallatin (1879), a staunch Adams man though serving as a cabinet member under the opposition, and John Randolph (1882), the temptuous antagonist of both John and John Quincy. Two others rounded out his efforts in biography, the unfinished or lost life of Aaron Burr and the late one on Cabot Lodge (1911), again enemies and friends of the Adams family. In the relation of man to his times he failed once more to find a form that would reveal the meanings he sought. Then his work as a historian was brought to an end with an exotic footnote, *Memoirs of Arii Tamai E* (1893), a search for the great theme of modern history in capsule form by placing in juxtaposition the international exploitation of Tahiti and reminiscences he recorded painstakingly from the last island queen. But his writing career was far from over.

If history could not be given significance by making it into a science, perhaps art could be made the vehicle of ideas. During the period of his laborious researches Adams threw off two novels, *Democracy* (1880) and *Esther* (1884), dealing with issues of the first importance: the corruption of government by business and the beginnings of religious skepticism as a result of scientific discoveries. Somewhat later he even tried his hand at poetry, notably his "Prayer to the Virgin at Chartres." But his writings in these genres give him no status in the realm of literature, for they are the work of a competent amateur rather than an inspired artist. Having other things to say that called for exposition, even argument, Adams also wrote a large number of essays, enough to fill a volume during his lifetime and two posthumous ones. But it is not as a essayist that he takes rank today as a literary author.

That claim, and it is a growing one, rests exclusively on two works written in his old age, *The Education of Henry Adams* (1907) and *Mont-Saint-Michel and Chartres* (1904). Both are highly personal books, one taking the form of autobiography and the other that of a summer tour in

France with his niece. One of their most striking features is that both are aimed at discovering the meaning of history, his perennial theme. If he could not find it in chronological sequence or the lives of other men, in ideological fiction or polemical essays, maybe he could find it in the story of his own life, if seen imaginatively and aesthetically. Their other striking feature is the emphasis on form in both prefaces. If he could find the right forms he could at last express what he had to say.

Though the *Education* was written second and as a sequel to *Chartres*, it is the best one to begin with for several reasons. It takes up the story of America's past where Adams' formal histories leave off and brings it right down into the twentieth century. It appeals more directly to modern readers, as a consequence, having an impact as dramatic and timely today as when first issued. It fits more closely with an American literary tradition, one that includes Franklin's *Autobiography*, Thoreau's *Walden*, and Mark Twain's *Life on the Mississippi*. But it is more successful as a piece of literature than the first of these three books, more ambitious and significant in scope than the other two. It is the classic example in America of the full-scale autobiography shaped by the creative imagination into a work of art.

I

Henry Adams launched his *Education* in its posthumous edition with two prefaces. One he wrote for his editor, H. C. Lodge, to sign, when the book was published six months after his death in 1918. The other is the acknowledged author's preface to the privately printed edition, dated February 16, 1907. Both are crucial to an understanding of the book's method and meaning. In the first he defines his purpose: to treat man as a force, which can be measured only by "motion from a fixed point." This leads to his concept of how the two books are linked, by suggesting as a subtitle for *Chartres* "A Study of Thirteenth-Century Unity" and for the *Education* "A Study of Twentieth-Century Multiplicity." With the aid of these two "points of relation," he said, he could project his lines forward and backward indefinitely. But the second book proved more difficult to write than the first.

The major problem posed by the *Education* was "the usual one of literary form." There are many statements in the letters to support this prefatory aside. To William James he wrote, "As for the volume, it interests me chiefly as a literary experiment, hitherto, as far as I know, never tried or never successful. Your brother Harry [Henry James the novelist] tries such experiments in literary art daily, and would know instantly what I mean." To a young painter he said:

> Between artists, or people trying to be artists, the sole interest is that of form. Whether one builds a house, or paints a

picture, or tells a story, our point of vision regards only the form—not the matter. [The *Education* has] not been done in order to teach others, but to educate myself in the possibilities of literary form. The arrangement, the construction, the composition, the art of climax are our only serious study. . . . The Confessions of St. Augustine [was] my literary model.

This point is followed up in a second letter to James:

Did you ever read the Confessions of St. Augustine, or of Cardinal de Retz, or of Rousseau, or of Benvenuto Cellini, or even of my dear Gibbon? Of them all, I think St. Augustine alone has an idea of literary form—a notion of writing a story with an end and object, not for the sake of the object, but the form, like a romance. I have worked ten years to satisfy myself that the thing cannot be done today. The world does not furnish the contrasts or the emotion.

In his preface Adams made explicit the differing problems facing the modern author and his classic model: "St. Augustine, like a great artist, had worked from multiplicity to unity, while he, like a small one, had to reverse the method and work back from unity to multiplicity. The scheme became unmanageable as he approached his end." But there is always irony or ambiguity in Adams' references to his life and writings as "failures." The failure here referred to is clearly that of literary form. His revolutionary "dynamic theory of history" simply could not be rendered dramatically through his own life story, so that in the last three chapters the chosen device of autobiography broke down into something like expository essays.

Yet in spite of his protestations that the *Education* remained "unfinished," Adams did not forbid its publication after his death, and during his life he himself had printed a small edition for private circulation. The author's preface to this is chiefly concerned with the use of autobiography as a literary form. Of the two models there mentioned, Franklin is singled out as the only American guide but is dismissed as being only a model of "self-teaching," not for "high education." Rousseau's *Confessions* is played with at some length but only to set it up as a monumental warning against the ego: "Since his time, and largely thanks to him, the Ego has steadily tended to efface itself, and for purposes of model, to become a manikin on which the toilet of education is to be draped in order to show the fit or misfit of the clothes."

Those who have pondered the two prefaces will certainly not expect the book they introduce to be a straightforward and personal narrative of Henry Adams or a mere surface picture of the nineteenth century world he lived in, much as they may serve for its outward subject matter. In the passage just quoted, the verbal play alone should alert readers to the possibility that in the following pages imagery and structure may have as much to do with meaning as facts and ideas or historical events and persons. The author of these prefaces is clearly one who uses language like a poet. Perhaps his purpose was not to record his life and times as a factual story, but to compose a book that would suggest larger meanings. Two passages from Adams' letters confirm this. To this novelist James he wrote punningly of the *Education*, "The volume is a mere shield of protection in the grave. I advise you to take your own life in the same way, in order to prevent biographers from taking it in theirs." To the psychologist James he added, "With this I send you the volume. . . . I feel that Sargent squirms in the portrait. I am not there." This cryptic reference to a contemporary portrait painter, whose work he thought mannered and either idealized or distorted, implies that his own work is so far from a self-portrait that the real Henry Adams is conspicuous by his absence.

The *Education* may be thought of, therefore, as a fiction that uses autobiography as a mere starting point. The first problem in escaping from the limitations of such a literary device is how to achieve the proper distance from one's materials, how to arrive at meanings that are objective and universal while taking full advantage of the drama afforded by a narrative of personal experiences during a crucial period in history. Adams' strategy for this, in the preface, is to make a play on the "Clothes Philosophy" that forms the center of *Sartor Resartus*, though without naming this influential book of the early nineteenth century. In it language was described as the clothing of thought, and body as the clothing of soul, the universe itself being but "the living garment of God." For the transcendental Carlyle clothes were mere appearances covering the true Reality, the one thing worth studying. Adams reverses this, saying that, for him, "The object of study is the garment, not the figure. . . . The tailor's object, in this volume, is to fit young men, in universities or elsewhere, to be men of the world, equipped for any emergency; and the garment offered to them is meant to show the faults of the patchwork fitted on their fathers."

Thus the persona Henry Adams, who is written about in the third person as the subject of the *Education*, has been reduced to a tailor's dummy, even to the mannequin used by window dressers and artists. He is reduced still further by a final meaning of the term "manikin": a little man or dwarf. Such is the shrunken status of Everyman in the modern world. Nineteenth century discoveries in geology, astronomy, and biology had pushed the history of the earth back from thousands to millions of years, located it as a mere speck on the periphery of the Galaxy, and assigned man only a relative superiority over other animals—all of which destroyed the myth of a special creation and of man, fashioned in God's image, as lord of all creatures. A similar thing had been happening in the changing concepts of the human world brought about by the trend toward collectivism in society and the new theories of behavioral psychology, which turned man into a pawn moved by external and internal forces beyond his control.

In the drift from a humanistic to a deterministic view of himself modern man had indeed become a manikin, so that Adams' emphasis is shifted from autobiography to history. Even in this he allows himself an artist's freedom, saying that the tailor can adapt the clothes as well as the model "to his patron's wants," that is, to the reading public he is trying to reach. And since in this elaborate conceit language is the "clothing of thought," literary form rather than content is once again emphasized as the key to meaning. Having achieved complete detachment from his materials, Adams can now select and maneuver them at will. The facts of his own life and of the historical period through which he lived can be used or omitted, heightened or played down, reshaped in any way dictated by his artistic purpose. And having freed himself from the literal Henry Adams, his task is to create a persona to take his place: "The manikin, therefore, has the same value as any other geometrical figure of three or more dimensions, which is used for the study of relation. For that purpose it cannot be spared; . . . it must have the air of reality; it must be taken for real; must be treated as though it had life." Such is the animated puppet that is moved through the experiences of a long and complex education.

One of the advantages of using autobiography as a literary device is that the narrator who is telling his own story has already lived through all the experiences down to the last page before he begins to write the first one. Because of this he can render the meaning of his life by the form and expression he chooses to give it. In general, the two chief masks in the book are (a) the subject Henry Adams, who is passed off as a manikin for easy display, and (b) the narrator Henry Adams, who is the objective author commenting on his whole past career. But the former becomes an endless variety of personae as (b) tries to reconstruct (a) at the several stages of his education: as child, student, diplomatic secretary, historian, consultant to statesmen, commentator on modern man and his civilization. This continues right on down to the time when the aging subject merges with the narrator, the dispassionate old man seeking to make his autobiography yield the greater truth of his education.

In the shifting perspectives of the book the narrator's role is complicated still further by the several "voices" through which he can speak. Is it the historian who is proving the muddleheadedness of British politicians during the Civil War, or the scientific determinist who has taken the stance that history is chaos rather than sequence? Is it the postgraduate student or the later historian-turned-artist who finds the chief value of his foreign education in the discovery of Reubens and Beethoven? It is crucial to decide which voice of Henry Adams is speaking at any given point. It is equally important to remember that not only the objective narrator but each changing subject persona is a pose, none of them corresponding exactly to the factual Henry Adams at any stage. They are a series of masks assumed under the shifting mask of the speaker. Thus the whole narrative is removed from the mode of strict autobiography and becomes a fictive account in the best and deepest sense of that term.

In addition to the various voices of the narrator there are other ways in which the style is modulated, notably the shift from that of a detached intellectual to that of one emotionally involved. The bulk of the book is written in the former style: factual for the narrative parts, dry and sharp in the commentary. This gives a tone of authority to the whole. The vignettes are detailed, the portraits clearly etched, the chronicle straightforward, the conclusions faced unflinchingly. Readers are aware that many things have been left out, of necessity, and that the opinions are controlled by a personal value system. But here is a writer, they are convinced, who can record his own life truthfully and evaluate it without self-inflation or apology. The book gains in dependability even from the one way in which it seems to depart from the truth—Adams' tendency to be much too hard on himself. His unique heritage is played down by understatement, his personal abilities and accomplishments undercut by constant deflation. Everyone knows, on the contrary, that his position as an Adams was unrivaled in nineteenth century America, and the book itself is evidence of his high intelligence and extraordinary learning.

This mode of negation is not the result of an absurd modesty. In his letters as well as his books Adams assumed the roles of arrogance and humility at will. Admitting his error in a political prediction once, he declared, "Hitherto in my life I have always been right; it is other people who are wrong." Yet ten days later, in obvious reference to both *Chartres* and the *Education*, he could say:

> Vanity is a danger I can hardly fear now; on the contrary, self-deprecation has always been my vice, and morbid self-contempt my moral weakness, as it was in that of the 12th-century mystics, which is the bond of sympathy between us; but we each recoup ourselves by feeling a calm, unruffled, instinctive, unfathomed skepticism about the existence of a world at all. . . . There are but two schools: one turns the world onto me; the other turns me onto the world; the result is the same. The so-called me is a very, very small and foolish puppy dog, but it is all that exists, and it tries all its life to get a little bigger by enlarging its energies.

Even in the letters it is the author rather than the person who is writing.

In the *Education* this mode of negation is a conscious strategy that pervades the whole book. All the chief personages are treated with the same irony, all the main events viewed with the same skepticism. The drift to collectivism is accepted as inevitable, the individual as overwhelmed by the forces of determinism—not just Adams alone. The "personal failure" theme, therefore, is not a reflection of any failure in his own life but is used to dramatize his pessimism over the loss of values in the modern world, the impending failure of civilization itself. It is a literary device used deliberately for reader-irritation, to keep raising the question: "What does this pessimist with impossibly high standards really want?" By the end of the book it is clear what he wants: to expose relentlessly the fraudulent aspects of modern society and to shock man into awareness of his plight, so he can meet his doom with self-respect and even try to control it with confidence and intelligent purpose. Instead, "the menagerie is chewing its tail in religious silence," Adams concludes, while the universe either runs down or explodes.

The ground tone of the book is set by this objective analysis of his life and times. It is for this reason that the subjective passages stand out with such dramatic effect. They are few and brief, but they always come at crucial stages in his career. As each one occurs it is dismissed as accidental education, or "education only sensual." At the time, the persona is blind to any value it may have in fitting him for his world. But the wary reader soon becomes aware, as the author has been all along, that until Adams can bridge the gap between intellect and emotion he will not have any education at all. Those who take the book as literal autobiography can be easily misled into concluding that the author was simply a cold intellectual, even a sour old man, who occasionally gave vent to extravagant feelings. But the literary student will recognize these as contrasting styles deliberately played against each other for strategic purposes. The subjective episodes, all but submerged under the objective surface, provide a measure for one of the book's most important meanings: that modern man's dependence on fact and reason has been largely responsible for the fragmentation of his world. He has lost the capacity to feel—the capacity for war and worship, for love and art—that brought unity out of multiplicity in the medieval world of *Chartres*.

Equally important is the clue to Adams' method of dramatizing his autobiography offered by these subjective passages. Two of them are available in the following selections for readers to analyze. The first occurs when, as a young man, he visits Antwerp Cathedral on the way to graduate studies in Berlin (Chapter 5). Prostrating himself before Reubens' "Descent from the Cross," he tries to use this painting as a doorway into the lost religion of the Middle Ages. There is no biographical evidence that he ever had such an emotional experience. But there is ample evidence in the text of the *Education* to show how this highly subjective episode fills out a major theme of the book: the disappearance of religion in the modern world. The second comes at the age of thirty-two, when he witnesses the death of his sister in the terrible convulsions of lockjaw (Chapter 19). His personal grief and shock are played up to the full as the dramatic cause of his abandoning orthodox attitudes toward God and

nature, leading him to embrace the modern belief in scientific determinism. But this reorientation is conspicuously absent from the letters of
1870, which record the actual experience with clinical detachment.

This particular subjective episode also shows why Adams rejected
some of his autobiographical materials and used others. His grief and
shock over personal loss could have been illustrated far more dramatically
by the death of his wife in 1885, without need of literary heightening.
After thirteen years of happy marriage, Marian Adams, suffering from
melancholia, took her own life. Her husband was broken in fragments,
and he only found some degree of wholeness again after years of wander-
ing and searching for peace. Yet this entire segment of his mature
career—all the happiness and the pain (not to mention his great achievement as a historian)—is omitted from the *Education*. Chapter 20 ends just
before his marriage in 1872; Chapter 21 takes up the narrative again
under the title "Twenty Years After (1892)," with no comment on the
hiatus. As an artist he chose to bypass the tragic end of his marriage and
transfer its powerful emotional impact to a previous event, the death of
his sister, on which it was easier to gain perspective. Besides, the chief
literary use he wanted to make of his confrontation with violent and
meaningless death was that chaos rather than sequence is the law of
nature, even as he intended to prove it is the law of history. It was more
strategic to fix this turning point in his thinking by a dramatic episode of
1870, just prior to his assuming the role of professional historian, rather
than by his wife's suicide in 1885, long after he had begun applying his
"scientific" theory of anarchic forces in nature to the historical process.
These are some of the ways by which Adams transformed his
autobiography into a work of art and gave it meanings far transcending
the personal. Interested students can discover many others for themselves
and find out how they work to achieve the literary form the author was
seeking.

II

A number of patterns mesh together to give the *Education* its over-all
structure. Most obvious of these is the story line, which creates the effect
of a chronicle from childhood to old age. But this autobiographical pattern, at most a surface device, is breached more often than the casual
reader may notice. Many chapters, scattered throughout the book, drop
the personal narrative for broader topics—international diplomacy in
London during the Civil War, the breakdown of American government
and society during the Reconstruction, the impact of new discoveries in
science and inventions such as the dynamo, and so on. The last three
chapters abandon the story line altogether, with the frank admission that
he can formulate his radical theory of history only by shifting to the essay

form. Autobiography is bypassed even more by the omission of many significant matters, as a check with the actual record will show. Virtually nothing is told about Adams' affectionate relation with family and kin, or his intimate and wide-ranging friendships—except for the public life of previous Adamses and the careers in politics and science of two close friends, Hay and King. In sum, he left out all the subjective parts of his life, all the emotional and humanizing aspects, unless he could fit them into the design of his "education." The most notable omission is of the entire account of his marriage and its anguished aftermath, as shown above. This skipping of the whole period of his prime, from age thirty-four to fifty-four, breaks the book into two parts, even as his wife's death had broken his life.

Adams once described the *Education* as a centipede that crawls twenty chapters downhill, then fifteen chapters up a little "for the view." This whimsy is the clue to a patterning much more important than the autobiographical one, as far as structure is related to meaning. The first part is his search during youth and early maturity for a career in the world appropriate to his heritage. The second, after a gap of twenty years, is the retired historian's quest to understand the breakdown of his world into multiplicity. In the one he defines his aim as being "to control power in some form." For the other, he sees the need of redefining his goal: "to react with vigor and economy . . . and by choice" to the forces that are turning an ordered world into chaos. Most of the personal narrative comes in the first part, most of the commentary in the second. There, having given up action, he can turn to theory and try to draw conclusions from the meaning of his life. The relation between action and theory establishes the relation of the two parts. As might be expected, all the subjective episodes are in part one, since feelings are the result of personal experience. Part two is almost wholly objective, limited to facts and ideas, as he turns himself into a representative manikin of the collapsing modern world.

This balancing of modes in the overall structure is repeated on a smaller scale in the arrangement of the first twenty chapters, which follow the chronological order fairly closely. Chapters 1 through 6 make a distinct unit, dealing with the years of his formal education from grammar school in Boston through post-graduate studies in Berlin. The failure of this attempt to prepare himself to be one of the "men of the world, equipped for any emergency" is dramatized by "Treason," in which the America of his heritage is rent asunder by the violence of Civil War. Thus Chapter 7 forms a link with the next group, eight chapters dealing with his experiences in England as Secretary to the American Minister, in which he is educated by public affairs as a spectator. There the multiplication of forces beyond man's control, in politics and economics as well as war, suggests the impending breakdown of all Western civilization. At the end of his English residence he tries to convert himself into a

Darwinist, applying the principles of biological evolution to society, in a desperate attempt to find a new faith in order and unity that will replace the lost one of religion. So the last of these chapters, "Darwinism," leads into the final group of five centering around the Washington years when he becomes a reformer and writes essays on current events. But this evangelism is short lived. The weakness and drift under President Grant strike him as "evolution in reverse," and social Darwinism is soon rejected as a practical program for hastening ultimate perfection. The railroad conspiracy and the gold scandal show that corruption is widespread. The outbreak of the Franco-Prussian War extends this chaos in society to the international scene, and the death of his sister in the same year suggests that anarchy is the law of nature too. As his ordered world falls into fragments he withdraws to a professorship at Harvard. His "failure" there is that of one expected to teach history as meaningful sequence when he is convinced it is essentially "incoherent and immoral."

The chronicle of his early life thus divides itself naturally into three sections: his formal schooling, his education by public affairs as a spectator, and his experiences as a participant who fails to find his proper role. But this structure by outward events is far less important to meaning than the dramatic juxtaposition of subjective and objective experiences, whereby the rare emotional passages achieve their effect by being sounded against the hard factual narrative that gives the book its tone. The first and third sections gain their special significance through experiences that appeal to feeling only, as previously indicated. His formal education reaches its climax not in university studies but in the discovery of painting and religion at Antwerp Cathedral, symbolizing medieval unity, and in the discovery of Beethoven in a Berlin beer garden, when a "prison-wall that barred his senses on one great side of life suddenly fell." Shortly afterward in Rome, as he meditates on the decline of classical and medieval culture, based on art and emotion, he can only ask the agonized question "Why?"

In the long middle section there are no such strong subjective passages, since it is devoted to analyzing problems in society and government, as he tries to fit himself for a traditional Adams role in the world. There are incidental experiences in England that raise the unsolved issue of unity again, as in the meeting with Swinburne, when he envies the fusion of mind and sensibility achieved by the poet; or that reveal his internal conflicts, as when his mind tries to embrace evolution as a "new form of religious hope" though his instinct rejects it because he can only perceive time as motion and change. But on the whole these chapters are concerned with ideas and facts, and as such they form the objective core of part one.

The third section returns to the use of climactic emotional experiences for achieving meaning. Just as intellect fails to find any vestiges of an ordered world in post Civil War America, so on the death of his sister the previous coherence of his personal life is ruptured by the "insanity of force" that is nature. Ignorant of the value of "education only sensual," the persona requires twenty more years of experience before he is able to "restore the finite to its place." The very next scene, the last subjective moment in the book, suggests a possible way for doing this. An enthusiastic new friendship with the geologist King, begun in the Rocky Mountains of Colorado, gives promise that somehow the outward beauty and the inner chaos of nature can be reconciled, that by a synthesis of science and aesthetics man may impose unity on his experience. On this hopeful note the first part of the *Education* comes to an end.

The persona has now been established as a manikin for the study of relations—between feeling and intellect, unity and multiplicity, the past religious phase of history and the present mechanical one. The last fifteen chapters, in which he crawls back uphill for the view, are unrelieved by any dramatic emotional episodes. They continue the objective narrative that was the staple of part one also, but with much less emphasis on personal experiences, in order to display the social and scientific forces that move the manikin through the modern world. On the surface they seem like a proliferation of illustrations of multiplicity. But as he learns to incorporate sensual experience in his total education, he is able to work out the new theory of history that concludes the book. This conclusion is far from being a victory over the anarchic forces of society and nature. Man cannot hope to control them, or even to stop the drift toward multiplicity. But he can set himself the task of understanding them so he can unify his own experience, if only by expressing it in a work of art based on a new theory of history. This would be the intelligent use of doom, as one critic has phrased it. "Unity is vision," Adams said flatly, and by implication reality is—and always has been—complex and chaotic. The only question is, "Can modern man impose his vision of order on the chaos of the world as effectively as medieval man did?"

Part two of the *Education* is structured most effectively by the full development of two patterns: the manipulation of time, and the creation of images to symbolize the phases of history. Both had been used in part one, though sparingly. From the beginning Adams extends his life span over three centuries, pretending that though he lived in the nineteenth century he was educated for the eighteenth and so unfitted for the twentieth. By an ingenious trick of telescoping time all three are made to exist simultaneously. The eighteenth century came to an end in 1848, he declares theatrically, when ex-President Adams collapsed on the floor of Congress. And since this was the very date of Marx's *Manifesto* and the outbreak of revolutions all over Europe, the same year ushered in the twentieth century. Thus the nineteenth, which comprises virtually the whole education of the persona, vanishes before it fairly begins.

This time game is proved "scientifically" in the book's penultimate chapter by applying the "Law of Acceleration" to history. The religious phase had dragged itself out over so many millennia, refusing to admit its own decline and death, that the mechanical phase burst on the scene fully formed—long prepared for by the admission of reason into St. Thomas' theology, which made way for Newton and applied science. This squeeze play reduces the nineteenth century to a mere point in time between the two great phases of history. Of course it could be argued that the grandfather, last embodiment of the great family tradition, did die in 1848 and Adams was simply reporting that fact. But a more historically precise date for the end of the Federalist era would have been 1829, when John Quincy was defeated by the new Jacksonian democracy, or even 1801, when John Adams was defeated by Jefferson. It was simply more appropriate for the author's literary purposes to choose the date in mid-century and so bring the demise of the eighteenth into dramatic juxtaposition with the rise of Communist theory and the drift toward twentieth-century collectivism.

These three centuries, lumped together to form the modern world of the persona, are expanded as well as collapsed at will. Adams refers to Quincy, where he began his nineteenth-century boyhood, as not only "colonial" but "troglodytic." At the age of thirty, meditating on the fossilized *pteraspis* recently found near Wenlock Abbey, he accepts this shark out of the Silurian age as his first ancestor. In his prime, with the discovery of anarchic force as the true reality behind the appearance of order, he does not hesitate to project his lines forward and predict the exact year in the twentieth century when the world will blow up or grind to a halt.

Another use to which he puts this maneuverable time scheme is in linking his two books as sequels. The ratio of change, so slow throughout most of recorded history, is now accelerating at such a dizzy speed he can bring the medieval and modern periods together. The three-century unit of the *Education* is paralleled by the three chosen for *Chartres*. During the eleventh, twelfth, and thirteenth centuries the religious power that had given unity to civilization for so long reached its highest expression, then began to show signs of breaking down. In the nineteenth century the persona Henry Adams is watching this process work itself out in the fragmentation of the modern world even as he clings to the illusion of an ordered one he has inherited. In Chapter 25, "The Dynamo and the Virgin," as his education enters the twentieth century, he tentatively brings the two poles of history together, in more than the title. The love of Mary he traces back as a sexual force to Venus, even to Eve. Then with the decline of Mariolatry, he blasphemously offers up a scientific prayer to the dynamo. In a later chapter, "Vis Nova" (The New Power), he adds a comic footnote in the episode where he visits the shrines of the Virgin in an automobile.

To make concrete his dramatic handling of time, Adams creates a number of striking symbols. Most effective is his violent yoking of the central symbols of Christianity with two drawn from modern technology. The Cross to which Christ was nailed had brought salvation, so elevating the worth of all men and uniting them in the brotherhood of love. It is a constant in the religious world of *Chartres*, almost nonexistent in the secular one of the *Education*. But it does appear twice, with telling effect: in the experience at Antwerp Cathedral as a young man and in that of the old man at the Paris Exposition, where it is described as "a revelation of mysterious energy" now largely lost to man. In bold contrast to the Cross he sets up the railroad, running all through the nineteenth century, that nails man to its crossties and brings death to the individual. As it comes into full power during the decades after the Civil War, it emerges as a symbol of the new industrial energies drawing all human movement to itself in a novel kind of unity, yet one that offers, paradoxically, only the anonymity of a collective society. It represents the victory of Boston over Quincy, of a mechanistic civilization over a traditional humanistic one.

The second pair is his most daring conjunction of symbols. So furiously is the law of acceleration operating that the mechanical phase of history is hardly established before it is replaced by the "supersensual" one, railroads by dynamos and radium, which dramatically reveal the progressive degradation of energy and the instability of matter itself. Having failed to find any meaningful sequence in history or society—"while the mere sequence of time was artificial, and the sequence of thought was chaos"—Adams turns at last to study the sequence of force. But by 1900 he finds "his historical neck broken" by energies that are anarchical and totally unsuspected, giving history a new phase by rupturing the unity of natural force. He knows he can never understand this until he can learn to relate the power of the dynamo in the twentieth century to that of the Virgin in the twelfth. "He made up his mind to venture it; he would risk translating rays into faith."

The only common value he can find to measure the difference between faith and force is their attraction on his own mind, as representative of the mind of other men. He knows that electricity could no more have built Chartres Cathedral than worship of the Virgin could have led to the invention of the dynamo. "The force of the Virgin was still felt at Lourdes, and seemed to be as potent as X-rays; but in America neither Venus nor Virgin ever had value as force," though modern man's blind obedience to scientific power suggests the terms of a new worship. Perhaps a parallel is possible, and the dynamo can be shown to be a "moral force" much as early Christians felt the Cross. Thus he sets the terms of his "scientific" experiment. If he could show that Cross and railroad, Virgin and dynamo, are all symbols of power worshiped by man—differing from each other only because they are the expressions of different epochs—he might be able to show that history does have sequence. If love of the Virgin, symbolizing medieval religion even more powerfully than the crucified Christ does, had led to a new synthesis in the theology of St. Thomas, then understanding modern force might lead to a synthetic theory of history couched in scientific terms and so acceptable to modern man. First, by using the feeling self as a center to measure the forces of Virgin and dynamo, representing two poles of history, he might be able to give meaning and unity to his own experience. Then this private synthesis could be extended to a public one. The search for a new dynamic theory of history is the goal of part two of the *Education*.

Chapters 21–35 divide themselves into three sections, the three phases of his search. In the first five, the decline of art symbolizes the change that has come over Adams' inherited world and his isolation from the new industrial one that has replaced it. His education as an Adams fitted him for the eighteenth century rather than the twentieth, his temperament for art rather than science. Yet, because the persona has been part of the very historical process causing his alienation from the modern world, he is peculiarly qualified to analyze it. And he does achieve some sense of personal unity as he learns to fuse feeling with intellect, solving the problem that had proved a barrier to his earlier education in part one. Though the succeeding chapters record the drift to multiplicity in differing areas—government, science, his personal life, and so on—they are united by a common concern: to achieve the artist's vision of order and impose it on the disorder of the contemporary world. Searching for peace (after the death of his wife), Adams begins his far-flung travels. First he goes to the Orient where he discovers the ancient past, then to the South Seas and primitive art. The meeting with the painter La Farge, who goes with him on these trips, is crucial. From him he learns that the aesthetic sense is another way of knowing, opposite to reason, and this enables him to discard the idea that sensual education is valueless. Then comes his exploration of the cathedrals in Normandy, where his study of medieval art gives him "a new sense of history," a conviction that it can be understood intuitively as well as intellectually.

Meantime he has been striving to keep abreast of the modern world—the chaos of politics and economics in Washington, the dynamos first glimpsed in Chicago. By the time of the Paris Exposition in 1900, when he can fathom the meaning of these new machines representing the anarchic forces released by science, he is ready to write his climactic chapter "The Dynamo and the Virgin." Believing with Bergson that the intuition must find the goals for the mind to analyze, he first allows himself to feel the relations between these two symbols of power, then uses his intellect to measure the degree of their attraction on men and their influence on history. Just how significant the role of feeling is in establishing the book's meaning he made explicit in a letter several years after its publication:

> I like best Bergson's frank surrender to the superiority of Instinct over Intellect. You know how I have preached that

principle, and how I have studied the facts of it. In fact I wrote once a whole volume—called my *Education*— . . . in order to recall how Education may be shown to consist in following the intuitions of instinct.

But the book's chosen method dictates a rational, even scientific, "demonstration" of his conclusions, though they have been arrived at intuitively. This requires him to undertake a new kind of education. Convinced that "the alternative to art was arithmetic," he plunges into statistics to chart the present and the immediate future.

Chapter 26, "Twilight," is a transitional one in which he tries to relate the pattern of his personal experiences to the whole movement of contemporary history. The next six chapters form the second group, setting forth the views of the Conservative Christian Anarchist, a fictive role he creates for himself as one who perceives order and chaos simultaneously everywhere. In the first three he sees the impending conflict between Imperial Russia and the West as one between inertia and acceleration, unity and multiplicity, but every effort to fuse these contradictory forces breaks down. The Russo-Japanese War, in which the new scientific forces are being applied to instruments of destruction, actually raises the question of the survival of civilization. In the second three chapters he tries to work this out "scientifically." All the forces making for unity are discussed in "Vis Inertiae," all the forces of chaos in "Vis Nova," with an attempted resolution in "The Grammar of Science." But each chapter reaches the same conclusion: it is a "toss-up between anarchy and order." So long as man could face the chaos of reality and still impose on it his vision of an ordered world—religious in the Middle Ages, political in the founding of the American Republic—he could achieve at least the illusion of unity. But even his capacity for creating illusions may be lost in the flood of new forces overwhelming him now. This first of the twentieth-century world wars, coming right on the heels of Adams' vision of the dynamo and radium in 1900, seems a direct application to human society of the anarchy being unleashed by scientific discovery. Chapters 27–32 are his attempt to resolve the conflict between man's fading dream of unity and the fact of multiplicity made vivid by science.

The final section of the *Education* is a triad of chapters in which the retired historian makes a last heroic effort to come to terms with the chaos of the modern world. Having felt the power of the Virgin and the dynamo as personal experience, he extends them from private to public history by making them into symbols of unity and multiplicity, so as to prophesy the future as well as understand the past. It is in these three concluding chapters that Adams says his literary form failed him, the chosen device of autobiography having to be replaced by expository essays. As he wrote to Barrett Wendell, a professor of literature at Harvard, "I found that a narrative style was so incompatible with a didactic or scientific style, that I had to write a long supplementary chapter [actually three] to explain in scientific terms what I could not put into narration without ruining the narrative." The main outlines of this synthesis can be pondered by students in the last selection from the *Education*, "A Dynamic Theory of History." The next chapter, "A Law of Acceleration," presents elaborate statistics from the history of science to substantiate his theory; and the process by which power is increasing in a geometrical ratio is imaged as a comet ready to explode. In the final chapter the reader is told he must begin his education where Henry Adams' leaves off, in the age of supersensual chaos.

Several passages from the letters will throw light on this complex argument and furnish evidence that its real method is literary rather than scientific, its purpose moral rather than historical. Just as the *Education* was being brought to its conclusion, Adams sounded his stoical note of hope in the face of impending doom:

> What is the end of doubling up our steam and electric power every five years to infinity if we don't increase thought power? As I see it, the society of today shows no more thought power than in our youth, though it showed precious little then. To me the whole lesson lies in this experiment. Can our society double up its mind capacity? It must do it or die; and I see no reason why it may not widen its consciousness of complex conditions far enough to escape wreck; but it must hurry. Our power is always running ahead of our mind.

And even during the composition of *Chartres*, several years earlier, he was already projecting the dilemma that would be posed at the end of the *Education*:

> I apprehend for the next hundred years an ultimate, colossal, cosmic collapse; but not on any of our old lines. My belief is that science is to wreck us, and that we are like monkeys monkeying with a loaded shell; we don't in the least know or care where our practically infinite energies come from or will bring us to. . . . It is mathematically certain to me that another thirty years of energy development at the rate of the last century, must reach an *impasse*.
>
> This is, however, a line of ideas wholly new, and very repugnant to our contemporaries, . . . I owe it to my having always had a weakness for science mixed with metaphysics. I am a dilution of Lord Kelvin and St. Thomas Aquinas.

Aquinas' philosophy makes the final chapter of the *Chartres*. Kelvin's Second Law of Thermodynamics brings the *Education* to its conclusion. A third letter, written just after he had completed one book and was beginning the other, makes it clear how the two books were linked in his mind:

> I am trying to work out a formula of anarchism; the law of expansion from unity, simplicity, morality, to multiplicity,

contradiction, police. . . . The assumption of unity which was the mark of human thought in the middle ages has yielded very slowly to the proofs of complexity. The stupor of science before radium is proof of it.

Chartres and the *Education* were planned and executed as sequels. Only by reading them as such can the student grasp their full significance.

III

The best approach to Adams' intentions and methods in *Mont-Saint-Michel and Chartres* can likewise be picked up from comments in his correspondence. To a medieval historian, H. O. Taylor, he wrote (with a copy of the book):

> I have no object but a superficial one, as far as history is concerned. To me, accuracy is relative. I care very little whether my details are exact, if only my *ensemble* is in scale. You need to be thorough in your study and accurate in your statements. Your middle ages exist for their own sake, not for ours. To me, who stand in gaping wonder before this preposterous spectacle of thought, [the conceptions of modern scientific philosophers,] . . . the middle-ages present a picture that has somehow to be brought into relation with ourselves.

Here Adams explicitly disclaimed the role of historian, just as in the letters quoted previously he denied that he was writing autobiography in his *Education*. His purpose in the *Chartres*, he said, was to create a structure—"a picture" of the past—that would help man to reorient his thinking today. Some five years later he commented to A. S. Cook, another medievalist:

> I wanted to show the intensity of the vital energy of a given time, and of course that intensity had to be stated in its two highest terms—religion and art. As our society stands, this way of presenting a subject can be felt only by a small number of persons . . . . the one-in-a-thousand of born artists and poets.

To Taylor again, in a letter near the end of his life, he made a statement that clarifies his use of religion as one of the two main themes in his book:

> Logically the religious solution is inadmissable—pure hypothesis. It discards reason. I do not object to it on that account: as a working energy I prefer instinct to reason; but as you put it, the Augustinian adjustment seems to be only the Stoic, with a supernatural or hypothetical supplement nailed to it by violence. The religionists preached it, and called it Faith.

His real purpose was to grasp medieval unity through the vision of an artist, the historian's view being inadequate and the religious one lost to modern man.

Adams' bantering complaints about the dwindling audience today—especially for books on art, poetry, and religion—reflect his deep concern over the alienation of the artist in the modern world. But he played the game with zest. Both of his novels were published anonymously, the second one even "suppressed," as an experiment with the reading public to see if an unadvertised book would sell. His last two works, which he considered his greatest achievement, were issued only in limited editions for private circulation. And his pessimism about the plight of the serious author prompted him to mockery in his comments on them. To an English friend he wrote, "I hardly think my *Education* is fit for any public." As for *Chartres*, he declared to William James, "The last three chapters are alone worth reading, and of course are never read." It was of this book ("the only book I ever wrote that was worth writing") that he said jocularly at the time of its first publication, "I deny that it is a book; it is only a running chatter with my nieces and those of us who love old art." Then he added with comic exaggeration, "It was meant only for . . . women, [since] men no longer read at all"—meaning that their reading is confined to the factual and scientific.

These frivolous remarks were addressed to one of those bright young women who formed a coterie around him in his old age, one of the "nieces in wish" to whom he dedicates his pages in the preface to *Chartres*. There he gives free play to his banter about the shrunken relation of author to reader, saying the only one possible now is between an uncle and his niece. "Nieces have been known to read in early youth, and in some cases may have read their uncles." But this is to be a book in the guise of a tour to the cathedrals of Normandy. "For convenience of travel in France," he adds, "the nieces shall count as one only. . . . One niece is much more likely than two to listen. One niece is also more likely than two to carry a kodak and take interest in it." But even with a captive audience of one there are limitations: "One cannot assume, even in a niece, too emotional a nature, but one may assume a kodak." This little fiction establishes the point of view for the whole book. In talking about religion and art today, he implies, one is limited to addressing a feminine sensibility; and the camera suggests the value of pictures to stimulate the emotional response if it should need bolstering. Narrator and niece are summer tourists and so need not take anything too seriously—architecture, theology, history. They may come back simply with a feeling or a picture, but the garrulous uncle reserves the right to slip in some comments on its meaning. The last words in the preface are "the uncle talks:" . . . All that follows is what he says, certainly the most rewarding "running chatter" a niece ever listened to.

Chartres adopts the mode of a travel-guide-book as a literary device in much the same way that the *Education* uses autobiography. The fictional sightseeing trip through the cathedral country of France furnishes at most a mechanical structure. Even this outward form is abandoned midway, the tour proper coming to an end with Chapter 10. The second half of the book is a tour of medieval civilization—its history, poetry, religion, and philosophy—rather than of architectural shrines. So it is a travel book in two ways far transcending a mere guide for tourists. It is an imaginative journey across the *"pons seclorum*, the bridge of ages, between us and our ancestors,'' into the emotional and intellectual world of the Middle Ages, as Adams says in the opening chapter. It is also an attempted pilgrimage, he says near the end, across the *"Pons Sanctorum*—over which only children and saints can pass''—though he undertakes it as a pilgrim of art, not of faith. In part one the stones of architecture are used to build a foundation on which the drama of medieval civilization can be acted out in part two, as a recent critic has pointed out. The architecture provides a vocabulary which becomes metaphor later on. The tour in space becomes a journey in time. The shift from tourist geography to poetic history marks the shift of interest from the two famous shrines of the title to the whole of French medieval culture.

The first part of the book is divided into two distinct sections. Chapters 1–4 are focused on the eleventh century and are concerned with action, the church and state militant. This was the period of the early crusades and the conquest of England. With the zeal of converts the Normans boldly asserted their new faith in the one and only God, not the Trinity or the Virgin. They symbolized the Christian soldier's union with Him in the fortress abbey at Mont-Saint-Michel. The last of these chapters forms an architectural transition from Romanesque to Gothic, and a geographical transit from Normandy to the Ile de France. The second section, Chapter 5–10, is centered on the twelfth century and concerned with feeling, worship of the Virgin as symbolized by the great era of cathedral building that culminated at Chartres. As intercessor, Mary harmonized man's acts with God's will, thus bringing unity out of multiplicity. The two sections differ in that one approaches God directly, the other through love of the Virgin; one expresses its faith in acts, the other in art. But they are more like each other than what follows, since both are simple assertions of unity needing no rational proof.

This alternation between masculine and feminine emphases is reversed in the second part, which likewise divides itself into two sections. Chapters 11–13 are devoted to women and the dominant role they played in the history, poetry, and miracles of the period. These recreate medieval society as reflected in literature and legend. Mary is still a constant referent, but as her power declines she tends to be analyzed as a human and sexual force rather than a divine one. This prepares for the breakdown of intuitive faith in the thirteenth century, the focus of Chapters 14–16. This final section is concerned with reason and the reassertion of unity through the doctrine of the Trinity. The scholastic philosophers did not assume God but tried to prove Him, notably in the *Summa Theologiae* of St. Thomas Aquinas. Yet the conclusion they sought was but the starting point of the eleventh and twelfth centuries. In part one the narrator tries to adopt the medieval viewpoint of feeling and faith. In part two he shifts to the rational analysis of a modern commentator. But both perspectives are present throughout, though the presumed unity achieved by act, intuition and reason in the Middle Ages can be understood by the narrator only aesthetically.

Such is the substantive "argument" of this difficult book. But far more complex patternings enrich its structure and meaning. For Adams said of *Chartres*, in the same letter defining his intent and method in the *Education*, that it too had "not been done in order to teach others, but to educate myself in the possibilities of literary form"—his sole interest being, once again, not the matter, but the style, the structure, and the art of climax. Of the many literary devices employed, one of his most effective is the maneuvering of time. As in the *Education*, *Chartres* also spans three centuries, but each has a differing conception of unity, so that the Middle Ages tend to become a period of motion and flux like any other. To create the illusion of unity artistically (the religious unity of Christian belief being hard for modern man to grasp) he constantly telescopes time, each section of the book displaying all three centuries.

For example, though the solid masculine foundations that make the abbey church distinctive are eleventh-century, its glorious Merveille dates from the twelfth, and its crowning cloister from the thirteenth. Adams insists on the harmony of all three, saying that the "restrained strength of the Romanesque married to the graceful imagination of the Gothic" makes an ideal union. So he can assert dogmatically, "The whole Mount kept the grand style; it expressed the unity of Church and State, God and Man, Peace and War, Life and Death, Good and Bad; it solved the whole problem of the universe. . . . God reconciles all. The world is an evident, obvious, sacred harmony." But further additions to Mont-Saint-Michel were made in the fifteenth century that shattered this harmony, Adams admits, and the only way he can preserve his fiction of unity is to say the Middle Ages had ended long before that date. He makes his point by a prophecy of impending disunity as extravagant as his previous claim of unity had been: "Not till two centuries afterwards did the Mount take on the modern expression of war as a discord in God's providence. . . . [The châtelet] jars on the religion of the place; it forebodes wars of religion; dissolution of society; loss of unity; the end of the world."

Similarly, in the last section, the resort to reason that undermined the unity of a religion based on faith is focused on the great work of Aquinas in the mid-thirteenth century. Yet this tendency is shown to have been under way for a long time, dating back at least to the end of the eleventh when Abélard launched his attack on orthodox theology, using the new weapon of scientific logic. It is true he was defeated ultimately by Bernard, the champion of intuition, and there was a short-lived transition (1140–1200) during which the French mystics tried to reconcile reason and emotion as a dual way to God. Yet it was Abélard's insistence on proving unity that re-emerged more than a century later in Thomism. Thus the forces of disunity were actually at work all during the twelfth century, fixed by Adams as the high point of medieval unity. This glorious period of the Transition, dominated by worship of the Virgin, forms the vital center of his book and provides its artistic unity. Yet it is shown as only an unstable equilibrium of the components of the eleventh century's unquestioning belief and the inroads of rational doubt in the thirteenth. Medieval unity he finally admits was a vision, not a fact. But it was this continuing effort to impose order on chaos, and the faith that it could be done, which distinguished the world of *Chartres* from that of the *Education*.

A far more subtle time strategy is the pervasive ambiguity in Adams' treatment of youth and age, the present world of the tour and the past as embodied in the shrines being visited. The key to the first ten chapters, where he tries to translate himself from modern fact and reason to medieval feeling, is given in a paradox: "The man who wanders into the twelfth century is lost, unless he can grow prematurely young." The contrast is set up in the preface by the fictive tourists themselves, the old uncle and the young niece. This device is most prominent at the beginning of Chapters 1 and 6 and at the conclusion of Chapter 10. It is exactly at these crucial points that the ambiguity of old and young is most emphatic. In the first two (the entrance to the Mount and to Chartres Cathedral) the imaginative act by which the narrator seeks to recover the vision of youth in the Middle Ages is rendered by invoking the famous "Ode: Intimations of Immortality." In the third (just before the tour proper ends) the full effect of the literary parallel is revealed: through it Adams' entrance into medieval religious art is made possible. By becoming a child again—following both Wordsworth and the Biblical prescript for entering the kingdom of heaven—he can at last experience Chartres in its glory. A detailed study of the analogy will prove rewarding.

This ambiguous play back and forth from age to youth is part of the over-all strategy of shifting between objective and subjective modes. The predominance of one over the other is reversed in *Chartres* from what it was in the *Education*. There the style was mainly dry, hard, and sharp because the persona was exploring the unknown, pitting his intellect against the hopeless multiplicity of the modern world. Here the style is mainly warm and lyrical, giving a sense of re-exploring the familiar to recover a lost unity, the beauty of art if not religion in the Middle Ages. Though the narrator pretends at times to concern himself with historical and architectural facts, and so manages to slip in a great many documentary details, he quickly discounts them as of no interest to mere tourists—just as he had dismissed the subjective episodes in the other book as accidental education. Subjectivity is pervasive in the first half of *Chartres*, especially at every crucial point, with the uncle insisting on an emotional response in himself and in his niece. As niece fuses with uncle, so the reader fuses with both. At the outset he declares his purpose is "to catch not a fact but a feeling." And by the end of part one of the tour there is a flat statement that feeling must prevail:

> We have set out to go from Mont-Saint-Michel to Chartres, . . . trying to get, on the way, not technical knowledge; not accurate information; not correct views either on history, art, or religion; not anything that can possibly be useful or instructive; but only a sense of what those centuries had to say, and a sympathy with their ways of saying it.

Then he carefully disavows any devotional intent: "We are not now seeking religion. . . . We are only trying to feel Gothic art."

In the next five chapters, however, as the appeal to emotion is emphasized, the tour is rendered increasingly in religious terms for dramatic effect. By the device of growing prematurely young and learning to feel again, uncle and niece are transformed in gradual stages from modern tourists into medieval pilgrims. Surrounded by the full glory of Chartres Cathedral in "The Court of the Queen of Heaven" (Chapter 10), their identification with the "crowd of kneeling worshippers" becomes complete, and a twelfth-century sacrament is enacted in the present tense. As they lift their eyes "after the miracle of the mass," they see a vision far above the high altar: "There is heaven! and Mary looks down from it, into her church, where she sees us on our knees, and knows each one of us by name. There she actually is—not in symbol or in fancy, but in person." This vision should not be taken as spiritual autobiography, of course. This event took place in Adams' study, not in church. It was created for the sake of its function in the book: a means of access into the medieval world of art and feeling. Even so, the recovery is only transient. As he slips back into the role of twentieth-century tourist, the narrator comments on his "experience" in the past tense:

> It was very childlike, very foolish, very beautiful, and very true—as art, at least; . . . when we rise from our knees now, we have finished our pilgrimage. We have done with Chartres. For seven hundred years Chartres has seen pilgrims, coming and going more or less like us, and will perhaps see them for another seven hundred years; but we shall see it no more, and can safely leave the Virgin in her majesty, . . . looking down from a deserted heaven, into an empty church, on a dead faith.

The literary brilliance of this fictive scene consists in the blasphemous shock of dropping the narrator's spiritual progress at its climactic moment. Thereafter the personal story becomes secondary. But the vision has enabled the twentieth-century tourist to see beyond architectural surfaces and so to understand the drama that was acted out between the eleventh and thirteenth centuries.

This is the substance of the second part of *Chartres*. There the mode of presentation changes radically, as Levenson has demonstrated. The action of moving from one architectural shrine to another, which gave the structure to part one, was no longer possible when he turned to exploring the monuments of literature and philosophy, to show how religion permeated medieval society and held it together in a unity. Similarly the narrator's role shifts, and the speaking uncle subsides into a choric figure commenting on the human actors as they perform their parts on the stage of the medieval imagination. It was easier to make their actions dramatic when they were drawn from actual history, as in Chapter 11. This one, "The Three Queens," serves the additional purpose of linking the two halves of the book, as the narrator points out, by "the coincidence that while the Virgin was miraculously using the power of spiritual love to elevate and purify the people, Eleanor and her daughters were using the power of earthly love to discipline and refine the courts." Even when the characters were drawn from fiction and legend he could let them speak from texts that were inherently dramatic, as in the next two chapters showing the dominance of women in secular poetry and the Virgin's pervasive influence in popular accounts of her miracles. But the philosophic texts that were his only documents for the last triad of chapters offered meager possibilities, Levenson continues, and more ingenious tactics were necessary to dramatize his conclusion. For the conflict of reason and intuition, he does not hesitate to invent an imaginary debate between Abélard and his opponents. For the final scholastic synthesis, he avoids a formal analysis of Aquinas' writings and interprets them instead as an elaborate metaphor: a Church Intellectual that paralleled the design of the Church Architectural. And by showing its builder in the process of creating his philosophic edifice, he makes a heroic effort to translate theology into drama.

As the talking uncle becomes more and more a commentator on the main action of medieval history in part two, he becomes less and less aware of his listening niece. But the narrator-auditor device is picked up again in the last chapter to round out the tour. There, in comparing the *Summa Theologiae* to a Gothic cathedral, he declares that the equilibrium of each structure is precarious, showing "the visible effort to throw off a visible strain":

> Faith alone supports it, and if Faith fails, Heaven is lost. . . . The delight of its aspirations is flung up to the sky.

> The pathos of its self-distrust and anguish of doubt is buried in
> the earth as its last secret. You can read out of it whatever
> pleases your youth and confidence; to me, this is all.

So the book ends with the uncle resuming his proper role as the rational
old man, but not without a challenge to his niece, and all who are young
enough, to find if they can a new faith that will unify their world.

If historians rebuke Adams because his concept of medieval unity
does not fit the facts, scientists and theologians balk even more at his
proposition that St. Thomas' introduction of reason into religion paved
the way for Newton and modern multiplicity. It is argued outright in
"The Virgin and the Dynamo," urged suggestively in *Chartres*. Both the
Summa and the late Gothic cathedral, he says in the latter, were "ex-
cessively modern, scientific, and technical"; yet the result was "an art
marked by singular unity, which endured and served its purpose until
man changed his attitude toward the universe." The medieval vision of
unity reached its peak and began its decline simultaneously in the rationalism of the thirteenth century. "From that time, the universe has
steadily become more complex and less reducible to a central control."

Adams was clearly more interested in his art than in his argument.
For despite his complaint that the literary form of *Chartres* (like that of
the *Education*) fails toward the end, as the fictional device of the tour
gives way to three essays on the scholastic synthesis from Abélard to
Aquinas, he was never more artful than in these final chapters. Under the
pretense of expounding theology, he creates in them a drama of the
debates illustrating the movement from instinct to reason during the Middle Ages, an ideological counterpart of the architectural metaphor of the
transition from Romanesque to Gothic. So they complete the artistic unity
of his tour of the French cathedrals, forming a capstone to the structure of
Chartres. At the same time they provide the link with his next book. The
pilgrim, again turned tourist, continues his journey beyond the last page
right back into the modern world of doubt and loss, and we next hear him
speaking as the persona of the *Education*. In a letter to another and
greater creator of fictions, Henry James, he made explicit this relation
between the two books:

> I note for your exclusive use the intent of the literary art-
> ist—*c'est moi!*—to make this volume a completion and
> mathematical conclusion from the previous volume about the
> Thirteenth Century,—the three concluding chapters of this be-
> ing only a working out to Q.E.D. of the three concluding
> chapters of that.

It is when they are read thus, as sequels, that *Mont-Saint-Michel and
Chartres* and *The Education of Henry Adams* seem most fully what they
are—created works of art.

"Henry Adams: The Limitations of Science"

Howard M. Munford*

I

Concerned more than any other figure of the America of his genera-tion with the whole reach of science, Henry Adams toward the end of his life expressed the results in his culminating "dynamic theory of history." He announced the theory in his presidential communication to the American Historical Association in 1894, played variations on the theme in his two late pamphlets, "The Rule of Phase Applied to History" and "A Letter to American Teachers of History," but gave it its fullest formula-tion in the final chapters of *The Education*. It seems strange that this book, starting out autobiographically, and which, like Franklin's *Autobiography*, we are told, was designed to serve as a handbook for young men, should culminate on this abstract level. The explanation un-doubtedly is that Adams wanted to force his readers, the young men of the dawning century, to come to terms with the most pervasive influence in their world. Regardless of the social role they might find themselves play-ing, they could not be effective without a fundamental understanding of the nature of science. Yet one must add another failure, probably his greatest, to Adams's own record of frustrated aspirations. The new men of the twentieth century have almost totally misunderstood the lesson he would have had them learn.

Most readers have seen the theory as Adams's effort to apply the laws of physical science to the course of history. Historians especially have tended to read it as a serious effort to convert history into a science, while expressing, frequently, from their present-day relativistic approach, the futility of such an attempt. The more discerning have been rightly mystified that such a critical and informed intelligence should have gone down the sterile way of scientism. "How did it happen," asked Carl Becker, "that a mind so critical of all religious and political dogmas could have accepted so readily, so naïvely, the dogmas of natural science?" An

*Reprinted from *The Southern Review*, N.S. 4 (Winter, 1968), 59–71.

unquestioning confidence in the generalizations of science is indeed inconsistent with everything we know of Adams.

Some recent appraisals by literary scholars are more discerning. Sensitive to the strategies of art and shades of irony they are in the process of seeing the main effort of Adams's later work as being directed actually toward opposing the excessive claims of science in the interest of doing justice to and reasserting other more vital claims of human experience. Ernest Samuels in the final volume of his superb three volume biography sees Adams as trying to "impale [science] on its own dilemmas and contradictions." J. C. Levenson sees the dynamic theory as being chiefly heuristic, designed "to stimulate younger men and make them seek better answers than his own." Samuels, however, questions the soundness of Adams's understanding of science and his grasp of the problems involved, concluding that his theory falls finally into incoherence because he could not "state his problem or wholly know what he himself meant." One can appreciate Samuels' conclusion in light of Adams's exasperatingly involved procedures in *The Education*, but aspects of the dynamic theory which have not been sufficiently considered indicate that Adams did know what he meant, and what he meant would come close to satisfying the most hard-headed and rigorous of contemporary critics of science.

Adams was himself to blame for the misreading. Any inquiry pushed to its limits, he had found, inevitably leads to contradiction. He developed his method of speaking in paradox to express this fundamental truth. Moreover, he found himself resorting to the standard method of art of saying one thing in terms of another but compounded the difficulty by seeming to assert the truth of both terms of the formulation even though one negated the other. Irony suited the temper of his mind, but this was irony prolonged and elaborated to an extent that was to tax the understanding and try the patience of even the most attentive and sympathetic readers. Temperament and mannerism account, perhaps, for some of this but, actually, Adams found himself resorting to extremes of irony and paradox because of a peculiar position he was in with regard to the question of science and the extent of its hegemony. Looking back on his earlier work as an historian, he had come to realize that he had made an enormous mistake. He had somehow to rectify that mistake, convey what he had subsequently come to see, and no ordinary means would be adequate.

In his monumental *History of the United States* Adams had made a supreme effort to convert history into a science by trying to detect the universal laws determining the course of history. The theme which unites the nine volumes is the discrepancy between what Jefferson, Madison, and Monroe wanted and tried to do and what they had to do. History's solutions to America's problems went counter to the most deeply held beliefs and strenuous endeavors of these early Americans.

To the extent that he was the child of his age, Adams should have been gratified with this seemingly necessary conclusion. The advanced thought of the time was insisting with increasing emphasis that science could and should be applied to any and all phenomena including man, society, and the course of history. There was no logical reason for divorcing the laws of human development from the laws governing the rest of the universe. If atoms and molecules blindly run, as Whitehead observed characterizing nineteenth-century thought on the matter, and man is composed of atoms and molecules, why then, man also blindly runs. But even as Adams was drawing together the results of his vast and painstaking investigation and giving *The History* its final form, he was appalled at the measure of his apparent success. The protagonists of his historical drama, he said unhappily in a letter, were "like mere grass-hoppers kicking and gesticulating on the middle of the Mississippi River. . . . They were carried along on a stream which floated them, after a fashion, without much regard to themselves. . . . I am almost sorry that I ever undertook to write the History." Yet, however unwillingly, he carried *The History* through to completion on the lines seemingly dictated by the evidence. He had too much invested to let it drop. Moreover, he was uncertain at this point about what had gone wrong although he was beginning to feel what he later, in 1901, confessed to Henry Osborn Taylor: "Never did a man go blind on a career more virtuously than I did."

Adams seems to have been registering his dismay at what he was doing in the novel he wrote in deepest secrecy while in the process of working on his *History*. *Esther* (1884) is a study of the feminine sensibility cast adrift in a world where the old values have been dissolved by science and whose deepest cravings can find no satisfactions in the new dispensation. "I care more for one chapter, or any dozen pages of *Esther*," Adams wrote in 1891, "than for the whole history."

Adams was indeed on the horns of an intolerable dilemma. The weight of scientific evidence behind the vision of the universe imposed upon the modern consciousness seemed overwhelming, yet, as with Esther, the instinctual, emotional side of his nature revolted. How could he continue to contribute to a view of the universe and human nature toward which he was so deeply antipathetic? "All a historian won was a vehement wish to escape," as he later confessed, yet his restless, inquiring intelligence, his obsessive desire to understand the world and his place in it would permit no escape. Adams finally resolved the dilemma by immersing himself even more deeply in the question and painfully working his way through the corpus of the latest scientific thought until he came out on the other side. He came out into a post-Newtonian universe with a view which no longer necessarily involved the pessimistic conclusions of the earlier world view of science and which, fully understood, indicated what had been wrong with his earlier methods and assumptions.

II

On the most obvious level, the dynamic theory is a report on the course of contemporary developments. Adams must have had himself in mind when he describes in *The Education* the kind of newspaperman who is "more than most men a double personality; and his person feels best satisfied in its double instincts when writing in one sense and thinking in another." Adams was, in an important sense, this kind of reporter, as Levenson has remarked. He was witnessing and recording a revolution in society and the lives of men, and he saw where this revolution was destined to lead if it continued along the lines already established.

After observing the movement of science, then, he submitted his report. The dominant pattern was that of the release and utilization of power. The development of the mechanical energies of steam and electricity and, at the time Adams was writing, of the new energies of radioactivity, was determining the course of social development, and these energies were multiplying at a speed of "vertiginous violence" which spelled ultimate disaster on a global scale. These energies were manifesting themselves in giant industrial complexes which were "wrenching" the American mind out of old directions into new ones of the utmost inhumanity. The young man who wished to participate in these developments would have to be "educated" accordingly; he must therefore himself be regarded as "a certain form of energy; the object to be gained" in such an education was "economy of his force." To this extent the individual *was* under the dominion of the mechanical laws of science.

Adams, however, was writing one way and not only thinking but feeling another, and he expressed his feelings unambiguously. In the chapter of *The Education*, "The Grammar of Science," where he describes the universe as science explains it, his most emphatically expressed conclusion is that "He repudiated all share in the world as it was to be, and yet he could not detect the point where his responsibility began or ended." Not only in this passage, but throughout the rest of the book, his extreme revulsion of feeling toward what he saw and what he himself was ostensibly doing is unmistakable. But in light of this revulsion of feeling, he worries about what his responsibility is. The question posed by the dynamic theory is in what respects it fulfills his responsibility in the face of his own recognition of the way in which science was producing a kind of society which outraged the instinctual and emotional side of his nature.

The purpose of *The Education* is avowedly didactic. He is trying to present a "working model" for education. He had it heavily on his conscience that the teacher affects eternity and "never knows where his influence stops." The terms in which Adams, in his role of teacher, conveys the lesson to be learned from the theory indicates the way in which he intended it to influence the future and fulfill his responsibility.

In the final chapter, Adams states the lesson he would have his "scholars" learn. His dynamic theory, he says, "tended to encourage foresight and to economize waste of mind. If it was not itself education, it pointed out the economies necessary for the education of the new American." Not in itself the sum of education, the theory indicated the kind of education which the new Americans must achieve if they were to succeed in the terms provided by the world in which they lived, or, as he says elsewhere, if their minds were "to react, not at haphazard, but by choice, on the lines of force that attract their world." The terms provided by the twentieth century world were wholly scientific and industrial.

Here the reader must keep in mind Adams's habits of irony. Throughout the development of his theory Adams has been pointing out that the forces he has been reporting are multiplying at a rate which threatens catastrophe. If the young men learn, as they should according to this view, how to "diminish friction, invigorate the energy" so as to get in line with these forces and contribute to their movement, they are hastening that very catastrophe. The education he is ostensibly presenting as a model for the American born into the new century is right from one point of view, the point of view of success, but frightfully ominous from another.

Adams alerts the reader to the double-edged nature of his prescription by wryly remarking that "naturally such an attitude annoyed the players in the game." Elsewhere he says, "Historians were not exempt from the passion of baiting their bears." Of course! The new Americans, the scientists, the captains of industry, managers of the new technology, and those bent on succeeding in the age's terms would not appreciate being told that their efforts were rapidly bringing them in sight of their own doom and that the more successful they were, the sooner the end would come. As a Harvard professor he had in his history seminars engaged in the method of outrageous statement to court opposition and stimulate discussion. Perhaps he hoped the same method would be effective in this book designed to be a handbook for the young men of the new society.

There is a confusing term he uses to describe himself and his poetic friends, Bay Lodge and Trumbull Stickney. They were, he said, "conservative Christian anarchists." Adams uses the term rather playfully to convey several contradictory attitudes, but what he meant by calling himself an anarchist is clear enough. "As anarchist . . . he was bound to accelerate progress; to concentrate energy; to accumulate power; to multiply and intensify forces; to reduce friction, increase velocity and magnify momentum, partly because this was the mechanical law of the universe as science explained it; but partly also *in order to get done with the present which artists and some others complained of.*" (My emphasis). There is nothing in the new scientific, industrial order a humane and sensitive man would wish to preserve. The impending catastrophe would destroy the new order and give man a chance to return to primitive beginnings.

The very terms he uses in this passage as a means of "getting done with the present" are the same terms he uses to describe the kind of education the young man of the new America needs if he is to succeed. The irony of the formulation on this level is unmistakable and takes on the proportions of a hoax. In this way he baited his bears.

III

Baiting bears satisfies one's instinct for sport; it is "amusing," to use one of Adams's favorite words, but how does it fulfill one's responsibility, particularly if one sees himself playing the role of teacher? What is the lesson he would have had his "scholars" finally learn?

A phrase from the passage previously quoted in which Adams expresses his anarchistic impulse indicates the most significant aspect of the theory, the one through which he is fulfilling his responsibility as teacher and critic. The young man who followed the prescription for education he had ironically given and who would therefore all unconsciously, perhaps, find himself playing the role of anarchist would like Adams himself be "bound to accelerate progress . . . *partly because this was the mechanical law of the universe as science explained it.*" (My emphasis.) Attention is focused on the nature of scientific explanation.

The subtlest part of the theory lies right here. Adams presents it in such a way as to raise the whole question of the epistemology of science; he phrases it in a way to provoke the attentive reader to question the validity of his assumptions and the nature of his method. To the extent that he was being scientific, one would be forced to question the validity and assumptions and nature of science itself.

Adams was formulating his theory in the period characterized by Whitehead as being "one of the dullest stages of thought since the time of the First Crusade . . . because it was an age of successful scientific orthodoxy undisturbed by much thought beyond the conventions." The philosophy of science, as we construe that term today, had scarcely made an appearance. A naïve realism characterized the thought of the scientists to the extent that they considered the epistemological problem at all. The concepts of science, it was believed, provided the "true" picture of the real world. Or, as Abel Rey, the French historian and philosopher of science, summed up the situation: "Traditional physics . . . ascribed to its theories an ontologic value, and these theories were all mechanistic. Traditional mechanistic physics was supposed above and beyond the results of experience, to be the *real* cognition of the material universe. This conception was not a hypothetical description of our experience; it was dogma."

Adams, with his sense of the main issues of the modern world, quickly found his way to those four thinkers who were beginning to challenge this orthodoxy. *The Education* records the centrality of J. B.

Stallo, Ernst Mach, Henri Poincaré, and Karl Pearson for the determination of Adams's final position. Different as these challengers of scientific orthodoxy were in important respects, what they did have in common, and what Adams fastened upon, was their assertion of the provisional and subjective nature of scientific concepts. With almost shocked incredulity he read Pearson's *The Grammar of Science* and learned that his and the world's assumptions about scientific truth had apparently been false. Pearson, Stallo, Mach, and Poincaré indicated that the so-called scientific laws which the world, including the scientists, had thought of as representing the unveiling and explaining of an objective order of reality and of being cognitions of the universe were nothing of the sort. They were "fictions" or "conventions," devices of thought, inventions, tools for achieving certain desired results. What they revealed was man's desires and what they chiefly explained was the mind of man.

"Is science true?" plaintively asks Esther. "No," replies Strong, her scientist friend. "Then why do you believe in it?" "I don't believe in it," he replies. "Then why do you belong to it?" "Because," he says, "I want to help in making it true."

Adams in his dynamic theory was indirectly but centrally doing just this: trying to show in what respects science is or is not true. He constructed an elaborate theory ostensibly "scientific" to explain the course of history. What has been insufficiently noticed is how Adams, at every step in the process, carefully calls attention to the limitations of the method he is pursuing and the special, restricted nature of the "truth" he appears to be promulgating. He invites, he deliberately tries to provoke, the reader's skepticism toward what Rey called the "ontologic value" of his own theory, and by implication, all scientific theory.

He begins the process in the Editor's Preface bearing Lodge's name but written by himself. He quotes a passage from *The Education* in this preface which he therefore indicates is of central importance. "Any schoolboy," the quoted passage begins, "could see that man as a force must be measured by motion from a fixed point." Later, in the same passage he points out that in developing his theory, he is not "assuming anything as true or untrue, except relation." The passage concludes by saying the theory is "subject to correction from any one who should know better." Already he has invited the reader to raise questions about his main assumptions and the nature of his theory.

One is the huge and really unfounded assumption on which the "schoolboy" bases his theory, that man is a force which can be measured mechanically. He asks his readers to recognize this when, in a passage later in the book, in which he announces his intention of framing a dynamic theory, he reverts to the schoolboy image and says, "Any schoolboy could work out his own problem if he were given the right to state it in his own terms." Adams, like the schoolboy, arbitrarily selects his own terms. Other terms could be selected and another explanation devised if the choice were different. As he says elsewhere, there are "indefinite possible orbits" which could be assumed and used.

All through the development of his theory he puts the reader on his guard in this way. Chapter XXXIII, which is devoted to the theory, begins by stating: "A dynamic theory, like most theories, begins by begging the question." It is with this warning which in effect says flatly he is making his basic assumptions wholly without proof and assuming in advance the answers he is ostensibly seeking, that he prefaces the statement central to his theory: "Man is a force." In the second paragraph of the same chapter, in asserting that man is controlled by natural forces, he again says this is something he "takes for granted." If the framers of "the atomic theory; the correlation and conservation of energy; the mechanical theory of the universe; the kinetic theory of gases, and Darwin's Law of Natural Selection," could build up "so many and such vast theories on such narrow foundations as to shock the conservative and delight the foolish," he could do likewise.

In the second place, Adams assumes nothing "as true or untrue except relation." Throughout he keeps repeating that his dynamic theory is not to be taken as true in any objective sense. Discussing the intention of the theory he says, "One sought no absolute truth. One sought only a spool on which to wind the thread of history without breaking it." At the conclusion of Chapter XXXIII he states that whatever value the theory has "is wholly one of convenience." In what sense, then, is the theory meant to be true? Adams wants his readers to see it is only a device which he uses to achieve certain anticipated results and its only test is convenience for his own purpose.

Furthermore, in announcing his attempt at a dynamic theory Adams says he is going to "*invent* a formula of his own for *his* universe." (My emphasis.) That phrase holds the key: the consciously subjective nature of what he was doing. The explanation which he may provide will have to be "invented," not discovered, and it is everywhere insinuated that this is true of the formulae and concepts of science.

He is direct enough when he concludes that "the scientists had reduced their universe to a series of relations to themselves." In referring to the new scientific order he comments, "Man knew it was true because he made it and he loved it for the same reason." His most explicit statement along this line comes in the late pamphlet, "The Rule of Phase," in which he was continuing to play with his dynamic theory: "Religion," he wrote, "is the projection of mind into nature in one direction, as science is the projection of mind into nature in another. In neither case does, or can, the mind reach anything but a different reflection of its own features."

As a child of the eighteenth century who "greatly preferred his eighteenth-century education when God was a father and nature a mother, and all was for the best in a scientific universe," it was an agonizing lesson finally to be forced to accept the implications of his new understanding of the nature and limitations of science. Gone was any possibility of science's revealing objective truth; gone was any possibility of its revealing an order or unity inherent in the universe. He had sadly to face the existentialist situation and conclude that logically all one could assume was "Chaos is the law of nature, order is the dream of man."

These seemingly pessimistic conclusions, however, provided Adams the opportunity of resolving the dilemma he had faced in writing the *History*. He had been trying to be scientific on the terms provided by the scientific orthodoxy of the nineteenth century. On these terms he had been forced to treat man as a helpless instrument of universal natural law. His new view of science no longer made necessary the deterministic conclusions logically involved in the earlier assumptions.

Man, according to his later view, is an active, interested being whose relations to the universe are true to the extent that he is concerned about them. The nature of his chief concerns will determine the kind of order he creates. His chief concern in the previous two centuries had been, as *The Education* makes clear, the creation and wielding of power which had resulted in the scientific-industrial order of the twentieth century. On one level, the dynamic theory seems to be saying this order has been produced by the inhuman working out of inexorable forces. On this other level, man is actually an agent of nothing but his own interests. For the young man of the new century to accept these forces as inexorable and to become their agent is to deny his own humanity.

This view seems to indicate that Adams was in the process of going down the road to that form of idealism which plagues the modern consciousness. With the waning of traditional beliefs and the development of the idea that man's relation to objective reality is factual only to the extent he is concerned about it, objective reality tends to dissolve and nothing is left but the ego. At that point, as T. S. Eliot was fond of remarking, the ego assumes an enormous and alarming importance. Adams did not go that far. He may have discarded the naïve realism of Newton, Bacon, and Darwin, he may have become convinced of the subjective nature of scientific knowledge and religion, but he was still painfully aware there was a reality outside of himself with which he and society must contend. His deep social concern, his sense that he was a man acting in and for the world out of the world's need, precluded the solipsistic conclusion.

Adams's idea was close to that being formulated by Santayana at about the same time. Santayana was to say that modern philosophy teaches our idea of the so-called real world is a product of the imagination. The question is which imaginative system one will trust. He thought no system is to be wholly trusted, including that of science, but all systems can be used and, up to a point, trusted as symbols. Science expresses our dynamic relation to surrounding reality. Philosophies and religions, where they do not misrepresent these same dynamic relations, express destiny in moral dimensions by using mythical and poetic images. This is essentially Adams's point in his assertion that religion and science are projections of the mind into nature in different directions.

Lewis Mumford could well have been recapitulating Adams's point of view when he said, in an address in 1956: "We deceive ourselves if we believe that this technological civilization, this so-called atomic age, is purely the product of external circumstances and forces, independent of the human will . . . . The world is in fact a wish-fulfillment, attached partly to a normal desire for order, for power, for knowledge, and partly to a neurotic [sic] desire for security . . . along with paranoid delusions of grandeur and desires for domination. In any event, the self out of which our machine-conditioned culture sprang was not the whole self: like all the other transformations of man it brought forth and expressed only a part of man's . . . possibilities." That Adams was fully aware of an aspect of man's nature not expressed in the scientific-industrial order and victimized by that order is amply manifest in his celebration of woman and what she stands for in the companion-piece to The Education, Mont-Saint-Michel and Chartres.

This view raises a question. The present scientific industrial order senselessly multiplying power at a rate rapidly bringing us toward ultimate catastrophe has been produced by man's desire for power. Is Adams suggesting that although man is responsible for his own world he is also immutably its victim? The pessimistic air which pervades The Education suggests this, but another possibility is left open. From his treatment of the masculine-feminine theme we are made aware of other equally vital concerns of man. Where the industrial order, a manifestation of the masculine principle, has created "a country-side filled with scrap iron, scrap paper, and cinders," the twelfth century, when the feminine influence had been paramount, had produced man's greatest art and "left every remote village strewn with fragments which flashed like jewels." What possibilities remained for the artistic and feminine side of man's nature to produce an order more humanly satisfying than the scientific?

In 1910, in a letter, he gave his not very positive answer: "My idea is that the world outside, the so-called modern world can only pervert and degrade the conceptions of the primitive instinct of art and feeling, and that our only chance is to accept the limited number of our survivors—the one-in-a-thousand of born artists and poets and to intensify the energy of feeling within that radiant center."

Adams's view of science does open the possibility of redoing, remaking, reforming the world in light of consciously held human aims to which imaginative fictions and forms could give emotional and aesthetic support. This is, it seems, the chief significance of his dynamic theory: clearing the way for a possible reordering of society along more humane and emotionally satisfying lines than those provided by an uncritical acceptance of the order provided by science.

"Henry Adams and the Art of Politics"

J. C. Levenson*

The Henry Adams of the reading public seems almost too various to be real: he covers a full 180 degrees from politician *manqué* to master of symbolist art. But the two extreme positions can be said, after all, to lie in a simple straight line. The idea of politics as an art clarifies at once Adams's relation to twentieth-century estheticism and to his eighteenth-century political inheritance. More particularly, the idea of the politician as artist discloses the vital bond between the narrator and his subject-matter in the *Education*. Thus Henry Adams the historian, over years of thought and study, came to have more and more reservations about his grandfather's actual career in politics, but Henry Adams the didactic autobiographer presented his highest model of civic man in the figure of this same grandparent. In the familiar anecdote from the *Education*, John Quincy Adams enacts a fable of "negative capability" as he puts down his six-year-old grandson's rebellion and takes the unwilling boy to school. As the story is put, the great spokesman of freedom suppresses the "inalienable rights of boys," but acting out such a contradiction as might have wrecked his moral and rational world, he plays his role admirably—in silence, without irritable reaching after fact and reason, without temper or cant. In the *Education*, the political artistry of such exemplary figures as John Quincy Adams, Thurlow Weed, or John Hay is artistry indeed: it rests upon disinterested perception of what is; accepting what the eye sees, the artist in politics learns to negate subjectivity, to give up preconceptions, to live with mysteries that outreach logic. And the family likeness of the political and the artistic imagination is evident in other ways. Adams's painter friend La Farge, for instance, educates by the very fact of his easily "carrying different shades of contradiction in his mind"; the lesson Adams draws is that "the mind resorts to reason for want of training." Moreover, politician and painter, in Adams's view, share an intellectual characteristic with the scientist, whose procedures depend on "self-restraint, obedience, sensitiveness to impulse from without." All three types resemble each other and, naturally enough, the

*Reprinted from *The Southern Review*, N.S. 4 (Winter, 1968), 50–58.

"historian" protagonist who conceives the three in accordance with his canons of education. But the "historian" of the *Education* is different from the professional scholar who in fact wrote the *History*, just as the presidential grandfather of the *Education* is different from the John Quincy Adams of political actuality. In the fable, said the fabulist, "the tailor adapts the manikin as well as the clothes to his patron's wants"—except that half a century after Carlyle, the clothes philosophy was being replaced by an art philosophy.

Passive perception, the quality shared by artists and other men of achievement, accounts for one side of Adams's ideal intellectual hero, but not for all. Even when obstacles to seeing are cleared away, there is danger that experience may accumulate merely "inert facts." The negative virtue is not enough. What is needed more, Adams argues, is the active, or "reactive," mind. Reaction is what he tries to teach the young, though action comes more naturally to them. The condition of such action may be energy or illusion, naïve self-assertiveness or doctrinaire commitment. Only an occasional Thurlow Weed, the perfect political manager, could keep self out of the game and undeluded by high claims or causes, play men like cards, each at his relative value. For most, purposeful action seems to be lost with the passage of time. The young are fortunate in their unity of vision. In Adams's words, "the mania for handling all the sides of every question, looking into every window, and opening every door, was, as Bluebeard judiciously pointed out to his wives, fatal to their practical usefulness in society." The *Education* ambiguously suggests that the uncomplicated life in which "every problem had a solution," was the eighteenth century, historically considered, as well as youth, subjectively remembered. Certainly the perceiver changes at least as much as his object: "The older the mind, the older its complexities, and the further it looks, the more it sees, until even the stars resolve themselves into multiples. . . ."

The complex mind in the pluralistic universe is not, however, doomed to helpless passivity. By calculating his drift, a man may learn to choose his direction. Attuning his responsiveness to higher and higher forces, he may invent and try out working patterns of experience. So the artist-politician sees a chance for international accord and seizes the moment for restricting violence. So, in a different way, the artist-historian glimpses a configuration in the way he has felt his world and invents a "dynamic theory" to express his vision. To establish an organized peace or a general theory by which to educate future peacemakers—such are the imaginative designs which old men may secretly nourish. The assertion of vital will is different from that of a "Gargantua-Napoleon-Bismarck," the measure of youthful ambition. Old men, their eyes trained upon the distant stars, no longer measure their ambition by the great bells of Notre Dame.

But the works of the constitutive imagination are fragile. Try John

Hay's Open Door, for example, and it comes off on its hinges. Try Henry Adams's historical formulas, and whatever you find them to be, they are not science. Try science itself, and Adams will quote the scientist's disclaimer to having found unchangeable truths: "All that we win is a battle—lost in advance—with the irreversible phenomena in the background of nature." After the clearing away of egoistic distortions, after the reactive apprehension of the world, and after the imaginative leap to an idea of order, the only certainty is ultimate failure. Strongly as Adams puts the case for Hay's political artistry or his own boldly sketched historical generalizations, he leaves no doubt that the real work never is, but always to be done. Death, not completion, sets the end to labor and life.

Education, then, proceeds in Adams's dialectic from ignorance and egoism to perception and synthesis, though with failure in some sense the final word. But if the effort to run order through chaos cannot hope for a permanent victory, its value is real nonetheless. Despite the end in failure, the pattern is not morbid. Adams establishes a heroic and tragic conception of intellectual man which replaces—or, better, transforms—a heroic and illusory conception of political man that was his eighteenth-century heritage. His figure of the artist as hero fits the twentieth-century as he presented it and as we have had to live in it, but the artist-hero is not, in this case, one more instance of the esthetic movement. As a model of responsible intelligence in politics, this figure reminds us that Adams was revising for the new age his oldest ancestral beliefs. Indeed, if we wish to understand how radical the change and how essential the continuity, we must look back to his earlier work and resee it in the light of the later.

What we discover in looking backward is that the dialectic of the *Education* can be a useful guide to Adams's own development. His being born, as he said, in the eighteenth century, accounted for his first political philosophy. This centered on the ideal of the statesman, an aristocrat by nature, whose governance derived from character and training rather than from vested feudal powers. Henry Adams evoked an old Adams-Jefferson relation when he described the simple industrial classes, agriculture, handwork, and learning, as having always resisted the nineteenth-century forces of change which were "capitalistic, centralizing, and mechanical." The old leadership enforced—with the consent of the governed—the moral law, right reason, and the United States constitution. Of the New England worthies of his father's generation, Henry Adams observed: ". . . They were statesmen, not politicians; they guided public opinion, but were little guided by it." Reasoning *a priori* from the laws of Nature and of Nature's God, such doctrinaire leaders seemed to impose their will on history.

Seemed to impose their will on history, the *Education* would have us say; but the young Henry Adams took a less ironic view of his eighteenth-century Arcadia. In the *History*, the election of 1800 is treated as having voted out the age of statesmanship: Jefferson, the last American leader whose individual actions can shape the course of national development, follows public opinion and virtually dismantles the government. To the historian, Jefferson failed of responsible statesmanship most evidently in not sticking to his preconceived ideas of strict construction; Jefferson's not pressing for a constitutional amendment to confirm the Louisiana Purchase was in the *History* an instance of moral slackness, although Henry Adams might later have seen this as measuring the drift and holding one's tongue in the face of contradictions.

The author of the *History* dispensed justice with little mercy. For hastening the end of the moral law and the Constitution, Jefferson was a failed hero; for trying to brandish America's puny power in the grand-scale contests of Napoleonic Europe, Jefferson was a mock hero; at best, he had a post-heroic individual importance only because he represented an American type. The transition from statesmanship to social typicality was truly revolutionary. For though the "reign of politics" in the national consciousness did not end at once, social history was now what counted. The American people gradually filled the vacuum left by the cutting down of government: they placidly defeated the Burr conspiracy by ignoring it; they solved the problem of geographic overextension by moving steadily westward and by producing from their ranks the inventors who transformed rivers into steamboat highways; by their technical adaptability and their resources of leadership, they survived the test of war. As statesmanship became less effective, the American people became more important in the shaping of history. The heroic view gave way to the patriotic, the democratic, the scientific, and the historian turned his attention from the conduct of affairs to the "economical evolution of a great democracy." Adams's nationalism made the *History* more of a rising than a falling action. But in his adjustment to the passing of the statesman ideal, he seemed tacitly to adopt the very theory which he elsewhere disapproved, namely, that the American democracy could accomplish by popular action what hitherto had always been the responsibility of government. In the course of writing the *History*, he put less and less emphasis on the side of Jefferson which envisioned a positive program of social development under national political leadership. Instead, he seemed to accept a laissez-faire theory of politics as not only a fact of American life, but very much a benign fact. He made his great work the obituary of political history and an invitation to evolutionary social science.

In this respect, the *History* is Henry Adams's farewell to politics in much the same way that *Democracy*, as H. D. Aiken argues, is his farewell to reform. In his temporary abandonment of an eighteenth-century civic conscience, he came abreast of his times, as we like to say. The well-adjusted historian gave his moral proxy to evolutionary science, and admitted anxiety only on the questions that genteel cultivation might raise. He concluded his final volume by suggesting that the remaining unknowns of American progress were chiefly the problems of unpurged manners, material affluence, and cultural mediocrity. What he neglected to hint at was a subject he knew as well as anyone then alive, that post-Jeffersonian laissez-faire made possible new, vast concentrations of power which wholly changed the social basis of American democracy. The first effect of his giving up ideological politics was general acquiescence.

If anyone ever lacked the acquiescent temper, however, it was Adams. Belief in inevitable, unguidable, cosmic progress was out of character for him; he entertained the idea—it should be noted—during the years after his wife's death when his spirit ran lowest. Then, as his nineteenth-century world showed signs of collapse, he began to cheer up considerably. The Panic of 1893 and its political consequence, the triumph of McKinley, helped give him a new surge of vitality. His talks with Brooks Adams re-started historical speculation, the triumphant gold standard taught him that industrial capitalism had vanquished agrarianism forever, he learned to see in the American landscape, how "agriculture had made way for steam; tall chimneys reeked smoke on every horizon, and dirty suburbs filled with scrap-iron, scrap-paper and cinders, formed the setting of every town." In such a world he gave up at last his eighteenth-century model of the ideal state and accepted as given the new forces which made up the empire of Coal: Big Business and government regulation, Big Labor and the welfare state. Democracy in the old egalitarian, decentralized meaning of the term was no longer a possible issue. American agrarianism was like the utopian anarchism which he termed "a bourgeois dream of order and inertia." Given the actual clash of terrific forces, the relevant political questions had less to do with democracy than with keeping the peace. No one could dismantle the industrial machine or fend off its incursions on both liberty and law. But the forces might be controlled. Whether socially managed power be called socialistic did not matter; for his American readers, Adams saw, a more understandable and less offensive term might be McKinleyism— "The system of combinations, consolidations, trusts, realized at home, realizable abroad." And domestic policy being so nearly settled, the crucial problems lay abroad.

International conflict was the ultimate challenge to foresight, management, and political deftness. Greater organization was the constant alternative to greater risk of catastrophe, and so long as intercontinental disaster was staved off, it would be because either military or industrial force organized an international system. For America, as Adams saw it, the choice between gunpower and peaceable industry as the basis of an ordered world was the crucial choice.

The choice was real, and the task of controlling the forces could be reasonably undertaken. When we ask what gave Adams his idea of possibility, what made him think that even in the twentieth-century multiverse the political art could still be effective, the answer lies in his having developed a new idea of what the mind could do. The answer is suggested in his prescription for the administrator he wanted, a man with "medieval qualities of energy and will." It is suggested more clearly still in his dissociating himself from the prevailing commitment to acquisitiveness and political jobbery all around: his own commitment, he averred, was to "medieval pursuits like politics and poetry." He had progressed from the doctrinaire Puritan rationalism of his ancestors through a faith in democratic progress which was, I have contended, insufficiently critical; and in his now becoming committed to politics again, he started with new conceptions, developed in his study of the Middle Ages. In the course of writing *Mont-Saint-Michel and Chartres*, he first worked out his ideas of education. The Normans, as he then saw them, showed the naïve energy of the young, and twelfth-century Frenchmen, still more wonderfully, repaid the Virgin for her inspiration with the single-minded commitment that made the greatest monuments of Europe. But he was not completely at home in the world of the once-born. There were unsure touches in his idealized picture, as in the self-identification of the narrator with a twelfth-century peasant mother praying for her dead child. Adams in the *Education* described the climax of the earlier book when he imagined "himself three hundred years old, kneeling before the Virgin's window in the silent solitude of an empty faith, crying his culp, beating his breast, confessing his historical sins," and he meant no irony in the description. But he had the good sense always to prefer his last three chapters in which he presented the challenge of the multiverse in medieval terms. Those chapters shift the motive of the *Chartres* from trying to enter an imagined Other-world to accepting This-world, real and chaotic, and honoring the effort to hold it together as well as one can. At its best, the incursion of experience that outran logic was represented by the Virgin and Saint Francis: "Both were human ideals too intensely realized to be resisted merely because they were illogical. The Church bowed and was silent." The pluralistic Church of the twelfth century was a model, as the late R. P. Blackmur argued, of "The Harmony of True Liberalism." To serve such an ideal in the actual world, Saint Thomas devised—in Adams's view—a philosophy for Church and State, a Church Intellectual that men could enter, a structure in which "science and art were one." The spire which crowned the structure was man's free will; the difficulties of construction, of logic were risked because "Saint Thomas needed to fill his Church with real men."

Free will was necessary to the religious architecture of the thirteenth century—and to the political art of the twentieth, as Adams conceived that art. But if the historian's medieval reflections gave him a clue to his own age, they did not give him a set formula. In the medieval case, aspiration to God drew men into Aquinas's church; in the modern age, fear of destruction, a "force from behind," drove man to seek the control of violence. Even so, there was choice. Adams's catastrophism, in history as in geology, was not simply an optimistic theory of evolution turned on its head. On the contrary, catastrophism—the chance for unpredicted and apparently unpredictable change—upset nineteenth-century determinism altogether by making room for novelty. Along with seeing what must be, passive perception can spot the point of contingency and define the locus of genuine choice. Hope comes into being along with fear, and it is fear, not doom, that Adams was preaching in the *Education*.

His figure for free will came now from science rather than architecture: the comet which, approaching the sun, must unpredictably wheel in its course or be destroyed. The typographical error which deletes that *or* at the point where logically choice may enter, is still repeated in recent editions—as if editors and printers conspired to keep doom in the air and responsible will out of the discussion. For responsible will, as Adams defines it, requires an arduous education: one must learn to efface the ego, sharpen the senses, open the mind, hold one's tongue, not care for the stakes but watch the game and wait. Even so, there are differences in attainment. John Hay represents the political art at its most advanced: his perception is keen as it must be in a Secretary of State, who "exists only to recognize the existence of a world which Congress would rather ignore." But even a Secretary of State, the man in government who most ought to take the long look ahead, is a practical man, and "practical politics consists in ignoring facts." When education and practicality part company, the "historian" must know that it is time to detach himself from established power. Impractically he may then spend his strength merely in trying to order his own consciousness and by writing, create a way of seeing for his race. The character called Henry Adams becomes thus the artist-hero of our times. But the writer Henry Adams joined the esthetic movement with reluctance: he would rather serve on earth than reign in the ideal world of his art. The old artificer, preaching silence, alienation, and cunning, betrays an eighteenth-century wish for usefulness that we hardly expect in so modern a work of art. To take that side of him seriously would be to couple delight with terror.

"Henry Adams"

J. C. Levenson[*]

Henry Adams once tried lightly to explain how it felt to be the heir of Presidents and the inheritor of a pew in the granite church of Quincy, Massachusetts. Since few Americans are aware of hereditary pew holding, much less of President grandfathers, explanation was in order—and misunderstanding was to be expected. Adams' anecdote was to become an essential datum in the popular interpretation of his literary and historical work:

> The Irish gardener once said to the child: "You'll be thinkin' you'll be President too!" The casualty of the remark made so strong an impression on his mind that he never forgot it. He could not remember ever to have thought on the subject; to him, that there should be a doubt of his being President was a new idea. What had been would continue to be. He doubted neither about Presidents nor about Churches, and no one suggested at that time a doubt whether a system of society which had lasted since Adam would outlast one Adams more.[1]

Since *The Education of Henry Adams* became a posthumous best seller almost at the same time as Brooks Adams published *The Degradation of the Democratic Dogma* (Brooks's tendentious title and dark introduction set the tone for his collection of Henry's late, and often gloomy, speculations on historical development), it was easy to simplify the complex artist by reference to the cranky theorizer. The shortest way through a difficult book was to suppose that the gardener's words traumatized Henry Adams, prefigured a life of frustration at not becoming President of the United States, and led to final sublimation in an apocalyptic vision of cosmic disaster. By this view, the spoiled child of the republic became father to the man, and Adams' argument that anarchic twentieth-century society would have the power and might have the stupidity to blow up the world could be put off as the outrageous fantasy of a decadent and a sorehead. Nowadays, when the spoiled-child interpretation is more easily caricatured than believed in, the task remains to find some better way of

*Reprinted from *Pastmasters: Some Essays on American Historians* edited by Marcus Cunliffe and Robin W. Winks, pp. 39–73. Copyright © 1969 by Harper & Row Publishers, Inc. By permission of the publisher.

157

connecting Adams' individual experience with his intellectual achievement. In a sense, we must reinterpret the incident in the garden which brought him the awful knowledge of historical change. What impressed Adams himself in the incident was not a shock of personal disappointment. Rather, he emphasized the way a child can expose what an adult might conceal, principally the assumption that the world is likely to go on as it is now or, even better, as it used to be. Standing for naïve blindness to the real changes of history, the child of the anecdote represents the vague attitudes of people in general. More specifically, the child—with his President grandfather and family pew—represents an immediately felt relation to church and state. The controlled multiplicity of the figure is evidence of rational skill rather than off-guard confession on the part of Henry Adams, but like any good symbol it says more than may have been consciously intended: the encounter with the Irish gardener announces that for Adams the age of politics is over. This theme runs through almost all of Henry Adams' mature work until the *Education;* and even in the *Education*, the passing of the age of statesmanship, ideally set in the eighteenth century, is his recurrent subject.

But Adams' response to this subject was by no means a matter of misery and lamentation. In the most grand-scale projection of the theme, in his *History*, he seemed to argue that the successful establishment of a democratic republic made politics obsolete; in the American democracy men behaved patriotically by giving up an archaic concern for public affairs and turning their energies to their individual tasks. Adams' own practice in accordance with this teaching was singularly successful, enough so that he may be said to have eluded the spell that was cast on him in the Quincy garden. That he attained the presidency of the American Historical Association is worth taking seriously as something more than an ironic fall: for once, an Adams, though he might repel popularity and avoid honors, could not prevent official recognition of what he did for his country. Moreover, the subjective importance of his work was as great as its objective value: of the many characters which he showed the world, that of professional historian was perhaps the closest to the center of his being. The point may be argued from his own usage in the *Education*, where his epithet for himself was "the historian," but there is no need to settle for his own testimony when the externally verifiable facts of his biography are so persuasive. Until he became a historian, Adams lacked a calling. Given the custom of the country whereby men define themselves by the work they do, not even the heir of Presidents was exempt from the popular pragmatism. To be without a calling was, to some degree, to lack an identity. The story of Henry Adams' education is his learning to give up the expectation of a career in government and, after the loss of childhood security and hereditary self-conception, his making an identity of his own by becoming "the historian."

Adams shifted his ambition from politics to history by a very gradual process. At Harvard, he was elected Class Orator for 1858, but he took the success to be literary rather than political. He did not for that reason think of a literary career, for he then conceived of literature as the product either of Sketch-Book sensibility or of Concord uplift, and his practical temperament rejected both. On the other hand, he did not follow the family pattern of going on at once to study law and prepare himself for an eventual career in public service. He chose the more roundabout course of going first to study the civil law in Berlin. There, instead of perfecting his scholarly preparation, he found himself to be less serious than he expected—and less gifted in the German tongue. Though he worked at the language, it was a case of German for German's sake: there was no visible progress in the law. As an innocent abroad, he learned that behind the appearance of a great university were such realities as stuffy halls, mumbled lectures, and the opportunity for a graduate student to drift at pleasure for as long as the money kept coming from home. When the money stopped coming, he returned to read law in Boston. But he soon dropped one family tradition in order to follow another, giving up law in order to serve as his father's confidential secretary, first in Washington and then for seven years in London. There the wavering toward and away from politics continued. As the son of the Civil War Minister to Great Britain, he was an apprentice diplomat; as an anonymous correspondent for the Boston *Courier* and the *New York Times*, he was a semiprofessional maker of public opinion; as an avid student of history and political theory, he was training himself to be the philosophical statesman of the future. On the other hand, he was given to speculation on the mysteries of his own consciousness and of the cosmos, he suffered and triumphed with the vicissitudes of clubland society as well as the Union cause, and his meeting the poet Algernon Charles Swinburne impressed him even more than his meeting John Stuart Mill. Although politics was the end in view for the young Henry Adams, it was not the only end.

Back in Washington, after the Grant administration made it shockingly clear that it had no openings for junior statesmen, he stayed on as a political journalist, and his staying may be regarded equally as his sticking with politics in an unofficial role or as his orderly retreat from youthful hopes to alternative possibilities. The same ambiguity persisted when he accepted an assistant professorship of history at Harvard in 1870: part of the attraction of the post was that along with it he undertook the editorship of the *North American Review*, and his Cambridge obligations did not keep him from continuing as an organizer of an Independent movement that tried to exert leverage on both political parties. There was no irrevocable commitment involved with his move to Harvard. His family, in their urging him to accept the position, evidently thought it was time for him to exchange public for private ambitions, but he himself came to that view slowly and not so much by deliberation as by the commitment which comes with effort and experience. Nevertheless, by the time he returned to Washington in 1877, the change had come. Although playing politics remained his avocation, understanding American political history was his certain work. And in his enthusiasm for the task, he assumed the characteristic which, in his *History*, he would someday argue to be quintessentially American: having given up an archaic concern for political power, he performed the highest patriotic duty by turning his energy to individual ends. By returning to Washington *as a scholar*, he was helping to make it into a great capital:

> One of these days this will be a very great city if nothing happens to it. Even now it is a beautiful one, and its situation is superb. As I belong to the class of people who have great faith in this country and who believe that in another century it will be saying in its turn the last word of civilisation, I enjoy the expectation of the coming day, and try to imagine that I am myself, with my fellow *gelehrte* here, the first faint rays of that great light which is to dazzle and set the world on fire hereafter. Our duties are perhaps only those of twinkling, and many people here, like little Alice, wonder what we're at. But twinkle for twinkle, I prefer our kind to that of the small politician.[2]

Unlike Prescott, Parkman, and Bancroft, Henry Adams was a professor before he was a historian. In this respect, he belonged to the new generation that was fixing norms for academic professionalism in America. But the lines between generations, especially in his case, were blurred. He went to Harvard as an amateur and, after his seven years' labor there, he resigned in order to pursue history as an independent man of letters. Moreover, he tended to classify himself intellectually as well as socially with the older group of gentleman scholars, Like his distinguished elders, he made his own collection of original documents on which to base his work. Financially able to conduct research on both sides of the Atlantic, he made good use of his social position to win access to archives in Paris and Madrid—and Washington, too—which had never before been opened to historians. Wherever he worked, he left busy scribes behind him to gather his harvest, quite in the grand style of the independent scholar. But there were other kinds of research, beyond anyone's private means, which suggest some of the differences that the new organization of historical study made. A simple instance occurred when Adams, happily independent and working at his summer residence in Beverly Farms, exercised the privilege of a sometime faculty member and arranged with the Harvard library for shipment upon shipment of old newspaper files. Just as great institutional libraries now stood in contrast to even the best individual collections, so also the mass of historical information began to exceed the resourcefulness of the individual researcher. Adams' reading in depth in the period of his *History* was a different kind of study from the exhaustive search of archives: going through state papers, one assumes a fixed limit to the possibly relevant primary sources, whereas the materials of social history are virtually inexhaustible. In practice the questions of the researcher limit the data he takes in, but the old idea of scholarly authority makes the researcher constantly try to extend his powers of absorption and intelligent discrimination. The shift from political to more broadly social history implies professionalization in two respects, the pooling of resources in great libraries and the constantly increasing number of mutually dependent researchers who try to keep up with the materials. In addition, these technical changes accompany and perhaps encourage a shift of scholarly interest from the premodern era with its limited surviving evidences to the modern, post-1789 period, for which there are superabundant materials. In all these respects, Henry Adams was a representative scholar. His liberation from politics, in his professional as in his personal life, was gradual and incomplete, to be sure, but he had a deep underlying awareness of the changes that were required of his profession by the modern world. He wrote to this effect in a letter to Parkman:

> The more I write, the more confident I feel that before long a new school of history will rise which will leave us antiquated. Democracy is the only subject for history. I am satisfied that the purely mechanical development of the human mind in society must appear in a great democracy so clearly, for want of disturbing elements, that in another generation psychology, physiology, and history will join in proving man to have as fixed and necessary development as that of a tree; and almost as unconscious.[3]

Apart from the rather dated notions of social science which so often catch the eye in this letter, it is well worth noting the plain central statement that names democracy as one more reason why political history is to be supplanted by social. Ironically, Adams' gloomy prognosis for political history was based on a political premise—namely, the Jeffersonian and in general the American assumption that stateless society was the ideal liberal and democratic order. Along with professionalism and modernism, a sense that democracy was—and ought to be—the main direction of the age affected Adams' historical practice and set him apart from the old school.

Political history was hard to escape. As a mode of historical writing, it preceded the making of the professional academic discipline with professional standards. It originated in a classical concern for statecraft, whereby history served to instruct a ruling prince or a governing class. But the classical conditions of statecraft changed: the highly rationalized eighteenth-century balance of power, which seemed to Gibbon the greatest European achievement since the Pax Romana, depended on the coexistence of modern nation-states; with no central force for order, it blew apart under the pressure of revolution. In 1815 much was restored, but the Metternich concord of nations, which replaced the abstract symmetry of pre-Revolutionary Europe, only half-concealed the new forces. In this nineteenth-century environment, a generation of historians arose who were more concerned for the nation than for the state; in the general revival of medieval studies which then took place, they sought national origins rather than political wisdom. In the United States, however, the Middle Ages were not so visible as in Europe, not so tangibly present in the daily experience of the nation, and so the historian's situation was less hospitable to nationalism. By a survival of eighteenth-century cosmopolitanism and a stretch of the visual imagination, Americans could include in their own premodern history the age of the conquistadors or the general rise of Protestant liberalism; but the cultural distance between Prescott's and Motley's subjects and their audience meant that their histories, picturesque, dramatic, and scholarly as they were, did not compel the deepest involvement. For premodern history, Bancroft and Parkman found the more effective American subject by turning to the colonial period. Bancroft, arguing from impressive research to a few simple generalizations, set the scheme of patriotic liberalism for generations of textbook writers and, indirectly at least, stimulated wave after wave of scholarly revisionism. Bancroft survives mainly as an influence; Parkman survives in his own right for having fashioned a history of great and complex meaning out of virtually definitive knowledge of his subject. That he saw America as an integral part of European civilization established a breadth of view which made it easier for Adams to set his *History* in its international context. Yet Parkman's most characteristic accomplishments in defining his subject differ so much from Adams' at so many points of correspondence that the older historian seems to have been an ironic model for the younger. Parkman was remarkably nonpartisan in treating the major conflict of his story, since his love of so-called medieval qualities of manhood made him see an almost chivalric contest between France and England, with little point to the choosing of sides, even though patriotic liberalism gave the slight emotional odds to England. Parkman, as he rendered the leading figures of his story, wrote from a sense of epic greatness and a conviction that he could supply numerous examples from a heroic age, now utterly past. Parkman, at his most original in discovering the relation of his subject to his own time, made the great American forest his peculiar symbol of value, evoking a love for untouched nature and a regret that the "progress" of organized society should displace it. By contrast, Henry Adams was to make progress his subject and ignore unimproved nature except as a logistical problem. He was at one with Parkman in focusing on the development of national institutions and the problem of political and military hegemony over the North American continent, but he was to be antiheroic in tone and would direct his analysis toward the future, not the lost past.

Romantic history, like earlier history, was political; realistic history was even more so. The organization of academic scholarship, the textual criticism of documentary evidence, and the élan of finding that earlier histories did not stand up before a search for the way things, really happened gave the intellectual advantage to realism. His youthful sojourn in Berlin spoke well of Henry Adams' historical instincts: he had found the very center of the new movement. Even though he had got only a vague conditioning rather than a real training there, the rigorous young professor of Anglo-Saxon law stood for German rather than, say, British standards and methods. He read widely in the German authorities and studied Old English charters in the German critical fashion; he established a graduate seminar along German lines and, from its program of research, produced the first Harvard Ph.D.s in history; with his best students as fellow contributors, he published in 1876 *Essays in Anglo-Saxon Law*, an early monument of collaborative scholarship. The progression of his interests also followed the pattern of the new academic orthodoxy. He started as a medievalist, moved on to American Colonial history, and completed the move from medieval to early modern to modern history by setting up a course on the history of the United States from 1789 to 1840. Whether the rigor of his studies ought to be ascribed to German academicism or simply to the New England background, the energy and intellectual forcefulness were certainly his own. He made his teaching of medieval institutions less remote by getting his students to regard it as a special training in Anglo-American law. In the Colonial period, he made himself expert enough to stand as authoritative critic of Bancroft's volumes as they came to hand; eventually, old Mr. Bancroft himself was using Adams as a private critic of his draft text. In the national period, he got into the controversial questions of American particularism and Federalist separatism: he not only reviewed his student Henry Cabot Lodge's *Life of George Cabot*, but also rebutted it with overwhelming evidence in his 1877 volume, *Documents Relating to New England Federalism, 1800–1815*. The realistic history which Adams produced as an academic scholar was legalistic, exacting, and of interest principally to the historical profession. Above all, it was as thoroughly political as history had ever been. At his most modern, in his pragmatic view that his history courses might serve to educate future lawyers, he was also closest to the most traditional motive of historical study, namely, the education of a governing class. The particular pride he took in Lodge—historian, lawyer, and active politician already showing the signs of future leadership—was not simply that of a nineteenth-century academician; the friendship between teacher and student was classical and New Englandly, also.

The immediate effect of professionalization was to make history more rather than less political: the watchword of the day became Edward A. Freeman's "History is past politics, politics is present history." Adams, who conducted his researches in that faith, was part of an academic vanguard. He became, as he ironically boasted, the modern authority on "sac and soc." He had traced that verbal formula to the point where its two terms stood for intelligibly different feudal rights, and yet he was uneasy at the pedantic nature of his achievement. He lacked a legal theory like that of his friend and colleague Oliver Wendell Holmes, Jr., for whom the disclosure of historical origins was a step toward making the law more pliable to current historical needs. But politics served Adams, as legal philosophy served Holmes, to provide a context of meaning. His studies took on life when, writing about Anglo-Saxon courts, he showed how judicial history might be seen as past politics. He seemed to project his own concern with Jeffersonian America back to the England of Alfred the Great: as he told the story, the chance for a national, secular judicial system in a strong, free nation-state was lost because Alfred failed to establish institutional means for prolonging the national power beyond his own reign. Later in his career, Adams would suggest a similar argument against Jefferson's failure to consolidate gains that depended at first on his influence as a popular leader. Anglo-Saxon England provided him with an occasion for defining the responsibilities of statesmen and measuring the cost of what they left undone. His political concerns, local and recent as they were in origin, helped him to form a comprehensive and focussed view of his subject; yet his faithful labor at the intricacies of legal history helped him to establish his subject as something other than the projection of a merely topical interest. Between the two aspects of his medieval study, its topicality and its remoteness, he attained intellectual liberation and professional authority: he learned to know a world not his own. He had respect enough for the facts to let that world stand in its own right, and at the same time he had personal interest enough to make it imaginatively his. To paraphrase his own comment on the use of learning languages, a second history doubles a man. Whatever the limitations of political history, within those limitations Adams mastered a field of learning that did not merely broaden his view of his own society, but gave him a new perspective altogether.

In his Harvard years, Adams made little effort to get beyond the history of past politics. As a teacher of medieval history, he read Ruskin and prepared lectures on Gothic architecture, but such excursions were few. When he had trained a successor to take over his medieval courses, he himself turned to American Colonial history, a field where he was apparently content to ask traditional questions. One reason he could so easily settle for narrow limits was that cultural recognition scarcely required a conscious effort; ancestral ties and tangible monuments provided all the topicality he needed. When he noted, for example, that New England had produced men who were intolerant even for their age, to reconstruct that age and the local frame of mind did not require a great leap of historical imagination. When Lodge succeeded him as the instructor of American Colonial history and produced his *Short History of the English Colonies in America*, he dedicated the book to Adams; the acknowledgment of debt implied a common, and traditional, definition of the subject. Moreover, the close connection of Lodge's *Cabot* and Adams' *Documents* indicates that the presentness of their grandfathers' political battles was a lively part of the two men's historical interest. Indeed, Adams' last official act in his professorship was to propose that Lodge also have a course in American history after 1789 so that, as he wrote to President Eliot, the rival views might serve "to stimulate both instructors and students, and to counteract . . . the inert atmosphere which now pervades the college." Having been as aggressive as possible in presenting his proposal as a practical device for teaching, he went on to suggest that it was also a device for applied libertarianism: "His views being federalist and conservative, have as good a right to expression in the college as mine which tend to democracy and radicalism."[4] Within the limits of political history, Adams had arrived at a conception of his discipline that was extremely modern in its relativism. Implying that, along with the scientific establishment of the data, the values of the inquirer had much to do with what the past seemed really to be like, Adams was already transcending the assumptions of old-fashioned realism. In his conception of historical knowledge, he responded to a philosophical revolution that was in its earliest stage, even though, in his idea of what facts a historian is concerned to deal with, his commitment to politics appeared to be fixed.

Since, as Adams early observed, values condition any inquiry into the past, it is important to note that he declared himself to be a democrat and a radical. His affirmation deserves to be taken at face value even though it is hard to fill out the meaning of the terms. Since he did not always share the sentiments and ideas by which American democrats or radicals are conventionally classified, his statement of belief is often ignored or dismissed as insincere. He never idolized those who labor in the earth or in the shop, he only respected them as men. He never cherished a dream of the barricades, for to him the revolutionary impulse (which he too sometimes felt) was essentially anarchic. He seriously thought that in this country democracy had once and for all taken possession of the national government and that secession movements, after 1798, were right-wing revolutions, antidemocratic and antilibertarian in nature. These democratic and unionist convictions were the widely shared convictions of his generation, a generation that fought to preserve the national government in the trial of civil war. But as the historical interpretation of the Civil War has undergone successive revisions since then, the sense of democratic nationalism has become harder and harder for later generations to recover. Without such a recovery, however, we can understand neither Adams nor his age.

The great beliefs that carry nations through wars do not lead quickly

and clearly to practical programs for reorganizing society in the aftermath of wars. So with Adams, his great beliefs came in the postwar period
to appear very much like the politics of respectability. Democracy, the
Union, and the moral law came down in practice to a few rather prosaic
articles of belief. Hard money, for example, once the common-sense
economics of agrarian and popular movements, was in the post-Civil War
years the policy of the financially conservative upper middle class.
Although Populist-influenced students tend to view hard money as anti-
agrarian in intent, Republican bankers were following a path that Jacksonian planters had been over before them: they hoped that reason and
morals and the "free" operation of the economy would bring under control the enormous industrial expansion which their policies were also
abetting. Postwar capitalists, if they were to be judged by their official
reasoning, were not very different from prewar planters. In both cases,
the ideal of regulation—*without regulators*—bespoke a faith in the so-
called normal market and an assumption that if only men would behave
morally, which was to say naturally, they would have the best of all possible economies. Other parts of the early Adams program have become
dated less than his fiscal policy but still, understandably, lacked wide appeal in his time. On the question of civil-service reform, it is self-evident
that the merit system would be less popular than the earlier shibboleth of
rotation in office. Even though the administrative branch might claim to
be much less corrupt than the legislative, still it was clear that the
bureaucracy had to be rationalized, if only for the sake of getting a
moderate efficiency. But the moralism of the reformers implied that one
need only cure the symptoms of corruption in order to restore a normal,
righteous order. The reform effort assumed an ideal republic under the
Constitution, once attained, recoverable now, potentially stable if not absolutely unchanging, and it reasoned as if individual moral defect was the
only cause of social change. Adams, by the 1890's, would radically change
his political ideas to take other social forces into account, but in the 1870's
and 1880's, when he was at work on his *History*, he was only beginning to
find his way around the traditional American assumptions and his intellectual findings were not immediately converted into political terms.
Yet he did support criticism of the classical economic case for limiting
wages; and writing to a friend in England, he advised that raising wages
and subdividing capital were a social and political necessity: "Your
working-men, as a class, are still too poor."[5] But when he wrote thus, he
seemed not to realize the implication of his own advice, namely, that in
an industrial age equality is not providentially given—as it had been,
evidently, in the American past—but has to be achieved by rational
political effort. But even though he had not thought through all the implications, his instinct of statecraft stood him in good stead. His conception of political possibility, lively enough when he thought of British
politics, logically contradicted the ideal of the unregulated market and

kept him from ever accepting outright the norms of the Manchester economists. There was justice in his later claim that "he had never in his life taken politics for a pursuit of economy," and if, for a time, he accepted the passing of statecraft, he did not do so for the sake of an abstract market ideal. Rather, the position he took in his middle years was that in America the end of positive government had done what Jefferson said it would, namely, make possible the rise of a great democratic society. The social, not the economic, effects of negative government reconciled him to the facts of American political history.

The Jeffersonian faith that the less governed the better, although it was a dubious guide to political justice in the 1870's and 1880's, served Adams very well as an interpretive principle for early nineteenth-century history. It was possible, in other words, for the historian to function without first having solved all the current problems of the political theorist or the social scientist. Nevertheless, Adams' or any other historian's sense of his own age is crucial to his work; it balances his having a second past and keeps him a historian rather than an antiquarian. The response to one's own time may be in large part unstated. A reservoir of conviction is in fact better than a set of pat answers, since ideological neatness may keep a historian from learning anything that he cannot account for a priori. Sure solutions to present problems can be very well dispensed with, but a clear sense of the problems themselves cannot, for it is the urgent pressure of unsolved problems that leads to the search for a relevant past.

In this respect, Adams was fortunate that his professorship entailed his being editor of the *North American Review*. Thanks to his extraordinary energy, he managed, along with his regimen of study and research, to give the *North American* a last great period before the age of quarterlies finally waned. He not only knew but also helped elicit the best thought of his countrymen on the leading issues of the day; and in the interplay of editor and writers, some of his leading historical ideas took shape. The occasion of the national centennial in 1876 led him to his largest undertaking in contemporary history, for he decided to present a survey by experts of the nation's progress in science, political and economic thought, religion, law, and education. This survey of 1876 supplied him with questions that he would later put into his own surveys of 1800 and 1815 that begin and end his *History:* he could discern the trends of so short a span as fifteen years only because he looked forward to the present as well as looking back to a more distant past. And the findings of Simon Newcomb, William Graham Sumner, Daniel C. Gilman, and the rest concerning America's first century are interestingly close to Adams' findings about the American democracy's first decade and a half. Their collective report found that politics had decayed and was beset by corruption, but in the other fields a special kind of progress could be noted. Adams, if not his contributors, could see that the changes closely followed the pattern which Tocqueville had described a generation before. The higher arts and more theoretical areas of knowledge—science, theology, political economy—required the kind of sustained, disinterested, and costly effort that might be looked for in aristocratic societies; in America, they tended to fall into neglect. On the other hand, except in politics there were compensatory advances in the direction of practicality, mildness, and short-run benefit: technology rather than science, general morality rather than theological distinction, universal schooling not matched by progress in higher education. The experts who took part in Adams' survey were more effective, perhaps, when they criticized than when they praised, but the kinds of progress which they recorded were evidence of the rise of a great democracy.

Before the centennial year was over, Adams used the *North American* as the platform for both his farewell to politics and his profession of faith. In his caustic essay "The Independents in the Canvass," he scored off both parties and the reformers as well, denouncing corruption and ritual promises of mended ways, on the one side, and on the other, naïveté and ineffectuality. But his more important contribution to the October, 1876, number was a review of von Holst's *Constitutional and Political History of the United States.* Moving to the international scale restored his breadth of view: while closeness to politics at home could engender disgust, criticism from abroad roused his national feeling. Since the outside critic in this instance represented the highest Germanic scholarship, Adams' professional mettle was challenged along with his patriotic self-esteem. So the occasion prompted him to discover more than he might otherwise have done of the implications of his own beliefs. He found that, with all due respect for von Holst's strictness and learning, he had to suggest that there were limits to the intellectual usefulness of legalism and moralism and the demand for perfect logical consistency in men or institutions. Distinguishing between the judgments of a German professor and "those of a politician who is forced to act within the limitations of the possible," he disclosed a political flexibility in his own mind that was at odds with the moral rigidity of the would-be reformer. He advocated logical rigor as strongly as ever, but in putting his own professional judgments up against those of the foremost institutional historian in the field, he spoke up for the other kinds of perception which had to be practiced along with "microscopic analysis." The intangibles of national feeling and general forces had to be taken into account, he argued, and the fallacy of applying perfectionist criteria had to be understood. Against what he took to be the antidemocratic tenor of von Holst's argument, he counterattacked sharply:

> One of the most bitter charges brought by Dr. v. Holst against the American political system is that it destroyed the idea of representation, and degraded representatives into mere mouth-pieces of their immediate constituents. And now he

takes the broad ground that self-government is impossible because a majority of the legislature, influenced thereto by a few strong-willed men, did what he is violent against them for not habitually doing, that is, adopted a measure [the war declaration of 1812] without waiting for a mandate from their constituents. . . . From internal evidence it seems probable that the sentiment is intended solely for a German audience, and that its aim is to demonstrate that Prince v. Bismarck is essentially as good a representative of self-government as Washington and Madison.[6]

Adams expanded on what von Holst left out—the establishment of the Constitution and the emergence of the nation—until he recognized that he was writing a kind of "centennial oration" of his own.[7] The warm rhetoric of his review and the hammering ironies of his essay on the Independents defined the range of pride and indignation that he carried with him from his life as politician, editor, and professor to his labors as an historian during the next span of his life. Characteristically, his hammer was more noticed than his bellows: his publishers did not like the anti-Republican remarks in "The Independents in the Canvass," and Adams felt obliged to resign from the *North American*. He was evidently as glad to leave the editorship as to give up trying to rally the now-dispersed reformers, and he was also ready to quit Boston and Harvard, where he found too little genuine intellectual friction to strike the sparks of originality. He expressed his exasperation with the placidity of his academic life somewhat more fully than he did his gravitation to Washington for its politics and society and the professional ambition which he scarcely formulated even to himself. But with the chance to edit the Gallatin papers and write the biography of Jefferson's great Secretary of the Treasury, he made the break from teaching and moved back to the national capital. He went this time as a committed historian, more detached from politics and yet more deeply concerned with political questions than he had ever been.

The *Life of Albert Gallatin*, with its three accompanying volumes of his papers, was of a scope and detail beyond anything Adams had touched before. The subject freed the biographer equally from the academicism of Anglo-Saxon law and the provincialism of New England Federalist controversy. Gallatin's career in Congress, in the Treasury, and in diplomatic service, based as it was on careful mastery of the public business, led Adams into the exhaustive study of legislative, administrative, and diplomatic processes; and permitted him to develop the kind of historical authority which can only be built upon such study. Nothing less than presidential papers could have been more important for leading the historian into the intricacies of Jeffersonian democracy and early nineteenth-century American history; and before coming to them, it was

worth while for Adams to have the view from one step away and to formulate his main questions independently of the central figures whom he
would examine later. Gallatin's only limitation as a subject was his exemplary virtue, which revived for Henry Adams some of the perfectionist
longings which he had exorcised in his review of von Holst. Gallatin
proved to be the one statesman of the era whose greatness never diminished under scrutiny, the only one whom he admired without reservation
even when he knew all there was to know about him. His own forebears
John and John Quincy Adams came in for their share of his stern
judgments, but Gallatin consistently provided an ideal standard of
political behavior. Evidently the highest rational standards were attainable in this one instance, anyway, but so much the worse for that. The
moral of the story, as Adams privately summed it up for Lodge, seemed to
be the vanity of party politics. The ex-politician wrote to his highly
political student: "The inevitable isolation and disillusionment of a really
strong mind—one that combines force with elevation—is to me the
romance and tragedy of statesmanship."[8] At the very moment when the
historian's grasp of his subject was first opening out to its full scale, he was
also the biographer who narrowed his focus to the individual and saw
with unique clarity the fine shadowed lines of missed aims, lost zeal, and
gathering weariness.

The tragic theme which Adams imputed to his biography of Gallatin
is important if only because it contrasts with the rising action of his
History, in which the emergence of American democracy sets an affirmative tone and the shortcomings of statesmen are treated satirically
rather than pathetically. In part the difference is accounted for by the
nature of the two works: in a biography, what a man seeks and fails to attain is lost with the finality of individual life; in a history, groups of men
who do their work partially and are thrust aside are succeeded by others
who do the same. Men are mortal, but politicians as a class go on forever.
Beyond that, the idea of an emergent nation coming into its first youth is
the very opposite of pathetic. The conception of social progress that
Adams had in his *History* excluded a conception of tragedy such as he
tried to build into his *Gallatin*, and conversely, the interpretation of
events which lent itself to Adams' tragic view of the *Gallatin* had to be
revised before he could write the *History*. This difference of argument
arose, I would further argue, because Adams felt too close to Gallatin to
perceive political meanings other than those which came out of the actual
party conflicts. The political problem is set forth in his summary of where
Republican controversialists of 1800 stood on the ultimate political issue:
"The interests of the United States were too serious to be put to the hazard
of war; government must be ruled by principles; to which the Federalists
answered that government must be ruled by circumstances."[9] In the
event, war was the great externally imposed limitation on Jeffersonian

hopes and ideals, but this formulation from the *Gallatin* was too patly dualistic to cover all the elements of the case as Adams himself presented them. For he had previously said that, in the contest of principles, the very real battle of the 1790's had been won by those who wished the new nation to be ruled by the people themselves and had been lost by those who were blind to the power of that principle in the public forum. And by the end of the biography, Adams could observe that the democratic ideal had won so complete a victory that "there was no longer any essential disagreement among the people in regard to political dogmas."[10] In this fundamental respect, then, Adams ignored the triumph of principle over circumstance in order to get to another aspect of that ambiguously worded conflict in which the result was just the reverse. With slightly altered emphasis, Adams could suggest that the model society which the Jeffersonians sought to create was a utopian illusion: "Mr. Gallatin, his eyes fixed on the country of his adoption, and loathing the violence, the extravagance, and the corruption of Europe, clung with what in a less calm mind would seem passionate vehemence to the ideal he had formed of a great and pure society in the New World, which was to offer to the human race the first example of man in his best condition, free from all the evils which infected Europe, and intent only on his own improvement."[11] The hope for a New World to contrast with the Old was generous, humane, and in tune with the people's actual feelings, but the keeping of peace—good in itself and necessary to popular economic development—was not simply a matter of choosing goals and wishing hard. Peace-keeping was also a practical problem. The means which the Jeffersonians counted on, economic sanctions and diplomatic manipulation of the balance of nations, were inadequate to the task, for neither Napoleon nor Canning calculated national interest on the basis of short-term trade advantages, and in any case trade—or even peace—with the United States did not weigh decisively in the councils of the great powers. The belief that the world would follow reason and interest and leave the United States in peace proved untenable, and the Republicans had then to deal with the circumstances of international embroilment and actual war. Gallatin saw that leadership had passed from the Treasury, where the chief planning of domestic policy had been done, and in such a time, when he could serve his country best in diplomacy, he was only too happy to take on a new role. As the chief negotiator of the Treaty of Ghent, he proved himself once more to be the main reliance of the Republican administration. After the war was over, however, he stayed in the diplomatic service rather than re-enter the political arena: "Riper, wiser, and infinitely more experienced than in 1800, Gallatin had still lost qualities which, to a politician, were more important than either experience, wisdom, or maturity. He had outgrown the convictions which had made his strength. . . ."[12] What Gallatin had lost was the key to political success, "that sublime confidence in human nature which had given to Mr. Jefferson and his party their single irresistible claim to popular devotion."[13]

The *Gallatin* is a work of enduring scholarly value because Adams analyzed the governmental process so precisely and showed in such detail the impact of democratic policy and of foreign complications on American institutions in their formative years; but his interpretive confusions proved that it was not so easy for the historian to shift from microscopic to general views. Circumstance turned out to be stronger than principle, he argued, but he had not yet comprehended his own demonstration that principle was one of the circumstances which affected political events. He attributed to Gallatin more world-weariness and loss of conviction than the documentary evidence supported, thus disclosing his own perplexity about the relation of belief to action. He seemed unbelievably antirational in declaring Gallatin's mind to have been strongest when least experienced, unless he was deviously saying simply that men's energies decline as they get older. He also suggested, more believably, that Gallatin's improving mind had little to do with his deteriorating political position; when the Secretary of the Treasury, beset by faction, stepped aside as a political leader, Adams commented: "There are moments in politics when great results can be reached only by small men—a maxim which, however paradoxical, may easily be verified. Especially in a democracy the people are apt to become impatient of rule, and will at times obstinately refuse to move at the call of a leader, when, if left to themselves, they will blunder through all obstacles, blindly enough, it is true, but effectually."[14] The unstated assumption that the nation could do what its government could not do would come to the surface in the argument of the *History*, but even in this early form it ambiguously suggested both an affirmation of national spirit and an admission of collective blindness. The ideas which Adams tried out on his material seemed often to lead to contradiction, and yet they had one thing in common. In one way or another, they all expressed a disenchantment with politics which he would have to learn to qualify before he could make his mastery of political history complete.

Democracy, the novel which Adams wrote for recreation while completing work on the *Gallatin*, confirms this sense of where Adams stood at the end of the 1870's. Behind its bright ironies and lively incidents, there is disenchantment—and a touch of pathos. The heroine, Madeleine Lee, widowed, lonely and restless, goes to Washington to see power at close range and is almost beguiled into marriage with the impressive but corrupt Senator Ratcliffe. When she discovers that she has almost, for motives she is shrewd enough to question, condoned what she judges to be morally insupportable, her revulsion makes her flee. She can conceive no middle ground between perfectionism and total corruption. Her recoil is, as Henry Aiken has suggested, that of the middle class abandoning politics to the politicians; and despite the presence in the novel of a historian who preaches faith in democracy as the ground for putting up with the defects of American government, there is room to question whether Adams saw his heroine's moral shock in historical perspective. In *Democracy* even more than in the *Gallatin*, there is an antipolitical sentiment that exceeds the rational implication of the materials presented. Adams could not yet claim the breadth of moral perspective which he had commended in the von Holst review.

Adams' departure for Europe in the spring of 1879 conveniently marks a new stage of his career. He had seen the *Gallatin* volumes through the press and sent the manuscript of his novel to Henry Holt for anonymous publication. Of these works, the former established Adams' unique scholarly authority in his field, and the latter gave proof that he had imaginative energy to spare. Manifestly, he was ready for a greater undertaking than anything he had yet done; and as he set about his search of European archives, he now mentioned a professional purpose that he had never before stated. To James Russell Lowell, who helped him get access to state papers in Madrid, he wrote: "I want to tell the whole truth, in regard to England, France, and Spain, in a 'History of the United States from 1801 to 1815,' which I have been for years collecting material for."[15] In thus announcing his long-nourished project, he was right to connect Europe with "the whole truth" as he conceived it. Simply in personal terms, his national consciousness came to complete expression only when challenged from abroad. He needed to respond to von Holst as well as to his fellow Independents, as it were: concerned with American affairs by themselves, he was always the stern analyst; when international comparisons were in question, he showed a warmer side. As a descendant of John Yankee, he had a natural affinity for the old American theme of the transatlantic contrast. But professionally even more than temperamentally, he needed to deal with Europe in order to get the whole truth. The enlargement of significant context was crucial: he arrived by his own path at Ranke's view that nation-states, while they might be the units of historical consideration, could be considered only as interrelated parts of general history. And on the scale of the general historian, he once more proved his authority. The transcripts he had made in 1879, now in the Library of Congress, have been so complete a resource for his successors in the field, that only in the last decade has research begun to frame questions which expand the range of scholarly relevance and lead to the gathering in of new evidence. In theoretical and technical as well as more or less unconscious ways, Adams' researches in Europe indicate the emergence of a master.

It was after conducting his exhaustive search of state papers and political documents that Adams began systematically to read through old newspapers and to study the various sources of social and cultural history. Whatever his convictions about the future of historical writing, he himself worked to transcend political history, not abandon it. With his intellectual powers asserting their control over more and more material, he thought about the Jeffersonian era in a different way. The passing of an age of politics, so that the time was out of joint for the Gallatin of his portrait (and for the heroine of his novel), no longer seemed a matter of pathos. The change Adams described was easier to accept when thought of as part of a larger movement, and the pattern as he now conceived it brought him once more to a view like that of Ranke. The great German historian believed that the beginning of the nineteenth century separated an epoch of dynastic conflict, in which the foreign policy of the leading states was the basic subject for historical study, and a modern age in which nations turned inward and fixed their primary energies on material growth, the development of science, constitutionalism, and popular struggles for power. In Adams' version, this shift in subject matter implied a necessary change in historiography, a new form of social history to go with the new content. Even more important, he gave a special American slant to the pattern, so that the theoretic contrast between the Old Regime and the modern era was reinforced by the spatial and cultural polarity of Europe and America.

While these general ideas were giving shape to the *History*, the minor works that came from Adams' hand, while not so clever or arresting as *Democracy*, showed his greater sureness of purpose. His broadly satirical biography of John Randolph (1882) hit its target so hard that the echoes of the impact can still be heard. His candor in paying off an old family score is almost disarming, as if the book were an exercise in raillery; but a tone of bitterness comes in when the story turns to what Adams regarded as the unnatural marriage of the states'-rights philosophy to the slavery interest. When, as on slavery, he could see an issue clear, Adams showed no inclination to be politically uncommitted. On the other hand, his second novel, *Esther*, published pseudonymously in 1884, showed that he could represent a world bigger than that which was bounded by politics and political disillusionment. The conflicts of science and religion, reason and emotion, which he built into his plot, bespoke an awareness of tragic losses and withal, a sense of how the spirit may accommodate to the nature of things. He himself had to accommodate, the next year, to the calamity of his wife's suicide, by which, as he said, half his life seemed cut away. For bearing that loss, one of his resources was the professional discipline he had cultivated so long and well. Though the élan had gone out of his life, he continued for almost five more years in the work he had begun, and despite his belief that his writing must show the ebb of spirit which he dated from that moment, he sustained his conception to the end. In 1889 he brought out the first two of his nine volumes; by the summer of 1890 he had seen to the last details of maps, indexes, and revision; before the last volumes were published in 1891, he had fled to the South Seas and begun the long struggle with the problem of who he was when he ceased to be a historian.

Composing his *History* at the height of his powers, Adams framed the conception he would hold to: he viewed his subject as fundamentally a rising action. In his mind, the emergence of the American nation was one and the same story as the taking shape of American democratic society. He argued, in effect, that before 1800, when there had been an active political culture, there had been neither an American nation nor an unquestionably established democracy. The other side of his argument was that after 1815 there was a nation and a democracy in America, but very little of politics in the old sense. Between those dates occurred the passing of the reign of politics, of which he would be the chronicler. Since he wrote primarily as a political historian, the negative side of his ironic subject is what first meets the eye, not the rise of democratic nationality but the fall of statecraft. But the reader's difficulty, if it exists, is with form and not with content. Certainly Adams did not delimit the period of his narrative in order to be gloomy. On the contrary, had he extended his survey but a few years longer, he would have had to include the debate over the Missouri Compromise, that "firebell in the night" which startled a tranquil nation with its signal of disaster; but Adams regarded the Civil War as the *other* great story of nineteenth-century America, a story which he left to his friend John Hay, the biographer of Lincoln. Although the *History* contains evidence enough of Adams' antipathy to slavery and racism, there were few occasions when he needed to do more than touch upon those tragic themes. Irony, not tragedy, set the tone of his account. The decline of politics and the rise of democracy would have been a pessimistic subject from an eighteenth-century Tie-Wig point of view, but Adams was far from being a Federalist. He referred to eighteenth-century norms for satirical effect, but they were not the only political standards by which he invited his readers to judge the action. On the other hand, his affirmation of democratic nationality was for the most part indirect. Following his brother Charles' advice to "suppress the patriotic glow,"[16] he understated his favorable judgments and let the facts, subtly ordered, speak for themselves. But the principal irony, beyond his satire and his indirection, is at his own expense: anxious to write the history of a nation, he was trained—in what he thought was an outworn convention—to write the history of a state. His originality lay in accepting his limitations and thereby making the most of his talents. In his magnificent introductory chapters, he pointed the way to his successors as he used new methods and new materials, but in his main narrative, he narrowed his subject to the fate of politics during an era of emergent nationality.

How could social history turn into politics? Adams was able to modulate from one form to the other because he redefined the key term.

Distinguishing between politics in the sense of statecraft and the political character which is deducible from the underlying economic and social institutions of a country, he gave his first attention to the more fundamental. At the very beginning of his work, he presented the economic and social conditions of 1800 and the irreducible question of physical survival. That the American people could hold together a continental nation despite enormous natural obstacles was, he argued, truly in doubt. There were no known means of maintaining communications, much less a social organization, over such distances. The accumulated experience of civilized man offered little help with this problem of space, and where the great powers of the Old World had made almost no progress, the Americans gave no sign that they would be capable of a new departure. Compared with the nation-empires of France and Britain, they certainly had no advantages in the power they could bring to the task. Yet a difference in "political arrangement" seemed to the Americans themselves to be revolutionary in its potential effect, and if the people thought so, then the social historian would be justified in exploring the idea. Adams instinctively adopted the principle of taking point of view into account, and he thereby established a basis for writing political history: if politics occupied the minds of the people, then political history was in this case popular intellectual history.

The popular point of view was by no means the only criterion for including data. Adams felt obliged to record both what people believed they were doing and what in fact they accomplished through their political effort; a discrepancy between intention and event might prove an irony at the expense of the people or their government or both. But such a discrepancy suggested that there were causes which shaped events but escaped the consciousness of the time, unknown forces beyond anyone's control that could affect the course of things in essential ways. The social and economic force which Adams had in mind this early was technology, but he was still very far from conceiving it as the occult mechanism which he later symbolized in the Dynamo. His symbols in the *History* were the steamboat, first of all, the factory elevator, the pivot gun, and the tall-masted sloop; and these were the symbols not of occult power but of human art. Moreover, the popular sense of democracy as a social force was confirmed paradoxically. Adams listed the spiritual successors of Benjamin Franklin—Eli Whitney, Oliver Evans, Robert Fulton, and others—and he made it clear that while the ordinary people seemed unaware of change, it was from their ranks that the agents of change came: "All these men were the outcome of typical American society, and all their inventions transmuted the democratic instinct into a practical and tangible shape. Who would undertake to say that there was a limit to the fecundity of this teeming source?"[17] Economic equality and social freedom were, for Adams, the essential characteristics of the

American democracy as it confronted the physical challenge of mastering a continent. That the people should have thought of political, rather than economic and social, arrangement as accounting for their strength would prove wrong if the term referred to statecraft. For the ultimate historical test of physical survival, however, the historian confirmed the popular belief that democracy, in the sense of equality and freedom, made the difference between defeat and triumph.

Adams' own complex attitudes are woven into the fabric of the *History*. He managed at once to express the convictions of an American democrat and to study the limitations of American political democracy, and his personal commitment did not temper his rigor. But the author's views must be distinguished from those of his characters. Jefferson's opponents, useful because they registered his every inconsistency or ineptitude in the strong clear language of interested observers, do not speak for the historian himself. Their pungent criticism, right by the canons of logic and strict morality, was often wrong in a broader sense, for the trouble with Federalist opinion in general and New England judgments in particular was a tendency toward doctrinaire rigidity. Those so-called practical men understood the world's experience too well to believe that it could change. Refusing to share Jefferson's "illusions" about the nature of man and the possibilities of society, they also could not see that Jefferson spoke for the beliefs and hopes of most of his countrymen. Given the blindness of contemporary observers, the historian had to make explicit his own insight. He concluded his magnificent introductory survey of the social and intellectual scene in 1800 with a chapter on "American Ideals," which is crucial for all that follows. The chapter shows his imaginative penetration of the substance of things hoped for by the Jeffersonians, and it further shows his commitment to the proposition that beliefs can affect the course of events. Insofar as he argued that what was in men's minds could make a difference in their destiny, he freed himself as never before from the imputation of simple materialistic determinism. His historical practice was thus committed to an articulate and self-conscious version of the faith that had motivated the American democrat of 1800. Writing of that hypothetical representative man, Adams declared that "his dream was his whole existence" and that his enemies, instead of sneering at the hard money-getting American of their caricature for his materialism, should have noticed that, even on his sordid side, he was rather, the "victim of illusion":[18]

> The men who denounced him admitted that they left him in his forest-swamp quaking with fever, but clinging in the delirium of death to the illusions of his dazzled brain. No class of men could be required to support their convictions with a steadier faith, or pay more devotedly with their persons for the mistakes of their judgment. Whether imagination or greed led

them to describe more than actually existed, they still saw no
more than any inventor or discoverer must have seen in order
to give him the energy of success.[19]

In his own version of the "will to believe," Adams linked the ordinary
citizen and his American dream with the "visionary" inventor who reversed the meaning of practicality by seeing more in his world than
experience-so-far could attest. Indeed, he went on to suggest that Emerson in his field, Robert Fulton in his, and Jefferson in the area of politics
all represented the same visionary aspect of the national character. If
"down to the close of the eighteenth century no change had occurred in
the world which warranted practical men in assuming that great changes
were to come,"[20] then the energizing faith of the Americans proved to be a
historical fact of the greatest importance.

The American faith of 1800 was to be tried by the political experiment: could ordinary men, left in peace to pursue their own interests,
make a free nation out of the virtually unorganized, geographically
overextended, technically unequipped republic? Freedom, for the Jeffersonians who were assuming office, virtually came down to the one great
objective of leaving men alone. In domestic politics, this meant the
removal of those vested powers and artificial restraints by which government had inhibited the enterprise of private individuals. In reducing the
activity of government, however, they neglected to cut its legal powers,
and most notably, given their professed fear of monarchism, they did
nothing to limit the executive authority which a President might exercise.
In foreign policy, Jeffersonianism meant a single-minded pursuit of
peace. The peace policy extended the principle of negative freedom,
being left alone, to the international scene, but it was especially cherished
because of its implications for domestic policy: a military and naval
establishment would be a costly burden and an artificial class interest imposed on the free development of society. Through the intricate chronicle
of the many activities of the Jefferson and Madison administrations,
Adams traced the working out of this American experiment. He took
careful account of the centrifugal pressures of American society and of the
actual danger from the clashing imperial forces of the Napoleonic era,
and he showed how often the Jeffersonians defied logic, experience, and
common sense in their sanguine hopes for national security without
governmental effort. His ironical argument seemed to be that, despite
multiplied errors of judgment and act, the confidence was justified by the
event. But even though the experiment was on the whole a success, the
lesson was ambiguous. Adams bore witness to the historic efficacy of the
Jeffersonian faith, but he offered little encouragement for anyone to expect future survival on a basis of faith alone.

The Jeffersonian intent could be summed up in a sentence: "Congress
and the Executive appeared disposed to act as a machine for recording

events, without guiding and controlling them."[21] But the first important action of the *History* pointed in just the opposite direction. The Louisiana Purchase, in Adams' view, had an importance for American history comparable only to that of the Declaration and the Constitution. In seizing the opportunity to buy Louisiana from France, Jefferson acted on the assumed existence of sovereign powers, and he implicitly gave up the idea of restricting government to the expressly delegated powers of the Constitution. Not only constitutionally, but geographically and socially too, his act put an end to any real hope of establishing a limited federal state on the model he had set forth in the 1790's. By 1803, barely two years after his coming to office, the experiment in minimal government and social decentralization was over, logically speaking. Moreover, Jefferson and Gallatin seemed to perceive the direction society might then take, for as soon as cost cutting and tax cutting had the effect of bringing increased revenues to the Treasury, they proposed to expand governmental activity. Not that they reverted, in their swing back to positive government, to a policy of military and naval build-up: they proposed national sponsorship of economic and educational improvements, namely, a national road and canal system and a national university. The proposals of 1806 and 1808 were never realized, because of legislative and popular indifference as well as increasingly complicated foreign relations; that is, in an interpretation of the event that Adams had revised since writing the *Gallatin*, the trouble lay not only with the harsh circumstances of world affairs, but also with the persistence of outworn ideas among Jefferson's fellow democrats in Congress and out. The nation generally remained firm in the ideology of 1800, even though Jefferson proved that a politician could have more important qualities than consistency, such as the capacity to learn and grow.

But the circumstances which outran plans and foresight did not always offer an opportunity for growth, and Jefferson did not consistently grow. His early success led him into circumstances which were far more equivocal. When American expansionism turned toward Florida, Spain would not sell. Claiming that West Florida had been included in the Louisiana Purchase, the Americans argued a fictitious point that could only be made good by armed intervention. Intending to bluff but not to fight, they found themselves embroiled in the diplomatic conflicts of Europe, where negotiations were habitually backed by force. While Jefferson spoke of "the effect which the strong language toward Spain was meant to produce in the Tuileries,"[22] Talleyrand spoke of the attention he expected the American government to give to "the events of the last campaign."[23] The contrast was heightened by the crossing rhythms of the narrative: while Jefferson moved with incredible slowness to put down the Burr conspiracy, Napoleon disposed the armies of France with speed that was equally remarkable and, between his overpowering campaigns against Prussia and Austria, found time to issue the Berlin Decree and assert absolute control over foreign commerce with Europe. Jefferson also had to deal with British blockades and impressment of seamen off American ships, and Orders in Council which virtually asserted absolute control over foreign commerce at sea. On the domestic front, meanwhile, the breakup of his congressional support into Old Republicans (defenders of the states'-rights principles of 1798) and New left him without legislative managers—and often without legislative support—for his administration. The historical challenge, it thus turned out, was not whether he could enact his vision of positive government, but whether he could "save the country from faction at home and violence abroad."[24]

The problem of survival had been recast as a problem in politics, but Adams invited the reader to consider whether politics was of prime importance. Although the state was threatened with collapse or destruction, society in every other respect seemed healthy. Apparently the people might succeed where their political leaders failed. Engrossed as they were with their daily tasks, they moved unconsciously toward the great goal of converting American society into something new: in Ranke's terms, the historical phases shifted from the primacy of foreign policy to material development; in Herbert Spencer's sociology, man was advancing at last from the military to the industrial stage of civilization; in Adams' own language, the practice of statemanship was becoming less important than the evolution of democracy. The Burr conspiracy, in his view, was defeated by the same public indifference that caused the Jeffersonian program of internal improvements to languish and expire. Moreover, nonpolitical history, like political history, could be something more than a negative force. The experiments of Fulton, followed step by step, marked the approaching time when the Western territories would be brought within reach of the coastal settlements, and the problem of holding the vast country together would be solved. Also, the strength that internal development would draw from the steamboat might prove to be the nation's best ultimate defense. The difference between social history and political was pointed up by Adams, as he juxtaposed the humiliating *Chesapeake-Leopard* encounter and Fulton's first public demonstration with the *Clermont*. The *Chesapeake*, forced to strike its colors under fire and yield four seamen to the British boarding party, took the center of public attention, but the historian suggested that had the *Clermont* been noticed and its significance appreciated, the public might well have ignored the British attack. It was ironic that men sought political solutions to political problems, but the spell of the past still held men's minds.

But Adams' comment—"The reign of politics showed no sign of ending"[25]—had another meaning, whether he fully intended it or not. He went on writing political history not only to be ironic or because he was the prisoner of his professional technique. Rather, he recognized that long-range prospects and underlying causes do not free men or nations from the necessity of dealing with an immediate challenge. He was never so beguiled by the idea of social evolution as to think that eventual progress would make up for the actual catastrophe. Napoleon and Canning might be scornfully regarded as medieval and barbarous, but so long as Americans must live in the same world with them, the historian must assert the primacy of foreign policy. Perhaps the most remarkable thing about the *History* is that it is a study of middle-class pacifism and American isolationism written at just that time when the peace of Europe seemed most assuredly to be organized as economic competition and when the internal development of the United States seemed most remote from foreign entanglements. Looking back to the Napoleonic era from the 1880's, Adams learned from historical study to ask disturbing questions before actual events forced them on more complacent minds.

Jeffersonian foreign policy was founded on the same basic premise as domestic, namely, that letting people or nations pursue their own concerns in peace is not only the most desirable but also the most efficacious course. The United States asked nothing except to be let alone, and if other governments were not enlightened enough to do so, then the natural operation of the free market could be counted on to bring them into line. The waste and destructiveness of war were avoidable when the means of peaceable coercion were at hand for the control of possible aggressors. In a sentence which Adams thought important enough to quote twice over, Jefferson declared: "Our commerce is so valuable to them, that they will be glad to purchase it, when the only price we ask is to do us justice."[26] When, by 1807, both England and France made it impossible to hope that foreign commerce could be protected by the automatic operation of interest, the embargo transformed the policy of negative government into its opposite. Collectors of customs, governors, and court officials could not enforce the law without troops and vessels actually patrolling the coastwise trade and the avenues to Canada. States' rights and decentralized government were contradicted more directly than in the matter of the Louisiana Purchase, and this time the ideal of statelessness was contradicted on a consistent, daily basis. Measuring the costs of peaceable coercion as against war, Adams found that "personal liberties and rights of property were more directly curtailed in the United States by embargo than in Great Britain by centuries of almost continuous foreign war."[27] The constitutional cost was matched by an economic one which could be figured with respect to government revenue and the reversal of capital expansion, but Adams regarded the moral cost as greater still:

> If war made men brutal, at least it made them strong; it called out the qualities best fitted to survive in the struggle for existence. To risk life for one's country was no mean act even when done for selfish motives; and to die that others might more happily live was the highest act of self-sacrifice to be reached by man. War, with all its horrors, could purify as well as debase; it dealt with high motives and vast interests; taught

courage, discipline, and stern sense of duty. Jefferson must
have asked himself in vain what lessons of heroism or duty
were taught by his system of peaceable coercion, which turned
every citizen into an enemy of the laws,—preaching the fear of
war and of self-sacrifice, making many smugglers and traitors,
but not a single hero.[28]

Finally, there were the political costs: at home, each major sectional interest was alienated from Jefferson's administration, and abroad the
United States lost the chance to stand at the head of the popular movement which even then was beginning to rise against Napoleonic tyranny.
Though Adams conceded that the mild pressure of economic sanctions
might work if applied much longer than military force, he did not sympathize with Jefferson's reluctance to see the embargo lifted. Believing
that the "experiment" in peaceable coercion had been worth trying, he
also believed that it had failed.[29]

The meaning of the failure was war. American pacifism and isolation
proved untenable, and the American people must no longer shun "the
common burdens of humanity" or hope to evade "laws of Nature."[30] But
nothing could hurry the event: the Madison administration seemed to
drift toward collapse, and only the arrival of a new generation in Congress restored energy to government. When war finally came, Adams
treated Madison's hope that it would create a strong national spirit to
back the government as a parody of Hamilton's militaristic philosophy.
But only a parody. Given the mediocrity of political leadership, Adams
once more argued that the people took over the functions of saving the
state: "Not so much the glories as the disgraces of the war roused public
sympathy; not so much the love of victory as the ignominy of defeat, and
the grinding necessity of supporting government at any cost of private
judgment. . . . The slow conviction that come what would the nation
must be preserved, brought one man after another into support of the
war, until the Federalists found their feet in quicksand. The 'crisis' produced the opposite effect to that which Burke's philosophy predicted."[31]
Tracing the conduct of the war in detail, the historian did have victories
as well as defeats to relate, but the one general triumph he claimed was
that of the people rising to the ultimate challenge. Under analysis, that
triumph was due to such national traits as adaptability and quickness,
that is, capacity for organizing and deploying their force as needed and
speed in mastering the technology of war, whether with such old weapons
as artillery and ships of the line or such new inventions as the pivot gun
and the fast schooner. The demonstration of national character through
military history is, as I have argued elsewhere, one of Adams' great
technical feats; but he did not stop with social history even when he found
such a device for presenting it. The people triumphed also by producing
the men who were needed, such generals as Jacob Brown and Andrew
Jackson, such diplomats as William Pinkney and Albert Gallatin. In

generalship and diplomacy he found the last irreducible areas of statecraft, in which the individual still counted. At the very moment when he was clinching his argument that national character, primarily formed by social democracy and an industrial bent, accounted for national survival, he also asserted the older belief that the individual handling of power made a real difference in how events came out.

Adams was not contradicting himself. Rather, he was finding the point at which historians, like politicians, must accommodate their principles to circumstance. Just as events tended to outrun ideologies, historical evidence tended to outrun historical preconceptions. Hence Adams' contrast between the lawyer's argument and the historian's: "The lawyer is required to give facts the mould of a theory; the historian need only state facts in their sequence."[32] In his rigorous commitment to describing how things really happened, he disproved a good many theories, both Federalist and Republican, and left few standing without need of qualification. His own conception that social forces were the determinants of social events he found qualified by the "element of individuality," which he regarded as the "free-will dogma" of historians.[33] It was only a modest qualification, to be sure, for what he mostly showed was how limited was the freedom of action which a diplomat might have. But given the pressure of long-term causes, the momentum of past actions, and the tangle of recent negotiations, there was always room for a new departure. When President Madison was ready for a more positive stand, Pinkney in London brought issues to a head by exerting his initiative within the narrow limits set by his instructions from Washington and the situation at hand. When the nation urgently needed peace, Gallatin at Ghent gradually assumed leadership of the American delegation, harmonizing sectional claims and dissuading his colleagues from untenable demands until the Americans and the British could agree on terms of armistice. It was an inconclusive treaty, but "in referring all their disputes to be settled by time, the final negotiator, whose decision they could safely trust,"[34] the American mission returned the major issues from the political arenas of war and diplomacy to the impersonal working out of social evolution. The interest of the negotiation lay in the fact that the more precisely Adams defined the restrictions that bound his diplomatic figures, the more surely he demonstrated the power to act which remained to them within the art of the possible. As he had commented on a William James proof of free will, it seemed "a very microscopic quantity": "Although your gift to the church seems to me a pretty darned mean one, I admire very much your manner of giving it, which magnifies the crumb into at least forty loaves and fishes."[35] He too magnified the crumb and thereby made the free-will element of the *History* the center of interest. And the interest was not simply metaphysical. His major underlying thesis took a political form: when men do not exert their conscious wills, they are not left alone but caught in the natural drift toward violence; in a world where war is the historic condition which societies have had to undergo, peace does not come with wishing but has to be made. This is the work of "practical politics." It lacks the grandeur or assurance of the old-style moral statesmanship, "being commonly an affair of compromise and relative truth," but it is "a human attempt to modify the severity of Nature's processes."[36]

Adams considered that, once the Treaty of Ghent was signed, America was free to direct its full energies inward to the development of the continent. The historian's mind turned inward, too, and he concluded as rapidly as he could with a survey of the economic, intellectual, and social situation of 1815 and the direction which the evolution of American society had seemed to take. For him, the nature of American democracy and its survival were settled, the last phase of dramatic—that is, drama-tizable—history had passed, and the future belonged to demography and econometrics as far ahead as he could see. Though he still had questions to raise about a nation that had taken shape as intelligent and quick, mild and peaceable, he tried to convey a sense of evolutionary fixity in his clos-ing chapters. But the facts which he had so strenuously labored to set in order did not fit the mold of a theory. Even as he turned his back on political history, he taught more lessons about its possible usefulness than he himself altogether fathomed.

More than ten years' sustained concentration on the *History* left Adams exhausted, and his own personal disaster left him cut off from much of the active life he once had relished. As he went into virtual retire-ment, his professional activity was reduced to the scale of gesture. His presidential message to the American Historical Association in 1894 (not delivered in person, but sent as a letter from Mexico) and his article on "Count Edward de Crillon" for the first issue of the *American Historical Review* in 1895 suggested between them that his generalizing and his em-pirical faculties had somehow shrunk apart. Thinking that the profession had been too long regarded as safe and harmless, he spoke up for the "four out of five serious students of history" who had felt the ambition to reduce their subject to the working out of scientific laws, and he ambiguously en-couraged the young to move into a realm of ideas where their work would be at once dangerous and responsible.[37] On the other hand, in offering a minor correction of the *History*, he expressed concern that "at the most moderate estimate the historian can hardly expect that four out of five of his statements of fact shall be exact."[38] He managed to affirm both mean-ings of scientific history—interchangeable generalization and factual ac-curacy—and at the same time to cast doubt on the attainability of either.

But the silence to which he then pledged himself was not to last. He had ahead of him the remarkable second career that produced *Mont-Saint-Michel and Chartres* (1904) and the *Education* (1907), books that made history his very personal subject. In these works, history *as it had been felt* meant as it had been felt by him, and yet each depended on the author's impressions being founded on a prior professional mastery of his subject. The *Chartres* could make its unique contribution to medieval cultural history only because Adams had previously learned with such pains the way in which illusion may be a social force: "Illusion for illusion, courteous love, in Thibaut's hands, or in the hands of Dante and Petrarch, was as substantial as any other convention;—the balance of trade, the rights of man, or the Athanasian Creed."[39] And the late R. P. Blackmur read a political moral in Adams' treatment of the medieval church; the catholicity with which the church accommodated those forms of devotion that seemed to exceed the bounds of orthodox theology thus appeared as "The Harmony of True Liberalism." The *Education* also, though its form must be described as something quite other than history, deals with historical subject matter and develops motifs from Adams' earlier work.[40] Inviting "active-minded young men" to attend to the problem of how to control power, the book suggests that neither teacher nor student will turn out to be a "Gargantua-Napoleon-Bismarck."[41] Yet there is a new urgency in the relation between the two. As the autobiographical protagonist of the narrative assumes the identity of the "historian," he moves upon an international scene that is radically changed from the placid 1880's: in time of peace he had insisted on mankind's common destiny of having to deal with war; now acutely conscious that man had entered a century of total war and potential global catastrophe, he sought the clue to running order through chaos. As a historian, his duty was to set his own experience in order even though, in the nature of things, his Dynamic Theory was more useful as a model of inventiveness than as a mold to contain the whirl of facts and forces. As a teacher, his duty was to teach the intelligent mind how to react, and his hope was that the effort of the historian would be matched, in political man, by the effort to make peace.

Notes

1. *The Education of Henry Adams* (Boston, 1918), p. 16.

2. Adams to Charles Milnes Gaskell, Washington, November 25, 1877, in Worthington Chauncey Ford, ed., *Letters of Henry Adams*, 2 vols. (Boston, 1930, 1938), 1: 302.

3. Adams to Francis Parkman, Washington, December 21, 1884, Harold Dean Cater, ed., *Henry Adams and His Friends* (Boston, 1947), p. 134.

4. Adams to Charles William Eliot, Boston, March 2, 1877, in Cater, ed., pp. 80–81.

5. Adams to Gaskell, Beverly Farms, Mass., September 24, 1882, in Ford, ed., *Adams*, 1: 339.

6. "Von Holst's History of the United States," *North American Review* 23 (1876): 355–56.

7. Adams to Henry Cabot Lodge, Beverly Farms, Mass., August 23, 1876, in Ford, ed., 1: 296.

8. Adams to Lodge, Paris, October 6, 1879, in Ford, ed., 1: 314.

9. *The Life of Albert Gallatin* (Philadelphia, 1879), p. 273.

10. Ibid., p. 561.

11. Ibid., pp. 272–73.

12. Ibid., p. 559.

13. Ibid., p. 560.

14. Ibid., p. 432.

15. Adams to Lowell, Paris, September 24, 1879, in Cater, ed., p. 92.

16. Henry Adams, *History of the United States During the Second Administration of Thomas Jefferson: 1805–1809*. (Privately printed, John Wilson and Son, University Press, Cambridge, Mass., 1885), p. 227. One of six copies printed from the draft text of the *History*, this volume was sent to Charles Francis Adams, Jr., for critical comment and returned to the author with marginal annotations (Massachusetts Historical Society).

17. *History of the United States*, 9 vols. (New York, 1889–1891), 1: 182–83.

18. Ibid., 1: 172.

19. Ibid., 1: 174.

20. Ibid., 1: 60.

21. Ibid., 1: 242.

22. Ibid., 3: 114.

23. Ibid., 3: 387.

24. Ibid., 3: 124.

25. Ibid., 4: 135.

26. Ibid., 1: 214, 217.

27. Ibid., 4: 273.

28. Ibid., 4: 277.

29. Ibid., 4: 272.

30. Ibid., 4: 289.

31. Ibid., 7: 70.

32. Ibid., 3: 45.

33. Adams to Samuel Jones Tilden, Washington, January 24, 1883, in Cater, ed., p. 126.

34. *History of the United States*, 9: 52.

35. Adams to William James, Beverly Farms, Mass., July 27, 1882, in Cater, ed., pp. 121–22.

36. *History of the United States*, 8: 20.

37. "The Tendency of History," in Brooks Adams, ed., *The Degradation of the Democratic Dogma* (New York, 1919), pp. 126 ff.

38. *American Historical Review* 1 (1895): 51.

39. *Mont-Saint-Michel and Chartres* (Boston, 1933), p. 224.

40. *Education*, p. x.

41. Ibid., p. 4.

"The Hamlet in Henry Adams"

Charles Vandersee*

The world is a fit theatre to-day in which any part may be acted. There is this moment proposed to me every kind of life that men lead anywhere, or that imagination can paint. By another spring I may be a mailcarrier in Peru, or a South African planter, or a Siberian exile, or a Greenland whaler, or a settler on the Columbia River, or a Canton merchant, or a soldier in Florida, or a mackerel fisher off Cape Sable, or a Robinson Crusoe in the Pacific, or a silent navigator of any sea. So wide is the choice of parts, what a pity if the part of Hamlet be left out!

> HENRY DAVID THOREAU, diary entry for 21 March 1840; first published in the *Atlantic Monthly*, January 1905.

The aim of the artist is psychologic, not historic truth.

> JAMES RUSSELL LOWELL, 'Shakespeare Once More' (1868).

I

As Thoreau recognized in 1840, America was not a land likely to produce Hamlets. The mood of the country was expansionist and brash, the summons of the West being responded to with fervor and the needed technology for a bustling nation rapidly developing. 'Puritan fanatics like Goodyear brought to the vulcanization of rubber the same intense passion that Thoreau brought to Nature', Lewis Mumford has observed (*The Golden Day*), and it hardly needs adding that the national passion which was to gain the ascendancy was decisively that for rubber. It was not that Americans were incapable of serious reflection and patient philosophizing. But one undertook such concerns at his peril, and in direct opposition to the frenetic spirit prevailing in his compatriots. As soon as America spied a thinker, it grew apprehensive. Thus Emerson, though issuing a bold manifesto in his famous 'American Scholar' address of 1837, felt himself called upon to operate from a defensive position also. With ill-concealed sarcasm he noted his countrymen's excessive alarm.

*Reprinted from *Shakespeare Survey* 24 (1971), p. 87–104, by permission of Cambridge University Press.

Our age is bewailed as the age of Introversion. Must that needs
be evil? We, it seems, are critical; we are embarrassed with
second thoughts; we cannot enjoy any thing for hankering to
know whereof the pleasure consists; we are lined with eyes; we
see with our feet; the time is infected with Hamlet's unhap-
piness,
'Sicklied o'er with the pale cast of thought.'

Paradoxically, *Hamlet* was popular in America at this time (as
throughout the century), perhaps because of Hamlet's very contrast to the
admired national types.[1] The young, literate, and introspective Prince
would have been an odd bird indeed to American audiences, and his play
a glimpse of the pathos and tragedy that seemed, from a New World point
of view, to be receding happily into the very distant past. To be sure,
there were some cultivated men on the Eastern seaboard for whom the
play was filled with power rather than merely curiosity. One such was the
former President of the United States, John Quincy Adams. Turned out of
office by the Tennessee democrat, Andrew Jackson, Adams was reduced
to the office of Massachusetts Congressman in 1839 when the
Shakespearian actor James H. Hackett wrote to ask his opinion of Hamlet.
Widely known as a Shakespeare buff, his idolatry beginning in childhood,
Adams was eager to reply. His habit was to rise at 4 a.m. in order to take
care of his private correspondence before going off to the Capitol, and the
letter he wrote runs to seven printed pages. To him, Hamlet was 'the per-
sonification of a *man*, in the prime of life, with a mind cultivated by the
learning acquirable at a university, combining *intelligence* and *sensibility*
in their highest degrees, within a step of the highest distinction attainable
on earth, crushed to extinction by the pressure of calamities inflicted, not
by nature, but against nature—not by physical but by moral evil'.[2]
Just at the time Adams declared his enthusiasm for Hamlet, and
Thoreau feared his absence in America, there was born in Boston the
thinker and writer who was to become the American Hamlet. This was,
oddly enough, John Quincy Adams's grandson, Henry Brooks Adams,
born in 1838. *The Education of Henry Adams*, immodestly but accurately
called by its publishers, 'quite simply the greatest autobiography of
American letters,' has also and accurately been termed 'the
autobiography of an American Hamlet'.[3] It was the climax to a literary
career that had included two novels (*Democracy* and *Esther*), two
biographies, the masterly nine-volume *History* of Jefferson and Madison,
and *Mont-Saint-Michel and Chartres*. By a fitting coincidence Adams was
in the process of writing his *Education* in the very year, 1905, that
Thoreau's diary reference to Hamlet appeared in print for the first time.
Whether Adams saw this plea is not known, but what is perfectly clear is
that Adams intended to portray himself as a Hamlet figure, that
unlikeliest of characters in nineteenth-century America. Four allusions in
the *Education* help make this clear, two of them occurring as Adams

neared Hamlet's own age of thirty. Both passages allude to lines from
Hamlet's famous soliloquy on indecision:

> Thus conscience does make cowards of us all;
> And thus the native hue of resolution
> Is sicklied o'er with the pale cast of thought,
> And enterprises of great pitch and moment
> With this regard their currents turn awry,
> And lose the name of action.   (III, i, 83–8)

The first instance referred to the English anti-slavery 'eccentrics' of
the 1860s, men such as Henry Reeve of the *Edinburgh Review*, whom
Adams had known when he spent the Civil War years in London as
secretary to his father, the American minister to the Court of St. James's.
As Adams recalled them forty years later, these men had the virtue of
moral earnestness, but it was cancelled out by dogmatism and cautious
reserve. Idealists they were, but rigidly so, and as a consequence they
turned out to be 'mute and useless' in the political arena. 'As a class,'
wrote Adams, 'they were timid—with good reason—and timidity, which
is high wisdom in philosophy, sicklies the whole cast of thought in action'
(192). Such men were 'the followers of Tocqueville, and of John Stuart
Mill,' and Adams, as he wryly confessed elsewhere,[4] felt himself one of
them. Later on in the *Education*, when he described how his own days of
backstage politics and muckraking journalism ended, and his 'nervous
energy ran low' (316), the Adams of the *Education* came to look more and
more like these English 'eccentrics'.

The second passage had to do not with politics but with evolutionary
theory. Like other thinking young men of the 1860s, Adams had come
under the spell of Darwinism—everybody's 'new hobby' (231)—and the
idea of progress that it implied. To most intellectuals the Darwinian
scheme was one more truth happily discovered in an increasingly com-
prehensible world. An interval of Hamlet-like introspection revealed to
Adams, however, that he himself cared nothing about how true the
hypothesis was, but only about how interesting it was. He concluded, uncomfortably, that 'he was a Darwinian for fun.'

> Mr. [Charles Francis] Adams, the father, looked on [this at-
> titude] as moral weakness; it annoyed him; but it did not an-
> noy him nearly so much as it annoyed his son [i.e., Henry],
> who had no need to learn from Hamlet the fatal effect of the
> pale cast of thought on enterprises great or small. He had no
> notion of letting the currents of his action be turned awry by
> this form of conscience. To him, the current of his time was to
> be his current, lead where it might.   (232)

The 'conscience' of which Adams spoke was a name for mental
scrupulousness, or what he here described as a 'mania for handling all the
sides of every question, looking into every window, and opening every

door' (232). James Russell Lowell, in his 1868 essay, 'Shakespeare Once More', was to point out to American readers that Shakespeare's 'conscience' meant 'consciousness'.[5] The *Zeitgeist* would not, as Adams foresaw, tolerate excessive consciousness—a Hamletizing scrutiny of its fashionable dogmas or its frenetic enterprises. It was 'fatal' to one's 'practical usefulness in society' (232). Adams's vow, therefore, was to circumvent the temperamental Hamlet in himself and to adopt, with proper seriousness, the dogmas and attitudes of his time. It is this temperamental Hamlet in Adams that we shall be exploring, in so far as Adams enforces the parallel on his readers in the *Education*, a highly stylized portrait of himself.

Adams's own awareness of the parallel is sufficient to evoke scrutiny, but the very circumstances of his life, as he chooses certain details and incidents for the *Education*, offer striking parallels to Hamlet's, and thus provide a most intriguing context within which to study the temperamental affinity. Both Hamlet and Henry Adams were royal personages, Hamlet literally and Adams as a member of a three-generation dynasty that had supplied the United States with two presidents. ('You'll be thinkin' you'll be President too!' the Irish gardener had told young Henry [16].) Both men in young manhood found 'the times out of joint', Hamlet in the reign of his murderous uncle, and Adams nervously watching from London as the Civil War turned the nation into a battlefield. Both voiced despair in the middle of a glittering world, Hamlet amid the drunken revelry that gained the Danish court notoriety (I, iv, 8–22), and Henry Adams amid the boisterous Gilded Age of American plutocracy as well as *fin-de-siècle* Paris. Both were university scholars, one gracing Wittenberg as student and the other Harvard as both student and professor of medieval history. Both had loves who died tragically, the fair Ophelia driven to madness and the witty but suicidally disturbed Marian, whose presence in the *Education* is established only by enigmatic references to her tombstone in Rock Creek Cemetery (329). Both men had close friends who functioned as important foils in their life stories: Hamlet's Horatio and Henry Adams's political confidant John Hay. Both believed themselves forced into situations requiring redress, and both undertook it with pathetically mixed results. Hamlet succeeded, circuitously, in revenging his father but died himself; Adams failed to reform a corrupt American government and thus to render viable his family's political ideals, but he survived to write his testament of failure. Both were victims of education, Hamlet suffering from information conveyed him by his father's ghost, Adams tormented by a harrowing vision of the future havoc that science seemed to be calling down upon the world. Finally, and most significant (since the aforementioned correspondences are more curious and informative than really meaningful), both men were tormented by the twin curses of the brilliant and sensitive mind: conscience and consciousness. The two men were, in these respects, near twins in temperament, as many of the most famous passages in the *Education* hint. Adams, for example, claimed to have spent much of his time as a Harvard undergraduate in 'desultory and useless reading' (60), and he later described himself as a typical Harvard student of that era: 'perhaps his worst weakness was his self-criticism and self-consciousness' (65). In the *Education* the theme of his life as professor, journalist, and 'stable-companion to statesmen' (317) turns out to be failure, and not only his famous failure to be educated for life in a modern multiverse. Involved also is his failure to profit from the advantages handed to him, and the failure of his country to persist in the ideals and moral standards of its founders.

II

In the *Education*, the memoirs and the moral fable of the Hamlet who survived, the conscience we encounter is active but ineffectual, and the operation of consciousness is at best inconclusive. For more than one reason Adams divided his book into two chronological parts, omitting the years between 1872 and 1891. Part one, from birth in 1838 to the corrupt Washington of 1871, deals with Adams's formidable New England conscience and its contribution to Adams's extraordinary discomfort and failure of sorts. Part two, from 1892 until the death of John Hay in 1905, is concerned with consciousness and its role in alienation. As in *Hamlet*, these two leading themes artfully interweave in the *Education*. But the emphasis in the beginning is on conscience (accompanied by ignorance), whereas the last half of the book develops the idea of consciousness (or awareness) and leaves the reader to make his own inferences about the place of conscience.

The conscience of Henry Adams is the 'instinctive' morality that imbedded itself in his character from earliest infancy. This, at least, is what Adams insists that we understand:

> Resistance to something was the law of New England nature; the boy looked out on the world with the instinct of resistance; for numberless generations his predecessors had viewed the world chiefly as a thing to be reformed, filled with evil forces to be abolished. (7)

The word 'instinct' is one of Adams's carefully chosen words; elsewhere he refers to his 'nervous system' (148), reinforcing the idea that moralism is something he was born with, an aspect of innate temperament. Insuperably and unchangeably moralistic, this 'nervous system' unfitted him for viewing politics as a mere game or as an impersonal power struggle. Politics could only be seen on the lofty plane of statesmanship: how to administer with justice and prudence the affairs of the people. ' 'Tis sweet and commendable *in your nature*, Hamlet,/To give these mourning duties to your father', remarks Claudius (I, ii, 87–8; italics mine). The acknowledgment of Hamlet's innate temperament is the same thing Adams seeks from his reader, and it is from this point that the tension in the *Education* begins to mount. For Adams's notion of being born into a Boston morality has a great deal to do with duties to the fathers, not alone the Adams line of statesmen but the 'moral tradition' of New England. Yvor Winters, with his customary thoroughness, has traced the genealogy of this tradition back six centuries to 'the paternity of Ockham',[6] but one need not be quite so precisely concerned with origins. Adams himself was inclined to delve much farther back than the Middle Ages when seeking certain of his moral principles, political ethics in particular. 'It was the old Ciceronian idea of government by *the best* that produced the long line of New England statesmen', remarked Adams in fixing on perhaps the central tenet of his political morality (32, italics Adams's). Speaking more generally, his moral principles went back even further: 'he inherited dogma and *a priori* thought from the beginning of time' (26). Adams's whimsical point here is to stress firmly the impact of traditional values upon himself. Whether one liked the idea of being bound by fixed standards of ethics or not, one *was* bound. 'Grant's administration outraged every rule of ordinary decency' (280), Adams bluntly asserted later in the book. 'The moral law had expired—like the Constitution'. This is virtually the same decisive tone of voice used by Hamlet in referring to his own land under a corrupt and sinning sovereign: ' 'Tis an unweeded garden,/That grows to seed' (I, ii, 135–6).

For our purposes the implications of such a conscience require attention in order to see why Adams is able to use Hamlet as a spiritual point of reference but at the same time is unwilling to draw a detailed parallel. Looked at in broad terms, the *Education* has a tension that most life studies do not, and certainly most Victorian-era biographies do not. The usual life has as its beginning focus of interest the question, 'What *can* I do?' as opposed to Adams's implied question, 'What *must* I do?' The typical American questions go on something like this: What am I fitted for? Where do my talents lie? How can I get somebody to recognize my worth? Where can I get some leverage? How far can I finally get? The narrative is of a struggle to get a place, to rise in esteem and worldly goods, to place oneself in as prominent a place as possible within the endlessly expanding American economy. Obstacles can always be overcome (or else the route easily changed); opportunities are as frequent as the rising of the sun. Adams is noticeably different. The question compulsively raised in the whole first section, 'What *must* I do?' means, in Adams's own phrases, 'What do my "New England nature" and my peculiar "nervous system" *compel* me to do in life?' Far from becoming the American self-made man, which John G. Cawelti has recently well characterized,[7] Adams is in quite a different situation. He has *been* made and shaped already; he is not entrusted with making himself. The breath of life called 'education' simply needs to be breathed into his well-shaped Boston nostrils, and thus his pre-existing shape will be filled out.

If his attitude seems dutiful and deferential—even fatalistic—we should immediately recognize a second implicit question that Adams raised, one which will seem as arrogant as the first question is modest. If one has New England values imbedded, *a priori*, in one's 'system', and if one also finds these values subsequently confirmed empirically (e.g. the 'slave states', glimpsed at the age of twelve, represent 'the sum of all wickedness'), then other questions must perforce arise: Not only, 'What must *I* do?' but then 'What must *they* do?'—*they* being, at various times, the Confederate leaders, Grant and his cabinet, the general American public, and the various foreign powers (especially the English ministers), all of whom seemed to lack the Adams/Boston ethical nervous system. That question leads, as a necessary consequence, to two others, much more painful: 'Why aren't they doing it?' 'How can I get them to do it?' To sum up, the leading moral issues in the life of Adams as depicted in the *Education* disregard entirely the ultra-American question, 'Where am I going and how fast will I get there?' in favor of a more complex question filled with a great many more dramatic possibilities. 'Where do *we all have* to go, and how do *I* get us started?' This question accounts for the rich interplay of tensions in the first part of the book, and contributes as well to the surprising modernity of the book, which made it a sort of bible early in the 1920s to a series of lost Americans for whom the Horatio Alger values had paled.

Here in basic outline is Hamlet unmistakably, though Adams avoids a direct comparison. Personal career and wellbeing are secondary; the important thing is to be where one's moral influence can operate, where one can act out one's ethical imperatives. Hamlet abandons Wittenberg, ostensibly at the request of Claudius and his mother, but also in order to stay in Denmark and keep an eye on the suspicious couple. Adams in his early twenties follows his father to London as legation secretary for eight long years, doing secret and propagandistic journalism for part of that time, in order to keep an eye on Gladstone, Russell, and Palmerston. Neither young man worries about gaining a foothold on the ladder of life; his place is virtually guaranteed. Claudius acknowledges Hamlet as 'chiefest courtier', and Adams remarks apropos of his own auspicious family name: 'His social position would never be questioned . . . Never in his life would he have to explain who he was' (64). The role of *son*, the role of *a priori moralist*, the role of *keen observer*—these are the key similarities, to which must be added the gilt setting: for Hamlet the king's court; for Adams, access to the most crucial diplomatic post of the Civil War and later, briefly, admission to the confidence of high Washington officials during the Reconstruction era (243–82).

From here the pattern in Adams's *Education* diverges slightly from *Hamlet*. The revenge and subterfuge which are so important for Hamlet are played down in the *Education*, though they were fully present in Adams's life and quite often can be discerned between the lines of the *Education*. Adams devotes two striking pages, for example, to his extensive but anonymous journalism in 1860–1 (120–1). On some thirty occasions he had sent indiscreet dispatches from London, which editor Henry Raymond of the New York *Times* gladly and prominently published. For the American minister's son to be using pen and ink at the Legation for purposes of criticizing England in a home newspaper was dangerously indiscreet. Moreover, his advice to the North is rightly understood in retrospect as an attempt to stage a play that would catch the attention (if not necessarily the conscience) of the Queen's ministers. Adams stressed the need for military victories, for immediate emancipation of slaves, for anything that would make the North appear strong and thus keep Foreign Secretary Russel from supporting the Confederacy.[8] This Hamlet-like subterfuge Adams passed over quickly in the *Education*, and he omitted entirely his one great effort to revenge his fathers. This was the now-famous biography of John Randolph, which he published in 1883. The outspoken Randolph, a Virginian, had been a bitter enemy of John Adams and John Quincy Adams both, and family enmity (compounded by regional suspicion) had remained inflamed over the decades. Henry Adams's scorn is amply evident throughout the book, as he portrays to the point of caricature the madness and ill temper of Randolph. Adams's biographer refers to the book as his 'golden opportunity' for revenge against the man who had denied his grandfather re-election as President. The eccentric Virginian appears in *John Randolph* as an irresponsible Quixote and a jealous Iago; in private Adams called him a 'lunatic monkey' and complained about having been 'obliged to treat him as though he were respectable'.[9] Randolph's moral failure lay in traducing the Adamses' standards of statesmanship: he was 'violent, tyrannical, vicious, cruel, and licentious in language as in morals'—'unintelligible and monstrous' to what Adams called 'a New England man'. To Adams's considerable satisfaction, the book sold well.

But again, within the pages of the *Education* both the filial revenge and the behind-the-scenes contriving are underplayed, lest the Hamlet analogy appear too blatant. The conscience-laden Hamlet that remains is the observer, the lamenter, and the would-be reformer. A. C. Bradley in 1904, the year before Adams wrote the *Education*, speculated of a younger Hamlet that 'Doubtless in happier days he was a close and constant observer of men and manners'.[10] The Adams of the *Education* uses the image of a card game to make the same point about himself: 'Probably no child, born in the year [1838], held better cards than he . . . As it happened, he never got to the point of playing the game at all; he lost himself in the study of it, watching the errors of the players' (4). The moral errors were those that were especially noticeable, and Adams throughout the book vivified them by making them visible to the eye as well as referring to them abstractly. Slavery, seen in Maryland in 1850, struck him in this manner:

> The railway, about the size and character of a modern tram, rambled through unfenced fields and woods, or through village streets, among a haphazard variety of pigs, cows, and negro babies who might all have used the cabins for pens and styes, had the Southern pig required styes, but who never showed a sign of care. This was the boy's impression of what slavery caused . . .   (44)[11]

The seasoning he underwent in London during the Civil War, being privy to his father's diplomacy, gave him a chance to observe the presumed duplicity of Earl Russell. This too had a visual embodiment: '*Punch*, before 1862, commonly drew Russell as a schoolboy telling lies, and afterwards as prematurely senile, at seventy' (164). The horrifying scandals under Grant's administration likewise were visible to the eye, in Adams's two vivid metaphors:

> The worst scandals of the eighteenth century were relatively harmless by the side of this, which smirched executive, judiciary, banks, corporate systems, professions, and people, all the great active forces of society, in one dirty cesspool of vulgar corruption . . . already he [Adams] foresaw a life of wasted energy, sweeping the stables of American society clean of the endless corruption . . .   (272–3)

To function as 'close and constant observer' was thus literally to confront evil with the senses as well as with the mind. We recollect Hamlet vividly speaking of the 'salt of most unrighteous tears' and the 'incestuous sheets' of his mother, and the 'funeral bak'd-meats' that 'Did coldly furnish forth the marriage tables' (I, ii, 180–1).

The next step for a moralist beyond mere observation is protest—some verbal articulation of outrage. Adams's chapter 'Free Fight' (1869–70) begins with remarks about his 'splenetic temper' (269) in the face of the 'unnecessary evils' of nature—bad climates and the differentiation of sexes. Behind this banter (not too far removed from Hamlet's discerning of camels, whales, and weasels in the clouds), lay the serious moral outrage over existing political evils. Adams again used journalism as the outlet for his anger and devotes the chapter to two scandalous occurrences in particular. One was the notorious and brazen effort by financier Jay Gould to corner the US gold supply in 1869, which Adams wrote up for the *Edinburgh Review*. The other scandal was within the government itself, as executive, legislative and judicial branches all engaged in mutual destruction. The Senate chamber was a particular focus for this national chaos, being 'a scene of irritated egotism that passed ridicule.

Senators . . . picked quarrels with each other, and no one objected, but they picked quarrels also with the Executive and threw every Department into confusion' (278–9). The newspapers, reported Adams, 'discussed little else than the alleged moral laxity of [President] Grant, [Congressman] Garfield, and [Speaker of the House] Blaine' (280). Adams himself summarized it all in a long and angry essay for the *North American Review* ('The Session').

His intent was destruction, annihilation of the evil itself and thorough reformation of the men. Both articles struck their mark, but with little consequence. Hamlet's dramatic simulation of his father's murder had at least the effect of interrupting the performance and driving his uncle from the audience. Adams's articles were instantly read widely and pirated by other periodicals, and the 'Session' piece dealing with Congress was even 'reprinted by the Democratic National Committee and circulated as a campaign document by the hundred thousand copies' (292). The moral effect, however, was nil. Readers he had, but the cry of conscience, the 'active enmity' toward corruption that the articles represented (281), failed to arouse the American public. 'Not one person, man or woman offer[ed] him so much as a congratulation, except to call him a begonia' (292). Begonia was the epithet applied to him by a Wisconsin senator, evidently in scornful measurement of the weakness of a moral stance in the America of 1870—an 'unweeded garden' if ever there was one. Or, to use Adams's own specific allusion to *Hamlet*: 'On the whole, even for Senators, diplomats, and Cabinet officers, the period was wearisome and stale' (295).

The conflicts thus set up between the New England conscience and the succession of British and American politicians do not, as in *Hamlet*, lead into violent combat and a spectacular denouement. 'Barren and dangerous' the Washington politicos might be (297), but Adams does not emerge as a knight to combat them in the political arena directly or as a shrewd gamester to defeat them with clever strategy. His moralizing is verbal and direct, much as the Hamlet who cries to his mother, 'O shame! Where is thy blush?' But none of the soiled politicians find themselves convicted—none cries that his heart is cleft in twain. A mere 'begonia', Adams is not even honored with an attempt to be bought off, much less exalted, like Hamlet, with a commission to have his head struck off. For all practical purposes, except for one transitory political campaign, he is ignored. The first half of Adams's book ends with Adams quite resigned to failure. 'Henceforth, he went on, submissive' (313). This is the last line of the last chapter in the first section, appropriately titled 'Failure'. We recognize that the Hamlet analogy which up to now has seemed so plain is an analogy concerned specifically with temperament, which Adams wisely refuses to carry into plot or structure. Hamlet plunges on; Adams withdraws from the struggle.

III

What occurs in the second half of the *Education* is therefore not a heightening of the specific moral tensions and conflicts of the first part. Instead, it is an attempt to examine thoroughly the world in which they take place, the world in which 'moral law' seems to have expired. This examination shows us the other aspect of Hamlet's character residing in Adams, the quality of consciousness and awareness. We see Adams putting forth this trait for our consideration as we begin the chapter entitled 'Twenty Years After'. The year is now 1892, and Adams's days of journalistic activism and moral outrage have been left behind. The twenty years had been spent teaching medieval history at Harvard, editing the illustrious *North American Review*, writing nine volumes of American history, and quietly penning two novels. 'Henry Adams thought his own duties sufficiently performed and his account with society settled' (315–16). There is thus a distinct chronological separation that Adams insists upon: one's hereditary 'duties', moral and vocational, occupied the first half of life, and now to be undertaken is serious thought, the painful exertion of the intellect. The mind as active probing agent takes over to replace the mind as passive repository of *a priori* morality. As noted, this sharp dichotomy perhaps more than anything else prevents Adams from enforcing the Hamlet analogy step by step throughout the *Education*. In *Hamlet*, conscience and consciousness exist inextricably; it is ludicrous to try to think of Hamlet relaxing his vigil or becoming 'submissive'. Adams, with a whole lifetime to portray, finds the dichotomy structurally important, in setting off his life into distinct phases. Yet in the long run the reader cannot help noticing that Adams wants things both ways. He wishes to emphasize consciousness in the last half of his life, yet he makes plain from the beginning that a predisposition toward that consciousness does exist from boyhood. 'Restless-minded, introspective, self-conscious' are the adjectives Adams applies to himself and his brothers from childhood on (28). As early as the fourth page of his narrative he stresses that in him were intensified certain New England traits, 'the habit of doubt; of distrusting his own judgment . . . .; the tendency to regard every question as open . . .' (6). In short, we are to understand that a predisposition to selfconsciousness and mental awareness exists in Adams from boyhood, even if this seems to be operating only at half-capacity during the first three-and-a-half decades of his life. The critical and questioning faculty, dormant and unaware of the right questions to ask, coexists in the boy and man with an unthinking *a priori* moralism. Contradictory as this sounds—a habit of distrust going along with unquestioning assent—Adams seems to insist upon it. His reason becomes clear only in the second part of the book. We need only contrast two passages, the first from chapter two:

> Viewed from Mount Vernon Street [the Adams boyhood home], the problem of life was as simple as it was classic. Politics offered no difficulties, for there the moral law was a sure guide. Social perfection was also sure, because human nature worked for Good, and three instruments were all she asked—Suffrage, Common Schools, and Press. On these points doubt was forbidden.   (33)

On these principles, and with faith in this Mount Vernon trinity Adams had operated, unconscious of their virtual obsolescence, until the decade of the 1870s. One might very well be born with a propensity for doubt, but doubt stopped at these three icons. The Adams of 1892, however, was beginning to wake into full consciousness, and with consciousness the secure icons of youth vanish in a mist of uncertainty. The second passage is from chapter 21:

> The new world he faced in Paris and London seemed to him fantastic. Willing to admit it real in the sense of having some kind of existence outside his own mind, he could not admit it reasonable [i.e. by his old Mount Vernon standards] . . . As he saw the world, it was no longer simple and could not express itself simply. It should express what it was; and this was something that neither Adams nor [his friend John] La Farge understood.   (317)

Two ideas are here for our attention. First, the consciousness which had always existed, but only in latent form, now arouses itself. Second, the stimulus for this arousing is the very newness of the modern world, which has become so striking as finally to make an impact on the mind. It is this acute awareness of the 'new world'—and the *sudden* awareness, Adams would have us believe—that defines the consciousness of Adams, his own peculiar 'pale cast of thought' that kept him for the remaining twenty-odd years of his life trying to find scientific and social patterns to deal with this newness.

The fruit of this contemplation finally turned out to be a theory of history that would account for the direction of history if not for its details. We recall that Hamlet, in the speech Adams has twice referred to, meditates on the likely consequences of consciousness: 'enterprises of great pitch and moment . . . lose the name of action'. Hamlet does not articulate in the speech the path he himself follows, a path which unites thought with action, which puts consciousness to active use so that effective action may follow. That is also the path that Adams follows in the last half of the *Education*. It is the quest to find out what is going on in the world, so that one can deal with it. Hamlet follows the movements of the King, has clandestine conversation with the Queen, interrogates Rosencrantz and Guildenstern, and in general conducts himself as a sleepless and earnest one-man intelligence-gathering agency. And he is finally able to have his acquired knowledge consummated in action. Adams moves on a philosophical level. He tries to find out what is going on in terms of science and history. And the final result of his efforts culminates not in action for himself but in a gentle hope that others may benefit. If man wishes to lead a successful life, his only hope lies in this very consciousness or awareness, not in mere action alone, which is the flaw of most Americans (297), and not in mere reflex response to *a priori* morals. The famous lines of the preface express quite clearly the intended link between Adams's theorizing and a later generation's practice that might follow from it: the 'object, in this Volume, is to fit young men, in universities or elsewhere, to be men of the world, equipped for any emergency' (xxiv). Thus it is here again clear that the basic temperament of Adams is akin to that of Hamlet, and in a general sense their aims are similar. Only at the end is there a sharp divergence, for if Adams had pushed the analogy too far he would have had to make his book a tragedy. As we shall later spell out, this is by no means the logical outcome or the chosen intent.

The temperamental affinity of Adams with Hamlet, as an inquiring spirit determined to find out what is going on, begins to develop in the second chapter of the second section of the *Education* (chapter 22). Here Adams talks about 'a starting point for a new education' (337), about seeming 'to feel that something new and curious was about to happen in the world' (338), about discovering that 'life had taken on a new face' (339). The year is now 1893, notable to Adams for a panic in Wall Street, a world's fair in Chicago, and the reappearance in his life of his iconoclastic brother Brooks, 'a vigorous thinker who irritated too many Boston conventions ever to suit the [Boston] atmosphere' (338). These three novelties combined to suggest to Adams more things than he had dreamed of in his philosophy before. The panic seemed to demonstrate that even the shrewdest and wisest men of the world—those who manipulated money—were victims of 'some very powerful energy at work' which 'nobody understood' (338). The Columbian Exposition in Chicago, with its anachronistic architecture and fantastic Midway, was an 'inconceivable scenic display', an utterly chaotic 'Babel of loose and ill-joined . . . vague and ill-defined and unrelated thoughts and half-thoughts and experimental outcries' (340). As for Brooks, he brought to Adams a new hypothesis, or 'law of history', that seemed to prove the real nature of things to be 'instability' tending toward 'anarchism' (339). In short, when the dormant mind woke up in 1893 it found that the world it looked upon was chaos. One seems for the moment, at this critical point in the *Education*, to be transposed out of *Hamlet*, where 'the time is out of joint', into *Lear*, where 'all's cheerless, dark, and deadly'. Is chaos the law, or is there order in the chaos? This was the question to occupy Adams until he wrote the *Education* in 1905–6 and then for some ten more years.

It must be noticed that Adams's pursuit of scientific and metaphysical truth is on a different plane from Hamlet's pursuit of existential truth. To seek to discover how the world runs is a different problem from trying to find out what is on Claudius's calculating mind and what is making Gertrude act the way she does. Yet the alertness of the intellect is the same, and, more important, the self-conscious aspect of the pursuit looms large in both minds. Both Adams and Hamlet keep holding open house in their minds, as it were, pointing out to the audience how well aware they are of what they are doing and what they hope to accomplish by it. We readily accept the device of soliloquy in *Hamlet* as one convention that places us in the self-revealing mind of the speaker, but we have in addition such self-conscious interior revelation as Hamlet's declaration of awareness to Guildenstern: 'You would play upon me . . . you would seem to know my stop, you would pluck out the heart of my mystery . . . you cannot play upon me' (III, ii, 380 ff.). Or, the self-conscious explanation of his destined role, spoken to Gertrude after having stabbed Polonius:

> Heaven hath pleas'd it so,
> To punish me with this [Polonius] and this with me,
> That I must be their scourge and minister.
>
> (III, iv, 173 ff.)

The maps of Adams's mind and charts of his mental voyaging during the late years are open for inspection on page after page of the *Education*, the author being, as he frankly admits, 'engaged in studying his own mind' (434). The closing chapters of the *Education* give us a sense of isolation, a feeling that Adams as an old man is gradually withdrawing into the dark recesses of his mind to commune with himself and with whatever wisdom is available between the pages of books. 'He got out his Descartes again; dipped into his Hume and Berkeley; wrestled anew with Kant; pondered solemnly over his Hegel and Schopenhauer and Hartmann . . .' (431–2). The names of scientists further sprinkle his perplexed pages: Gibbs, Pearson, Stallo, Haeckel, Mach, Poincaré. The conflict which Adams is thus engaged in as he nears the climax of his book is one which involves the clash of competing theories, a combat of abstractions rather than a duel with rapier and dagger. Adams himself was uncomfortable with his ending; to try to tack an argumentative conclusion onto a book that has been predominantly narrative seemed an error of form.[12] But there is consistency of theme, as the consciousness latent in the 'eighteenth-century' Boston child from the beginning becomes an active and struggling force seeking mastery of twentieth-century chaos the world over. Fully aware that consciousness 'makes cowards', Adams and Hamlet both set up strong resistance to this tendency.

IV

Specific focus on these two traits of temperament, conscience and consciousness, is to suggest why it is that readers over the years have sensed an affinity between Adams and Shakespeare's Hamlet. The extended comparison does not exhaust the similarities, for in addition to the biographical parallels mentioned earlier one can without much difficulty construct a much longer list of temperamental and emotional affinities. Such a list is attempted by an affectionate reader of the Adams self-revealed in his published letters, as distinguished from the highly stylized view that Adams gives of his life in the *Education*. Louis Kronenberger declares:

> If Henry Adams was Hamlet in that he lacked the resolution to help avenge the murder of his grandfather's and his great-grandfather's dreams; if he was Hamlet in that he, in the *Education*, like the Prince of Denmark in his soliloquies, had a fine gift for dramatizing himself, if he was Hamlet in possessing a reflective and humorous nature, veined with sensibility and streaked with cruelty and disgust, and masculine in its thinking and feminine in its emotions—if he was Hamlet in all these things, he was Hamlet in one thing more: in relishing his privileged place in life . . . year after year Henry Adams crossed to Europe on luxury liners and for months on end moved about Europe at least as much prince as Hamlet—in a succession of splendid hotels and country houses, and in an atmosphere not always so conspicuous for seriousness of thought or loftiness of purpose . . .

Kronenberger is wrong in his initial statement, regarding a lack of resolution to avenge his ancestors, as we have noted above. But the rest of his remarks, pertaining as they do mostly to Adams's life rather than to his book, suggest further lines that might be followed if one were to read between the lines for a more extensive parallel between the two men. Briefer analogies by other scholars are also suggestive. Ernest Samuels, whose three-volume biography is authoritative, observes Adams's 'Hamlet-like indecision which was the other side of his passion for dogmatic generalization'. This is in reference to Adams's skeptical ambivalence toward the scientists he was reading and from whom he was deriving his law of history. Grant C. Knight, apropos of the same scientific researches, intriguingly suggests that Adams was 'a "Hamlet" substituting the second law of themodynamics for a father's ghost'. Richard Chase, in his dialogue, *The Democratic Vista*, has one character remark: 'Adams is the most famous example of the modern American Hamlet, whose character and thought are finally neutralized by contradictions, rather than being inspirited and enlivened by them.'[13]

All of this is not to say that *The Education of Henry Adams* cannot be understood without reference to *Hamlet*. The point is rather that an understanding of how *Hamlet* lurks inside and underneath Adams's moody life story is to approach that subtle book with the alertness that it demands, and moreover to gain at least a small sense of what the great

English playwright meant to this American whose whole life was lived within the drama that political history provides. 'Toward the real artists', Adams once wrote to the woman he loved, 'I take no attitude except that of staying quiet on my knees, as I do before Shakespeare and Rembrandt and George Washington and you.'[14]

Having made this far an excursion into the effect of Hamlet on Henry Adams, we have still not discussed the most significant reference to the play in Adams's *Education*. This is a particularly important one because it occurs in the last paragraph of the book, at the very point at which a reader is compelled to inquire 'What now?' What is the prospect for the future, now that Adams's consciousness has chastened us into awareness of our chaotic modern world? How does he get himself out of the book, having built up not to Alger-like success but merely to a sort of hesitant affirmation after talking almost endlessly of 'failure'? That *Hamlet* should have occurred to him as an exit device is for several reasons not at all surprising, as a bit of investigation into cultural and personal history will suggest.

In 1904, the year before Adams wrote his book, A. C. Bradley published in England his famous lectures on *Shakespearean Tragedy*, where he noted that *Hamlet* was the most popular of Shakespeare's plays on the English stage at the end of the nineteenth century.[15] This was true in America as well as England, and had been for some time. Boston alone, for example, had the chance to see eleven stagings of the play between 1870 and 1876, the years that Adams had taught at Harvard.[16] Adams's teacher, James Russell Lowell, was one of the many American critics who studied the young Dane and the troubling play that recounted his irresolution. Lowell, in fact, apparently valued *Hamlet* highest among Shakespeare's plays, if we judge by the length and passion of the *Hamlet* section in his 1868 essay 'Shakespeare Once More'.[17] In America at large during Lincoln's time there was 'widespread knowledge' of the stock situations in *Hamlet*, says a historian who has studied the matter. McGuffey's famous Readers, as one contribution to this knowledge, presented for young readers Hamlet's speech concerning Yorick's skull, marked with the desired inflections and pauses.[18] Practical young Americans at the time of Adams's boyhood were thus doubly enriched—encountering principles of elocution along with their exposure to great dramatic literature. It was this haphazard familiarity with the great lines from *Hamlet*, parroted in the schools, that Mark Twain exploited in perhaps the most comic scene of *Huckleberry Finn* (published 1885, but set in the 1840s): the charlatan duke's rendition of 'Hamlet's soliloquy', which turns out to be a preposterous pastiche (chapter 21).

Mid-century in America, the period of Adams's collegiate years, had seen the rise to fame of Edwin Booth, the illustrious son of Junius Brutus Booth and brother to John Wilkes. Edwin Booth's *Hamlet* was in the repertoire of his first visit to Boston in the spring of 1857, when he was twenty-three and Henry Adams in the audience was nineteen. Newspaper reviews of his performance were mixed. The Boston *Transcript* reviewer reported that Booth indeed looked the part of Hamlet, but that the production on the whole was barely an average job. A correspondent to the *Transcript*, however, asserted that Booth's Hamlet was 'beautiful'—not so much in energy expended but in intensity of portrayal.[19] When Booth returned to Boston with Hamlet in November of 1859, Mrs. Julia Ward Howe poured out nineteen effusive stanzas on the performance, which Lowell published in the *Atlantic Monthly* under the title 'Hamlet at the Boston'. Two of her romantic quatrains give an idea of why Booth's powerful characterization lingered in the memory:

> And, beautiful as dreams of maidenhood,
> > That doubt defy,
> Young Hamlet, with his forehead grief-subdued,
> > And visioning eye.
>
> . . . .
>
> 'Tis with no feigned power thou bind'st our sense,
> > No shallow art;
> Sure, lavish Nature gave thee heritance
> > Of Hamlet's heart.[20]

A junior at Harvard in 1857, Henry Adams saw Booth's first Hamlet at the Boston Theatre and came away from it moved by the sheer theatricality of the young Edwin. Adams was to see *Hamlet* twice more very soon, once in 1858 in Berlin and once in 1860 in Düsseldorf. The Berlin performance, probably starring Louis Dessoir, reminded him of Booth's triumphant debut in Boston. In a letter to his family he drew a comparison between Booth's production and the one he had just seen at Berlin's *Schauspielhaus*: The German version

> was well done; remarkably well done. Setting aside the scenery, which is always perfect here, it was an exceedingly well acted piece. But Dessoir was not equal in stage effects to Booth and I've seen Mrs. Barrow [of the Boston Theatre permanent repertory company] do Ophelia much better than the little Fräulein Fuhr, who didn't at all satisfy me.

There was also, he observed, a loss in the translation; 'the German spoils it to an Englishman. The speech " 'Tis not alone my inky cloak, good mother" begins in the German "Gnädige Frau". The whole thing sounds flat to me in German.'[21]

Of his theater experiences during those two years in Europe, this was quite the longest response that Adams set down in writing. There is little doubt that the play itself had something to say to him—something he did not try to explain but only hinted at when he described Bogumil Dawison's performance in Düsseldorf, his third *Hamlet* in four years: 'It was a very remarkable rendering, something entirely new and very striking, but repulsive and painful. I don't want to see it again and yet it showed more genius than any I ever saw.'[22]

No wonder, then, with the early imprint of at least three *Hamlets* on his mind, Adams dropped fragments of the great Shakespearian lines into his letters and writings during the late 1850s and 1860s. Probably it was Booth's Hamlet, or perhaps an early reading of the play, that came to mind in January of 1858 when he delivered a college oration at festivities of the Hasty Pudding Club. In 'The Cap and Bells' he made reference to the scene at Yorick's grave and to the 'great revenge' contemplated by Hamlet in his 'half-real madness'.[23] A letter to his brother from Washington in 1861 made semi-comic use of Hamlet's speech to Horatio in I, v, 129–31: 'I for one am going upon the business or the pleasure that shall suit me, for every man hath business or desire such as it is, and for my own poor part—look you—I will go write an article for the *Atlantic Monthly*.' Ophelia's mad song from act IV comically launched a spirited letter to his brother in 1862:

> Good morrow, 'tis St. Valentine's day
> All in the morning betime.
> And I a maid at your window
> To be your Valentine.

The same 'undiscovered country' lines from Hamlet's soliloquy that would later give Howells the title for a novel provided Adams in 1866 with a humorous reflection upon his brother:

> Charles and his wife are so happy in Italy that I could envy them if it were not for that 'something ere the end', that un-discovered country from whose bourne no bachelor returns makes me rather 'accept the ills I have, than' the rest— Hamlet's logic is good for more cases than suicide.

In 1867, looking at the wretched state of post-war politics, he complained to his brother, 'The world is out of joint, and Hamlet was a damned fool for trying to set it right instead of trying to make money on it.'[24] Oddly enough, it was during this very decade that Adams had an excellent chance to contemplate his grandfather's spirited affection for *Hamlet*. In 1862 James H. Hackett published in New York a little volume with a long title, *Notes and Comments upon Certain Plays and Actors of Shakespeare*, which included the long letter about *Hamlet* that John Quincy Adams had written him in 1839. 'I look upon the tragedy of *Hamlet* as the master-piece of the drama—the master-piece of Shakespeare—I had almost said, the master-piece of the human mind', enthusiastically declared the ex-President and then-Congressman (p. 192).

Saturated in *Hamlet* at an early age, it is no wonder that at the other end of his long life Adams should find the words and situations of Hamlet coming back upon him. His first visit to the real Denmark had been in

1862, two years after his Düsseldorf *Hamlet*. Nearly forty years elapsed before his second visit, in 1901, as the *Education* was possibly beginning to germinate in his mind. In the early autumn of that year he boarded a ship in Sweden and crossed the Baltic Sea 'to Helsingfors where Hamlet's father's ghost was sitting on his terrace waiting'. Early in 1904 the Ghost reappeared, as Adams, now sixty-six, contributed to the memorial volume put out by the Century Club in New York in honor of the late Clarence King. The brilliant geologist King, who was to figure so prominently in the *Education*, had in 1894 gone with his friend Adams to visit pre-revolutionary Cuba (*Education*, 349) and had gregariously roamed about in the wilds becoming friendly with the brigands and conspirators of the island. The incongruous situation amused Adams, as he depicted himself and the ebullient King: 'There were two elderly men; bald-headed [Adams]; gray-haired, or at least sable-silvered, like Hamlet's father [King], literary and scientific gentlemen . . .'[25]

Twice, therefore, in four years the Ghost of Hamlet's father had made its appearance in the mind of the ageing Adams. Was he the Hamlet perceiving this ghost? We may guess that the implication was intended, and that to close friends and correspondents this role was not a new one for Adams to adopt. At least twice in the 1890s he had made the persona quite explicit. Writing in 1891 to his closest friend, Elizabeth Cameron, wife of a Pennsylvania senator, he had lamented their impossible relationship. 'Why send you what I have written in this letter? I know it cannot give you pleasure, and is likely to give you pain . . . I cannot with propriety lead a life fit for you to associate with. I must be a nuisance to you and myself—like Hamlet . . .'' Here the Hamlet persona thus had a very personal implication, opening up a realm additional to the political and moral implications that we have already noticed in the *Education*. Traveling in France in 1899, Adams was still writing to Mrs. Cameron, though he had managed to stabilize his romantic feelings. He could now jest about his passion for 'twelfth century churches and literature', and declare of himself to Mrs. Cameron, nineteen years his junior: 'I am a sexagenarian Hamlet with architectural fancies.'[26]

Adams published his *Education* privately in 1907, in 100 copies for friends. Presumably most were keen enough to perceive both Hamlets, the romantic 'nuisance' and the political moralist, though the former is quite absent from the text. For the rest of us, the Hamlet of the *Education* is the man who tried heroically to consummate a difficult relationship between himself and the world, between conscience/consciousness and the recalcitrant circumstances of an amoral and chaotic world. Possibly aware that the psychological resemblances between himself and Hamlet in the *Education* were becoming too striking, Adams at the end backed away. Throughout the book he had been adhering, in effect, to his mentor Lowell's dictum that 'the aim of the artist is psychologic, not historic truth',[27] but even so he could hardly so disregard history as to end the book on a fully tragic note. He had not, after all succumbed; his mind in its quest had invented a great formula, a 'Dynamic Theory of History' (473),and had in fact seemed to see a bit of light flickering at the end of the historical corridor. Perhaps the modern mind *could* deal with the remarkable new forces and energies that seemed to buffet from all sides: 'Thus far, since five or ten thousand years, the mind had successfully reacted, and nothing yet proved that it would fail to react—but it would need to jump' (498). Adams himself is thus left wearied by mental struggle but in fact quite alive and even hedgingly triumphant. The death that marks the end of the book is that of Adams's longtime friend, John Hay, and it is not a tragic death. No Hamlet, Hay in eight years as Secretary of State 'had solved nearly every old problem of American statesmanship, and had left little or nothing to annoy his successor' (503). Never introspective, Hay had had brilliant success in the active world as poet, editor, businessman, biographer, and statesman. Yet Adams, in what is perhaps one of the two or three artistic blunders of the *Education*, tried in the last sentences to shift the role of Hamlet from himself to Hay. Hay, the cheerful man of affairs and symbol in the book of cynical politician but also devoted public servant, prepares to die, and in doing so echoes Hamlet. To which Adams responds as Horatio:

> when the treatment ended, three weeks later, and he [Hay] came on to Paris, he showed, at the first glance, that he had lost strength . . . He was conscious of it, and in his last talk before starting for London and Liverpool he took the end of his activity for granted. 'You must hold out for the peace negotiations' [of the Russo-Japanese War], was the remonstrance of Adams. 'I've not time!' he replied. 'You'll need little time!' was the rejoinder.   (504)

'Had I but time', was the way Hamlet put it, in Shakespeare's words. Fixing on Hay's remark as a fortuitous way to lead himself out of the *Education*, Adams somewhat incongruously moves into the final paragraph of the book with himself still in the role of Horatio, survivor:

> There it ended! Shakespeare himself could use no more than the commonplace to express what is incapable of expression. 'The rest is silence!' . . . It was not even the suddenness of the shock, or the sense of void, that threw Adams into the depths of Hamlet's Shakespearean silence in the full flare of Paris frivolity in its favorite haunt where worldly vanity reached its most futile climax in human history; it was only the quiet summons to follow—the assent to dismissal.   (504–5)

Perhaps, indeed, it was not so severe a mistake suddenly to throw over Hamlet and close out the narrative as Horatio. For Adams no doubt had in mind the succeeding words of Horatio: 'Let me speak to the yet unknowing world/How these things came about'. Moreover, as the ambiguous reference to 'Hamlet's Shakespearean silence' suggests, Adams was possibly trying to play both roles at once.

In the final analysis, however, the importance of the Hamlet persona in the *Education* has to do neither with the facts of John Hay's life nor with Adams's apparent switch in roles at the end. The larger implications are suggested by Lowell and Thoreau, the authors providing epigraphs for this study. Writing in 1840 as an American fully cognizant of the new nation's great destiny, Thoreau registered a mild and even humorous dissent, as was his custom. He pointed to the bustling, active world of whaling, homesteading, selling, fighting, fishing, sailing—and included in his Whitman-like catalog of possibilities the fantasy of carrying mail in Peru or falling victim to a Siberian exile. But he reserved the end of his list for the least likely possibility to entice a young American (Thoreau was twenty-three): 'what a pity if the part of Hamlet be left out!' One might read about Hamlet in school readers, but the very idea of an American boy growing up that way! Esther Dunn points to the manner in which McGuffey handled Shakespeare's biography in his Readers—stressing his good marriage, his joint-ownership of a theater, and the fact that he 'accumulated some property'. *There* was Shakespeare; there was nothing of the Hamlet in the man who wrote *Hamlet*—school children, please note. Apprehensive parents were alerted by James Russell Lowell, lover of Shakespeare and well acquainted with the reflective life in his capacity as Smith Professor of French and Spanish at Harvard, but at bottom a practical man. Toward the end of the 1868 essay already cited, 'Shakespeare Once More', Lowell made a remark which hits strikingly close to the Henry Adams temperament and is almost a verbal foreshadowing of Adams's self-deprecating description of himself as failing to play his hand in the card game of life. It was not of Adams, Lowell's student of ten years before, that he was speaking, however. Lowell was cautioning against a Hamlet tendency that seemed to be catching on in America generally in the Gilded Age, not just among thin-lipped Bostonians. A modern American reader cannot help respond with a feeling of irony and may well rub his eyes in disbelief, but here is what Lowell was writing: 'It is certainly curious how prophetically typical the character [of Hamlet] is of that introversion of mind which is so constant a phenomenon of these latter days, of that over-consciousness which wastes itself in analyzing the motives of action instead of acting' (*Among My Books*, p. 225). Thoreau thought the absence of this phenomenon a pity in America; to Lowell, even in the middle of a business-oriented era, it was nothing but waste.

To have examined one such figure out of the era under discussion (Adams was two years old as Henry Thoreau wrote in his journal), is to consider the reality of the tension in America between act and thought, even in Adams's lifetime (1838–1918), an era usually understood in terms of enterprise, aggrandizement, decisiveness, and 'get-up-and-go'. The Hamlet side of the American character, as we see it cropping out in such diverse literary characters as James's Lambert Strether, Howells's Silas Lapham, and the 'I' in Emily Dickinson's poems is—Lowell notwithstanding—the side of America that can increasingly be seen as more attractive and even necessary than the average citizen has learned to acknowledge. Society, that is, does not remain humane unless consciousness and conscience are sensitively functioning at all levels. Consciousness provides imaginative awareness not only of different possibilities for growth and change but of their respective implications and of the need for choice, while conscience keeps pace, ready to take stands based on considered principle and to pass moral judgment on public actions.

It might well be argued that there is thus a kind of ideal, Platonic Hamlet toward which men aspire, which neither Shakespeare's Hamlet nor the Henry Adams of the *Education* is able really to be. Neither man, admirable in many ways, will serve us adequately as a model. The Hamlet temperament is one that too easily debases itself into either gothic monomania or cynical passivity. Toward the latter Adams tended in real life, and of the former in America Faulkner gives us a picture in the haunting figure of Henry Sutpen, who murders his sister's suitor in Mississippi in 1865 (*Absalom, Absalom!*): 'that gaunt tragic dramatic self-hypnotized youthful face like the tragedian in a college play, an academic Hamlet waked from some trancement of the curtain's falling and blundering across the dusty stage from which the rest of the cast had departed . . .'

That, however, is another story. Meanwhile, the Henry Adams whose conscience cried out to save his morally floundering nation and whose consciousness incisively discerned what are still central problems of a technological society is perhaps the most poised and balanced—and therefore useful—reincarnation of Hamlet that America has yet produced.

Notes

1. See Esther Dunn, *Shakespeare in America* (New York, 1939), pp. 209, 211, and elsewhere; Robert Falk, 'Shakespeare in America: A Survey to 1900', *Shakespeare Survey 18* (Cambridge, 1965), pp. 102–19.

2. To James H. Hackett, 19 February 1839. Hackett, *Notes and Comment upon Certain Plays and Actors of Shakespeare, with Criticisms and Correspondence* (New York, 1863), p. 193.

3. Halford Luccock, *Contemporary American Literature and Religion* (Chicago, 1934), p. 137. *The Education of Henry Adams* was published privately in 1907 and by Houghton Mifflin (Boston) in 1918. Later printings, including the Modern Library edition, have the same pagination. Page references are in parentheses.

4. Years later Adams wrote to Charles Milnes Gaskell, an English friend: 'Our epoch of John Stuart Mill and de Tocqueville and Henry Reeve and the Duke of Argyll, is as far away as that of Rousseau and of John the Precursor. What is to happen next does not necessarily

concern us' (10 March 1902). *Letters of Henry Adams 1892–1918*, ed. Worthington Chauncey Ford (Boston and New York, 1938), p. 377.

5. 'Shakespeare Once More', *Among My Books* (Boston, 1870), p. 213. Originally published in *North American Review*, 106 (April 1868), 629–70.

6. 'Henry Adams, or the Creation of Confusion', *In Defense of Reason* (New York, 1947), p. 391. 'The history immediately relevant to an understanding of Adams's mind might be said to begin with the first great theological critics of Aquinas, especially with Ockham' (*ibid.* p. 374). See also Austin Warren, *The New England Conscience* (Ann Arbor, 1966), pp. 170–81, for discussion of Adams's moral heritage.

7. *Apostles of the Self-Made Man* (Chicago, 1965). Cawelti rightly points out that Adams in his best known novel, *Democracy*, deals with self-made men in the realm of American electoral politics (p. 267).

8. Ernest Samuels discusses this phase of Adams's life in *The Young Henry Adams* (Cambridge, Mass., 1948), pp. 97–112. Adams also wrote letters to the son of Secretary of State William H. Seward as a part of his quiet but determined activism. They are printed with an introduction in Charles Vandersee, 'Henry Adams Behind the Scenes: Civil War Letters to Frederick W. Seward', *Bulletin of the New York Public Library*, 71 (April 1967), 245–64.

9. Ernest Samuels, *Henry Adams: The Middle Years* (Cambridge, Mass., 1958), pp. 186–7. Adams, *John Randolph* (1883; rpt New York, 1961), pp. 25, 184.

10. *Shakespeare Tragedy*, 2nd ed. (London, 1905), p. 114.

11. I am quoting a less familiar passage to make the point. Most readers of the *Education* will also recall his famous analogy between the badness of the road that leads to Mount Vernon and the evil of Southern slavery (47).

12. Mixing 'narrative and didactic purpose and style' is something that 'cannot be successfully done'. 'I found that a narrative style was so incompatible with a didactic or scientific style, that I had to write a long supplementary chapter to explain in scientific terms what I could not put into narration without ruining the narrative.' To Barrett Wendell, 12 March 1909, in *Henry Adams and His Friends: A Collection of Unpublished Letters*, ed. Harold Dean Cater (Boston, 1947), p. 645.

13. L. Kronenberger, "The Letters—and Life—of Henry Adams, *Atlantic*, 219 (April 1967), 83. Samuels, *Henry Adams: The Major Phase* (Cambridge, Mass., 1964), pp. 383, 25. G. C. Knight, *The Strenuous Age in American Literature* (Chapel Hill, 1954), p. 145. Luccock, *Contemporary American Literature and Religion*; R. Chase, *The Democratic Vista* (Garden City, 1958), p. 41. A list of similarities, both basic and trivial, could carry on endlessly. It is not surprising to find the authors of a recent study-guide to the *Education* asking as their first practice question why Henry Adams could 'be considered a Hamlet figure'. Their prefabricated answer is rather more intelligent than occur in most books of this kind, and it makes, among other obvious points, the observation that 'although the man Adams was known to be fond of society, the speaker that one finds in the *Education* is quiet, withdrawn, and meditative, much like Hamlet. Adams is also given to soliloquies, or long periods of vocal soul-searching—in a very real sense, the entire *Education* can be considered an extended soliloquy on Adams' view of society'. James and Colette Lindroth, *The Education of Henry Adams* (Monarch Notes and Study Guides, New York, 1966), p. 70.

14. To Mrs. J. Donald Cameron, 28 December 1891, in Adams Papers, Massachusetts Historical Society, Boston. Quoted by permission.

15. *Shakespearean Tragedy*, p. 91.

16. Eugene Tompkins, *The History of Boston Theatre, 1854–1901* (Boston-New York, 1908).

17. See also Falk, 'Shakespeare in America: A Survey to 1900', p. 114.

18. Dunn, *Shakespeare in America*, pp. 281–2, 233–5. See, for example, *McGuffey's New Fifth Eclectic Reader* (Cincinnati, 1866), p. 34.

19. Eleanor Ruggles, *Edwin Booth: Prince of Players* (New York, 1953), pp. 85–9, 96.

20. 'Hamlet at the Boston', *Atlantic Monthly*, 3 (February 1859), 172–3. Booth's Hamlet was to become 'a national institution, a legend'. See Charles H. Shattuck, 'Edwin Booth's *Hamlet*: A New Promptbook', *Harvard Library Bulletin*, 15 (January 1967), 20.

21. To Charles Francis Adams, Jr, 17–18 December 1858, in *Letters (1858–1891)*, p. 8.

22. To Charles Francis Adams, Jr, 25 November 1859, in *Letters (1858–1891)*, p. 55.

23. 'The Cap and Bells', *The Harvard Magazine*, 4 (April 1858), 125.

24. To Charles Francis Adams, Jr, 13 February 1861, in *Letters (1858–1891)*, p. 88. To the same, 14 February 1862, in *A Cycle of Adams Letters 1861–1865* (Boston and New York, 1920), I, 112. To John Gorham Palfrey, 4 May 1866, in Cater (ed.), *Henry Adams and His Friends*, p. 29. To Charles Francis Adams, Jr, 16 February 1867, in Adams Papers, Microfilms (Massachusetts Historical Society, Boston, 1954–9), reel 581.

25. To Mrs. J. Donald Cameron, 28 September 1901, in *Letters (1892–1918)*, p. 355; Adams, 'King', in *Clarence King Memoirs* (New York, 1904), p. 174.

26. 10 November 1891 and 26 September 1899, in Adams Papers, Massachusetts Historical Society. Quoted by permission.

27. 'Shakespeare Once More', *Among My Books*, p. 208.

"The Education of Ernest Hemingway"

George Monteiro*

I

To native writers emerging in the 1920s *The Education of Henry Adams* (1918) spoke with an immediacy and an authority now difficult to reconstruct. Sherwood Anderson, whose own *Winesburg, Ohio* (1919) would soon become another model for young writers, was puzzled by Adams's book. But he was intrigued enough by it to grapple with its ideas in the pages of his own autobiography. Scott Fitzgerald, who as a child had known Adams, not only studied the *Education* but paid its author a writer's compliment by putting him into *This Side of Paradise.* At one point, in fact, Fitzgerald had even decided to call his first novel *The Education of a Personage.*[1] On the basis of the *Education* T. S. Eliot branded Adams a 'sceptical patrician', damning him as an ineffectual product of his New England heritage, but not disdaining, all the while, to snap up from the *Education* images and phrases for his own poetry.[2] Ernest Hemingway, who consciously sided with Eliot on absolutely nothing, would have found himself, had the occasion forced itself, hard put to disagree with Eliot's rather summary judgement of Adams. Nevertheless, all things considered, it remains my conviction that one important way in which Hemingway's work resembles Eliot's, and both resemble Fitzgerald's, is that in certain basic characteristics it is what it is because of *The Education of Henry Adams.*

Precisely when Hemingway discovered the *Education* is difficult to say. Reviewing Anderson's *A Story Teller's Story* in 1925, Hemingway wrote: 'all of my friends own and speak of "The Education of Henry Adams" with such solemnity that I have been unable ever to read it.'[3] Yet, this disclaimer notwithstanding, he could and did resent those reviewers of Anderson's book who, in his opinion, too readily and fashionably compared it to the *Education.* Years later Hemingway would get into the same act, only by then it would be James Thurber's autobiography that he would prefer to the *Education.*[4]

*Reprinted from *The Journal of American Studies* 8 (April 1974), 91–99, by permission of Cambridge University Press.

How much of Adams's book the young Hemingway had absorbed by 1925 cannot, with certainty, be determined, but we do know, at least, that Anderson's autobiography provided him with a generous excerpt from the *Education*. Hemingway's review of *A Story Teller's Story* makes the point that in the public market-place Anderson's book, good enough in its own right, has no difficulty standing alone:

> The reviewers have all compared this book with the 'Education of Henry Adams' and it was not hard for them to do so, for Sherwood Anderson twice refers to the Adams book and there is plenty in the 'Story Teller's Story' about the cathedral at Chartres. Evidently the Education book made a deep impression on Sherwood for he quotes part of it . . . 'A Story Teller's Story' is a good book. It is such a good book that it doesn't need to be coupled in the reviewing with Henry Adams or anybody else.[5]

The passage quoted by the bemused Anderson comes from Adams's showpiece chapter on 'The Dynamo and the Virgin':

> Singularly enough, not one of Adams's many schools of education had ever drawn his attention to the opening lines of Lucretius, though they were perhaps the finest in all Latin literature, where the poet invoked Venus exactly as Dante invoked the Virgin:—
>> 'Quae, quoniam rerum naturam *sola* gubernas.'
> The Venus of Epicurean philosophy survived in the Virgin of the Schools:—
>> 'Donna, sei tanto grande, e tanto vali.
>> Che qual vuol grazia, e a te non riccore,
>> Sua disianza vuol volar senz' ali.'
> All this was to American thought as though it had never existed. The true American knew something of the facts, but nothing of the feelings; he read the letter, but he never felt the law. Before this historic chasm, a mind like that of Adams felt itself helpless; he turned from the Virgin to the Dynamo as though he were a Branly coherer. On one side, at the Louvre and at Chartres, as he knew by the record of work actually done and still before his eyes, was the highest energy ever known to man, the creator of four-fifths of his noblest art, exercising vastly more attraction over the human mind than all the steam-engines and dynamos ever dreamed of; and yet this energy was unknown to the American mind. An American Virgin would never dare command; an American Venus would never dare exist.[6]

Anderson's choice of this passage shows uncommon good sense, for it neatly epitomizes Adams's findings. Adams draws the historical line of ultimate enervation from Venus (the force of pagan love) to the Virgin (the potency of sex in Christianity) to the dynamo (the symbol of asexual power). In this excerpt the reviewer, a young man 'commencing his education', as he would later put it,[7] found a workable focus for assessing life in the twentieth century.

II

From the beginning Hemingway was cautious about naming those writers who influenced him, a caution which frequently broke out into nasty denials, name-calling, and angry repudiations. He worked constantly and successfully at the difficult task of convincing his readers that his fiction, unlike that of some others, grew directly out of life *as lived*. And Hemingway's success at implanting this idea was indeed remarkable, if we can go by the little that students of his work have so far uncovered about his sources. It is small wonder, then, that so little has been made of the somewhat obvious links between the stories of *In Our Time* and the *Education*. Nick's family name is, of course, Adams. His father's given name is Henry. And Nick's 'journey' as chronicled from story to story can be, and has been, seen as one of 'education'.[8] Even Adams's third-person narration, appropriate to a self-proclaimed 'manikin' but atypical of most autobiographies, is reminiscent of the third-person narration Hemingway chose for the highly autobiographical Nick Adams stories of *In Our Time*. Even if it is argued that Nick is not to be taken as an intimate persona for Hemingway, it is still certain from the chronological scheme of the stories in which he figures that Hemingway's narrative models in this instance were the *bildungsroman* and its close cousin the autobiography. That the specific model in this case, if we can choose one, was *The Education of Henry Adams* seems particularly plausible when we note that an early draft of 'Indian Camp', the story which presents Nick at his youngest, carries the telling legend: 'Ernest Hemingway Chartres September 27, 1925,'[9] a date less than six months after the publication of Hemingway's review of Anderson's autobiography. That Adams was on Hemingway's mind is suggested by 'The Last Good Country', another early story but until recently unpublished. There Adams's longing regard for the great mediaeval cathedrals finds a clear echo in Nick Adams's wistful exchange with his younger sister over the cathedrals of Europe they have read about but not yet seen.[10]

More significant than the identity in names, the shared metaphor of 'education', similar interests in cathedrals, and the similarity of attitudes and narrative methods, however, is the point that in the *Education* Hemingway found an exact and exacting definition of the world his generation had inherited, along with a set description of the historical milieu in which he himself must live and work. Years before the outbreak of war in 1914 Adams had pointed out that the human mind was helpless before the multiplication of forces which inevitably defeated its most disciplined efforts. In Adams's bootless search for man's proper and dignified place in the twentieth century Hemingway found a precedent for his own form of postwar acedia—as he would anatomize it in 'Soldier's Home', that account of the returning veteran's inability to 'readjust'. In Adams's insistence upon the importance of man's rationality and his ability to conceptualize, despite his cold awareness of their rapidly diminishing efficacy, Hemingway found precisely the intellectual attitude that the traumatized Nick Adams, in 'Big Two-Hearted River', could not begin to entertain. Nick Adams's opposition to ratiocination is echoed as well, but with a difference, in Jake Barnes's tight-lipped counter to quests like that of Henry Adams for an exact knowledge of relationships among forces. Barnes begins by saying that he has no interest in searching for the meaning of existence. 'I did not care what it was all about', he insists. 'All I wanted to know was how to live in it'—that is, how to acquire an education practical to the extent that it would enable him to live out his life with some semblance of personal order. But then, in the precise tenor, if not the thrust, of Henry Adams's own expression of his dimming hopes, Jake adds, 'Maybe if you found out how to live in it you learned from that what it was all about'.[11]

The Sun Also Rises resembles the Education in still other ways, particularly in its opening pages. With Hemingway's title and first epigraph in mind, consider the relevance of this early sentence from the Education, with its own dark echoes of the human battles and races alluded to in Ecclesiastes: 'Had he been born in Jerusalem under the shadow of the Temple and circumcised in the Synagogue by his uncle the high priest, under the name of Israel Cohen', writes Adams of himself, 'he would scarcely have been more distinctly branded, and not much more heavily handicapped in the races of the coming century, in running for such stakes as the century was to offer . . .'[12] It may be only coincidental, of course, but one should not dismiss out of hand the intriguing idea that Adams's decision to talk about himself as the historical counterpart of the high priest's nephew, Israel Cohen—in a biblical metaphor which runs through the entire first chapter of the book, and which at several points alludes directly to Ecclesiastes—has some relation to Hemingway's decision to call his hero's alter ego Robert Cohn and actually to name his hero Jacob, which is, Brett Ashley observes, 'a hell of a biblical name'.[13] The book itself, as Hemingway would insist, was 'a damn tragedy with the earth abiding forever as the hero'.[14]

Hemingway's A Farewell to Arms, his next novel, resembles the Education in a more general way. Both books depict the withdrawal of individuals—Frederic Henry and Henry Adams—into spectatorship before a world hopelessly out of joint. Both books focus on the effect that the making of a separate peace has upon those who must make it. And both books deal with the death of love. It may well be that writers in the twenties would date the death of love from World War I. 'All the major writers recorded it, often in piecemeal fashion, as part of the larger postwar scene', Mark Spilka has written; 'but only Hemingway seems to have caught it whole and delivered it in lasting fictional form.'[15] Anticipating that select group, comprised—as Spilka sees it—of D. H. Lawrence, Eliot, and Hemingway, Henry Adams grasped the theme even more surely than Hemingway. The perception that the force of love—sacred and profane—had long since died to the Western world is recorded again and again in the *Education*, first printed in 1907. It is the point of the passage quoted by Sherwood Anderson.

III

Of all the Hemingway works indebted to Adams, however, the one most profoundly influenced by the *Education* is *Winner Take Nothing* (1933). For this, his third collection of stories, Hemingway took the title from the book's epigraph:

> 'Unlike all other forms of lutte or combat the conditions are that the winner shall take nothing; neither his ease, nor his pleasure, nor any notions of glory; nor, if he win far enough, shall there be any reward within himself.'[16]

Originally Hemingway was wont to pass his epigraph off as a quotation from some ancient volume on the game rules of mediaeval or renaissance sport. Later, however, he acknowledged that he had contrived the statement himself. This admission makes the excerpt particularly interesting in the context of Adams's influence on Hemingway. To convey his sense of man's fate in his own time Hemingway forged a passage of archaic English. Formally, the forgery reflects his curious sense of out-moded syntax and diction. In sentiment, however, the forgery is something else again. Its stoicism, rooted as it is in that sorrowful book, Ecclesiastes, is reminiscent both of Henry Adams's longing for the Middle Ages and his twentieth-century pessimism.

Besides 'Fathers and Sons', the Nick Adams story which closes the volume, there are four other stories in *Winner Take Nothing* which are pertinent here. In concert they display the various ways in which Christianity manifests itself in the twentieth century. 'God Rest You Merry, Gentlemen' takes up the pathetic results of a sixteen-year-old's desperate attempt to live up to Pauline strictures on sexual purity. 'The Light of the World', which Hemingway once put forth as his choice for the collection's opening story, focuses, finally, upon the relevation by a massive whore that her Christ is a dead prizefighter who once made love to her. 'The Gambler, the Nun, and the Radio', presenting the discovery that people have many opiates besides religion, has as its setting a Catholic hospital and as one of its characters a young nun who prays to the Virgin, rather indiscriminately, for her personal opiates, baseball and football teams, and a Mexican ('a bad one, a thoroughly bad one') suffering from peritonitis. A poor judge of character, she asks Frazer, the author's persona, to write 'something sometime for Our Lady', as currently honoured by the Notre Dame football team. He declines. 'I don't know anything about her that I could write. It's mostly been written already', he answers, adding, 'You wouldn't like the way I write. She wouldn't care for it either.'

Frazer had resisted the temptation to write about the Virgin, but, just as the young nun had predicted of Mr. Frazer, Hemingway had not. The story *he* had written appears in the same volume. 'A Clean, Well-Lighted Place', dealing with themes of sex and Christianity, is a key to the entire collection.

Spain is the setting of 'A Clean, Well-Lighted Place', precisely because of Hemingway's awareness that in the twentieth century Spain has been the one major European country where Catholicism of a heavily mediaeval cast remains a cultural, national, and personal force. But the story, for all its Hispanic aura, remains an American story of Adams-like acedia. For Adams the historian it was the discovery of the loss of human energy stemming from man's turning to the dynamo that energized his *Mont-Saint-Michel and Chartres* (1904) and the *Education*; for Hemingway the storyteller it was the somewhat analogous discovery that he lived in a world diminished by the loss of energy. And like Adams, Hemingway could neither believe nor come to terms with his nagging disbelief.

The deaf old man who walks unsteadily but with dignity provides Hemingway's café waiters with a subject that will allow them to reveal themselves. We soon learn that a week earlier the old man attempted suicide but that his niece discovered him in time to prevent his suicide. Her fear, presumably, was the Catholic's fear that in taking his life he would commit the unpardonable sin of despair. Speculating on the old man's difficulties, one waiter suggests that the old man would be 'better with a wife', but the other one thinks that 'a wife would be no good to him now'. If the younger waiter is in a hurry to get home because he does have a wife and a bed waiting for him (' "I have confidence" ', he blusters, ' "I am all confidence" '), the older waiter cannot resist the opportunity to undermine his companion's unexamined sureness by asking him, with some malice, if he does not fear going home before his usual hour. This insulting joke—especially insulting to a *macho*—reflects the uneasy attitude toward marriage and sex which filters through the story.[17] That sex and marriage—and, by implication, the family as well—are no longer the forces that once they were is suggested in the waiters' combined reaction to the soldier and the girl (wearing 'no head covering') who pass by in the street.[18] It all boils down, apparently, to whether or not the soldier 'gets what he's after' before the guard picks him up.

The narrative then moves toward culmination: the dramatization of the older waiter's own anxiety. Fearing darkness, he is 'unhurried', we are told, and reluctant to close up. It is only as he makes his slow way home, however, that he holds that discourse with himself which spells out the nature of his own difficulties. He breaks out into summary statement first—and then into parodic prayer:

> It was all a nothing and a man was nothing too. It was only that and light was all it needed and a certain cleanness and order. Some lived in it and never felt it but he knew it all was nada y pues nada y nada y pues nada. Our nada who art in nada, nada by thy name thy kingdom nada thy will be nada in nada as it is in nada. Give us this nada our daily nada and nada us our nada as we nada our nadas and nada us not into nada but deliver us from nada; pues nada.

Then, echoing the Adams who in his own time had felt the personal necessity to construct his own 'Prayer to the Virgin', but whose historical and intellectual neck had already been broken, he tells us, at the sight of the dynamo in all its force and massive reality, Hemingway's waiter begins a similar prayer to the Virgin—'Hail nothing full of nothing, nothing is with thee'—only to break off abruptly when he recognizes that, ironically, at that very moment he too stands directly before an engine whose existence cannot be denied: a steam pressure machine, Adams's dynamo, diminished, of course, but no less real, has invaded the bars themselves in the form of an elaborate mechanism for the making of coffee. Like Adams, he 'turned from the Virgin to the Dynamo as though he were a Branly coherer'.[19] Like Adams, Hemingway's waiter can no longer trust in the Virgin's power and efficacy. 'All the steam in the world', lamented Adams, 'could not, like the Virgin, build Chartres', for 'symbol or energy, the Virgin had acted as the greatest force the Western world ever felt, and had drawn man's activities to herself more strongly than any other power, natural or supernatural, had ever done'.[20]

The peculiar force of Hemingway's story stems ultimately from the author's decision to locate his nihilistic theme in the consciousness of a café-waiter. It would startle no one to discover a philosopher or a metaphysician concerning himself with such matters as the meaning and purpose of the universe, but that a waiter could be plagued with such awesome thoughts would, under ordinary circumstances at least, defy credibility. One contemporary review of the *Education* distinguished between the common man and the man of genius:

> The common man . . . adapts himself to circumstances, and, whether he tends bar or serves as a college president, he generally obeys the injunction, 'Whatsoever thy hand finds to do, do it with all thy heart.' In his obedience, there is a certain instinctive faith—a faith in the rationality of the universe, in something that gives measure and direction . . .

But the man of genius, he concludes, 'can live only by making the problem of the universe his own aching, personal problem'.[21] As Hemingway's
story indicates, profound concern with 'the problem of the universe' is not
at all a surefire touchstone in distinguishing either between the common
man and the man of genius, or between the historian and the barman.

Sometime after the publication of *Winner Take Nothing*, and in the
midst of a world-wide depression, Hemingway turned from depicting individuals paralyzed by acedia to depicting beings who somehow manage
to win out. The boy-man Francis Macomber achieves his masculine
manhood even when death follows hard upon its achievement. In full
view of Mount Kilimanjaro Hemingway's apostate writer works through
to an eleventh-hour redemption by facing up to his past life. Robert Jor-
dan, organizing a last-ditch action of doubtful public importance, comes
to the buoyant and lyrical conclusion that 'the world is a fine place and
worth the fighting for'.[22] In retrospect, it can be seen that Hemingway's
work from this point on increasingly insisted upon defining a form of
stoicism that proved to be life-sustaining in an age of many apostasies, not
the least of which were his own. Henry Adams's masterpiece—an act of
life performed when its author, almost the age of Hemingway's old man
of dignity and, like him, already in the care of nieces,[23] was approaching
his seventieth birthday—presented a life of stoic searching. But there is an
important distinction to be made between these two stoics and their individual codes. Under pressure building up over a lifetime Adams forged
a personal code of honesty—to his thought. Responding to pressures of
equal intensity, Hemingway constructed a personal code of honesty—to
his emotions.

Postscript. In 1944 Hemingway was looking around for a respite from the
war. He opted for Mont-Saint-Michel, intending to 'hole up and write for
a few days', as he announced, in 'this old hang out of Henry Adams'.[24]

Notes

1. *The Letters of F. Scott Fitzgerald*, ed. Andrew Turnbull (New York, 1963), pp.
137–8; and Henry Dan Piper, *F. Scott Fitzgerald, A Critical Portrait* (New York, Chicago
and San Francisco, 1965), pp. 45 and 47.

2. 'A Sceptical Patrician', *The Athenaeum*, No. 4647 (23 May 1919), 361–2.

3. *Ex Libris* (March 1925), 176–7; reprinted with an introductory note by Matthew J.
Bruccoli, 'A Lost Book Review: *A Story-Teller's Story*', *Fitzgerald/Hemingway Annual 1969*
(Washington, D.C. 1969), pp. 71–4.

4. Audre Hanneman, *Ernest Hemingway: A Comprehensive Bibliography* (Princeton,
1967), p. 269.

5. *Fitzgerald/Hemingway Annual 1969*, p. 72.

6. *The Education of Henry Adams* (Boston and New York, 1918), pp. 384–5. In *A Story
Teller's Story* (New York, 1924), pp. 378–9, the text is quoted with slight modifications.

7. *A Moveable Feast* (New York, 1964), p. 85.

8. Two critics have called the stories 'educative' in the Adams sense. (1) Carlos Baker
suggests that the Nick Adams stories 'might be arranged under some such title as "The Educa-

tion of Nicholas Adams" ', but he does not tackle the question of influence (*Hemingway: The Writer as Artist*, third edition [Princeton, 1963], p. 128). (2) Roger Asselineau organizes several stories under the same rubric, 'L'Education de Nick Adams', in his two-volume Pléiade edition of *Oeuvres Romanesques d'Ernest Hemingway* (Paris, 1968), vol. 1, pp. 1–75. In an endnote Asselineau explains that he has adapted the title from Henry Adams (vol. 1, p. 1366).

9. Philip Young and Charles W. Mann, *The Hemingway Manuscripts: An Inventory* (University Park and London, 1969), p. 45.

10. Ernest Hemingway, *The Nick Adams Stories* (New York, 1972), p. 90.

11. *The Sun Also Rises* (New York, 1926), p. 148.

12. *Education*, p. 3.

13. *The Sun Also Rises*, p. 22.

14. Quoted in Baker, *Hemingway*, p. 81.

15. 'The Death of Love in *The Sun Also Rises*', *Twelve Original Essays on Great American Novels*, ed. Charles Shapiro (Detroit, 1958), p. 238.

16. *Winner Take Nothing* (New York, 1933). All further citations from stories in this collection follow this text.

17. That Hemingway himself shared the older waiter's joke is suggested by his rather startling note on the original manuscript of another Nick Adams story, 'The Doctor and the Doctor's Wife'. 'Don't feel disgraced if you're a cuckold', wrote Hemingway. 'Even a bull has horns' (*Hemingway Manuscripts*, p. 39).

18. That the girl wears no head-covering, an observation offered, ostensibly, as a realistic detail, takes us back to Saint Paul's injunction: 'every woman that prayeth or prophesieth with her head uncovered dishonoureth her head: for that is even all one as if she were shaven' (I Corinthians 11:5). Recall, also, that Jake Barnes makes a point of telling us that Brett Ashley was stopped just inside the church at Pamplona because she was not wearing a hat (*The Sun Also Rises*, p. 155), and that in *For Whom the Bell Tolls* one of the fascists' obscenities was to shave Maria's head.

19. *Education*, p. 384.

20. *Education*, pp. 388 and 388–9.

21. Anonymous, *North American Review*, 208 (December 1918), 925.

22. *For Whom the Bell Tolls* (New York, 1940), p. 467.

23. Adams presented *Mont-Saint-Michel and Chartres* (Boston and New York, 1913) as an uncle's long monologue to his nieces (p. xiv); see also Adams's *Letters to a Niece and Prayer to the Virgin of Chartres*, with a niece's memories by Mabel La Farge (Boston and New York, 1920).

24. Carlos Baker, *Ernest Hemingway: A Life Story* (New York, 1969), p. 406.

"The Education of Henry Adams: The Confessional Mode as Heuristic Experiment"

This essay is based upon a simple hypothesis: *The Education of Henry Adams*[1] is less a disguising of self-revelation as impersonal art than a disguising of impersonal and experimental art as self-revelation. The dual themes—life and art—run their criss-crossing courses through Adams's pages; but from beginning to end the book is conscious art. On the surface it mirrors those materials out of which it is fashioned: the catalogue of sensory and intellectual experiences which constitute human knowledge. To the degree that such experiences are personal, organized around a single life, they are described in familiar terms of the confessional mode, in the literary tradition of St. Augustine and Rousseau. Henry Adams's original contribution, however, his peculiar and highly artistic re-working of self-revelation makes the cumulative result something quite different. His book becomes first a pseudo-scientific exercise in evaluation, testing rather than relating what he has learned, and finally an heuristic experiment in literature, which directs attention to the audience and away from the subject. Instead of revealing himself to be a candid penitent, Adams employs the narrative of personal experience as a mask behind which to hide. The deceptive appearance of self-revelation shields him from the penetrating gaze of the world around, while he unobtrusively labors to convert a contrived case of personal failure into a method for producing a more-than-personal success—the education of his readers.

For those readers are *involved in* and not simply informed about the facts of Adams's life. Once the confessional mode is, in effect, outgrown by the maturing author, simple narration gives way to experimental techniques. A new mode of invitation and even provocation replaces at center stage the writer as subject with the reader as object and raises the artistic goal of the audience's self-instruction above that of the author's self-revelation. The repeated cry of "failure" becomes a signal for beginning a new chapter of human experience at the same moment that the word loses

*Reprinted from *The Journal of Narrative Technique* 4 (1974), 3–18.

its original significance as a pessimistic summary of an individual human life. Adams's portrayal of the basic divisions between life and art, confession and education, constitute, on the one hand, a denial of unity in the writer's experience and, on the other, an attempt to insure that a powerful impression of division will be reflected in the audience's understanding. This literary strategy of balance and division characterizes the whole of the *Education*.

Most readers have been more comfortable with the conventional appearance of the early chapters, the account of birth and boyhood, than with the puzzling speculations of the adult mind, recorded in the second part of the book, beginning "Twenty Years After" (Chapter XXI). Reassured by the authorially unauthorized insertion of the subtitle, "An Autobiography," these readers have insisted upon viewing the book as a chapter of New England confessional and more particularly, as a final installment of the four-generation Adams family chronicle. This interpretation, however, reveals only one part in the structural frame of the whole book, and that part is merely the foundation for Adams's more complex demonstrations. In short, the pose of self-understanding found in sections of the *Education* apparently devoted to conventional autobiography eventually becomes evidence of fraud. Like the presumption of Darwinism, self-revelation finally yields only the illusion and not the substance of order, and the unifying pattern of personal organization gives way to contradiction, paradox, and a realization that chaos inward and outward threatens individual sensibility.

In the process of this demonstration, the confessional habit that Henry Adams had inherited from his literary masters and from earlier members of his own family is made to parallel the verifiable sequence of entropy in family history. The great line which began with Presidents ends in an obscure failure. Moreover, the very act of writing about this Adams in the fourth generation evidences artistic entropy—the failure to sustain the inheritance of self-relevation as a literary mode. The seemingly unfinished product of Adams's art stands as proof of chaos. Nothing more, he insists, can be expected in an age that uses the truths of science to make ordered analysis impossible. The struggling figure of the eighteenth-century man seeks vainly to define his experiences of a lifetime in some mode of expression more modern and thus more adequate than that of confession and self-revelation. As he sets down in the older literary form his record of personal experience, Adams hopes to show the limitations of that very record and of the experience itself. The *Education* documents an attempt to understand its subject and at the same time denies the classic ideal of self-understanding, all the while thrusting experimentally toward the possibility of some more useful truth.

Adams's case for failure rests upon something more persuasive than a rehearsal of his singular experience. His demonstration displays the failure of a representative man, a failure based upon the inadequacy of *all* human education. Such failure, however, is shown to be not a conclusion but a prelude to a different kind of education, a heuristic process, activated among the special and highly selective class of readers to whom the *Education* is actually addressed, the "one [mind] in ten" that can react to, rather than simply accept, his message. Working upon this audience, Adams hopes to invite, agitate, and provoke individual participation and response. The author acts as teacher rather than narrator and uses his own confessional as a carefully censored casebook example, with the end in view of motivating the reader to surpass that example.

Elsewhere, in a different mode of literary expression, Adams was able to demonstrate that divided personal experience did not preclude unified artistic expression. A writer could be fair to both subject and audience; he could explore the complexities of life, make use of what he found as a basic schema for self-understanding, and still achieve unitary interpretation in art. Adams's poem "Buddha and Brahma" showed how:

> . . . we, who cannot fly the world, must seek
> To live two separate lives; one, in the world
> Which we must ever seem to treat as real;
> The other in ourselves, behind a veil
> Not to be raised without disturbing both.[2]

In one sense the *Education* never raises that veil, even when the book seems to be offering sincere confession. Its author knew that any satisfactory portrayal of himself would present a divided and contradictory nature. But on another level, the *Education*, like Adams's poem, shows that art makes possible some progress beyond the "impasse" created by asking "questions which have no answers." The perceptive reader was expected to recognize this possibility and make use of art to create for himself a unified interpretation of experience quite unlike the insistent polarity of Adams's view.

In order to succeed as heuristic art, the *Education* depends upon the audience, which must react to its message. The author's efforts to give shape to his materials, to order and structure the specific elements of the narrative, to select among the myriad details of personal experience—these things and more, however, combine to form a sophisticated literary method that tests the limits of what can be done to engage the reader's understanding. Before concentrating on the role of audience, then, it is necessary to look at some of the writer's strategies, the ways in which the lessons of the *Education* impose themselves upon our consciousness. Always, we must keep in mind that the clearest message from its pages is one of limitation, FAILURE, written large; and that, as a progressive teacher, Adams hoped to show as well as tell the story of his education.

On the surface the lesson of the *Education* may seem clear enough:

"Chaos was the law of nature; order was the dream of man" (*Education*, 451). Yet the limitations in man's knowledge of nature on one hand, and of human consciousness on the other gave dreams at least a tenable reality. Order was not impossible in art, especially if the artist could create a literary form adequate to convey the impression of anti-form in nature. Like a dream, the resolution of apparent opposites lay outside scientifically verifiable experience but not beyond possibility. Therefore, a part of the complete truth, as Adams formulated that truth, had to be suggested rather than recorded. For such a purpose only an experimental art that paralleled the experimentalism of psychology could be inclusive enough.

As a literary experiment in form, the *Education* has been greeted with skepticism and misunderstanding. The twenty year hiatus in chronology, the sharp narrative division between parts I and II, and the virtual disappearance of the central figure—all violate conventional expectations created by an ideal of the "well-made" book. However, form in the older style seemed to Adams as obsolete as other expectations based upon personal experience. Experiments required time for evaluation; but meanwhile, he could rely upon his own substantial practice as a writer to hypothesize and set in outline an organic aesthetic by which his book should be judged:

> The pen works for itself, and acts like a hand, modelling the plastic material over and over again to the form that suits it best. The form is never arbitrary, but is a sort of growth like crystallization, as any artist knows too well; for often the pencil or pen runs into side-paths and shapelessness, loses its relations, stops or is bogged. Then it has to return on its trail, and recover, if it can, its line of force (*Education*, 389).

The "lines of force" determined the final patterning of materials, as the artist responded to various influences upon his consciousness.

This psychology of art functioned also as a psychology of education, since artistic sensitivity was a prerequisite of understanding. Adams had already made this point in *Mont-Saint-Michel and Chartres*. Now, instead of relying upon medieval history and thought, his explanation drew from the modern intellectualism of twentieth-century science:

> Science has proved that forces, sensible and occult, physical and metaphysical, simple and complex, surround, traverse, vibrate, rotate, repel, attract, without stop; that man's senses are conscious of few, and only in a partial degree; but that, from the beginning of organic existence his consciousness has been induced, expanded, trained in the lines of his sensitiveness; and that the rise of his faculties from a lower power to a higher, or from a narrower to a wider field, may be due to the function of assimilating and storing outside force or forces (*Education*, 487).

Adams in these passages sought to expand the definitions of art and education beyond the range of traditional associations. Both hypotheses argue for organic rather than static expression and for demonstration rather than description. The organic "consciousness" can be "induced, expanded, trained in the lines of his sensitiveness" only by "forces" and not simply by reading stories.

First, however, the existence of such forces requires demonstration. That process repeatedly takes shape in a tripartite pattern: an explanation of past experience in traditional terms, followed by a declaration and exhibition of the inadequacy of such explanation, and finally, a series of conjectures about where this particular line of thought may be expected to lead in the future. Obviously, the writer's attempt to combine the philosophical materials of thought with the dramatic incidents from his life opened the possibility of literary failure. Adams accepted this risk, and then disposed of it with a characteristically veiled apology. He described his position as that of an heir to an ordered intellectual tradition which had maintained its unity until his father's generation but which had lost all coherence in his own time: "The Minister's mind like his writings showed a correctness of form and line that his son would have been well pleased had he inherited" (*Education*, 213).

As Henry never tired of pointing out, the eighteenth-century mind failed to meet the requirements of the nineteenth and twentieth centuries. In literature, the eighteenth-century form of personal narrative was inadequate to express the consciousness of the twentieth-century mind. But the artist had to begin with the materials passed to him. Thus, the book first appears to be a simple history of the titular character from birth to old age (with a strong suggestion of death in the later pages), and the reader's historical sense is constantly evoked by reference to centuries and geological periods: ". . . one's earliest ancestor and nearest relative . . . was *Pteraspis*, a cousin of the sturgeon, and whose kingdom . . . was called Siluria" (*Education*, 229). Simultaneously, however, Adams attempts to surprise or startle the reader who expects simple continuity by occasionally disregarding time sequence, by creating such interruptions as the twenty-year break between chapters XX and XXI. The hiatus in time parallels the omissions in geological evidence, and both refute the possibility of an orderly education. These deficiencies in any strict time organization become a part of Adams's lesson, presented to the reader by demonstration, as well as commentary. As he explains the lessons derived from those parts of his past which seem traditional and non-scientific,

> Historians undertake to arrange sequences,—called stories, or histories—assuming in silence a relation of cause and effect. These assumptions, hidden in the depths of dusty libraries, have been astounding, but commonly unconscious and childlike; so much so, that if any captious critic were to

drag them to light, historians would probably reply, with one voice, that they had never supposed themselves required to know what they were talking about. . . . Where he saw sequence, other men saw something quite different, and no one saw the same unit of measure. . . . Satisfied that the sequence of men led to nothing and that the sequence of their society could lead no further, while the mere sequence of time was artificial, and the sequence of thought was chaos, he turned at last to the sequence of force . . . (*Education*, 382).

As an Adams, the spokesman declared himself free of his inheritance in politics and religion; as a writer, he was by the same declaration freed from methods of expressing himself in any literary mode that depended upon the very sequences he found fault with.

Only in the final chapter of the book, "Nunc Age," does the reader realize what has happened to the child who was born into the Adams household in Chapter I. As a center of attention in the volume and as a representative of the Adams family, that figure has been made the victim of "the new powers that had been created since 1840, and were obnoxious because of their vigorous and nonscrupulous energy." Henry Adams as subject has been replaced and the "sequence of men" broken in the book just as the Adamses as an institution were replaced in society by the new forces which the childless writer tries to make graphic for his audience:

They were revolutionary, troubling all the old conventions and values, as the screws of ocean steamers must trouble a school of herring. They tore society to pieces and trampled it under foot. As one of their earliest victims, a citizen of Quincy, born in 1838, had learned submission and silence, for he knew that, under the laws of mechanics, any change, within the range of the forces, must make his situation only worse; but he was beyond measure curious to see whether the conflict of forces would produce the new man, since no other energies seemed left on earth to breed. The new man could be only a child born of contact between the new and the old energies (*Education*, 500).

The importance of family is stressed in the early chapters of the *Education* and almost totally ignored in the last sections. We recognize that when traditional forms of education are replaced by speculations about force, the author is using this sequence of ideas to represent a human process—maturation of the mind. Concomitantly, rhetorical emphasis upon Adams's individual identity diminishes as the consciousness is "induced, expanded, trained." Creation of this effect relies upon a complex narrative point of view and a developing rather than a static persona, to act as subject. The obvious device of third person narration not only provides a tone of scientific detachment but also serves in a larger way to keep the author separate from the subject figure. Adams is left free to comment as a retrospective observer, one who has completed an education and now is teaching the lessons he has learned. His commentary forms a sequence of model lessons, shaped to the purpose of the reader's education and not as a simple recounting of the author's personal experience.

What results is expansion of the narrative line into heuristic experiment aimed at the reader. Each lesson takes on symbolic value as its meaning expands beyond the normal limits of an incident in time, history, politics, or the author's personal experience. A sample passage will illustrate:

> The next day, when the boy went to school, he noticed numbers of boys and men in the streets wearing black crape on their arm [sic]. He knew few Free Soil boys in Boston; his acquaintances were what he called pro-slavery; so he thought proper to tie a bit of white silk ribbon round his own arm by way of showing that his friend Mr. Sumner was not wholly alone. This little piece of bravado passed unnoticed; no one even cuffed his ears; but in later life he was a little puzzled to decide which symbol was the more correct. No one then dreamed of four years' war, but everyone dreamed of secession. The symbol for either might well be matter of doubt (*Education*, 51).

The paragraph begins in simple narration, stressing the perception and then the limits of comprehension in "the boy." Retrospection allows the author to focus upon the education of the subject rather than upon the action described. The narrative persona plays both actor and observer; and the author's description of what has been learned is directed toward his readers as much as to the implicit question of cause. Finally, the problem of symbolic value—white and black—remains unsolved, a public as well as personal puzzle, which readers are invited to consider. Their experience, as much as his, is brought into play, and the narrative structure of the lesson prevents them from finding in the book merely what they might expect from Henry Adams, an attack on the evils of slavery.

Similarly, another device, introduction of a "manikin" figure under the name of Henry Adams, serves to protect the author from self-revelation by offering the disguise of personal experience as a covering for didactic art. From almost the first words of the book the reader is warned that he must not expect another confessional in the tradition of Rousseau. Adams's "Preface" declares that the *Confessions*, although written like the *Education* "in the manner of the eighteenth century," can be instructive in the twentieth century only when correctly viewed. Timely interpretation emphasizes limitations and not accomplishments, and makes the *Confessions* useful as a warning rather than a model.

> As educator, Jean Jacques was, in one respect, easily first; he erected a monument of warning against the Ego. Since his

time, and largely thanks to him, the Ego has steadily tended to efface itself, and, for purposes of model, to become a manikin on which the toilet of education is to be draped in order to show the fit or misfit of the clothes. The object of study is the garment, not the figure. . . .

The manikin, therefore, has the same value as any other geometrical figure of three or more dimensions, which is used for the study of relation. For that purpose it cannot be spared; it is the only measure of motion, of proportion, of human condition; it must have the air of reality; must be taken for real; must be treated as though it had life. Who knows? Possibly it had! (*Education*, x).

The manikin technique marks a distinct break with the literary mode of confession. As the author hides in his "garments," he hopes to turn the reader's attention away from "ego" and toward instruction instead of revelation.

Whatever "life" Adams noted in the manikin appeared to derive from forces outside human control. Forces produced change, and even "the man of science" stood "bewildered and helpless" before "the new class of supersensual forces." Attention to "garments" rather than to "ego" freed the author to follow forces when men failed him; yet his limited understanding made the testimony of the *Education* always incomplete. Adams, like other men, was left to ponder contradiction and paradox where he had expected to find unity.

The reader's lessons result from his tracing each specific sequence of experiences and incidents, organized according to general categories, such as politics, religion, and science. These lines of interest show change or development in thought; they are naturally preceded by the physiological and psychological experience of existence. The early chapters make clear that family origins explain in a fundamental way who Henry Adams is and what he can expect to learn. The larger thematic demonstration—the failure of personal experience—begins in this treatment of family inheritance: "Whatever was peculiar about him was education, not character, and came to him directly and indirectly, as the result of that eighteenth-century inheritance which he took with his name" (*Education*, 7). To Adams, such a legacy seemed a handicap and not an advantage, a source of contradictory experience rather than a unified interpretation of life. For the child born in 1838, he claims, contradiction was already in the blood; because of the marriage two generations earlier between John Quincy Adams and Louisa Catherine Johnson, the boy began his life (and thus his education) as a "half-exotic" New Englander. "As a child of Quincy he was not a true Bostonian, but even as a child of Quincy he inherited a quarter taint of Maryland blood" (*Education*, 19).

After introducing this hereditary accident as explanation, Adams begins to model a political sequence leading from facts about his family to feeling about the South and slavery. The conclusion, however, appears only at a much later stage of consciousness, one which will admit contradiction in place of singularity of impression. But the reader must be prepared in advance; and the author first labors to dispel preconceptions of unity and to replace them with a preliminary understanding of the divided consciousness that the persona will later illustrate. A summary description offers an explicit literary formula for what will follow: "Life was a double thing. . . . From earliest childhood the boy was accustomed to feel that, for him, life was double." What is not yet clear to the reader on page 9 is the implicit suggestion, the virtual impossibility of either a unitary summary of experience—any simple meaning in life—or of a unified form of expression. These ideas are organically present in Adams's words; the remainder of the book develops their implications. The author begins by anticipating the contradictions of the adult mind and the absence of a unifying system and ends his book having demonstrated both.

In the process, Adams's artistic method allows him freedom to expand the limits of his own experience, to criticize as well as narrate and finally to encourage further speculation from his readers. Finding himself "an eighteenth-century child" who could "never compel himself to care for nineteenth-century style" the author obscures his position by developing the contradiction and then making judgments of the moment according to either set of values, whichever suits his purpose. This method forestalls any charge of dogmatism and also allows the reader to form a judgment of his own, sympathetic or antithetic to Adams's. Education in the Adams family marks the first in a series of insufficient modes of training for life. After its inadequacy is established, the alert reader need only follow the path of development in order to test for himself the author's further conclusions.

One path is labeled "politics," and it leads toward a symbol of family expectation, "the White House." As his readers knew, "all the boy's family had lived there" (*Education*, 46). But the path doesn't end there. The way leads on into the South, and the boy's symbolic journey into political knowledge continues, beyond simple expectations, to a lesson in complication and paradox:

> Bad roads meant bad morals. The moral of this Virginia road was clear, and the boy fully learned it. Slavery was wicked, and slavery was the cause of this road's badness which amounted to social crime—and yet, at the end of the road and product of the crime stood Mount Vernon and George Washington (*Education*, 47).

The incontestable value of George Washington as symbol provides the lesson with its shock effect; at the end of the political road, Mount Vernon and George Washington contradict the otherwise clear moral of Virginia and slavery. The result is impasse. Education can go no further and still remain within the limits of Adams's experience: "In practice, such trifles as contradictions in principle are easily set aside; the faculty of ignoring them makes the practical man; but any attempt to deal with them seriously as education is fatal" (*Education*, 48).

With a sure hand Adams traces other lines of thought to the apparent finality of contradiction. Politics draw him to study men, and men lead him through old-fashioned history to genealogy, heredity, and (by means of Darwin) to science. Connecting politics and science, the author finally demonstrates that his attempt (like every other) to measure human experience must end in failure: "the progress of evolution from President Washington to President Grant, was alone evidence enough to upset Darwin" (*Education*, 266).

Again, the rhetorical and didactic force of Adams's statement depends upon a symbolic use of names, placed in shocking conjunction. As in the earlier quotation, Washington represents an absolute, this time of personal integrity, a historical point from which to measure. Grant stands as total contradiction. But much more is involved in this lesson: both symbols have a common value as men, and in that common role they must be studied, if they are to be meaningfully compared. The eighteenth-century mind was trained to measure men by the standards of history; the twentieth-century mind uses science. Some progress or at least some advantage might be expected. Yet even as Grant "upset" Darwin, so Darwin seems to have added nothing to Adams's education: "In theory one might say, with some show of proof, that a pure scientific education was alone correct; yet many of his friends who took it, found reason to complain that it was anything but a pure, scientific world in which they lived" (*Education*, 88). Theory, of course, was not enough in an age of pragmatic demonstration. Here, at a point early in the book, the study of science turns Adams away from any conclusion, to consider other modes of education.

Once the pattern of investigation leading to impasse is implanted in the reader's mind, the expectation of failure along each line of thought becomes an almost automatic response. Sometimes the demonstration begins in a neat summary of the manikin's total experience, as in the matter of religious faith: "Of all the conditions of his youth which afterwards puzzled the grown-up man, this disappearance of religion puzzled him most" (*Education*, 34). In this statement, the boy-man division of narrative point of view, the retrospective freedom to comment, and the enigmatic result are all included. But the simple narrative expression still lacks the force of demonstration, and Adams hopes to supply that by filling in the details a few at a time.

Another lesson in this sequence centers on the death of his sister; it begins to make its point with a description of her horrible suffering and painful death in the agonies of lockjaw. The scene is surely the most moving in the whole of the *Education*; yet Adams refuses to let it stand alone as a sufficient "show of proof," partly because the story of this personal loss cannot be told by means of commonly shared symbols, like the White House or George Washington. In fact, the author's distrust of emotion goes beyond any effort to protect himself against embarrassment. He shows an unwillingness to rely upon emotional communication between himself and his audience. To the description, he appends a specific moral which intensifies the lesson.

> . . . the idea that any personal deity could find pleasure or profit in torturing a poor woman, by accident, with a fiendish cruelty known to man only in perverted and insane temperaments, could not be held for a moment. For pure blasphemy, it made pure atheism a comfort. God might be, as the Church said, a Substance, but He could not be a Person (*Education*, 289).

In an age of science the distance between "blasphemy" and "atheism," "Substance" and "Person" must be measured in thought rather than feeling. By refusing to make his own position clear and by providing evidence, instead of hollow assertion, to answer the "why?" "this disappearance of religion puzzled him most," Adams involves the reader's judgment and at the same time hides his own feelings. In place of an answer, the author poses a new question, in terms intellectual rather than spiritual, general and no longer personal. The *Education* becomes a quest-in-being, and denies its own importance as an exercise in history.

Henry Adams characterized his book as an "experiment," and like "Education" in his title, the word remains difficult to define in the various contexts of his essays, letters, and books. Yet, as readers, we must take both words seriously. Almost as much as educational, the book is experimental. Therefore, at this point in the discussion, we turn to consider heuristic possibilities. First, it should be noted that the reactions of the audience were finally beyond the writer's control and thus outside the limits of personal experience. An experiment, in theory at least, renounces inductively any certain judgment about what may be proved. But even for the trained scientist, such a method is hardly incompatible with a general purpose—better understanding of himself and of the world in which he functions. For the writer of the *Education* the double concern with method and goal was fundamental.

So far this essay has suggested that Henry Adams made of the *Education* an artistic attempt to supplement the deficiencies he noted in his life. Adams addressed himself to the problems of literary art—a special art in this particular case, one that would conceal when it appeared to reveal and exhort even as it seemed to explain or despair. What remains unexamined is Adams's goal, the overall design by means of which the author meant to weld together life and art, incidents and lessons, in a demonstration quite different from conventional displays of knowledge. The "Preface" once again provides our starting point: "The tailor's object, in this volume, is to fit young men, in universities or elsewhere, to be men of the world, equipped for any emergency." For such an object, the narrative report of Adams's own experience would not suffice; the paramount theme of the book was education, and merely personal examples, like the general study of men, offered no useful key to a complex world. In Adams's words, "the twentieth century finds few recent guides to avoid or to follow." The familiar balance of "avoid" and "follow" indicates the doubly ambitious formula for a useful guide. Rousseau had spelled out a warning against ego, without showing a pattern for success. Adams demanded more.

As a professor at Harvard College and in his writings he had hoped to educate "young men," until they were able to continue by themselves and to surpass his example. The young Henry Adams had himself been tutored by his elders; John Quincy Adams enters the pages of the *Education* as a lesson in force, and Henry's father, Charles Francis Adams, illustrates a mental standard which the son could both admire and criticize:

> Charles Francis Adams was singular for mental poise—absence of self-assertion or self-consciousness—the faculty of standing apart without seeming aware that he was alone—a balance of mind and temper that neither challenged nor avoided notice, nor admitted question of superiority or inferiority, of jealousy, of personal motives, from any source, even under great pressure. This unusual poise of judgment and temper, ripened by age, became more striking to his son Henry as he learned to measure the mental faculties themselves, which were in no way exceptional either for depth or range. Charles Francis Adams's memory was hardly above the average; his mind was not bold like his grandfather's or restless like his father's, or imaginative or oratorical—still less mathematical; but it worked with singular perfection, admirable self-restraint, and instinctive mastery of form. Within its range it was a model (*Education*, 27).

"Instinctive mastery of form"—in art and life—remained as a goal for the son. But this Adams could not escape questions "of superiority or inferiority" and "personal motives." In a new generation the family mind turned upon itself, and "instinctive mastery" seemed almost impossible. Education by example, at least human example, was obsolete. But to learn about form was still the proper business of education, and more than anything else Adams made education the business of his life. Already he had played many roles in educational experiments—student, teacher, and observer. Now, he set out to show that a life-long concern with the methods of instruction was in fact worthwhile. As a sequence of thought or a line of force, education connected past and present and projected into the unknown future: "A teacher affects eternity; he can never tell where his influence stops" (*Education*, 300).

The problem remained one of identifying those students who could learn and the best methods of instructing them or, better, of letting them learn for themselves.

> Barred from philosophy and bored by facts he wanted to teach his students something not wholly useless. The number of students whose minds were of an order above the average was, in his experience, barely one in ten; the rest could not be much stimulated by any inducements a teacher could suggest. All were respectable, and in seven years of contact, Adams never had cause to complain of one; but nine minds in ten take polish passively, like a hard surface; only the tenth sensibly reacts (*Education*, 302).

That tenth mind was the target for Adams's teaching; to it the *Education* was directed. And, just as in his classes at Harvard, "Adams found himself obliged to force his material into some shape to which a method could be applied" (*Education*, 302–3). Only the reacting mind, Adams believed, could benefit fully from lessons, which became surface polish for the merely passive manikin:

> The object of education for that mind should be the teaching itself how to react with vigor and economy. No doubt the world at large will always lag so far behind the active mind as to make a soft cushion of inertia to drop upon, as it did for Henry Adams; but education should try to lessen the obstacles, diminish the friction, invigorate the energy, and should train minds to react not at haphazard, but by choice, on the lines of force that attract their world. What one knows is, in youth, of little moment; they know enough who know how to learn (*Education*, 314).

The *Education* becomes, from the didactic point of view, an exercise book for mental training. Instead of copying maxims or letters and learning by imitation from example, the exceptional student is expected to trace the lines of thought, to the point where the manikin reaches impasse. The rare tenth mind follows only to react against the example of the manikin. For that mind, Adams holds out a hope of being prepared "by choice" to "jump" and stay ahead of expanding force. Such a mind might succeed where Adams knew himself to have failed, might complete the patterning of life and experience with a mastery that would replace chaos with design—whether religious, historical, scientific, or artistic.

The book offered no metaphor of mastery because the radiating lines of force and thought led away from and not toward a center. Unlike the controlling comparisons in *Walden*, the seasonal cycle or the pond itself, the central figure in the *Education* seemed to represent life near its end, with little hope of continuation or renewal. Experience had led away from instinct, and time had played him false, even while it pretended to educate:

> Truly the animal that is to be trained to unity must be caught young. Unity is vision; it must have been part of the process of learning to see. The older the mind, the older its complexities, and the further it looks, the more it sees, until even the stars resolve themselves into multiples; yet the child will always see but one (*Education*, 398–9).

The reader might be luckier, but "Adams's instinct was blighted from babyhood" (*Education*, 387). His last years were spent in an attempt to recapture that sense of instinctive mastery which had been taken from him. Adams felt himself to have been victimized by his own education: "Of all studies, the one he would rather have avoided was that of his own mind" (*Education*, 432). Yet he had no choice. The sequence of forces or lessons had led directly to his own "life study":

> Metaphysics insisted on treating the universe as one thought or treating thought as one universe; and philosophers agreed, like a kinetic gas, that the universe could be known only as motion of mind, and therefore as unity. One could know it only as one's self; it was psychology (*Education*, 432).

As a metaphysician or philosopher or scientist Adams could proceed no further. But as experiment rather than exposition, the *Education* could stimulate instinct in directions where it could not control thought. A true "model" for "self-teaching" in the twentieth century must eschew reason and communicate as art. Adams found a model in St. Gaudens's statue at the grave of Adams's wife, a wife who is never mentioned in the *Education*. Before that timeless figure the manikin stands interested but questionless—his rational pursuit of knowledge held in abeyance, as instinct overwhelms thought.

> Naturally every detail interested him; every line; every touch of the artist; every change of light and shade; every point of relation; every possible doubt of St. Gaudens's correctness of taste or feeling; so that, as the spring approached, he was apt to stop there often to see what the figure had to tell him that was new; but, in all that it had to say, he never once thought of questioning what it meant. He supposed its meaning to be the one commonplace about it—the oldest idea known to human thought. . . . The interest of the figure was not in its meaning, but in the response of the observer (*Education*, 329).

Art alone could avert impasse and reawaken man's latent and instinctive mastery over chaos. But the act of responding, the direct personal involvement necessary for appreciation and education, was finally the business of the audience. What the writer had begun, only his reader could successfully complete.

Meanwhile, if Adams could not keep from making the materials of his life into the primary form of his book, he could at least use his artistry to protect himself against candid revelations. The cry of "failure" drowned out the small inner voice and forestalled curious probings of potential biographers. When he sent the *Education* to Henry James, Adams was moved to remark: "The volume is a mere shield of protection in the grave. I advise you to take your own life in the same way, in order to prevent biographers from taking it in theirs."[3] His experience as biographer had left Adams with a deep understanding of history; he knew that what he wrote in the *Education* would be balanced against what others thought and wrote about him. By "taking his own life," the author sought to protect rather than reveal himself for all time.

The ideal of balance gave final meaning to each of the roles Adams filled in life. As teacher, he was in need of a pupil; as writer, he required a reader. Without such completion, the voice of Henry Adams must remain a lonely cry of failure and despair in the wilderness of universal chaos. That possibility, he hoped desperately to avoid; that possibility, he was reluctant to admit in either life or art. For it was only as art that an account of his life could achieve the balance and meaning which demonstrated the alternative to failure. His message must have an audience.

An experiment with words, the *Education* would fail only when readers failed it. To make use of Adams's experience became the responsibility of his audience. The author had acted his self-defined role:

> All considerable artists make a point of compelling the public to think for itself, and their rule is to require each observer to see what he can, and this will be what the artist meant. To the artist the meaning is indifferent. Every man is his own artist before a work of art.[4]

Experimental and didactic, the *Education* is foremost a "work of art." Its lines of organization stretch from past to future, from writer to reader, from personal narration to individual application. As a total experience, the book depends upon what the audience can do with it. For the text itself is merely a part of the *Education*, and its statement remains unfinished. Only the reader can complete the lesson which Henry Adams began.

Notes

1. Boston and New York: Houghton Mifflin, 1918. All references in the text are to this edition.

2. *The Yale Review* (October, 1915), 82–89.

3. *Letters of Henry Adams,* ed. Worthington Chauncey Ford (Boston and New York, 1918), II, 495.

4. Henry Adams to E. D. Shaw, 20 December, 1904, *The Letters of Mrs. Henry Adams, 1865–1883* (Boston, 1936), "Postscript," pp. 458–9.

"Henry Adams's *Education* and Autobiographical Tradition"

Earl N. Harbert*

For readers who have been fascinated by *The Education of Henry Adams*, the most significant event of recent years was the appearance in 1973 of a carefully revised edition, corrected according to the author's final intentions and edited by Adams's chief biographer, Ernest Samuels.[1] At long last, and for the first time since the book was put on sale in 1918, the title page of the *Education* appears without the infamous and misleading subtitle, "An Autobiography." Those two words, added to the 1918 version without authorization from Adams himself, who died before that printing appeared, have been largely responsible for a general confusion about the author's intentions, and, in turn, for a profusion of conflicting opinions, comments, and judgments concerning the final success or failure of Adams's achievement. Yet, all together this almost uncollectable critical response to the book forms at best a partial truth; for by any conventional definition, at least, the *Education* must be seen to offer us something much larger than the usual understanding of "autobiography " allows. How the shade of Henry Adams, at his sardonic best, must relish the last of his many jokes—this one played unintentionally on the three generations of readers who have helped to keep the *Education* alive.

All this is not to say that the book is free of autobiographical influences. Quite the contrary: many scholars have noted the author's debts to Rousseau and Augustine, to the private literature of the Adams family, especially the diaries of John and John Quincy Adams; and to that peculiarly American strain of personal narrative which can be traced, with some variations, from the Puritans, through Jonathan Edwards and Benjamin Franklin, to Henry James and Henry Adams.[2] And convincing evidence of indebtedness to an autobiographical tradition is provided by Adams himself in his "Preface" to the *Education*, where he acknowledges a familiarity with a variety of personal narratives in the various forms of confessions, autobiographies, and memoirs, mentioning their authors by name. From the perspective of our usual interest in admitted and implied

*Reprinted from *Tulane Studies in English*, 22 (1977), 134–41.

influences, then, Adams's reliance on a great autobiographical tradition is well established. So a sound case can be made—for treating his book as an impressive extension of that older tradition into the twentieth century. But, in fact, the *Education* should also be thought of, at least in part, as the first modern American autobiography, a seminal volume, as important in its way as was T. S. Eliot's announcements of modernity in his best poetry of the same period. To realize just how modern the *Education* really is, a reader need only compare it with the *Autobiography* of Henry's older brother, Charles Francis Adams II, published in 1916.[3] Charles's book shows what the mere conjunction of the well-established family writing habit, with a prosaic tradition of memoir-writing, and a pedestrian historical outlook could be expected to produce in the work of an almost exact contemporary. Nowhere in Charles's *Autobiography* does one find the play of artistic imagination that stamps Henry's *Education* as a unique work of genius, an account that is at once both traditional and highly experimental. For the *Education* is an American classic, and readers must take it on its own terms or fail to comprehend its full meaning.

Nor was this uniqueness lost to T. S. Eliot himself. In one of the earliest reviews of Adams's book, titled "A Sceptical Patrician" and printed in the *Athenaeum* in 1919, the poet warned: "It is doubtful whether the book ought to be called an autobiography, for there is too little of the author in it."[4] Unfortunately, while most readers of the very popular *Education* have recognized its autobiographical possibilities, few have taken Eliot's warning seriously enough.

Aside from Eliot's cautionary advice, which Adams had no opportunity to read, any more than he had a chance to strike the misleading subtitle from later reprintings, there is abundant external evidence that the author did not plan his work as simply yet another contribution to the tradition of American autobiography. Here, Adams's personal correspondence is extremely useful in putting us on the track of his thoughts concerning the autobiographical form in literature, even before he began the *Education*. Writing to Henry James in 1903 about the latter's biography of William Wetmore Story, Adams said:

> The painful truth is that all of my New England generation, counting the half-century, 1820–1879, were in actual fact only one mind and nature; the individual was a facet of Boston . . . Type Bourgeois bostonian [*sic*]! A type quite as good as another but more uniform. . . . God knows that we knew our want of knowledge! the [*sic*] self-distrust became introspection—nervous self-consciousness—irritable dislike of America, and antipathy to Boston.
>
> So you have written not Story's life, but your own and mine—pure autobiography. . . . [5]

Later, after he had completed the *Education*, Adams sent a copy of the private printing to James in 1908, together with a letter that explained: "The volume is a mere shield of protection in the grave. I advise you to take your own life in the same way, in order to prevent biographers from taking it in theirs."[6] The truth found by biographers and autobiographers could prove to be "painful truth" indeed. As a biographer himself, Henry Adams knew this first-hand, having written the lives of Albert Gallatin, John Randolph, and Aaron Burr before he began the *Education*. Certainly the possibilities for using some version of autobiography as a "shield of protection" had occurred to Adams as early as 1891, when he wrote to his English friend, Charles Milnes Gaskell: "The moral seems to be that every man should write his life, to prevent some other fellow from taking it."[7] So Adams determined to take his own life in literature but in a unique way, as he turned a chronological narrative of personal experience into an autobiographical literary experiment.

In the *Education* itself, perhaps the most obvious signal of the author's extraordinary intentions may be found on the "Contents" page. Surely a superb historian like Adams could do better than to leave such a hiatus as that between Chapter XX, entitled "Failure (1871)" and Chapter XXI, entitled "Twenty Years After (1892)." For "protection," of course, he had seen fit to leave this period in his life blank—a gap that excluded every detail of his relationship with Marian Hooper Adams, the wife who is never mentioned in the *Education*. Gone too, along with the personal version of his marriage, is all pretense to confessional sincerity or historical accuracy and completeness. Instead, as Adams makes clear, the reading game must be played by the author's own rules.

Nowhere is this made so clear as in the "Preface" to the *Education*. From that point onward in the book, the introduction of a "manikin" figure called "Henry Adams" serves to protect the real author from excessive self-revelation, by offering the disguise of personal experience as a covering for didactic art. From almost the first word, the reader is warned that he should not expect another confessional in the tradition of Rousseau or of the American Puritans. For Adams, the *Confessions*, although written like the *Education* "in the manner of the eighteenth century," can be instructive in the twentieth century only when correctly viewed or read. Timely interpretation emphasizes personal limitations rather than accomplishments, and makes the *Confessions* useful as a warning and not as a model.

> As educator, Jean Jacques was in one respect, easily first; he erected a monument of warning against the Ego. Since his time, and largely thanks to him, the Ego has steadily tended to efface itself, and, for purposes of model, to become a manikin on which the toilet of education is to be draped in order to

show the fit or misfit of the clothes. The object of study is the garment, not the figure. The tailor adapts the manikin as well as the clothes to his patron's wants. The tailor's object, in this volume, is to fit young men, in universities or elsewhere, to be men of the world, equipped for any emergency; and the garment offered to them is meant to show the faults of the patchwork fitted on their fathers. . . .

The manikin, therefore, has the same value as any other geometrical figure of three or more dimensions, which is used for the study of relation. For that purpose it cannot be spared; it is the only measure of motion, of proportion, of human condition; it must have the air of reality; must be taken for real; must be treated as though it had life. Who knows? Possibly it had! [*Education*, xxx.]

Enter the manikin "Henry Adams" and exit all pretense of conscious self-revelation. As the author tells us 432 pages later,

Of all studies, the one he would rather have avoided was that of his own mind. He knew no tragedy so heart-rending as introspection, and the more, because—as Mephistopheles said of Marguerite—he was not the first. Nearly all the highest intelligence known to history had drowned itself in the reflection of its own thought, and the bovine survivors had rudely told the truth about it, without affecting the intelligent [*Education*, 432].

Here, the "painful truth" Adams first had described to James emerged more painful still. The source was not simply personal revelation of the usual kind—the embarrassing details of an outward life—but rather the traditional autobiographical practice of looking inward, and of telling truthfully what one has found. Far better to spare the pain and turn away from self, to teach, instead, in the words of the "Preface," ". . . young men, in universities or elsewhere, to be men of the world equipped for any emergency." And teach, Adams did in the pages of his book.

This is not the place to trace in detail the many lessons in politics, religion, philosophy, science, and art—which measure the author's didactic intention in the *Education*. These main lines of educative force also provide themes for the narrative; while the manikin's example demonstrates over and over the repeated "failure" of the subject ever to learn enough. Gradually, by accretion, this "failure" grows to seem conclusive—just as certain as the failure, in Adams's mind, of Rousseau in his *Confessions* to provide any effective guidance for modern man. Yet the larger, more general lesson here is one of change and not of failure alone; and to give it force, the author concentrates his attention on a central human figure, the persona Henry Adams, who grows from child to man as he tries out, for the reader's benefit, a variety of possibly educational experiences.

But finally the life of "Henry Adams" by itself does not teach enough to satisfy the author, who tells us why:

> Truly the animal that is to be trained to unity must be caught young. Unity is vision; it must have been part of the process of learning to see. The older the mind, the older its complexities, and the further it looks, the more it sees, until even the stars resolve themselves into multiples; yet the child will always see but one [*Education*, 398–99].

Experience has led the manikin away from unity and instinct, and time has played him false, even while it pretended to educate.

In the face of such change, man must seek to recapture a sense of instictive unity in art, as Adams hoped to do in his *Education*. For him, art was the only possible alternative to chaos, although for others who may be better educated than he, the author holds out another possibility of scientific unity, especially in the final chapters of his book and in his later essays. But the *Education* tells Henry Adams's story, beginning with his origins in "Quincy" (Chapter I) and "Boston" (Chapter II), and ending with the futuristic speculations that radiated from his mature mind. Put together in his way, the whole story is an experiment in didactic art—taking up in the twentieth century where Rousseau and Franklin left off. For, much as when he was a classroom instructor at Harvard College, the author of the *Education* still kept his faith in the timeless value of the teacher, who could shape human thought into worldly force, and effectively link the past and present with an uncertain future. As Adams wrote in the *Education*, "A teacher affects eternity; he can never tell where his influence stops" (p. 300). By reaching out to the "one [mind] in ten" that "sensibly reacts" to such teaching, the writer hoped to have his autobiographical lessons accepted by his readers in the same way that, in the "Preface," he claimed to use Rousseau's *Confessions*, as "a monument of warning against the Ego"(*Education*, 302, xxx).

Finally, only the vigorously reacting mind, Adams believed, could benefit fully from lessons which otherwise became surface polish for the merely passive manikin:

> The object of education for that mind should be the teaching itself how to react with vigor and economy. No doubt the world at large will always lag so far behind the active mind as to make a soft cushion of inertia to drop upon, as it did for Henry Adams; but education should try to lessen the obstacles, diminish the friction, invigorate the energy, and should train minds to react, not at haphazard, but by choice, on the lines of force that attract their world. What one knows is, in youth, of little moment; they know enough who know how to learn [*Education*, 314].

That rare tenth mind alone knows how to learn: it follows out Adams's lines of force and interest only to react against the egoistic example of the manikin. For that mind only, Adams holds out the hope of being prepared "by choice" to "jump" and stay ahead of the other expanding forces in the universe. Just such a mind might well succeed where the author knew himself to have failed; it might complete a patterning of life and experience with a mastery that would turn chaos into orderly design. Yet, so far as Adams could see in the *Education*, all education based on example—at least human example—was already obsolete. Traditional autobiography, like other forms of human experience, seemed to have reached the end of its usefulness, as education and as art.

What was left to Adams and to modern literature was experiment. So he attempted to turn his narrative of personal experience into something both artistic and useful. Alongside the warnings provided by the chronological gap in the narrative and by the manikin subject, the author developed a vocabulary of symbols, used to tie past experience to future possibility by drawing on instinct rather than reason. The most famous example, of course, is Chapter XXV, "The Dynamo and the Virgin," perhaps the best evidence that the *Education* can be read as modern art, as many anthologies testify.

I do not pretend in this brief survey to judge the *Education* either a failure or a success as art. Still it should be useful to point out that the overall effect of Adams's symbolic treatment—like the picture of the titular character in the book who is both manikin and tailor, and the impression created by the before-and-after organization—is once again to underscore division or contradiction in human experience, and to deny the possibility of unity in the "vision" of the aging author. Perhaps the "child will always see but one"; yet the reader of the *Education*, on the other hand, is left to yearn for such childish unity—in subject matter, organization, and conclusion. The book lacks even an imposed authorial unity, in the form of a single symbolic pattern; and the reader cannot order the various lines of force and thought by reference to some convenient symbol, like the pond in *Walden*.

For Adams, "Chaos was the law of nature; Order was the dream of man" (*Education*, 451). By telling us only what he wanted to about his own life, Henry Adams played the part of a natural man who yet remained always something of a dreamer. While he was a teacher, he was also an artist, who sought to make his own story into didactic art of a high order, still leaving all judgments about his ultimate success to his readers. Meanwhile, the lessons of his life became theirs to use as they saw fit. Properly, the final words about the didactic value of an autobiography might be expected to belong to the author, who could best summarize the meaning of his own life. But in Adams's case, the authorial strategy was different. At the time that he was writing his life story, the author of the *Education* showed that he was too nimble or too evasive to be caught without "protection" and a "shield" for the future. In a letter to E. D. Shaw, the artist managed to shift the burden of interpretation from intention to response, as he showed how he had made the substance of his own experience into a heuristic experiment, designed to test his audience rather than to reveal himself:

> All considerable artists make a point of compelling the public to think for itself, and their rule is to require each observer to see what he can, and this will be what the artist meant. To the artist the meaning is indifferent. Every man is his own artist before a work of art.[8]

Taken as autobiography, then, the *Education* is most of all "a work of art." The genius of Adams's experiment in modernity lies in his dramatic conversion of the narrative and didactic conventions he had inherited—the stuff of traditional autobiography—to his own unique purposes. For, while he kept the surface appearance of the narrative of personal experience, perhaps to convince the public that they knew exactly what he was doing, Adams also offered his readers full artistic license to make every one of them his own autobiographer.

Notes

1. *The Education of Henry Adams* (Boston: Houghton Mifflin, 1973). All quotations in the text are from this edition.

2. The scholarship on Henry Adams has been surveyed in two essays by Charles Vandersee, *American Literary Realism, 1870–1910*, Vol. II (Summer, 1969), 90–119, and Vol. VIII (Summer, 1975), 180–188, both titled "Henry Adams," and in my own chapter, "Henry Adams," *Fifteen American Authors Before 1900: Bibliographical Essays on Research and Criticism* (Madison: University of Wisconsin Press, 1971, 1974), pp. 3–36. For recent discussions of Adams as autobiographer, see: Mutlu Konuk Blasing, *The Art of Life* (Austin: University of Texas Press, 1977) and Thomas Cooley, *Educated Lives: The Rise of Autobiography in America* (Columbus: Ohio State University Press, 1976).

3. *Charles Francis Adams, 1835–1915: An Autobiography* (Boston: Houghton Mifflin).

4. 23 May, pp. 361–362.

5. Henry Adams to Henry James, 18 November 1903, *Letters of Henry Adams*, ed. Worthington Chauncey Ford (Boston: Houghton Mifflin, 1938), II, 414.

6. 6 May, Ford, II, 495.

7. 17 August, Adams Papers—Fifth Generation.

8. 20 December 1904, *The Letters of Mrs. Henry Adams, 1865–1883* (Boston: Little, Brown, 1936), pp. 458–9. Elsewhere, I have explored at length some of the demands that Adams makes on readers who actively respond to his experimental and metaphysical method; see esp. Chapter 5, "The Education of Henry Adams" in *The Force So Much Closer Home: Henry Adams and the Adams Family* (New York: New York University Press, 1977), pp. 144–200.

"Henry Adams: His Passage to Asia"

Margaret J. Brown*

Early in June, 1886, leaving behind his Washington home and keep-sakes of a vanished marriage, Henry Adams crossed the American conti-nent on a Union Pacific express. From San Francisco, he began his voyage to Yokohama, Japan. When the Pacific Ocean belied its name, Adams described himself and his traveling companion, John La Farge, in their torment of seasickness, as "two woe-begone Pagans, searching Nirvana."[1] The tongue-in-cheek comment hinted at an elusive goal: Adams was not to find the realm of absolute peace in Japan or elsewhere. But his journey to that country proved a significant part of his life-long quest for unity, for a meaningful order to human life and the universe itself.

In large part because of his travels to Japan and to many other coun-tries in the Orient, during a life spanning the years from 1838 to 1918, Henry Adams became an especially qualified observer of men and events. Moreover, he became a writer who, by virtue of his achievements and distinctive insights, maintains a unique place in American letters. His en-during passion—expressed in history, biography, novels, and poetry—was that his country fulfill its early republican ideals and develop a civilization that could equal or surpass the great civilizations of the past. His knowledge of American ideals and experience sprang from his own ac-complishments as author, editor, and teacher, and, in part, from his family inheritance as a great-grandson of the second President of the United States and a grandson of the sixth. As a historian, Adams sought not just to assess his country's beginnings but, more especially, to "align himself with the future"[2] by foreseeing America's relations with the rest of mankind, West and East, in a world many years beyond his time.

The insights of Adams into America's associations with Europe and his sympathies for the culture of that continent have been analyzed by a number of literary critics. They have tended to be preoccupied with the Henry Adams who, at the turn of this century, extolled the spirit and art

*This essay was written for inclusion in this volume. It is published with the permission of Margaret J. Brown.

of the medieval cathedrals of France. But they have paid much less attention to the Adams who followed his 1886 journey to Japan with a return to
Asia, deliberately setting out "after the manner of Ulysses, in search of
that new world which is the old."[3]

As the extensive writings of Adams demonstrate, his interest in the
East was vital. For almost half a century he expressed this concern in hundreds of letters and in such significant books as his novel *Esther* (1884),
The Education of Henry Adams (1907), and *Tahiti: Memoirs of Arii
Taimai* (1901), an important transitional work concerned with the effects
of European imperialism on the islands of Polynesia. In writing his
masterful evocation of medieval Europe, *Mont-Saint-Michel and
Chartres* (1904), Adams used comparisons with Oriental art to establish
perspectives on the value of twelfth-century Western art.

Even so "American" a work as the *History of the United States of
America During the Administrations of Thomas Jefferson and James
Madison* (1889–1891) shows the effects of its author's thought about the
Orient. One of the important themes of the *History* is the early
nineteenth-century relationship between America and Russia, a country
that Adams considered essentially "Asiatic" in spirit. In the final book of
his career, *The Life of George Cabot Lodge* (1911), Adams probed
Lodge's use of Oriental concepts in his poems and in his two most important plays, *Cain* and *Herakles*. The biography of Lodge stresses the ideals
of abnegation and self-sacrifice that Adams felt underlay the major
Eastern faiths.

The need to examine the influence of the East upon Adams's work is
part of a larger necessity: to investigate the effect of the Orient upon the
whole body of post-Civil War American literature. Although there has
been able analysis of the use of Oriental ideas by the transcendentalists
Ralph Waldo Emerson and Henry Thoreau, little critical work has been
done to explore the origins and uses of Eastern ideas expressed by late
nineteenth- and twentieth-century American authors.[4] As Eusebio Rod-
rigues observes,

> The extent of oriental influence on American writing and art
> all through the nineteenth century has yet to be charted. Ar-
> thur Christy in *The Orient in American Transcendentalism*
> (1932) has indeed surveyed and recorded the oriental in-
> fluences on Emerson, Thoreau, and Alcott. But the contours of
> orientalism on the American literary map of the latter half of
> the nineteenth century have yet to be traced and its impact on
> Henry Adams and his contemporaries has still to be evaluated.[5]

Of the generation of American authors who came to their maturity
during the Civil War, Henry Adams was one of the first to demonstrate a
desire to know the Orient. In September, 1869, at the age of 31, he wrote
a British friend, Charles Milnes Gaskell, that within two years he would

"go to the Pacific." Life in his ancestral home of Quincy, Massachusetts, Adams declared, was "pleasant" but "dead" and altogether on "too small a scale."[6] But the journey was to be delayed for many years, first by his acceptance in 1870 of a Harvard professorship and later by his marriage in June, 1872, to Marian Hooper. In the summer of 1885, he began planning with Marian to travel to Japan—one motive being to relieve her grief over her father's death. When Marian committed suicide in December, 1885, he felt a greater need than ever for travel, to assuage his own sorrow and to satisfy an intense intellectual curiosity that transcended personal agony.

In voyages made in 1886 and during 1890-1891, Henry Adams spent nearly two years exploring Japan, Polynesia (the Hawaiian Islands, the Samoas, and Tahiti), the Fiji Islands, Indonesia, Singapore, and Ceylon. But his passionate desire to see China, which he called "the great unknown country of the world," was never fulfilled. During August-September, 1901, he journeyed for hundreds of miles within Russia, and, as he had done on previous trips, Adams registered his immediate impressions in letters to friends. Later, he expressed in the pages of the *Education* his more carefully meditated ideas about Russia and its relations with America, to the end of the Russo-Japanese War.[7]

From a consideration of the Asian travels of Adams and of his writings, the central question evolves: What was he seeking in the thought and art of the Orient? Although Adams did not find in the East all that he sought, what he gained was of lasting value to him as a thinker and writer. A major motive for his interest in Hinduism and Buddhism was his desire to find a unifying system of belief, by which his personal life and the fragmented society about him could be made whole. His sense of a broken existence after his wife's death is revealed in the *Education*, which asserts that his life had been "cut in halves."[8] The realization that the tragic breaking of his marriage was only a part of the larger disintegration of society led him, in *The Education of Henry Adams* and in *Mont-Saint-Michel and Chartres*, to contrast a shattered twentieth-century world with a seemingly cohesive medieval culture. Adams believed that in Europe during the period from 1150 to 1250 A.D. the common devotion to one faith had helped fuse the individual man, the church, the state, and God Himself into a unity, an organic whole, But, in the nearly 700 years since that century, a rapidly accelerating development of mechanical and technological forces had intensified social conflicts and had fragmented community life. Adams called the resulting diversity of interests "multiplicity,"[9] and he sought a system of belief that would weld the diverging forces of society once more into a cohesive whole.

The writings of Adams give no evidence that he ever found, East or West, a fully satisfying twentieth-century system of thought by which social unity could be achieved. Nevertheless, he gained in many ways by his exploration of Eastern life and culture. The most important consequence was that he located some vital ideas which he could exploit as a literary artist. For example, Buddhist beliefs concerning Nirvana are used as a recurring theme in his letters, in *Esther*, and in *The Life of George Cabot Lodge*. The blending of Buddhist and Hindu teachings in the "Buddha and Brahma" poem, written shortly after Adams left Ceylon in 1891, helped him achieve a philosophical stance that reconciled Western ideas with those of the East.

As he traveled in the Orient, Adams grew in ways that directly affected his work as a writer. On his voyages to Japan and around the South Seas, he was accompanied by John La Farge, a noted American painter and authority on stained glass.[10] Under the tutelage of La Farge, Adams studied watercolor painting in the Pacific islands and developed the sense of tone that the *Education* declares was missing from his New England experience. His boyhood in Massachusetts had conditioned him to extreme contrasts, of summer heat and winter cold, of the glare of June sunlight on the hills near Quincy and the oppressive dark of November nights. But the almost infinite gradations of color, by day and night, in the South Seas forced him to make an acutely sensitive response. The psychological practice of reacting to "tone" helped prepare him for the nuances of medieval stained glass and, ultimately, for the writing of *Mont-Saint-Michel and Chartres*.

Moreover, Adams saw some striking parallels between the Polynesian islands and the medieval France portrayed in *Chartres*, as he demonstrated in a letter to Yale University professor Frederick Luquiens. While awaiting an article from Luquiens on the *Chanson de Roland*, Adams recalled the difficulties he had faced as history professor at Harvard in helping students comprehend medieval art:

> It is quite impossible for our society, young or old, to get its intellectual processes back to the state of mind in which society naturally expressed itself in . . . the *Chanson*, . . . or the church, and sang, or built, or fought, or loved as a habit, without necessary reference to practical use. I've seen such societies in the South Seas. . . .[11]

Adams admired early Tahiti and twelfth-century France for some of the same reasons: both societies had honored the aristocrat and extolled the devoted lover and the warrior. In writing his *Tahiti*, Adams recounted legends that exalted the great chiefs; in *Chartres*, he quoted poetry glorifying French heroes such as Roland.

Samoa, as well as Tahiti, lay within the scope of Adams's allusion to peoples of the South Seas that "sang . . . or fought, or loved . . . without necessary reference to practical use." His experience with the cohesive society of the Samoans helped him appreciate the organic soundness of the Norman culture that built Mont-Saint-Michel and created the *Chanson de Roland*. There were specific social resemblances—for example, between the function of a *tulafale*, or orator, in Samoa, who lauded the chiefs and encouraged his people to fight or to celebrate, and that of a jongleur like Taillefer, who composed songs about heroic deeds and sang the *Chanson* while Normans went into battle.

The exuberant life of the Samoans helped Adams to feel the youthful spirit necessary for apprehending the twelfth century, as epitomized by Chartres Cathedral: "when young it was a smile." He complained, while in Samoa, of the "child-like" mind of the women, but the ability of Adams to identify himself imaginatively with them actually aided him when he began writing about the early Middle Ages. He remarked in *Mont-Saint-Michel and Chartres* that a man could become young out of season, just as he could play with children. The image of the "eternal child" that recurs in the early chapters of the book may owe almost as much to the months Adams spent with the gay, good-natured Samoans as it does to his reading of William Wordsworth's poetry.[12]

His observations of the Samoans, as they performed dances that imitated the movements of birds or beasts and chanted their legends gave Adams insights into the primitive mind, a major concern of his when he tried to perceive how his European ancestors had felt. Having seen the flamboyant use of color in the dress and decorations of Pacific islanders, he could write with authority in *Chartres*, "Primitive man seems to have had a natural colour-sense, instinctive like the scent of a dog."[13] As a result of such understanding, Adams treated with sympathy the apparently child-like approach of the artists of Chartres, whose glass portrayed green horses or knights with blue faces.

During his stay in Polynesia, Adams met Ariitaimai, the last pure-blooded princess of Tahiti, whose peace-making efforts in 1846 had saved her countrymen from destruction by French conquerors. By making Adams an adopted member of her clan, the Tevas—the most important family on the island—and by revealing the genuine native life beneath a French-imposed culture, she helped him realize "the true inwardness of Tahiti."[14] With her aid, he wrote an authoritative history of her people and learned, he believed, what the "archaic woman" was. He had in mind the powerful heroines of antiquity, like Penelope, who had shown strength of mind and character in dealing with her suitors, and the formidable Hallgerda of the Icelandic *Njalsaga*.[15] Like her spiritual sisters of the epics, Ariitaimai seemed to him a striking contrast with modern women, who in Polynesia and in the West had suffered a loss of effective power.

The concept Adams held of the role of woman in society was tied to the unity-versus-multiplicity theme so crucial to *Mont-Saint-Michel and Chartres* and *The Education of Henry Adams*. He observed that medieval women like Eleanor of Aquitaine and Blanche of Castile had exerted a vigorous, creative influence upon the politics and art of Europe. Nineteenth-century American women, however, no longer acted as a cohesive force to hold family and society together but had, instead, become victims of "multiplicity."

The ideas of Adams about the Orient and about women merged when he linked the Virgin of Chartres with the mother goddesses of Asia. His interest in Mary as representing the unifying power of divine love was anticipated by his earlier reflections about Kwannon, the Buddhist goddess symbolizing compassion. The Asian deity became an important source of ideas for the monument to be placed at the grave of his wife. Inspired by the images of Kwannon that he saw in Japan and by other symbols of Buddhist art, he commissioned sculptor Augustus Saint-Gaudens to begin work on a memorial statue. Adams insisted that it "should fuse the art and thought of East and West," and in his thinking about the monument Our Lady of Chartres gradually became one with the merciful Virgin of the East.[16]

The worship of another important divinity of Japan, the Amida Buddha, as represented in the impressive statue of Buddha at Kamakura, also influenced the Adams memorial. In September, 1886, when Adams and John La Farge saw the thireenth-century bronze statue, their experience fulfilled years of expectation. An "Essay on Japanese Art," which La Farge wrote in 1869, comments on the "serene ideal of contemplation" shown in the "colossal statue of Daibutz."[17] The symbolism used in the sculpture shows that the Buddha, by the subduing of his will, has gained freedom from the limiting conditions of the material world and has achieved the ultimate spiritual peace of Nirvana. Hence, the statue itself is considered an embodiment of Nirvana.[18]

Adams wished his memorial to Marian to express this Buddhist concept: in an 1896 letter to a friend, he called Saint Gaudens' statue "the Peace of God" and insisted that "Petrarch would say 'Siccome eterna vita e veder Dio.' " According to Mabel La Farge, Adams returned from Japan "resolved to have the idea ["the peace of Nirvana"] embodied in a Western form of expression, that the Western world might understand and be consoled by it as he had been."[19]

Such insights were among the many personal and intellectual gains Adams made from his study of the Orient. One of the most important benefits was that he transcended the "regional angle of vision"[20] of his New England youth and reached for a world outlook. In growing beyond sectional prejudices to achieve a cosmopolitan mind, he was influenced by the example of distinguished forebears. John Adams, John Quincy Adams, and Henry's father, Charles Francis Adams, Sr., had each developed an internationalism of viewpoint by serving overseas as diplomatic representatives of the United States.

The thinking of John and John Quincy, in particular, had a significant effect upon Henry Adams's ideas about Asia. The emphasis in the *Education* on the future importance of Russia to America is consistent with John Adams's observation in 1814 that Russia is "a tremendous power whose future influence cannot be foreseen. . . . we ought to cultivate a good understanding with this power."[21] With John Quincy, who had become America's first Minister to Russia, Henry felt a special sympathy of mind, as is evidenced by his 1901 letters from Saint Petersburg and his *History of the United States*. In these writings, he recalled the achievements of his grandfather at the court of Czar Alexander I.

When the American Senate confirmed the appointment of John Quincy to Saint Petersburg in June, 1809, the United States faced two formidable powers in conflict with one another: Great Britain, intent on expanding its influence, and a Napoleon Bonaparte determined to keep American ships and products from entering the ports of Europe and Russia. Although Adams had to contend with a close French-Russian alliance, he persuaded Alexander to free American ships from confinement in Russian ports and, in 1810, to decree that American vessels could bring in a wide variety of products to Russian cities at low tariffs. At the same time, Alexander restricted French imports to luxury goods, which he taxed with heavy customs duties. According to the interpretation of Henry Adams, the Czar's sweeping concessions to the United States and his defiance of the French emperor gave John Quincy a "diplomatic victory . . . Napoleonic in its magnitude and completeness."[22]

But the success of the American Minister was undermined, as Congress declared war against England on June 18, 1812, and, shortly afterwards, Napoleon's army invaded Russia. In Saint Petersburg, John Quincy realized that his country had become, for all practical purposes, an ally of Russia's invader. When the Czar offered the services of his government to mediate between England and America, Adams quickly accepted, as did President James Madison, who dispatched peace negotiators to Europe.

The strategy used by the Russian army—of retreat and of giving battle only when necessary—proved so effective that the French forces exhausted their energies within five months after their invasion and had to retreat toward Paris. Recalling this history, Henry Adams in 1901 suggested that the endurance of the Russian people and their ability to wait might also exhaust American energies. Pondering the threat to the West of competition with such a people, he reluctantly conceded that "in the long run, the passive character exhausts the active one. Economy of energy is a kind of power."[23] Adams explained this idea, in part, when he referred to the "inertia" of Russia, or her capacity for moving slowly in an almost straight line of development. And he asked if this inertia could help her make a more durable progress than that of the rapidly changing United States.[24]

Despite this idea, Adams predicted that for the next one hundred years America, rather than Russia, would retain the leadership of Western Europe. He confessed his difficulty in prophesying, though, by saying that his "grandpapa, sitting here in his study ninety years ago, could see ahead to me now, better than I can see ahead to the year 2000. . . ."[25] This comment is one of several remarks in the August–September, 1901 letters, revealing the influence of John Quincy Adams upon the thinking of his grandson. Such statements help confirm Brooks Adams's observation that there was a kinship of mind between "these two powerful and original men" and that, intellectually, Henry's life was "a continuation of his grandfather's."[26] Especially in Saint Petersburg, with its daily reminders of John Quincy's efforts to aid America and Russia, Henry Adams seems to have felt a strong spiritual kinship with his grandfather.

In assessing the effect of his imaginative ancestors on Adams, the *Education* describes the emotional heritage bequeathed by John Quincy's wife, Louisa Catherine Johnson. Because she gave Henry his "quarter taint of Maryland blood," he was "not of pure New England stock, but half exotic."[27] To Louisa, he felt indebted for his capacity for sensuous response that his travels developed, especially those in the South Seas. His reaction to the flamboyant beauty of the Pacific islands was foreshadowed in a trip Adams made when twelve years of age to Washington, D.C., where he visited Louisa, and to the "slave state" of Maryland. In spite of his antipathy to slavery, the Southern atmosphere had a powerful emotional appeal, which he associated with his grandmother: "The want of barriers, of pavements, of forms; . . . the freedom, openness, swagger, of nature and man, soothed his Johnson blood."[28] Young Henry's reactions anticpated those of the adult Adams, who loved the luxuriance of the tropics and responded with delight to Hawaii, Samoa, and Tahiti.[29]

The boyhood trip south presaged a major change Adams made in 1877, when he resigned from the faculty of Harvard University and moved his household permanently to Washington. Eager for a larger life than Cambridge, Massachusetts, could offer him, he explained to Charles Milnes Gaskell, "I gravitate to a capital by a primary law of nature."[30] In his new residence, he became a warm friend of the most distinguished Oriental diplomats in America: Chinese envoy Chen Lau-Piu and Baron Kiyonari Yoshida, the Japanese Ambassador to the United States. Yoshida, who shared the interest of Adams in ethnology and archaic law, cordially invited him to visit Japan.[31]

The Washington circle of Adams included such outstanding American scholars of the Orient as Raphael Pumpelly, who made the first extensive geological survey of the Gobi Desert, and diplomat William Rockhill, who led expeditions to Mongolia and Tibet. In March, 1890, when Adams was considering a trip to Peking, he praised *The Life of the Buddha* (1884) by Rockhill and asked Rockhill to "give me a Chinese education."[32] During the Boxer Rebellion of 1900, when Rockhill served as Chief Advisor on the Far East to Secretary of State John Hay, he provided Adams with a direct, important source of information about international affairs.

Although Adams was an observer and not, like Hay or Rockhill, a participant in the Boxer crisis, such events intensified his interest in the Orient. He recalled that his plan to visit China in 1891 had been thwarted by widespread violence there. In the valley of the great Yangtze River, and in other areas of the country, the Chinese people fought against the seizure of their territory by foreign powers, who were dividing it into spheres of influence for commercial exploitation.

In 1899, John Hay considered America's interests to be threatened by this dismemberment of China. He urged Germany, England, Russia, France, Italy, and Japan to adopt his "Open Door" policy, by permitting in their respective spheres of influence equal trade opportunities for all nations. The six powers gave nominal agreement to Hay's request, but, as Adams commented, Russia, Germany and France went on "gorging plunder in Asia."[33]

The violence that accompanied the Boxer Rebellion gave European nations new justification for extending their power in China. In June, 1900, the Boxers, a nationalistic Chinese group protesting Western oppression, attacked the foreign legations in Peking and for eight weeks besieged over 500 men, women, and children, who had sought refuge in the British compound. As Hay dispatched American troops to save the legations, Adams concluded that joint military occupation by Europeans appeared inevitable, with each of the foreign countries, including the United States, choosing an area of China to control.[34]

But even as Adams contemplated possible moves of the great nations, he identified himself with the subjugated Chinese. To Hay, he described himself as a person

> . . . whose traditional sympathies are with all the forces that resist concentration, and love what used to be called liberty but has now become anarchy, or resistance to civilization; I who am a worm . . . am quite Chinese, Asiatic, . . . and anarchist. . . .[35]

Here, Adams barely avoided calling himself a "Boxer" as well, but he made clear his antagonism to a concentration of Western force in the Orient. The comment helps explain why he considered himself an "anarchist"—by his definition, a person who loves freedom enough to resist the encroachments of "civilization."

Although Adams applauded Hay's success in saving the legations in Peking, he saw with apprehension the numerous signs of expanding American power in Asia. While traveling in Polynesia, where he witnessed a shocking deterioration of native life, he had become skeptical about the benefits of Western influence. The Spanish American War intensified his concern for the Pacific peoples. In May, 1898, when it became clear that the United States would defeat Spain, Adams wrote Hay from Belgrade that President William McKinley presented more of a problem than the whole Balkan peninsula. What, Adams asked, would "the ambition of the man" require after the Philippines and the West Indies—Hawaii, China, the entire Far East?[36]

Because Adams feared the consequences of annexing the former Spanish colonies, he wanted peace to come quickly. He believed that the United States would endanger its own independence if it rushed into the vacuum created by the withdrawal of European nations from their Pacific possessions. In a prescient letter of November, 1898, Adams foresaw the disintegration of the French and British empires. America, he warned, could become fatally enmeshed in the colonial predicaments of these powers by supplying them with economic, political, and, finally, military help.[37]

The economic involvement of the United States in the Orient had already been long in the making. Cities like Boston and Salem had grown prosperous in the eighteenth and nineteenth centuries by means of their commerce with the East. Among those persons who contributed to the spread of American business influence in Asia were such prominent New Englanders as Captain William Sturgis, the maternal grandfather of Mrs. Henry Adams. Sturgis formed a Boston partnership that for several decades before the Civil War controlled more than half of the United States trade with the Pacific region and China.[38]

The success of American commerce helped create a receptive climate in the United States for the arts of the East. In 1876, the Philadelphia Centennial Exposition highlighted an exhibition of Japanese paintings that awakened considerable public interest in Japanese art.[39] Also indicative of a growing attention to Asia were the popular Lowell Institute lectures of 1881 in Boston. Professor Edward Morse, fresh from a teaching stint at Tokyo Imperial University, gave a series of programs on Japanese folkways, in which he praised the "beauty and dignity of the arts and life of *daimyo* and *samurai*."[40] Among the Bostonians strongly impressed by the message of Morse was a cousin of Marian Adams, William Sturgis Bigelow, who moved to Japan to study its religion and art. When Adams and La Farge visited that country, Bigelow acted as their translator and guide.

The New Englander who made the most outstanding contributions to Oriental studies was Professor Ernest Fenollosa, with whom Adams and La Farge lived in the summer of 1886, near the shrine of Nikko. A graduate of Harvard, Fenollosa had gone to Japan in 1878 to teach philosophy at Tokyo Imperial University. When the Japanese government appointed him Commissioner of Fine Arts for the Empire, he became the dynamic center of a movement to save the great feudal art of Japan from the destructive effects of an industrial revolution.[41] While doing this official work, Fenollosa began a private collection of Japanese paintings, which eventually became a possession of the Boston Museum of Fine Arts. Fenollosa's pictures—along with the thousands of art objects donated by Bigelow and Professor Morse—gave the museum "the richest collection of Japanese works of art to be found anywhere in the world, not excepting Japan."[42]

The letters of Henry Adams from Japan refer frequently to the ideas of Fenollosa and Bigelow on art and religion: both men were ardent converts to Buddhism. Bigelow became a Buddhist monk but expressed the beliefs of his adopted religion in only one literary contribution, *Buddhism and Immortality*. Adams read this work and wrote a congratulatory letter to Bigelow, thanking him for a copy and expressing "admiration."[43]

The conversion to an Eastern religion by Fenollosa and Bigelow was symptomatic of the crisis of faith experienced by many intellectuals in post-Civil War America. Their questioning of Western religious dogmas had at least two basic causes: (1) the conflict in ideas between Darwinism and scientific determinism on one hand and orthodox Christianity on the other, and (2) the belief that organized religion in the United States had lost its spiritual vitality and meaning.

That Henry Adams felt discontent with organized religion is evident in the *Education*, which states that he and all of his brothers and sisters found "Even the mild discipline of the Unitarian Church . . . so irksome that they all threw it off at the first possible moment, and never afterwards entered a church." Adams believed they were not alone in this reaction, that the "religious instinct had vanished" from American society."[44] Not until the fifth decade of his life, when he saw such great French churches as Chartres and Mont-Saint-Michel, did Adams himself develop a deep appreciation of the values and achievements of traditional Christianity.[45] During the early 1880's, he emphasized only its limitations, a point of view illustrated by his novel *Esther*, probably the most personal book he ever wrote. Its heroine asks for "spiritual life" but declares that she finds "nothing spiritual" in the church of her fiancé, the Reverend Stephen Hazard.[46]

A number of New Englanders shared Adams's dissatisfaction with orthodox Western faiths, including descendants of the zealous missionaries who had carried Christianity to Hawaii and the Orient. As Van Wyck Brooks describes the situation in *New England: Indian Summer, 1865-1915*, "The scholarly mind of New England was torn with doubts. . . . In the Unitarian form, the Christian faith had lost its positive content, and the sons of those who had hoped to convert the Asiatics were wondering if the truth was not in Asia."[47]

In reaction against the religious void in their lives, many Americans turned to the East for inspiration. The timely publication in 1879 of *The Light of Asia*, Sir Edwin Arnold's long blank verse poem interpreting the life of Buddha, helped launch the wave of interest in Oriental faiths. Lafcadio Hearn, in New Orleans, voiced the growing sympathy of many intellectuals for Buddhism when he declared that the 1883 editon of Arnold's poem

> has enchanted me—perfumed my mind as with the incense of a strangely new and beautiful worship. . . . Buddhism in some esoteric form may prove the religion of the future. . . . What are the heavens of all Christian fancies, after all, but Nirvana—extinction of individuality in the eternal interblending of man with divinity. . . .[48]

A preoccupation with Nirvana somewhat similar to that of Hearn appears in the writing of Adams during the 1880's. After his wife's suicide in December, 1885, he longed to achieve Nirvana, with its promise of extinction of self, of personal desires and suffering.

Complementing Adams's concern for Nirvana was his interest in the Hindu belief in Brahma. This interpretation of God harmonized with the scientific determinism he displayed in his United States *History* and offered a meaningful concept of unity. In exploring this Hindu philosophy, his blank verse poem "Buddha and Brahma" expresses the human need to achieve oneness with the divine spirit, or the "sole Thought." The poem deals with the same multiplicity-versus-unity thesis that dominates *Mont-Saint-Michel and Chartres* and *The Education of Henry Adams*. The *Chartres* says explicitly that "The attempt to bridge the chasm between multiplicity and unity is the oldest problem of philosophy, religion and science. . . ."[49] Both books emphasize the necessity to control a multiplicity of energies with one powerful unifying force. In Hindu faith, such a force is found in Brahma.[50]

The major character of Adams's poem, the Rajah, defines Brahma as "One thought containing all thoughts possible," not only those that limited human reason thinks true but also opposing ideas. The "single spirit" resolves all contradictions: "For Brahma is Beginning, Middle, End,/Matter and Mind, Time, Space, Form, Life and Death."[51] Adams's portrayal of Brahma suggests that he found in Hinduism the unifying idea he sought when he first began to explore the religions of the Orient.

As he ended his Pacific journey of 1890–91, the "one thought" of Brahma proved at least temporarily satisfying. However, his personal feeling of oneness with the "single spirit" ebbed when he returned to the Western world of multiplicity. He did not again express a philosophical unity comparable with that of Hinduism until, in *Mont-Saint-Michel and Chartres*, he described the organic unity of Thomas Aquinas's theology and the cohesive effect upon twelfth-century Europe of worship of the Virgin Mary.

The long-term quest of Henry Adams for a unifying system of belief in Eastern religions evidences that his concern for the Orient formed an important, enduring strand in his thought. He shared in the spiritual discovery of the Far East—made, not long after the 1854 opening of Japan, by some Occidentals with vision, including certain New England intellectuals and a few European authors. Although Adams could not know that America would fight three major wars in the Orient in the twentieth century, he emphasized the importance of Asian ideas to the United States. In so doing, he anticipated by 100 years the intense interest in the East shown by an increasing number of Americans of varied levels of education.

His conviction that understanding the Orient is essential was one reason he urged his countrymen to develop "a new social mind" that could deal effectively with the multiplicity of forces threatening destruction. Because technological power always runs ahead of mind, our society needs "to widen its consciousness of complex conditions far enough to escape wreck." Adams believed that Americans could manifest this necessary comprehension of an expanding world, but, mentally, they would have "to jump."[52] In enlarging his own understanding of the Orient and in a continuing ability to "align himself with the future," Henry Adams has become a fully Representative Man, who articulates the aspirations of a people.

Notes

1. HA to Theodore Dwight, June 28, 1886, *Henry Adams and His Friends*, ed. Harold D. Cater (Boston: Houghton Mifflin Company, 1947), p. 163 (hereinafter cited as Cater).

2. *The Education of Henry Adams*, ed. Ernest Samuels (Boston: Houghton Mifflin Co., 1974), p. 395.

3. HA to Sir Robert Cunliffe, January 17, 1887, Adams Papers, Massachusetts Historical Society microfilm, reel 599.

4. This statement takes into account the excellent collection of essays first published in 1942 in *The Asian Legacy and American Life*, which surveys the influence of the Orient on Western arts and thought. Arthur Christy's essay "The Sense of the Past" comments briefly on the effect of Asian ideas upon Henry Adams and a few of his New England contemporaries. In "The Orient and Contemporary Poetry," John Gould Fletcher discusses the influence of Chinese and Japanese literature upon the Imagist poets. *The Asian Legacy and American Life*, ed. Arthur E. Christy (New York: Greenwood Press, 1968). Two outstanding biographies, of author Lafcadio Hearn and Professor Ernest Fenollosa, include critical analyses of the influence of Asia upon their work. (Professor Fenollosa is noted for his scholarly writings on Japanese and Chinese art). See Lawrence Chisolm's *Fenollosa: The Far East and American Culture* (New Haven: Yale University Press, 1963) and Elizabeth Stevenson's *Lafcadio Hearn* (New York: The Macmillan Company, 1961).

5. " 'Out of Season for Nirvana': Henry Adams and Buddhism," *Indian Essays in American Literature*, ed. Sujit Mukerjee et al (Bombay: Pop. Prakashan, 1969), p. 180.

6. September 13, 1869, *Letters of Henry Adams (1858-1891)*, ed. Worthington C. Ford (Boston: Houghton Mifflin Company, 1930), p. 167 (hereinafter referred to as *Letters* I).

7. My definition of the "Orient" or the "East" must necessarily be a liberal one that includes the islands of the South Seas, Japan, China, India, and Russia. Although some twentieth-century anthropologists insist on sharp distinctions between the cultures of the

South Pacific and Asia, Adams believed that the origin of the Polynesians could be traced back to the Asiatic mainland and that they could provide important clues to the development of older civilizations on the mainland.

8. *Education*, p. 317.

9. Adams used an association of ideas to define the contraries of "multiplicity" and "unity," when he stated that the "task of education" was "running order through chaos, direction through space, discipline through freedom, unity through multiplicity. . . ." *Education*, p. 12.

See the "Editor's Preface" to the *Education* (p. xxvii) and *Mont-Saint-Michel and Chartres* for Adams's comments about "the unity of Church and State, God and Man" during the twelfth and thirteenth centuries (Boston: Houghton Mifflin Co., 1963), p. 44.

10. For both trips, to Japan and around the world, Adams paid the bills for La Farge and, equally important, provided the artist with the stimulus of an adventurous mind. As a result of their association, La Farge wrote two excellent books: *An Artist's Letters from Japan* (1897) and *Reminiscences of the South Seas* (1912). In *An Artist's Letters*, La Farge acknowledged his multiple debts to a man who "always set my mind sailing into new channels." (New York: The Century Co., 1897), p. 25.

11. July 5, 1905, *Letters of Henry Adams, 1892-1918*, ed. Worthington C. Ford (Boston: Houghton Mifflin Company, 1938), pp. 544-45 (cited hereafter as *Letters* II).

12. *Mont-Saint-Michel and Chartres*, pp. 88, 2; HA to Mabel La Farge, Jan. 19, 1891, *Letters to a Niece and Prayer to the Virgin of Chartres* (Boston: Houghton Mifflin Company, 1920), p. 39.

13. *Chartres*, p. 138.

14. HA to Elizabeth Cameron, March 16, 1891, *Letters* I, 476.

15. Adams discussed both these women in a December, 1876 lecture to the Lowell Institute on "The Primitive Rights of Women," published in revised form in his 1891 *Historical Essays*.

16. Ernest Samuels, *Henry Adams: The Middle Years* (Cambridge: Harvard University Press, 1965), p. 334 (hereinafter called *The Middle Years*), and Mabel La Farge, "A Niece's Memories," *Letters to a Niece*, pp. 14, 23.

17. "An Essay on Japanese Art," printed in Raphael Pumpelly's *Across America and Asia* (New York: Leypoldt and Holt, 1870), p. 202.

18. *An Artist's Letters from Japan*, p. 237. Cf. Percival Lowell's *The Soul of the Far East*, which calls the Kamakura Buddha "the living representation of Nirvana" (Boston: Houghton Mifflin and Company, 1888), p. 160.

19. HA to R. W. Gilder, Oct. 14, 1896, cited by *The Letters of Mrs. Henry Adams, 1865-1883*, ed. Ward Thoron (Boston: Little, Brown, and Co., 1936), p. 458; *Letters to a Niece*, p. 9. In *Esther*, Adams translated "*Siccome eterna vita e veder Dio*" to read "As sight of God is the eternal life." *Democracy* and *Esther* (Garden City, N.Y.: Doubleday and Co., 1961), pp. 268, 272, 364.

20. In "Henry Adams' New England View: A Regional Angle of Vision?" Earl N. Harbert discusses the "open and adventurous mind" of Adams, which enabled him to surmount family biases and regional prejudices. *Tulane Studies in English*, 16 (1968), 134.

21. JA to William S. Smith, March 2, 1814, Adams Papers, cited by Page Smith, *John Adams* (Garden City, New York: Doubleday and Company, Inc., 1962), II, 1096.

22. *History of the United States of America During the Administrations of Thomas Jefferson and James Madison* (New York: Albert and Charles Boni, 1930), V, 419.

23. HA to E. Cameron, August 21, 1901, *Letters* II, 340-41.

24. *Education*, p. 411.

25. HA to E. Cameron, Sept. 1, 1901, *Letters* II, 347-48.

26. "The Heritage of Henry Adams," *The Degradation of the Democratic Dogma* (New York: P. Smith, 1949), pp. 13, 103.

27. *Education*, p. 19.

28. *Education*, p. 45.

29. See HA's letter of April 28, 1894, to C. M. Gaskell: "I love the tropics, and really feel at ease nowhere else." *Letters* II, 46.

30. Nov. 25, 1877, *Letters* I, 302.

31. Samuels, *The Middle Years*, pp. 28, 290, 293.

32. HA to Rockhill, March 11, 1890, *Cater*, p. 189.

33. HA to E. Cameron, April 2, 1900, *Letters* II, 281.

34. HA to Hay, Nov. 7, 1900, *Letters* II, 299.

35. June 26, 1900, *Letters* II, 291.

36. May 5, 1898, *Letters* II, 176.

37. HA to W. C. Ford, Nov. 26, 1898, *Letters* II, 195.

38. Appendix I, *The Letters of Mrs. Henry Adams*, p. 466.

39. Chisolm, p. 36. The date of the Japanese exhibition at Philadelphia coincided with the publication of the first book by any Westerner on Japanese art—*A Glimpse at the Art of Japan*, by the American author James Jackson Jarves. See Van Wyck Brooks, *Fenollosa and His Circle* (New York: E. P. Dutton and Co., 1962), p. 6.

40. F[rederick] W. C[oburn], "Morse, Edward Sylvester," *Dictionary of American Biography* (1934).

41. Van Wyck Brooks, *New England: Indian Summer, 1865-1915* (New York: E. P. Dutton & Co., Inc., 1940), pp. 362–65. Fenollosa had a significant effect upon twentieth-century literature. His translations of fifty classical Noh plays, revised and published after his death by Ezra Pound as *Certain Noble Plays of Japan* (1916), became a major influence upon William Butler Yeats and the theatre of the West.

42. J[ohn] F. F[ulton], "Bigelow, William Sturgis," *Dictionary of American Biography* (1957).

43. HA to Bigelow, Dec. 26, 1915, Cater, p. 773.

44. *Education*, p. 34.

45. In August, 1895, during his first tour of Normandy, Adams became profoundly inspired by the majesty of Coutances Cathedral and the Abbey of Mont-Saint-Michel. Shortly afterward, going south of Paris, he made his first visit to Chartres. See his letter to Hay, Sept. 7, 1895, in which Adams describes the psychological effect of these tours: "my soul is . . . built into it [Coutances Cathedral]" and "Chartres . . . was fascinating." Cater, pp. 346–47.

46. *Democracy and Esther*, p. 369.

47. *New England: Indian Summer*, p. 360.

48. Hearn to W. D. O'Connor, 1883 (month and day omitted), quoted by Elizabeth Bisland, *The Life and Letters of Lafcadio Hearn* (Boston: Houghton Mifflin and Company, 1906), I, 291–92.

49. *Mont-Saint-Michel and Chartres*, p. 299.

50. Frederick Carpenter gives a pertinent definition of Brahma: "the impersonal creative force of the world." *Emerson and Asia* (Cambridge: Harvard University Press, 1930), p. 113.

51. "Buddha and Brahma," *A Henry Adams Reader*, ed. Elizabeth Stevenson (Garden City: Doubleday and Company, Inc., 1958), p. 345.

52. *Education*, p. 498, and HA to Gaskell, April 23, 1906, *Letters* II, 469.

INDEX

Adams, Brooks, 56, 84, 96–98, 113, 154, 157, 199, 250

Adams, Charles Francis, 3, 5, 38, 76, 84, 89–91, 124, 189, 204, 221, 224, 231, 248

Adams, Charles Francis, II, 5, 7, 77, 85, 91, 175, 237

Adams, Henry,
    As autobiographer, 4, 63–75, 118, 236–242

    As biographer, 2, 5, 6, 7, 41, 51–56, 77, 85, 93, 94, 98–99, 101, 116, 169–174, 194, 238, 244

    As essayist, 1, 5, 8, 9, 11, 41, 53–54, 85, 90–92, 98, 102–103, 116, 118, 147–148, 184, 195–196

    As historian, 3, 5, 6, 7, 10, 50–59, 85, 92–93, 97, 101–102, 109, 116, 120–121, 123, 127–130, 135–136, 139, 141, 150, 152–154, 157–183, 197, 205–206, 224–225, 243, 249

    As letter-writer, 3–5, 12, 44, 48, 50–53, 58, 64, 71, 84, 85, 90–91, 95–97, 111, 117–119, 121–132, 139, 149, 175, 202, 204, 205, 234, 237, 238, 242, 245, 249, 250, 251, 253

    As novelist, 3, 7, 10, 20–33, 76–83, 87, 93–95, 104–113, 116, 133, 143, 172–174

    Bibliography of, 3, 4, 7–9, 15, 40–41, 85, 115–117, 242, 244, 255–257

    Biography of, 1, 2, 3–13, 50–58, 76–83, 84–103, 104–106, 115–139, 140–149, 150–183, 188–208, 217–218, 236–242, 243–255

    Letters of (quoted), 5, 9, 12, 44, 48, 50–53, 64, 71, 84, 85, 97, 98, 104, 111, 117–119, 121, 129–130, 131, 135, 139, 142, 149, 160, 166, 170, 175, 202, 204, 205, 234, 237–238, 242, 243, 250, 251

Literary reputation of, 3–13, 36–43, 48–49, 50–61, 67–72, 78–83, 104–113, 115–139, 140–149, 150–186, 189–190, 211–218, 220–234, 236–242

Literary style of, 8, 9, 31, 33–35, 41, 42, 56, 64, 66–73, 78–83, 100–102, 115, 118–139, 140–149, 151–183, 187–208, 220–234, 236–242

Adams, John, 3, 5, 10, 38, 52, 57, 76, 88, 89, 104, 115–116, 124, 127, 152, 157, 170, 190, 194, 201, 221, 236, 243, 248–249

Adams, John Quincy, 3, 5, 10, 38, 40, 52, 56, 57, 58, 60, 76, 88, 89, 94, 104, 115–116, 124, 126, 127, 150, 157, 170, 188, 190, 194, 201, 204, 221, 227, 231, 236, 243, 248–249, 250

Adams, John Quincy, II, 91

Adams, Marian "Clover" Hooper, 5, 8, 9, 46, 58, 77, 79, 80, 82, 92, 93, 95, 104, 110–113, 123, 124, 174–175, 190, 233, 238, 245, 248, 252, 254

American Historical Review, 11, 184

Anderson, Charles R., 115–139

Anderson, Sherwood, 211, 212, 213

Aquinas, Saint Thomas, 46, 60, 127, 129, 131, 135, 138, 139, 155, 254

Athenaeum, 13, 81

Atlantic Monthly, 4, 79, 203, 204

Augustine, Saint, 63–75, 118, 220, 236

Bell, Millicent, 104–113

Blackmur, R. P., 36–49, 155, 185

Blaine, James G., 79, 94

Booklist, 12

Bread-Winners, The, 8

Brooks, Phillip, 82

Brown, Margaret J., 243–257

Brownell, William Carey, 8

"Buddha and Brahma," 86, 222, 246, 254

Burr, Aaron, 153, 179, 238

Adams's unpublished biography of, 116, 238

Cameron, Elizabeth (Mrs.), 44, 51, 58, 82, 95, 111, 205
"Cap and Bells, The," 204
Cellini, Benvenuto, 63, 64, 118
China, 87, 90, 245, 250–251, 255n7
"Civil Service Reform," 8, 33–35, 78, 91
Civil War (American), 3, 7, 37, 76, 120, 123, 124, 125, 128, 165–166, 175, 189, 193, 195, 244, 252, 253
Commager, Henry Steele, 50–61
Compton, Frances Snow (pseudonym for Henry Adams), 8, 81, 95
Confessions of St. Augustine, The, 63–75, 118
"Count Edward de Crillon," 11, 184
Cram, Ralph Adams, 85
Crane, Hart, 38
Critic, 10

Daily Courier (Boston), 5, 90
Darwin, Charles, 58–59, 77, 90, 91, 94, 125, 147–149, 189, 229, 253
Degradation of the Democratic Dogma, 98, 157
Democracy: An American Novel, 3, 4, 6, 7, 8, 10, 19–35, 42–44, 45, 56, 57, 76–83, 87, 93, 105, 116, 133, 153, 172–174, 188
Quoted, 21–35, 42–43, 53–54, 87
Dial (Chicago), 10
Disraeli, Benjamin, 20–21, 78, 93
Documents Relating to New England Federalism, 4, 163, 165
"Dynamic Theory of History, A," 72, 73, 97, 131, 140, 141, 147, 185, 206
Dynamo, the, 47, 56, 60, 69, 83, 86, 102, 110–112, 123, 127–130, 139, 175, 176, 212–213, 216, 217, 241

Education of Henry Adams, The, 3, 4, 5, 6, 8, 9, 11, 12, 13, 41–42, 45–48, 53–60, 63–75, 78, 79, 80, 86–87, 89, 90, 94, 97, 100–102, 105, 109, 112, 113, 116–119, 120, 128, 129, 130, 132, 133, 136, 139, 140, 141, 143, 145, 146, 147, 149, 150, 151, 152, 155, 157, 158, 185, 188, 189–206, 211–218, 220–234, 236–242, 244, 245, 254

Quoted, 11, 40, 43, 47–48, 51–55, 58–59, 64, 67–70, 72–73, 100–101, 105, 107, 109, 112, 117, 118, 119, 120–139, 143, 145, 146, 147, 148, 151, 158, 189–200, 205–206, 212, 214, 217, 223–233, 250, 255
Eliot, T. S., 13, 86, 148, 211, 215, 237
English Historical Review, 10
Essays in Anglo-Saxon Law, 163
Esther: A Novel, 3, 6, 8, 9, 10, 42, 44, 45–47, 51, 76, 78–83, 94, 96, 104–113, 116, 133, 142, 174, 188, 244, 246, 253
Quoted, 45, 105–106, 110–112, 146
Examiner (London), 5

"Five of Hearts, The," 82, 94
Fortnightly Review (English), 8, 19
Franklin, Benjamin, 63, 76, 117, 140, 176, 236, 240

Gallatin, Albert (see also Life of Albert Gallatin), 4, 7, 40, 41, 42, 56, 58, 77, 85, 169, 170–174, 179–183, 238
Garfield, James A., 35, 196
Gaskell, Charles Milnes, 50, 91, 244–245, 250
Gibbon, Edward, 64, 93, 97, 101–102, 118, 161
Gilson, Étienne, 72, 108
Grant, Ulysses S., 34, 39, 56, 76, 78–83, 92, 125, 159, 192, 193, 195, 196, 229

Hamlet, 100, 105, 187–208
Harbert, Earl N., 3–15, 220–234, 236–242
Harper's New Monthly Magazine, 10
Harvard College, 4, 6, 41, 50, 51, 56, 59, 64, 67, 76, 89–93, 113, 115, 125, 130, 144, 159, 163, 164, 169, 190, 191, 202, 203, 207, 231, 232, 240, 245, 250
Harvard Magazine, 90
Hawthorne, Nathaniel, 8, 86, 108
Hay, John, 8, 40, 42, 44, 56, 78, 79, 82, 85, 93, 97, 98, 124, 150, 151, 156, 175, 190, 191, 206, 207, 250–251
Hayes, Rutherford B., 76–81
Hemingway, Ernest, 211–218
"Henry Adams, December 1885," 1–2

History of the United States During the Administrations of Thomas Jefferson and James Madison, 4, 6, 9, 10, 11, 12, 44, 51–55, 57, 77, 81, 85, 93, 94, 95, 97, 101–102, 115, 116, 141, 142, 148, 150, 151, 152, 153, 159, 162, 166–167, 174–185, 197, 244, 249
Quoted, 52, 142, 171–172, 176–184, 249
Holmes, Oliver Wendell, Jr., 87, 164
Holt, Henry, 78, 80, 95, 173
"Housatonic" (*see* Smith, William Henry)
Howells, William Dean, 20, 31, 78, 85, 92, 93, 204, 208

"Independents of the Canvass, The," 168, 169

Japan, 243, 244, 252–253, 255n7
Jackson, Andrew, 52, 76, 89, 116, 127, 166, 182, 188
James, Henry, 7, 20, 31, 38, 78, 80, 84, 85, 92, 93, 94, 95, 104, 112, 117–119, 139, 208, 234, 236, 237–238
James, William, 64, 93, 117, 119, 133, 178, 183
Jefferson, Thomas, 9, 10, 38, 52, 57, 59, 76, 77, 85, 89, 101–102, 115, 127, 141, 152, 153, 154, 161, 164, 167, 169–172, 174, 177–183
John Randolph, 4, 7, 10, 42, 52–55, 77, 85, 94, 116, 174, 194, 238

King, Clarence, 79, 80–82, 93, 94, 95, 97, 110, 124, 126, 205
Koretz, Gene H., 63–75

La Farge, John, 48, 82, 95, 110, 112, 129, 150, 198, 243, 246, 248, 252
Law of Civilization and Decay, The 97
"Legal-Tender Act, The," 41
"Letter to American Teachers of History, A," 11, 47, 54, 98, 140
Levenson, J. C., 138, 141, 143, 150–156, 157–186
Life of Albert Gallatin, The, 4, 6, 7, 8, 10, 41–42, 52–55, 57, 85, 93, 116, 169–174, 179, 238
Quoted, 170–172
Life of George Cabot Lodge, The (*see*

also Lodge, George Cabot), 244, 246
Lodge, George Cabot, 98, 116, 144, 244
Lodge, Henry Cabot, 40, 51, 64, 92, 117, 146, 163, 164–165, 170
London Critic, 10
Lyell, Sir Charles, 54, 58, 91

Macaulay, Thomas Babington, 93, 101
McKinley, William, 43, 154, 252
Madison, James, 9, 10, 115, 141, 178–183, 249
Melville, Herman, 38, 86, 108–109
Memoirs of Marau Taaroa Last Queen of Tahiti, 11, 116, 244, 246–247
Monteiro, George, 211–218
Mont-Saint-Michel and Chartres, 4, 6, 9, 11, 12, 45–49, 55, 60–61, 64, 68, 69, 78, 83, 85, 86, 94, 97, 101–102, 105, 116–117, 120–139, 149, 155, 185, 188, 216, 223, 244, 245, 246, 247, 254
Quoted, 46, 49, 60, 117, 133, 135–137, 155, 247, 254
More, Paul Elmer, 88
Munford, Howard M., 140–149

Nation, 6, 7, 8, 10, 33, 85, 91
New England Quarterly, 72, 104, 114
"New York Gold Conspiracy, The," 41, 92
New York Semi-Weekly Tribune, 7
New York Times, The, 9, 10, 91, 159, 194
North American Review, 33, 41, 56, 76, 85, 91, 92, 159, 167–169, 196, 197

Origin of Species, The, 90

Parrington, Vernon Louis, 58, 102
Pearson, Karl, 145, 200
Petrarch, 45, 185
"Prayer to the Virgin of Chartres," 116, 217
"Primitive Rights of Women," 1
Principles of Geology, 91

Randolph, John, 5, 10, 42, 77, 89, 194, 238
Roelofs, Gerrit H., 67
Roosevelt, Theodore, 40, 43–44, 100

Rousseau, Jean Jacques, 58, 63, 64, 67, 100, 118, 220, 226–227, 231, 236, 238–240
"Rule of Phase Applied to History, The," 47, 54, 98, 140, 147

Saint-Gaudens, Augustus, 46, 95, 248
Samuels, Ernest, 15, 67, 76–83, 84–103, 141, 201, 236
Santayana, George, 38, 148
Schurz, Carl, 40, 79, 93
Second Law of Thermodynamics, The, 47, 54, 131
"Session, 1869–1870, The," 41, 91, 196
Shakespeare, William, 48, 90, 187–208
Smith, William Henry ("Housatonic"), 10
Spiller, Robert, 86
Symbols, Henry Adams's use of, 69–73, 83, 86, 102, 110–113, 123, 127–130, 134–136, 137–139, 155, 195, 176, 212–213, 215–217, 228–230, 241, 247–248

Taylor, Henry Osborne, 4, 11, 12, 48, 51, 92, 132, 142
"Tendency of History, The," 11, 85

Times (London), 5
Thurston, H. W., 10
Trollope, Anthony, 7, 20, 78
Twain, Mark, 38, 76, 85, 87, 117, 202

Vandersee, Charles, 1, 2, 15, 187–208
Virgin, The, 46–48, 56, 60, 69, 83, 86, 102, 111–113, 127–130, 134, 136–139, 155, 212–213, 215–216, 217, 241, 248, 254
"Visit to Manchester, A: Extracts From a Private Diary," 5, 6, 11

Ward, Mary A. (Mrs. Humphry), 8, 19–35, 78
Washington, D.C., 7, 22–35, 37–39, 50, 56, 76–78, 83, 85, 88, 93, 94, 95, 99, 129, 159, 172–173, 196, 243, 250
Weed, Thurlow, 150, 151
Wendell, Barrett, 64, 130
Whitman, Walt, 38, 100, 207
Winters, Yvor, 102, 108, 192
Wright, Nathalia, 72
Writings of Albert Gallatin, The, 52, 93

Yale Review, 86